Migrant Rights at Work

Public debates about the terms of membership and inclusion have intensified as developed economies increasingly rely on temporary migrant labour. While most agree that temporary migrant workers are entitled to the general protection of employment laws, temporary migrants have, by definition, restricted rights to residence, social protections and often occupational and geographic mobility. This book raises important ethical questions about the differential treatment of temporary and unauthorised migrant workers, and permanent residents, and where the line should be drawn between exploitation and legitimate employment.

Taking regulatory reforms in Australia as a key case study, Laurie Berg explores how the influence of immigration law extends beyond its functions in regulating admission to and exclusion from a country. Berg examines the ways in which immigration law and enforcement reconfigure the relationships between migrant workers and employers, producing uncertain and coercive working conditions. In presenting an analytical approach to issues of temporary labour migration, the book develops a unique theoretical framework, contending that the concept of precariousness is a more fruitful way than equality or vulnerability to evaluate and address issues of temporary migrant labour.

The book will be of great interest to scholars and practitioners of immigration law and employment law and policy.

Laurie Berg is a Senior Lecturer in the Faculty of Law, University of Technology, Sydney, Australia.

Routledge Research in Asylum, Migration and Refugee Law

Available titles in this series include:

Refugee Protection and the Role of Law
Conflicting Identities
Edited by Susan Kneebone, Dallal Stevens, Loretta Baldassar

Gender in Refugee Law
From the Margins to the Centre
Efrat Arbel, Catherine Dauvergne, Jenni Millbank

Forthcoming titles in this series include:

European Asylum Law and the Rights of the Child
Ciara Smyth

Asylum Law in the European Union
Francesco Cherubini

The Socio-Economic Rights of Asylum Seekers
Liam Thornton

Asylum-Seeker and Refugee Protection in Sub-Saharan Africa
The Peregrination of a Persecuted Human Being in Search of a Safe Haven
Cristiano D'Orsi

Migrant Rights at Work

Law's Precariousness at the Intersection of Immigration and Labour

Laurie Berg

Routledge
Taylor & Francis Group
LONDON AND NEW YORK

First published 2016
by Routledge

2 Park Square, Milton Park, Abingdon, Oxon OX14 4RN
711 Third Avenue, New York, NY 10017, USA

Routledge is an imprint of the Taylor & Francis Group, an informa business

First issued in paperback 2017

British Library Cataloguing in Publication Data
A catalogue record for this book is available from the British Library

Library of Congress Cataloging-in-Publication Data
Berg, Laurie, author.
Migrant rights at work : law's precariousness at the intersection of migration and labour / Laurie Berg.
pages cm. – (Routledge research in asylum, migration and refugee law)
Includes bibliographical references and index.
ISBN 978-1-138-80555-2 (hardback) – ISBN 978-1-315-75232-7 (pbk)
1. Foreign workers–Legal status, laws, etc.–Australia. I. Title.
KU1278.A44B47 2015
344.9401'162–dc23
2015003900

ISBN: 978-1-138-80555-2 (hbk)
ISBN: 978-1-138-71682-7 (pbk)

Typeset in Baskerville by
Fish Books Ltd.

Contents

Acknowledgements

In preparing this work, I have been fortunate to have received a great deal of warm counsel and encouragement. I would particularly like to thank colleagues at the Law Faculty, University of Technology, Sydney and Anti-Slavery Australia, who have created a stimulating work environment and immeasurably helped me deepen my thinking on the issues addressed in this book. I have benefited greatly from the knowledge and advice of others in the field, especially at the University of Sydney. I am indebted to Professors Mary Crock and Ron McCallum who have shared their wide-ranging academic knowledge and advice, and Professor Terry Carney for his unwavering wisdom, guidance and support. I am especially grateful to Professors François Crépeau, Cathryn Costello and Rosemary Owens AO and Dr Joanna Howe who offered generous and incisive feedback on drafts of this work.

Sincere thanks are also due to those who have given shape to this book in its final form. The editorial team at Routledge has been extremely supportive and a pleasure to work with, especially Mark Sapwell, Annabelle Harris, Karl Harrington, Damian Penfold and Abigail Pukaniuk. Thank you Glenda Browne for the index. I also thank Douglas McDonald, Costa Avgoustinos, Freya Newman and Katie Poidomani for their exemplary editing assistance.

My son Lou was born as I was finishing this book, bringing sparkling joy and inspiring me to stay attuned to what is most important. My deepest thanks go to my parents, Carol and Tony Berg, my friends and Annie for their unstinting support and for keeping me (relatively) sane through this journey. I will also always be tremendously grateful to the many migrant workers who have shared their difficult experiences living and working in this country. Their resilience and determination has guided this work.

Abbreviations

ACT	Australian Capital Territory
ACTU	Australian Council of Trade Unions
AFL-CIO	American Federation of Labor and Congress of Industrial Organizations
AFP	Australian Federal Police
AGD	Australian Commonwealth Attorney-General's Department
AIC	Australian Institute of Criminology
ALP	Australian Labor Party
ANAO	Australian National Audit Office
ASCO	Australian Standard Classification of Occupations
AWA	Australian Workplace Agreement
BVE	subclass 050 Bridging visa E
BVF	subclass 060 Bridging visa F
CDPP	Australian Commonwealth Director of Public Prosecutions
CFMEU	Construction Forestry Mining and Energy Union
CJSV	subclass 951 Criminal Justice Stay visa
CLR	Commonwealth Law Reports
Criminal Code	*Criminal Code 1995* (Cth)
CSOL	Consolidated Sponsored Occupation List
Cth	Commonwealth of Australia
DCNSW	District Court of New South Wales
DEEWR	Australian Department of Education, Employment and Workplace Relations
DEWR	Australian Department of Employment and Workplace Relations
DIAC	Australian Department of Immigration and Citizenship
DIEA	Australian Department of Immigration and Ethnic Affairs

DIBP	Australian Department of Immigration and Border Protection
DIMA	Australian Department of Immigration and Multicultural Affairs
DIMIA	Australian Department of Immigration and Multicultural and Indigenous Affairs
DILGEA	Australian Department of Immigration, Local Government and Ethnic Affairs
DHS	US Department of Homeland Security
DOJ	US Department of Justice
DOL	US Department of Labor
ENS	Employer Nomination Scheme
ESOS Act	*Education Services for Overseas Students Act 2000* (Cth)
EU	European Union
FCA	Federal Court of Australia
FCAFC	Full Court of the Federal Court of Australia
FCCA	Federal Circuit Court of Australia
FMCA	Federal Magistrates Court of Australia
FW Act	*Fair Work Act 2009* (Cth)
FWA	Fair Work Australia
FWAFB	Fair Work Australia Full Bench
FWC	Australian Fair Work Commission
FWO	Australian Fair Work Ombudsman
GATS	General Agreement on Trade in Services
GSM	General Skilled Migration Program
HCA	High Court of Australia
ICE	US Immigration and Customs Enforcement
IDC	Australian Anti-Human Trafficking Interdepartmental Committee
IELTS	International English Language Testing System
ILO	International Labour Organisation
Immigration Restriction Act	*Immigration Restriction Act 1901* (Cth)
IRCA	Industrial Relations Court of Australia
IRT	Australian Immigration Review Tribunal
IWWNs	Illegal Worker Warning Notices
JSCM	Australian Parliamentary Joint Standing Committee on Migration
MIAC	Australian Minister for Immigration and Citizenship
MIEA	Australian Minister for Immigration and Ethnic Affairs
Migrant Workers Convention	United Nations International Convention on Protection of the Rights of All Migrant Workers and Members of their Families

Migration Act	*Migration Act 1958* (Cth)
Migration Regulations	*Migration Regulations 1994* (Cth)
MILGEA	Australian Minister for Immigration, Local Government and Ethnic Affairs
MIMA	Australian Minister for Immigration and Multicultural Affairs
MIMIA	Australian Minister for Immigration and Multicultural and Indigenous Affairs
MOU	Memorandum of Understanding
MRT	Australian Migration Review Tribunal
MSL	Minimum Salary Level
NDIS	National Disability Insurance Scheme
NES	National Employment Standards
NESB	non-English speaking background
NSW	New South Wales
NSWCC	Compensation Court of New South Wales
NSWIRComm	Industrial Relations Commission of New South Wales
NSWLR	New South Wales Law Reports
NSWWCC	Workers Compensation Commission of New South Wales
OECD	Organisation for Economic Co-operation and Development
QADT	Queensland Anti-Discrimination Tribunal
Qld	Queensland
QCA	Queensland Court of Appeal
QSC	Queensland Supreme Court
RSMS	Regional Sponsored Migration Scheme
SA	South Australia
SAIRC	South Australia Industrial Relations Court
Slavery Act 2013	*Crimes Legislation Amendment (Slavery, Slavery-like Conditions and People Trafficking) Act 2013* (Cth)
SOL	Skilled Occupations List
Trafficking Protocol	United Nations Protocol to Prevent, Suppress and Punish Trafficking in Persons, Especially Women and Children
TSMIT	Temporary Skilled Migration Income Threshold
UN	United Nations
UNODC	United Nations Office for Drugs and Crime
UNTOC	United Nations Convention against Transnational Organised Crime
UK	United Kingdom
USA	United States of America
VEVO	Visa Entitlement Verification Online
Vic	Victoria
WA	Western Australia

WAIRComm	Western Australian Industrial Relations Commission
WCC	Workers Compensation Commission of NSW
WHMs	working holiday makers
WHV	subclass 417 Working Holiday visa
Workers Compensation Act	*Workers Compensation Act 1987* (NSW)
Worker Protection Act	*Migration Legislation Amendment (Worker Protection) Act 2008* (Cth)
WPTV	subclass 852 Witness Protection (Trafficking) (Permanent) visa
WR Act	*Workplace Relations Act 1996* (Cth)
457 Amendment Act 2013	*Migration Amendment (Temporary Sponsored Visas) Act 2013* (Cth)
457 visa	subclass 457 Temporary Work (Skilled) visa

Foreword

People migrate for a variety of reasons. Push factors include war, conflict, natural disasters, persecution, poverty and unemployment. A major pull factor is the need for migrant labour in destination states. Irregular migration is frequently a result of a lack of regular migration channels, particularly for low-skilled workers, despite an often unrecognised need for their labour in countries of destination and the resulting vast underground labour markets that attract them. Many people see migration as the only way to improve their social and economic situation, and sometimes they see no other option but to migrate or remain irregularly. Migrants, and particularly irregular migrants or migrants with a precarious residence status, are often willing to do the 'dirty, difficult and dangerous' jobs that nationals will not, at the exploitative wages that unscrupulous employers will offer.

Tensions between migrants and the local population have in many places been fuelled by the debate about national identity, and in some cases also by the economic crisis. Migrants are sometimes accused, including in the public debate and contrary to what social science demonstrates, of 'stealing' jobs by accepting lower wages and poor working conditions. However, states seem to invest very few resources in trying to reduce the informal sector and sanction 'irregular employers', who profit from the exploitative conditions of work to boost their competitiveness.

Generally, migrants are at heightened risk of exploitation and abuse in the workplace, due to: deceptive recruitment practices, both by employers and intermediaries; frequent lack of social support systems; unfamiliarity with the local culture, language, their rights at work and national labour and migration laws in the country of employment; limited or denied access to legal and administrative systems; dependence on the job and employer due to migration-related debt, legal status, or employers restricting their freedom to leave the workplace; and reliance by family members on remittances sent back home by the migrant. These factors are amplified by the discrimination and xenophobia that migrants are increasingly facing everywhere.

Factors which further contribute to exploitation of migrants in the workplace include: pressure to lower the cost of labour in highly competitive sectors; the absence of effective implementation of labour and occupational health and safety standards; and frequent lack of unionisation. This concerns sectors where migrants are frequently concentrated, such as agriculture, construction, hospitality, care-giving, domestic work and informal work (such as street vendors). Migrants routinely work long hours, including overtime for which they are often not paid, and sometimes do not get their breaks or leave entitlements. They frequently report having been misinformed about labour conditions and benefits, and left without access to medical care and consular protection. A key contributing factor of their exploitation is their general fear of being detected, detained and deported for real or imagined reasons, and their consequent reluctance to risk complaining, protesting or publicly mobilising, preferring very often the coping strategy of 'moving on'.

The United Nations General Assembly has requested all states 'to enforce labour law effectively, including by addressing violations of such law, with regard to migrant workers' labour relations and working conditions, inter alia, those related to their remuneration and conditions of health, safety at work and the right to freedom of association' (GA/RES/68/179). In the Declaration adopted by the General Assembly during the High-level Dialogue on international migration and development in October 2013, States agreed to promote and protect effectively the human rights and fundamental freedoms of all migrants, regardless of their migration status; to protect women migrant workers in all sectors, including those involved in domestic work; to respect and promote international labour standards and the rights of migrants in their workplaces; and to cooperate on labour mobility programmes.

Yet, to most migrants almost everywhere, such a programme would appear as a fantasy, as migrants' labour rights are almost systematically superseded by immigration enforcement considerations, due to the lack of effective oversight mechanisms.

Laurie Berg's book is a major contribution to the understanding of this complex and under-researched field of migration law. It fills a clear gap in the legal literature which has been pretty silent on the protection of labour rights for temporary migrant workers (with the exception of domestic work which has received some attention) and irregular migrant workers, generally considered as outsiders who do not really deserve the same level of protection that citizen workers would command.

Dr Berg very intelligently deconstructs the policy discourse to show how legal language is constantly used to legitimise or delegitimise certain avenues taken by migrants to find the protection they need. The choice of precariousness over vulnerability as a central concept, for example, was well explained and we should all refer to it in the future.

Berg has gathered an impressive range of sources to support her analysis. Her use of diverse policy and legal sources and her meticulous analysis of how procedures are conducted allow the reader to understand more fully the absence of coherent rule-of-law-based and human-rights-based procedural safeguards in favour of the migrant workers involved.

Berg seems to be extremely well informed and conscious of the necessary analytical nuances requested by a complex field where many factors constantly interplay: personal circumstances and motivations of the worker; role of intermediaries; moral fiber of the employer; regulatory environment; efficiency of oversight mechanisms, labour inspection capacity, media interest; labour action by unions or civil society organisations; role of international organisations…

It is an excellent idea to include personal stories at the beginning of each chapter – migrants are too often presented as an indistinct depersonalised threatening mass (we use a 'liquid language', probably reminiscent of ancient invasions, with words such as flows, waves, tides, trickling, containing…). It is good to be reminded that we are actually discussing people, i.e. individual persons, who have a history, parents, siblings, children, dreams, hopes, bruises, achievements, and who try their best to make sense of their lives and provide for their loved ones, just like any one of us.

Persons with disabilities have adopted the slogan 'Nothing about us without us', well, for migrants, due to their status as foreigners, migration policies are always crafted 'without them'. Berg emphasises the therefore essential responsibility of the state to provide an appropriate regulatory environment as well as adequate recourse mechanisms, in order to empower individual workers, *whatever their status,* to fight for their rights against unscrupulous employers or recruiters.

Berg develops much nuanced discussion on the access to permanent residence for temporary migrant workers. It is an essential element in recognising the dignity of temporary migrant workers who have dedicated years of work in the host labour market. However, the author rightly notes that this objective is also a factor in the precariousness of migrant workers, as they'll endure unfair conditions in order to make sure that the employer will not derail their access to permanent residence, this, the curse of the 'carrot of permanent residence'.

The analysis of the sponsorship system is also very interesting. Berg has rightly constructed a robust indictment of the sponsorship mechanism. The dependency of the worker on the sponsor is always a source of precariousness. Manifestly, although it is unsaid, it is intended so, as, otherwise, many temporary migrant workers would quickly quit the triple-D job for which they were recruited in order to transfer to a better job in the labour market – the precariousness is a condition for meeting the labour needs of low-profit-margins industries without raising their labour costs. We will need a thorough public debate as to how to keep these industries (construction, agriculture, hospitality, care-giving…) competitive, without doing this on the back of migrant workers.

The criminalisation of 'illegal work' removes substantive protections for irregular workers, such as workers compensation entitlements, unfair dismissal protections and restitution for labour, and weakens workers' remedies. The criminalisation process actually eliminates labour law as a framework for understanding the irregular worker's predicament. This is a worldwide problem – the criminalisation of irregular migration is a political tool used to fend off populist nationalist attacks and it is usually decided without any study of its actual consequences for all stakeholders.

The correlated issue of the mistrust of the migrant's agency is also constantly noted as a golden thread. It is indeed one of the key conceptualisation failures which comes from unacknowledged preconceptions. Either migrants are disloyal, if not criminal, and cannot be trusted to respect law and authority because they aren't citizens – or worse, migrants' rights are simply not the same as citizens' rights. Crudely put, 'human rights' are only for citizens.

Berg rightly and frequently underlines the role of the law of unintended consequences in policy making in this field. For example, stiffer penalties on employers for labour rights violations against temporary migrant workers may actually increase the precariousness of those workers as they have a lot more to lose (job and sponsorship) if the employer is fined. As well, the harsh treatment of irregular migrants who are detected, including arrest, automatic detention and swift deportation, without proper recourse or remedies, actually increases the hold of unscrupulous employers and entrenches the underground labour markets that the government says it wants to eliminate. Such counterproductive effects are a constant feature of migration policy making.

Only when we'll create the conditions for a serene debate on the need of most countries for migrants, and on the advantages of migration at all levels, without interference from border control obsessions and populist-nationalist rants, will we be able to factor in all the information we need to develop the human-rights framework for migration policies that will effectively protect migrants.

In the meantime, we need research such as this book to remind us, on the one hand, what the law is and how it should be applied, and, on the other, how our policies are creating intense suffering that we refuse to see and acknowledge.

François Crépeau
Hans & Tamar Oppenheimer Professor of
Public International Law, McGill University

United Nations Special Rapporteur on the
Human Rights of Migrants
Montreal, 23 March 2015

1 Migrant rights at work

Guo Jiandong died on 4 June 2007. He was 33 years old.[1] Felling cypress pine in a remote forest 700 km west of Brisbane, Australia, Guo was cutting a tree, which brushed a dead tree behind him and fell onto him, crushing his face into his chainsaw. 'He was in the foetal position', his workmate recalled. 'He was backing away. He was still crouching when a dead tree hit him across the back'. The man who trained him claimed that Guo had never used a chainsaw before arriving in Queensland. The local paper carried a brief report on the death but did not record Guo's name or his Chinese nationality. In the 18 months he spent in south-western Queensland, he had only met a few locals who knew him just as 'Go' or 'the Chinaman'.

Along with eleven other Mongolian men, Guo had borrowed around A$20,000 to pay agents in China to travel to Australia on a four-year subclass 457 Temporary Work (Skilled) visa, sponsored by their Australian employer. They worked up to 80 hours a week, and never fewer than 48 hours, for which they were paid roughly A$12 an hour (the national minimum wage at the time was A$13.47). They received no pay slips, and only found out how much they had been paid by checking their bank accounts. In spite of this, before Guo's death, the group made no complaints, nor sought to change their circumstances. At that time, under the 457 visa scheme, an employee who stopped working for an employer-sponsor had just 28 days to find a new job and sponsor or leave Australia.[2] The possibilities of a non-English speaking Mongolian finding alternative employment in Queensland were few.

An investigation by the Department of Immigration and Citizenship (DIAC, as it was known between 2007 and 2013) found that the workers' employer, NK Collins Industries Pty Ltd, failed to comply with its

1 Details of this account of Guo's death are drawn from: Matthew Moore, 'A Lonely Death Among the Pines', *Sydney Morning Herald*, 29 August 2007; Matthew Moore, 'Timber Workers Face Deportation to a Bleak Future', *Sydney Morning Herald*, 19 October 2007; Editorial, 'The Passport to Misery', *Sydney Morning Herald*, 22 October 2007.

2 This period was extended to 90 days in 2013 by *Migration Amendment (Temporary Sponsored Visas) Act 2013* (Cth), sch 2 (*457 Amendment Act 2013*).

sponsorship requirements. On 18 September 2007, DIAC cancelled NK Collins' sponsorship and barred it from sponsoring further workers for three years, on the basis that tree felling lies outside the scope of the occupations that had been nominated for the workers (wood machinists rather than tree fallers) in breach of their visa conditions.[3] DIAC also found breaches in relation to underpayment of the specified salary. As a result, eighteen other Mongolian timber workers faced financial ruin and removal to China because their visas depended on this ongoing sponsorship. The Migration Review Tribunal overturned the sanctions against the employer finding that the evidence did not support DIAC's findings.[4] On 21 September 2009, NK Collins was found criminally liable for failing to discharge its workplace health and safety obligations in relation to Guo, although in 2013 the Queensland Court of Appeal allowed an appeal against this conviction on the basis that the charges had not fully particularised the breaches.[5] The company went into receivership before the matter was reheard. While NK Collins was required to contribute to a superannuation account held in Guo's name, it is not known whether Guo's wife in Inner Mongolia received the death benefit to which she was entitled.

Guo's treatment lies at the extreme end of migrant worker abuse. There are approximately 232 million foreign-born workers in the world, an increase of 57 million since 2000. Of these, 60 million are in high-income countries: an average of 12 per cent of their labour forces.[6] The share of foreign-born workers in traditional immigration countries such as Australia, Canada and New Zealand is even higher. Guo's death speaks of the structural violence that can shape the lives of a significant subset of these migrants: those working on temporary visas or no visa at all.

His story illustrates a central dilemma identified by Castles and Miller on which temporary labour migration schemes are built: maintaining the well-being of a resident population that is economically productive but lacks political representation and access to all of the social and economic benefits enjoyed by full members.[7] By adding temporary workers to the labour force

3 *071776514* [2007] MRTA 809, [24]. 457 visa-holders must not work in a position inconsistent with that for which the visa was granted: *Migration Regulations 1994* (Cth), condition 8107(1)(b).

4 *071776514* [2007] MRTA 809.

5 See *NK Collins Industries Pty Ltd and Peter Vincent Twigg* (C/2009/56) Industrial Court of Queensland, 27 April 2010; *NK Collins Industries Pty Ltd v. President of the Industrial Court of Queensland* [2010] QSC 373; *NK Collins Industries Pty Ltd and Peter Vincent Twigg* (C/2009/56) (No 2) Industrial Court of Queensland, 22 March 2011; *NK Collins Industries Pty Ltd v. President of the Industrial Court of Queensland* [2012] QSC 147; *NK Collins Industries Pty Ltd v. The President of the Industrial Court of Queensland* [2013] QCA 179.

6 International Labour Organization, *Towards a Fair Deal for Migrant Workers in the Global Economy* (International Labour Conference, 92nd sess, Geneva, Report VI).

7 Stephen Castles and Mark Miller, *The Age of Migration: International Population Movements in the Modern World* (Palgrave-Macmillan and Guilford Books, 2009), 206.

without adding permanent residents to the population, temporary labour migration schemes disaggregate membership of a national labour market from membership in a national political community. Defying a view of the world as divided into neat and territorially bound national states exercising sovereignty over their clearly demarcated and homogeneous populations, the vulnerabilities that attend migrant labour illuminate broader dilemmas related to justice in a simultaneously globalised and bordered world.

In most liberal democratic countries, permanent residents are typically granted almost all the rights of citizens with the most frequent and significant exception being the right to vote and absolute protection against deportation. While most agree that temporary migrant workers are entitled to the general protection of employment laws that apply to every other worker, temporary immigration programmes by definition necessitate the restriction of rights to residence, occupational and geographic mobility, and full social protections. So where precisely should the differences between temporary and permanent residents lie? What further restrictions should apply to migrants who lack immigration authorisation altogether? Where should the line be drawn between exploitation and legitimate employment? What role, if any, should migrants themselves play in shaping these standards? These questions, the focus of this book, touch on deeply held beliefs about how a national community should be defined and to whom domestic legal protection should extend.

Unfortunately, clear antidotes are not readily apparent. International law espouses the principle of equality of treatment for foreign and domestic workers. However, no industrialised country has ratified the United Nations International Convention on the Protection of the Rights of All Migrant Workers and Members of Their Families, the human rights treaty that most explicitly and specifically articulates the protections for migrant workers.[8] Developed nations are also reluctant to ratify International Labour Organization conventions promoting protections for migrant workers, which articulate safeguards for social rights for migrants.[9] In any event, international human rights law arguably takes a highly ambivalent approach to migrant workers: embracing the principle of equality while also deferring to the sovereign discretion of states to set criteria for immigration admissions and provide for a range of different immigration statuses which correspond to differentiated rights.[10] Yet these questions are urgent as global migration becomes increasingly temporary and oriented towards labour market needs.

8 International Convention on Protection of the Rights of All Migrant Workers and Members of their Families, adopted by GA Res 45/158, UN GAOR, 45th sess, UN Doc A/RES/45/158, 18 December 1990 (entered into force 1 July 2003).

9 E.g. Migrant Workers (Supplementary Provisions) Convention, 1975 (ILO No 143) opened for signature 24 June 1975, 1120 UNTS 323 (entered into force 9 December 1978).

10 Laurie Berg, 'At the Border and Between the Cracks: The Precarious Position of Irregular Migrant Workers under International Law' (2007) 8 *Melbourne Journal of International Law* 1, 18.

International trend towards temporary labour migration

National immigration policies have always been strongly shaped by each country's legal and cultural context and their unique history of immigration. Still, there is a convergence internationally toward temporary labour migration policies, although thoroughgoing comparative research into migration law and policy is only just beginning.[11] Governments increasingly present such schemes as a 'win-win-win' for migrants, employers and the national economy.[12]

This has involved a significant shift, in English-speaking developed countries, away from family migration and humanitarian entrants towards *skilled* migration. The skill stream of permanent residency in Australia represented 65 per cent of the migration programme in 2004–5 compared with 34 per cent in 1997–8.[13] In the 1990s, when the North American Free Trade Agreement facilitated the outflow of many skilled Canadians to work in the United States (USA), Canada sought to fill skills shortages and develop the 'knowledge-based economy' by actively recruiting skilled professionals from Asia through a points system to select immigrants established in the 1960s.[14] Like Australia, skilled admissions comprised 63 per cent of new Canadian residents in 2011.[15] When Britain reformed its policy for admitting migrants from outside the European Economic Area (which includes the European Union and Iceland, Lichtenstein and Norway) in 2008, it reduced 80 admission streams to five major tiers, three of which relate directly to labour migration. The USA is the noticeable outlier here with a vast majority of the permanent residency 'green cards' granted still related to family reunion, a trend that is probably best understood in the context of stalled immigration reform in that country.

Giving precedence to labour-related entrants in these high-income countries has been accompanied by a shift toward *temporary* migration, allowing local employers to recruit and employ foreign workers, even among those countries that have traditionally encouraged only permanent immigration. In Canada the number of temporary workers increased threefold between 2002 and 2011 from about 101,000 to 300,000, many of which were

11 See e.g. Philip Martin, Manolo Abella and Christiane Kuptsch, *Managing Labor Migration in the Twenty-First Century* (Yale University Press, 2006); Martin Ruhs and Philip Martin, 'Numbers vs Rights: Trade-offs and Guestworker Programs' (2008) 42(1) *International Migration Review* 249; Stephen Castles, 'Guestworkers in Europe: A Resurrection?' (2006) 40(4) *International Migration Review* 741. The IMPALA (International Migration Policy and Law Analysis) project seeks to measure immigration policies in twenty countries: http://projects.iq.harvard.edu/impala/home.

12 Catherine Dauvergne and Sarah Marsden, 'The Ideology of Temporary Labour Migration in the Post-Global Era' (2014) 18(2) *Citizenship Studies* 224.

13 DIAC, *Population Flows: Immigration Aspects 2005–06* (Cth of Australia, 2007), 6.

14 Canadian Minister for Public Works and Government Services, 'Building a Strong Foundation for the 21st Century' (1998), 10.

15 Organisation for Economic Co-operation and Development, *Immigration Outlook 2013* (2013), 240.

in low-skilled jobs under specific schemes for seasonal agricultural workers and domestic care workers.[16] In New Zealand, temporary skilled entrants outnumbered permanent skilled entrants between 2004 and 2009, with 83 per cent of those selected for permanent skilled migration in 2006 coming from onshore.[17] In Australia, net arrivals of long-term temporary overseas entrants have exceeded net permanent migration since 1998–9.[18] The USA has relied on temporary work permits for far longer, driven mostly by employer sponsorship, with more than 20 non-immigrant programmes that permit foreigners to enter and work. Even so, in the USA, the number of new temporary workers entering on schemes such as the H-1B temporary skilled visa increased from around 50,000 annually at the beginning of the 1990s to 136,890 in 2010.[19] Issues relating to the precarious working conditions of temporary migrant workers, therefore, have great salience internationally.

The Australian case study: intersections between migration and labour

While such trends are common to migrant worker schemes worldwide, they arise in Australia in unique ways. This book, therefore, takes the Australian policy responses as its central case study. In contrast to many foreign settings, temporary labour migration and unauthorised work are very recent arrivals on the Australian policy landscape. It is only since the 1990s that Australia has seen exponential growth in temporary labour migration.

Previously, from its colonial origins in the 1770s – with the notable exceptions of Pacific Islanders indentured in Queensland and Chinese arrivals in the late nineteenth century – migration to Australia was overwhelmingly permanent.[20] The hallmark of the 'White Australia policy' from Federation in 1901 was that newcomers (initially overwhelmingly from Britain and later Europe) were courted both to meet labour shortages and facilitate nation building. They were treated as immediate members of the Australian community and were expected to integrate instantly into the domestic labour market. The permanent settlement of white workers and their families aimed to maintain Australia's 'British character' and create an

16 Institute for Research on Public Policy, *Roundtable on Temporary Migration and the Canadian Labour Market* (University of Ottawa, 30 April 2012).

17 Lesleyanne Hawthorne, *Competing for Skills: Migration Policies and Trends in New Zealand and Australia* (report for the New Zealand Department of Labour, 2011).

18 Peter McDonald, Siew Ean Khoo and Rebecca Kippen, 'Alternative New Migration Estimates for Australia: Exploding the Myth of a Rapid Increase in Numbers' (Working Papers in Demography No 89, Demography and Sociology Program, Australian National University, September 2003), 2.

19 US Citizenship and Immigration Services, *Characteristics of H-1B Specialty Occupation Workers: Fiscal Year 2012 Annual Report* (2012), 4.

20 Anthony O'Donnell and Richard Mitchell, 'Immigrant Labour in Australia: The Regulatory Framework' (2001) 14 *Australian Journal of Labour Law* 269, 271–8.

egalitarian national community respectful of workers' dignity.[21] Non-European migration was seen as anathema to cultural homogeneity and the maintenance of robust labour standards and was, therefore, prohibited almost entirely. Temporary migrant labour was prohibited except where it would demonstrably not put downward pressure on the 'Australian standard', the promise of decent working conditions produced through arbitration between employers, unions and the government.[22]

With the demise of the White Australia policy in the 1970s and significant deregulation of the Australian economy in the 1980s, entry was permitted to a much wider pool of applicants (especially from the Middle East and Asia) increasingly on a temporary basis. Australia's commitments to liberalise the short-term entry procedures for highly skilled personnel under Mode 4 of the General Agreement on Trade in Services (GATS) in 1995 marked the beginnings of a 'permanent shift to temporary migration'.[23] During the 1990s, the paradigmatic entrant to Australia was completely transformed from permanent resident to temporary migrant, and family-sponsored to skilled.

While Australia now emulates the global trend towards temporary migrant labour in many respects, it has maintained a deeply ambivalent attitude towards it. Australia has never instituted a lower-skilled temporary labour programme like 'guestworker' programmes in Germany or France in the 1950 and 1960s or the controversial Bracero programme in the USA, which brought up to 400,000 Mexican workers per year into agricultural labour between the early 1940s and 1964. Indeed, unlike Canada, Australia continues to eschew a dedicated lower-skilled migrant labour programme altogether, with the exception of a very small Seasonal Worker Program, overwhelmingly in horticulture, that was first piloted in 2008. At the same time, low-waged migrant labour *has* in fact proliferated, partly through the 457 Temporary Work (Skilled) visa (although, as the name suggests, this visa was established to permit *skilled* labour), and increasingly through immigration schemes with other stated purposes such as international students and working holiday makers (young people from industrialised countries on a cultural exchange in Australia). With the upsurge of such temporary entrants since the early 2000s, Australia has increasingly fostered pathways to residence for professionals while cementing the temporariness of less-skilled workers' stays.

Australia's highly controlled historical approach to cross-border movement has another rare legacy. Lack of contiguous land borders and an historical aversion to temporary residency have meant that the presence in

21 Myra Willard, *History of the White Australia Policy* (Melbourne University Press, 1923), 121.

22 Lenore Layman, 'To Keep Up the Australian Standard: Regulating Contract Migration 1901–1950' (1996) 70 *Labour History* 25.

23 Peter Mares, 'The Permanent Shift to Temporary Migration' in Suvendrini Perera, Graeme Seal and Sue Summers (eds), *Enter At Own Risk? Australia's Population Questions for the 21st Century* (Black Swan Press, 2010). See *Australia Schedule of Specific Commitments: Supplement 1*, GATS/SC/6/Suppl.1 (4 October 1995).

Australia of unauthorised migrants is extremely limited. Geographic isolation has facilitated an intense cultural commitment to strong immigration compliance measures that are, according to its own Auditor-General, 'arguably the most effective of any country in the world'.[24] Nevertheless, and perhaps inevitably with the escalation of temporary migration, numbers of unauthorised migrants in the community (mainly those who have remained in Australia after the expiration of valid visas) have been steadily rising to 62,700 in 2013.[25] Australia's ability almost entirely to prevent clandestine entry into the community and facilitate strict monitoring of arrivals and departures through a universal visa system have meant that Australia is uniquely placed to gather data about unauthorised *labour*, which also appears to be on the rise.

These changes to the profile of migrants in Australia took place against the backdrop of perhaps the 'most significant reforms to Australia's industrial relations system since its inception'.[26] Australia's protectionist approach to nation building and labour rights at Federation in 1901 had been achieved through a centralised process of tripartite arbitration and conciliation between government, trade unions and employer associations. The 1980s saw moves to consolidate Australia's integration into the global economy through deregulation of financial markets and lowering of tariffs. Bargaining at the workplace or enterprise level largely replaced industry-wide standards of pay and conditions and Australia's uniform labour protections have become increasingly complex and piecemeal. In other words, the upsurge in numbers of non-citizens working in Australia with increasingly precarious immigration status coincided with generally less robust industrial protections across the Australian labour market.

Thus, Australia's immigration policies and industrial relations arrangements have been inter-linked from colonial days. As temporary labour programmes toppled the historical pre-eminence of permanent labour migration, those working pursuant to temporary visas or without visa authorisation – as much as 6 per cent of the Australian labour market – have been left more susceptible than resident workers to the raw impact of a weakly regulated labour market. This 'perfect storm' has led to a proliferation of exploitative working conditions experienced by some non-citizens

24 Australian National Audit Office, *Onshore Compliance – Visa Overstayers and Non-Citizens Working Illegally: Department of Immigration and Multicultural and Indigenous Affairs* (the Auditor-General Audit Report No 2 2004-05 Performance Audit, 2004), 20.

25 Department of Immigration and Border Protection, *Australia's Migration Trends 2012-13* (2014) 77.

26 John Edwards, Ron McCallum and Michael Moore, *Towards More Productive and Equitable Workplaces: An Evaluation of the Fair Work Legislation* (Department of Education, Employment and Workplace Relations, August 2012), 34.

in Australia from around 2004.[27] A restaurant owner in Sydney's Blue Mountains employed an Indian worker on a 457 visa, on the basis that he would be paid nothing whatsoever for twelve months.[28] Another employer demanded A$30,000 from a migrant worker in exchange for sponsoring his application for permanent residence.[29] In another case, a family brought a young woman from Indonesia on a false passport and temporary visa to Yowie Bay as a 'housemaid'. Carrying out domestic and childcare duties 17 hour days, seven days a week, she received a total of A$5,190 for four years' work.[30]

Yet strong national consensus on Australia's protectionist approach to migration and labour, until very recently, has meant that mainstream policy debates about exploitation of temporary migrant labour are still undeveloped in this country. Amidst such reports of seriously exploitative workplaces, pressure has intensified to follow other English-speaking developed countries in tackling 'rogue employers' and giving succour to 'vulnerable migrants' through law reforms including criminal offences for human trafficking or tougher border control. Such assessments too frequently consider employment law and migration law in isolation from each other. Centring attention on an individual's vulnerability or unscrupulousness obscures the more systemic nature of problems facing immigrant workers. This treats the relationships between migrant workers and their employers as natural phenomena rather than seeing such relationships as *shaped* by government regulation of employment and immigration.

Migrant workers and law's precariousness

This book contends that the lens of 'precariousness' captures the problems of global labour migration better than the doctrine of equality or even human rights. It attends to the influence of immigration law beyond its functions in regulating admission to and exclusion from the country of employment and the local labour market. My central argument is that the frame of precariousness illuminates the damaging impact on temporary migrants of the intersections between employment law and migration law. This perspective is developed by tracking how immigration law and enforcement reconfigure the relationships between non-citizens and their employers, building precariousness into the working conditions of temporary and unauthorised migrant workers. This stems from two particular features of immigration controls: their coercive effect and the uncertainty

27 Mary Crock, Sean Howe and Ron McCallum, 'Conflicted Priorities? Enforcing Fairness for Temporary Migrant Workers in Australia' in Cathryn Costello and Mark Freedland (eds), *Migrants at Work: Immigration and Vulnerability in Labour Law* (Oxford University Press, 2014), 422.

28 *Freya v. Yoga Tandoori House Pty Ltd* [2008] FMCA 288.

29 *Shim v. JMNE Pty Limited t/as Wooden Bowl Restaurant* [2010] FWA 8230.

30 *Masri v. Santoso* [2004] NSWIRComm 108.

they engender. The force of immigration regulation can be so potent that specific efforts by employers to exploit migrant employees are redundant.

Conceptualisations of 'precariousness' first emerged in industrial relations literature to capture the transformation of previously guaranteed permanent employment conditions into more uncertain or exploitative jobs.[31] Precarious employment is shaped by a range of factors including employment status (i.e. self-employed or paid employment), form of employment (e.g. part-time, casual or permanent) and broader dimensions of labour market insecurity.[32] The frame of 'precariousness' has since been adopted in British and Canadian scholarship to describe the insecurity that can attend immigration status.[33]

The perspectives on the precariousness engendered by immigration laws in this book are expanded by drawing on the cognate frames of 'precariousness', 'vulnerability' and 'dependency' developed in feminist legal and political theories.[34] These take a more holistic approach to precariousness, recognising that insecurity is inherent in human life. All our bodies and lives are fragile and we are necessarily dependent on others and vulnerable in certain ways. At the same time, precariousness is seen as highly specific, and frequently produced in relationships (with others, with institutions and with laws). Informed by industrial relations, immigration and feminist approaches, this wider lens of precariousness foregrounds the highly particularised situations of migrant workers under employment and immigration laws.

This book proposes four windows into the precariousness produced through law. These are traced across chapters dedicated to temporary migrant labour, unauthorised migrant labour and trafficked labour. First there is the direct impact of visa conditions. The coercive effect of conditions of stay is inherent to temporary non-citizenship status. Time-limited visas enforce 'temporariness' (to use Dauvergne and Marsden's term).[35] This constraint is buttressed by the ubiquitous threats of deportation or removal, which force people to move against their will, and administrative detention,

31 E.g. Gerry Rodgers, 'Precarious Work in Western Europe: The State of the Debate' in Gerry Rodgers and Janine J. Rodgers (eds), *Precarious Jobs in Labour Market Regulation: The Growth of Atypical Employment in Western Europe* (International Labour Organization, 1989), 1.

32 E.g. Judy Fudge, 'Precarious Migrant Status and Precarious Employment: The Paradox of International Rights for Migrant Workers' (2012) 34 *Comparative Labor Law and Policy Journal* 95; Leah Vosko, *Managing the Margins: Gender, Citizenship and the International Regulation of Precarious Employment* (Oxford University Press, 2010), 102.

33 Matthew Gibney, 'Precarious Residents: Migration Control, Membership and the Rights of Non-Citizens' (Human Development Reports Research Paper No 2009/10, United Nations Development Programme, April 2009); Luin Goldring, Carolina Berinstein and Judith K. Bernhard, 'Institutionalizing Precarious Migratory Status in Canada' (2009) 13(3) *Citizenship Studies* 239.

34 E.g. Martha A. Fineman, 'The Vulnerable Subject and the Responsive State' (2010) 60 *Emory Law Journal* 251; Judith Butler, *Precarious Life* (Verso, 2004); Judith Butler, *Frames of War: When is Life Grievable?* (Verso, 2009).

35 Dauvergne and Marsden, above n. 12.

constraining the liberty of non-citizens suspected to lack a valid visa. Second are barriers to the enforcement of employment rights. The operation of immigration enforcement, or fear of removal or instability, can inject uncertainty into otherwise robust employment entitlements. Logistical hurdles frequently confront workers who attempt to pursue claims after departing their country of employment. Frequently little dispensation is offered to such claimants who fall foul of procedural requirements or lack information about commencing proceedings.

Third, immigration laws can significantly transform not only a migrant worker's felt experiences but also the legal context of their employment relationships. Immigration rules related to temporary or unauthorised status, and their enforcement, can vary the substantive legal content of protections afforded in other domains in complex and unpredictable ways. Fourth, various personal circumstances of individual workers can enhance precariousness. The effects of immigration regulation, of course, depend greatly on the varying elements of vulnerability that may attach to a migrant worker's personal circumstances: their nationality; relative position within the global economy; access to social welfare protections at home and domestic labour market options there; and pre-existing debts to off-shore agents and other family or financial obligations. Security in the migrant's stay in a country of employment frequently depends on their skills as well as employment opportunities in the relevant industry sector. These forces intensify the superior bargaining strength of employers and enable them to exploit a migrant worker's structural disadvantage, including insecurities the employer played no part in creating.

The lens of precariousness to interrogate questions of justice for migrant workers, therefore, acknowledges the agency of workers and employers in exacerbating or ameliorating exploitation. Undoubtedly, most migrants choose to move abroad for employment in order to advance their financial and professional goals and those of their families. Ong's phrase, 'flexible citizen', suggests migrants' ability to circumvent and manipulate state processes to personal advantage, since migrants make decisions about their lives and work like anyone else. At the same time, those choices may be misinformed, can involve substantial risk and cost and are constrained by structural forces including global economic inequalities and immigration controls. Using precariousness as a framing device broadens the scope of analysis to embrace the constitutive roles played by institutions, laws and other deployments of power in shaping 'people's motivations, desires and struggles and mak[ing] them particular kinds of subjects in the world', which are often obscured.[36] It points to the significance of considering the agency, voice and interests of migrants when thinking normatively about migrants' rights and the regulation of labour migration. It also suggests ways

36 Aihwa Ong, *Flexible Citizenship: The Cultural Logic of Transnationality* (Duke University Press, 1999), 5.

in which government action can either foster conditions of exploitation or promote workers' resilience.

A decade of regulatory reforms targeting migrant worker exploitation in Australia forms the core case study through which concerns relating to justice and precarious labour migration are traced in this book. Several of these have done much to ameliorate the precarious living and working conditions of temporary and unauthorised migrant workers. The temporary skilled migration scheme (centred in the employer-sponsored 457 visa) has been significantly reconfigured over time with innovative safeguards including a requirement that employers accord wages and conditions at the prevailing market rate, and a longer 90-day period between termination of sponsorship and visa cancellation.[37] The Fair Work Ombudsman (FWO), Australia's labour inspectorate, has made significant efforts to target the working conditions of migrants on temporary visas, monitoring industries in which these workers are prevalent and vigorously prosecuting labour violations. Information-sharing between the FWO and the Department of Immigration and Border Protection has also been significantly streamlined.[38]

Further, a suite of new human trafficking offences, introduced in 2013, target labour trafficking in a sophisticated way. Among other initiatives, a forced labour offence was enacted that takes a highly nuanced approach to assessing the circumstances in which coercion of temporary or unauthorised workers can occur.[39] New provisions require courts and, where appropriate, juries, to consider the complainant's social context, the subtleties of 'psychological oppression' and dependencies in worker-employer relationships when assessing the presence of coercion or force.[40] These amendments may allow juries more readily to apply trafficking offences. This may result in more suspected victims of labour trafficking or forced labour accessing support and immigration concessions to regularise their stay in Australia (with the possibility of eventual permanent residence).

However, other regulatory responses, devised in the name of protecting temporary or unauthorised workers, have arguably done much less to ameliorate their precarious work. Fault-based 'employer sanction' offences criminalising those who employ unauthorised workers were introduced in 2007 and extended and supplemented with civil penalty offences in 2013.[41]

37 *Migration Legislation Amendment (Worker Protection) Act 2008* (Cth) (*Worker Protection Act*); *Migration Amendment Regulations 2009 (No 5)* (Cth); *Migration Amendment Regulations 2009 (No 9)* (Cth); *Migration Amendment Regulations 2009 (No 5) Amendment Regulations 2009 (No 1)* (Cth); *457 Amendment Act 2013.*

38 *Migration Act 1958* (Cth), ss 140ZA and 140ZH.

39 *Criminal Code 1995* (Cth), ss 270.6A(1) and 270.6A(2) (*Criminal Code*), introduced by *Crimes Legislation Amendment (Slavery, Slavery-like Conditions and People Trafficking) Act 2013* (Cth).

40 *Criminal Code* ss 270.10 and 271.11A(2).

41 *Migration Amendment (Employer Sanctions) Act 2007* (Cth); *Migration Amendment (Reform of Employer Sanctions) Act 2013* (Cth).

Sharper penalties were also introduced in 2009 for employers who violated the terms of their sponsorship role under the 457 visa scheme.[42] These interventions fall short by constructing unscrupulous employers as the problem, and enforcement as the solution, leaving firmly in place the structural causes of precarious conditions for these workers. Migrant workers bear the greater cost of these immigration penalties, even where designed to target employers, because when the employment relationship breaks down, or a breach of immigration laws is detected (whether by the migrant, or the employer or both), it is frequently the migrant worker who has the most to lose. These laws accentuate the underlying power differential in migrants' precarious employment.

Other reforms increased the thresholds of required skills and English language ability particularly for applicants for the 457 visa scheme. These were justified as preventing exploitation of vulnerable workers by limiting their ability to participate under the scheme at all. Here again, it seems difficult to maintain that this change left vulnerable workers better off. In the name of protection, the government moved to exclude. Rather than enhance the agency or bargaining position of temporary migrant workers in Australia, these reforms shut down options for migrant workers (especially those on student or other temporary visas hoping to transition towards permanent residence, which are an increasing cohort of applicants for 457 visas). This illustrates Ruhs' observations about a 'blind spot in human rights-based approaches to migration', which frequently promote the rights of existing migrants without considering the consequences of policies for admitting potential future migrants who do not yet have access to labour markets of higher income countries.[43]

Finally, the book reconsiders the legislative amendments that sharpened labour trafficking crimes in Australia. While celebrating the focus on human trafficking for non-sexual exploitation, these offences have left unchallenged the ways that immigration controls can seriously constrain migrant workers' labour market options and larger social choices. These structural forces can organise migrant workers into situations of forced labour without any specific effort by employers to exploit them. By detaching forced labour from labour so completely, these laws missed an opportunity to understand how intersections between employment and immigration regulations can magnify migrant workers' vulnerabilities. In this case, justice for migrant workers may be better protected by providing them with particular rights reflecting their specific location rather than simply formally equal access to rights available to citizens and residents in host states.

The chief task of this book is diagnostic: its main orientation is not towards 'law reform'. However, it does seek to offer some insights into how to

42 *Worker Protection Act.*

43 Martin Ruhs, *The Price of Rights: Regulating International Labor Migration* (Princeton University Press, 2013), 9.

recognise and promote migrant workers' resiliency in relationships with their employers. To this end I recommend adjustments to immigration laws and processes that foreground participatory inclusion. These coalesce around three key objectives: (1) empowering migrants to give voice to their perspectives to shape policy formation; (2) the ability to participate in institutional structures that provide concrete redress (including a right to be present in Australia long enough to access legal institutions that are *here*); and (3) recognition of all workers (whether citizen, resident, temporary migrant or unauthorised) as active participants in the Australian labour market. This involves reducing dependencies on employers, enhancing labour market mobility and treatment of migrant workers as subjects of employment law as much as objects of immigration law. Overall, it is argued that migrant worker exploitation needs to be recast from an immigration law violation to a labour law abuse.

Overview of the book

Chapter 2 introduces the key conceptual concerns, drawing together hitherto unconnected theoretical perspectives on inclusion and equality from Europe and North America. It explores the debates around the ethical treatment of non-citizens. The theories of inclusion that provide the ethical drivers for the arguments in this book emanate from liberal nationalist debates about open and closed borders and deliberative democratic theories that have predominated in the USA. However, these theories have typically foundered in the context of short-term labour migration. It argues that instead of frameworks centred on open or closed borders, citizenship or equality, the ideas of *relational impact* and *participatory inclusion* are more helpful starting points for theorising inclusion of non-citizens. These perspectives are then connected with theories of precariousness and vulnerability in industrial relations and immigration scholarship and feminist theory, which have been elaborated in Canada and Europe. The precariousness analytic lens provides a way to move beyond the road block created by calls for equality between non-citizens and citizens, whose treatment under domestic laws after all can never be equal in all respects.

Parts I to III each consider a separate immigration context in which migrants in Australia work: Part I concerns the regulation of temporary migrant labour; Part II concerns unauthorised migrant labour; and Part III concerns the criminalisation of forced migrant labour. Each of these parts undertakes three tasks. First, each part provides an overview of the relevant Australian immigration law framework and how this intersects with certain labour law protections to produce precariousness. Second, each part contains a chapter in which relevant reforms to immigration law are considered in context. Third, where reforms have not adequately addressed the dynamics of uncertainty and coercion produced by immigration law, suggestions are made for adjustments to immigration or employment regulation that will better foster migrant workers' resilience. A brief note on this terminology: the distinctions between temporary, unauthorised and forced migration are not intended to suggest that these are discrete fields of human experience; to the contrary, these legal boundaries are far from fixed and overlap in their application to non-citizens. Nevertheless, the separation is helpful because it demonstrates how influential these constructed categories are in determining a worker's status and the protections or impairments which can result.

Part I introduces the Australian case study, unpacking the regulation and evolution of temporary labour migration in Australia, primarily through the 457 skilled work visa, international student visas and young working holiday makers. Chapter 3 charts the unique features of Australia's historical immigration policies, which have produced the current regulatory context. At Federation in 1901, the federal government articulated aspirations for the 'Australian standard' that involved universal citizenship and dignity of labour. This historical antipathy to segmented labour markets based on class (as in Britain) or race (as in the USA) goes some way to explain the specific challenges temporary immigration policies pose to presumptions about social justice and equality in contemporary Australia. Chapter 4 analyses significant legislative amendments to the 457 visa scheme in the last decade. The features examined here, including employer sponsorship, visa eligibility criteria such as occupational skill levels and English language ability, labour market testing and the availability of pathways towards permanent residence, are evident (and can be problematic) in many labour migration schemes around the world. This chapter recommends regulatory changes to better support the agency of 457 visa workers.

Part II explores the production of unauthorised migrant workers, and some unique features of the incidence and forms of unauthorised labour migration in Australia, as against Britain, Canada and the USA in particular. Chapters 5 and 6 consider the legal precariousness that flows when the legislative offence of unauthorised work in Australia intersects with employment law (including access to workers compensation, unfair dismissal and restitution), emphasising lines of reasoning that have developed in British jurisprudence. In both countries, the consequence is to leave unauthorised workers vulnerable to the raw effect of market forces unmediated by law. And, far from deterring unauthorised work, this case law provides employers with a windfall. Chapter 7 explores the introduction, in 2007, of offences criminalising employers' use of unauthorised workers. The analysis here on the deleterious impact of employer sanctions on unauthorised workers bears out the concerns expressed by migrant worker advocates in the USA and Britain about civil and criminal offences in those jurisdictions.

Part III takes up the regulation of forced migrant labour. Chapter 8 reviews reforms to Australia's counter-trafficking framework introduced in 2013. It suggests that, while Australian policy has historically echoed international efforts in de-emphasising labour trafficking, recent approaches manifest a growing consciousness of extreme labour exploitation. However, Chapter 9 argues that while these measures capture a clearer spectrum of exploitation in trafficking crimes, they do little to afford industrial justice or promote inclusion for workers who have not been subjected to criminal exploitation. It suggests that a more emancipatory approach to uncoerced migrant labour requires further immigration reforms. Advances made in the USA in this regard are presented as a model of better practice.

A conclusion in Chapter 10 draws together the key findings and theoretical questions that guided and challenged this study. This elucidates Australian reforms which have been innovative in protecting migrant worker rights and identifies policy settings in other jurisdictions that have done much to promote industrial justice for, and social inclusion of, temporary migrant workers.

2 Inclusion and precariousness

Jin Woog Kim worked up to 120 hours a week for two years for Rexma Pty Ltd at a factory in Revesby in outer Sydney after overstaying his tourist visa in 2004.[1] Kim was promised A$10 an hour but was often paid nothing at all, sleeping on a sofa bed in the factory at night. Still, he would have chosen to continue this arrangement, sending money home to South Korea. Instead, a plastic recycling machine tore the five fingers from his left hand in May 2006. Fearing liability and detection, the owner and operator of Rexma, Chung Byung Man, refused to arrange an ambulance, leaving a co-worker to call a taxi to take Kim to the hospital.

It was not the first time Kim had been injured at work: in March 2005 the same machine took the top off the middle finger on his right hand. After that first injury, his employer had docked Kim's pay to cover the medical expenses. Upon his second injury, Kim believes, Chung may have notified Australian immigration authorities, then the Department of Immigration and Citizenship (DIAC) (in 2013 renamed the Department of Immigration and Border Protection (DIBP)), of Kim's whereabouts in an effort to have him removed from Australia.

Months after the incident, Kim contacted the Construction Forestry Mining and Energy Union (CFMEU) after reading an article in a Korean-language paper. With their assistance, he learnt that his precarious circumstances weakened his legal claims, and he ultimately received only A$13,000 in workers compensation. This figure did not reflect the fact that he was supporting dependants in South Korea since he had no evidence of the remittance payments he had been forwarding: his unauthorised status in Australia had precluded him from using official channels. After a three month campaign, the union achieved a settlement of Kim's claim for the payment of unpaid wages, overtime and

1 Details of Mr Kim's story are drawn from Laurie Berg and Anna Samson, 'Space for Economic Migrants? Poverty, Migrants and Australian Civil Society' in Helmut Anheier, Marlies Glasius and Mary Kaldor (eds), *Global Civil Society Yearbook 2009: Global Civil Society and Poverty Alleviation* (SAGE Publications Ltd, 2009), ch. 8; Workcover NSW, Injured Person's Statement, File No. 2006/023747 (on file with author); Conversation with En Won Lee, organiser, CFMEU NSW (Sydney, 13 November 2006); Unions NSW Meeting Minutes, Meeting held 7 December 2006, Trades Hall Auditorium, Sydney, at 6:03pm.

other entitlements. Fortunately, Kim was not forced to seek remedies in court, where he may well have been unsuccessful given established legal principles in New South Wales denying unauthorised migrant workers unlawful dismissal protections,[2] and mandatory workers compensation entitlements,[3] on the basis that they worked without legal authority.

Rexma and Chung pleaded guilty to various health and safety offences, failing to: hold valid workers compensation insurance; implement necessary safety measures; and notify WorkCover of the incident.[4] Rexma was fined A$45,000 and Chung A$21,800.[5] In 2012, Chung was found guilty of further industrial safety offences, in 'not dissimilar' circumstances, after another worker's fingers and thumb were amputated in the same factory.[6]

While at an emotional level Kim's story can only illicit distress, stark ethical dilemmas also underlie his presence in a factory on the outskirts of Sydney. They animate questions surrounding how Kim was treated: by his employer as well as by Australian regulatory processes designed to keep workers safe. This chapter explores just how challenging it is to delineate with precision the ethical entitlements of migrants in a national workforce (both unauthorised, like Kim, and those working lawfully on temporary visas). In so doing, the chapter addresses two inter-connected normative questions: to whom should the protection of the law extend and what should be the nature of that protection?

Both are fraught and touch on deeply held beliefs about who we are in community with others. Many advocate for migrants' entitlements on the basis of the inherent equal rights of humanity under international human rights treaties. Others respond that while foreigners must enjoy certain legal safeguards, our primary concern must always be for resident workers. They argue that nationals and residents must take priority over temporary visitors in access to certain social benefits, such as unlimited mobility in the labour market and publicly-funded healthcare. This point is put even more strongly in relation to unauthorised workers like Kim, who are sometimes said to be 'strangers' to the social contract that binds the national community, with fewer entitlements than other foreigners because they lack the very right to be present.[7] These approaches are reflected in a longstanding – and

2 *Chen v. Allied Packaging Co Pty Ltd* (1997) 73 IR 53.

3 *Australia Meat Holdings Pty Ltd v. Kazi* [2004] QCA 147; *Yong Fu Zhang v. Mei Hu t/as Eden Furniture and the WorkCover Authority of NSW* [2006] NSWWCCPD 15. For a contrary approach see *Nonferral (NSW) Pty Ltd v. Taufia* (1998) 43 NSWLR 312.

4 *Occupational Health and Safety Act 2000* (NSW), ss 8(1) and 86; *Workplace Injury Management and Workers Compensation Act 1998* (NSW), s 244; and *Workers Compensation Act 1987* (NSW), s 155.

5 *Inspector Lai v. Rexma Pty Ltd* [2008] NSWIRComm 78.

6 *Inspector Cooper v. Chung* [2012] NSWIRComm 79, [22].

7 Peter Schuck and Rogers Smith, *Citizenship without Consent: Illegal Aliens in the American Polity* (Yale University Press, 1985), 130–40.

unresolved – ethical debate. Some philosophers, such as Hannah Arendt, view nationality as among the strongest sources of ethical bonds. Others insist that moral commitments must be universal in scope. At each extreme, these approaches prove inadequate in making sense of the complex relational dynamics at play when citizens and non-citizens coexist in a workplace or community.

This chapter proposes, as an alternative, three conceptual perspectives to unpack the relationships of justice between longer-term and temporary residents of a workplace, neighbourhood or national polity, and the legal regulation of both. The first, which I call *relational impact*, proposes that workers are owed certain standards of just treatment not so much because of their presence within national territory but because of residents' impact upon them within shared relationships. This draws from, and expands upon, a key premise of democratic theory, often known as the 'all affected principle', which suggests that a law or government policy is legitimate only if all who are affected by it have a right to be involved or consulted in its creation. This 'all' who feel the impact of law has generally been presumed to include only nationals whose 'consultation' chiefly takes the form of national elections. However, the temporary or unauthorised migrant worker, like Kim, is living both in their bounded political community of origin (for him, South Korea), their host state (Australia) and within a globalised economy. Kim vividly illuminates how people stand in dense relationships with others outside of, or across, national political communities, impacting upon one another in ways that produce conflict or achieve shared objectives. He also demonstrates just how greatly citizenship and national communities matter, as a question of law as well as pragmatics.

For the foreseeable future, institutions of national sovereignty are likely to remain intact: legal demarcations between citizens and non-citizens remain an inevitable part of the contemporary context. Nevertheless, a key argument of this book is that, at the very least, a government must treat with justice all those who are affected by its laws and policies. Non-citizens might be excluded from national electoral processes but, while living with shared duties to uphold the law, migrants (both authorised and unauthorised) are entitled to participate in shaping the law. How can migrants both be included as meaningful participants within a national community but also excluded as not (yet) citizens? To attempt an answer, it is necessary to see citizens and non-citizens alike as sustaining multiple ties to local communities, to workplaces, to laws and to national institutions. Inclusion of migrants may flow from their ties to a neighbourhood, a workplace, or a legal institution without legal citizenship or any formalised national membership.

The second lens, which I call *participatory inclusion* of non-residents, is connected to relational impact in that it captures an aspiration that migrant workers be invited and empowered to play an active part in shaping laws and policies that affect them. This frame suggests three standards directing policies toward migrant agency: (1) inclusion of migrant voices in policy formation; (2) access to effective redress via legal institutions; and (3) recognition of migrant workers as subjects of employment law as much as objects of immigration law. Participatory inclusion provides a way to evaluate how the interests of migrants and residents are affected by law.

But greater precision is required to evaluate law's impact on migrant workers. What sort of consideration of non-citizens' interests is enough for laws or workplace policies to be described as fair? How are migrants' and citizens' interests to be weighed against each other in circumstances where they conflict? Equality of treatment may seem an obvious touchstone for social justice. Arguments about the exploitation of migrant workers are frequently couched in terms of whether migrants are receiving comparable treatment to residents. However, as argued in more detail below, the equality standard founders in the context of migrants' rights because, within the sovereign architecture of national laws themselves, citizens and non-citizens are inevitably unequal in legal standing. This is why human rights law and the tradition of anti-discrimination laws in Anglo-American legal systems often break down when applied to protecting against differential treatment of non-citizens.

Therefore, I propose the third conceptual lens, *precariousness*, to understand how the working lives of migrants are structured by migration law and policies. Initially devised in industrial relations literature, a focus on 'precariousness' has more recently been applied in sociological work on immigration status in Canada and the United Kingdom (UK). I extend this literature by suggesting a more nuanced account of precariousness that includes the related concepts of 'vulnerability', 'dependency' and 'precariousness' developed in the feminist theory of Martha Fineman and Judith Butler. Fineman and Butler understand vulnerability, dependency and precariousness to define the very 'meaning of what it means to be human'.[8] Thus precariousness is universal and inevitable. Since our fate depends on the actions of others, the precariousness of each person's life can never be eradicated. At the same time, precariousness is complex and particular, and individual experiences of vulnerability vary since we are all differently situated in webs of economic and institutional relationships.

The lens of precariousness is helpful in better comprehending our real impact on the lives of others. It illuminates how temporary or unauthorised migration status can create, or perpetuate, migrant workers' vulnerability to exploitative employment. Examining how immigration status reshapes employment relationships provides room for reflection on the vulnerabilities of temporary and unauthorised migrants *as well as* resident workers. This analysis suggests how government intervention can create or allay dependencies between employer and worker, and intensify precariousness or alleviate it.

8 Martha A. Fineman, 'The Vulnerable Subject and the Responsive State' (2010) 60 *Emory Law Journal* 251, 266; Judith Butler, *Precarious Life: The Powers of Mourning and Violence* (Verso, 2004); Judith Butler, *Frames of War: When is Life Grievable?* (Verso, 2009), 134.

To this end, the first section of this chapter presents an overview of two dominant approaches to migrants' rights in liberal democracies: an ethics based on nationality and an ethics that reaches transnationally. It also reviews some recent ethical arguments that migrants' rights should be grounded in terms of time and place. The sections that follow propose instead the conceptual lens of relational impact, and explain how this focus on impact yields larger aspirations for participatory inclusion of migrants in communal decision making and legal structures for redress. The next section sets out the third conceptual lens, arguing that the impact of the law on migrant workers should be viewed in terms of precariousness. In the final section, this chapter begins to imagine what it might mean to accord significance to the relationships between migrants and residents (and the harms or benefits flowing from them) as much as to migrants' non-citizenship status. It explores, in particular, how immigration law can organise temporary and unauthorised migrants into coercive and uncertain employment relationships and begins to suggest some ways in which government intervention can more inclusively promote workers' agency.

Debates about the significance of nationality

A long lineage of political theory, especially within North America, explores how far a national community's moral responsibilities extend in the context of high levels of immigration and porous borders. Scholars (who might be described as 'nationalist') see core moral responsibilities as encompassing primarily co-residents in a fixed political community. Others (who might be described as 'postnationalist') advocate for justice derived from a cosmopolitan view of humanity and human rights. In this section, I provide a brief sketch of Hannah Arendt's argument for the significance of nationality before turning to scholarship that has greater faith in more universalised accounts of justice. I then explore the limitations of both for thinking through what legal and social protections are held by migrant workers who live and work in a country of employment for limited periods of time.

Hannah Arendt's political theory of the international protection of human rights centred on those excluded from citizenship. Her analysis in *The Origins of Totalitarianism* focused on a particular historical context of stateless people and refugees during and after World War Two.[9] From this perspective, she concluded that citizenship remained an essential precondition for enforceable rights. Stateless people were abject precisely because they had been deprived of a nationality and a sovereign state willing and able to guarantee their protection. As a result, they lost not only the benefits of freedom and justice in a society, but also the mutual recognition necessary for a political life, a 'place in the world which makes opinions significant

9 Hannah Arendt, *The Origins of Totalitarianism* (Harcourt Brace, 1951), 290ff.

and actions effective': that was their 'right to have rights'.[10] Because human rights proved meaningless as soon as they were needed, justice is shown to be secured primarily by membership in a common community with shared political institutions.

Many contemporary scholars likewise see nation states as the best form of stable democratic community.[11] Michael Walzer described membership in a bounded community as, itself, a social good that forms the fundamental basis for many if not 'all the other social goods', and memorably warned that without national walls the world may turn into a 'thousand petty fortresses'.[12] In the absence of national citizenship, religion, race and other groupings that are less democratic than national citizenship may become even greater organising principles. But within national borders, 'popular sovereignty' can flourish, allowing people to be both makers and obeyers of the law.[13] Just as important, fair distribution of resources and public assistance require delimited communities because the mutual trust and shared sacrifice needed for meaningful self-government cannot be achieved on a global scale. Again, Michael Walzer's rhetorical observation stands out:

> I am not a citizen of the world ... I am not even aware that there is a world such that one could be a citizen of it. No one has ever offered me citizenship, or described the naturalization process, or enlisted me in the world's institutional structures, or given me an account of its decision procedures (I hope they are democratic) or provided me with a list of the benefits and obligations of citizenship or shown me the world's calendar and the common celebrations and commemorations of its citizens.[14]

Walzer conceives the bounded nation as a prerequisite for struggles for justice. In terms of the focus of this book, the national border must be seen, at least in part, as productive of special social responsibilities nationals hold to one another beyond foreigners.

Others reject national citizenship as the proper outer limit of legal rights and moral regard. Diverse scholars, whom I categorise as 'postnationalist', but who describe themselves as 'transnational', 'postnational' or 'cosmopolitan', argue that the equal moral worth of all individuals means that differential ethical treatment of others cannot be based on accidental privileges of birth

10 Ibid. 296–7. See also Alison Kesby, *The Right to Have Rights: Citizenship, Humanity, and International Law* (Oxford University Press, 2012).

11 E.g. David Miller, *On Nationality* (Clarendon Press, 1995).

12 Michael Walzer, *Spheres of Justice* (Basic Books, 1983), 29, 39.

13 Jürgen Habermas, 'Citizenship and National Identity' in Bart van Steenbergen (ed.), *The Condition of Citizenship* (Sage, 1994), 20.

14 Michael Walzer, 'Spheres of Affection' in Martha C. Nussbaum and Joshua Cohen (eds), *For Love of Country?* (Beacon Press, 1996), 125.

such as nationality.[15] This normative commitment to personhood alone is reflected in highly evolved human rights frameworks that no longer rest on long-held assumptions that the most relevant subject for rights is the citizen of a territorial state. Indeed, global market forces (evident in trade regimes, global networks of communication and the ease of international travel) are increasingly compromising the autonomy of elected governments in any event. As a result, people worldwide have a growing awareness of their overlapping or concurrent allegiances and identities beyond the nation state.

Unfortunately, however, each of these accounts is too uncompromising and uncomplicated to assist in precisely delineating the rights of migrant workers. On the one hand, seeing the nation state as the starting point for all questions of justice seriously misapprehends the reality of contemporary human social interaction. Confining justice only to relationships between compatriots places too much moral weight on the national border. The picture of national communities at the heart of communitarianism seems unrealistically rigid, static over time and idealised. By living and working in a foreign country, migrant workers disrupt an absolute binary between citizens and aliens. It seems intuitively flawed to reserve every public resource and legal protection for citizens, while withholding them entirely from foreigners, especially when migrants are inevitably subject to criminal sanctions and civil law liabilities in their countries of employment.

At the same time, the postnationalist model is no less categorical. Clearly, globalisation has eroded traditional national control over trade, the natural environment and macro-economic processes. But formal citizenship continues to hold tremendous import: nations worldwide strenuously defend their prerogative to exclude unwanted immigrants from access to their sovereign territory and from the various services and goods associated with citizenship. To argue that legal entitlements within any nation extend to all of humanity as a matter of inalienable human rights seems too universal an account of relationships to assist in understanding what precise social entitlements a migrant worker is owed in their country of employment. All people may have a universal right to health,[16] for example, but this philosophical commitment does not necessarily assist in determining whether Kim, an unauthorised worker in a factory in the outskirts of Sydney, should be granted health care subsidised by the New South Wales state government, or

15 E.g. Nina Glick Schiller, Linda Basch and Cristina Blanc-Szanton, *Towards a Transnational Perspective on Migration: Race, Class, Ethnicity and Nationalism Reconsidered* (New York Academy of Sciences, 1992); Yasemin Soysal, *Limits of Citizenship: Migrants and Postnational Membership in Europe* (University of Chicago Press, 1994); Thomas Pogge, 'Cosmopolitanism and Sovereignty' (1992) 103(1) *Ethics* 48.

16 International Covenant on Economic, Social and Cultural Rights, opened for signature 16 December 1966, 993 UNTS 3 (entered into force 3 January 1976): art 12 provides that governments shall take progressive measures to the extent of available resources to protect the rights of everyone to the enjoyment of the highest attainable standard of physical and mental health.

only emergency health care, or none at all.[17] Neither nationalist nor human rights perspectives explain in detail what responsibilities are owed to people who lack the legal status of residents or citizens, but who nevertheless live for days, weeks or years within borders that are inevitably porous.

Neither approach grapples with the fundamental paradox, elegantly expressed by Linda Bosniak, that '[b]orders produce injustice, but also make possible the very contexts in which we pursue justice'.[18] National immigration and citizenship laws are meaningful because they create a bounded national society that can promote equality and social welfare. At the same time, nationals (almost universally in the Western world) live in dense relationships in neighbourhoods and workplaces that cross the notional and legal boundaries policed by immigration laws. In these relationships, citizens and non-citizens, resident, temporary and unauthorised migrants all impact upon one another in ways that produce conflict or harmonious shared objectives. Principles of justice are needed to guide such complex social relations within and across these permeable borders, including those between non-citizens and citizens.

To navigate the complex social realities produced by transnational immigration, various legal theorists and political philosophers, especially in North America, have attempted to bridge these nationalist and postnationalist approaches to justice. Some foreground *time*, arguing that non-citizens gradually accrue membership as they continue to reside in a foreign country. Others, including Bosniak, stress *place*: her theory of 'ethical territoriality' conditions citizenship-based rights on migrants' geographic presence on sovereign territory, regardless of immigration status or duration of stay.[19] Both acknowledge the core problematic that broader theories of nationalist and postnationalist approaches often obscure. They recognise both the state's need for boundedness, as far as stability of law, democratic processes and government authority are concerned, but also the new forces of international immigration and the devolution of political power that have been triggered by globalisation. While these are attractive, I will suggest that these perspectives actually remain caught in this same false binary between absolute membership and absolute exclusion. I consider each approach in turn before considering their limitations.

17 The International Convention on Protection of the Rights of All Migrant Workers and Members of their Families, adopted by GA Res 45/158, UN GAOR, 45th sess, UN Doc A/RES/45/158, 18 December 1990 (entered into force 1 July 2003): art 28 delimits the right to emergency medical care for migrant workers 'that is urgently required for the preservation of their life or the avoidance of irreparable harm to their health on the basis of equality of treatment with nationals' regardless of irregular immigration status.

18 Linda Bosniak, 'Arguing for Amnesty' (2013) 9(3) *Law Culture and the Humanities* 432, 442.

19 Linda Bosniak, 'Being Here: Ethical Territoriality and the Rights of Immigrants' (2007) 8(2) *Theoretical Inquiries in Law* 389.

The first view proposes that full community membership for immigrants should turn not on citizenship or immigration status, nor nationality or ethnicity, but on duration of residence.[20] Most prominently, Joseph Carens has argued that length of time of residence should be singularly decisive.[21] In his view, having been resident for an extended period, an individual eventually crosses a threshold that entitles her to virtually the same legal status as citizens (and subjects her to the same obligations). Why base membership rights on duration of residence? Carens' argument is that over time resident non-citizens inevitably become enmeshed in a dense network of social associations and gain identities tied up with citizens. These ties create an interest in being able to continue to reside in that community and the 'state, which has enabled them to acquire that vital interest by admitting them, has an obligation to protect their interest by granting them a legal right to remain'.[22] Migrants must be accorded far-reaching membership rights after a certain threshold of permanent residence, which for Carens is variously asserted to arise at '[t]hree to five years', 'five years or so' and 'ten years at the most, probably five'.[23]

Between arrival and citizenship, Carens proposes an incremental accretion of membership rights over time: from 'civil rights' for those physically present with temporary or unauthorised immigration status ('simply because they are human beings'), to 'civil and social rights' (including the right to join a trade union) for those who have a right to ongoing residence.[24] In other words, reciprocal ethical obligations flow from the reality of a non-citizen's physical presence, but legal immigration status also plays a significant role.

Linda Bosniak eschews this 'status-based approach', which accords different people differentiated rights depending on the status assigned to them by nation-centred immigration law or their duration of residence. Instead, for her, core membership rights should attach purely to geographical presence within a country's territorial boundaries irrespective of duration of stay, social ties or immigration status.[25] Her approach 'accords legal and ethical

20 E.g. T. Alexander Aleinikoff, *Semblances of Sovereignty: The Constitution, the State and American Citizenship* (Harvard University Press, 2002); Ruth Rubio Marin, 'National Limits to Democratic Citizenship' (1998) 11(1) *Ratio Juris* 51; Rainer Bauböck, *Transnational Citizenship: Membership and Rights in International Migration* (Edward Elgar, 1994).

21 Joseph Carens, *Immigrants and the Right to Stay* (MIT Press, 2010), 50. Note that previously, Carens has argued in favour of open borders and the virtually unqualified rights of unauthorised migrants without regard to time: Joseph Carens, 'Aliens and Citizens: The Case for Open Borders' (1987) 49 *Review of Politics* 251.

22 Joseph Carens, 'Citizenship and Civil Society: What Rights for Residents?' in Patrick Weil and Randall Hansen (eds), *Dual Nationality, Social Rights and Federal Citizenship in the US and Europe: The Reinvention of Citizenship* (Berghahn Books, 2002), 100, 102-3.

23 Ibid. 102; Joseph Carens, 'The Case for Amnesty: Time Erodes the State's Right to Deport' (2009) 34(4) *Boston Review* 7, 10.

24 Carens, 'Citizenship and Civil Society', above n. 22, 101, 106.

25 Bosniak, 'Being Here', above n. 19, 410.

significance to "hereness", appropriately focusing on the social fact of a person's presence rather than on the legal formality of status to anchor basic constitutional recognition'.[26] This territorialism sits well within a liberal democratic framework since it embodies ethics of both 'inclusiveness and equality: it is the ground (both literally and figuratively) of national community belonging'.[27] But, although Bosniak rejects immigration laws as the proper basis for membership, this privileging of territory does in fact derive from legally constructed categories that are far from universal, although she does not directly acknowledge this provenance of her theories. Instead, she simply notes that the 'fact of sharing territorial space' sits comfortably within international law (since territory is relevant to the scope of sovereignty within the Westphalian state system) and American constitutional jurisprudence (since territory serves as a jurisdictional threshold).[28] Indeed, the connection between territory and *citizenship* has specifically been constitutionalised in the USA, where birthright citizenship is held by anyone born on US territory.[29] But, importantly, the legal significance of territory is far more culturally contingent than Bosniak allows and, for example, is less pronounced in Australia: statutory-based citizenship, for instance, is not granted to a child born on Australian soil unless one parent is a resident or citizen of Australia.[30] Such cultural variation might diminish the universal power of a territorial-based ethics of membership.

Judy Fudge notes that much advocacy for migrants' rights problematically tends to collapse into normative claims about either universalist human rights or citizenship.[31] Fixing membership on time and place seems a neat antidote. These approaches challenge nationalist thinking by treating membership as a social fact rather than legal formality, and extend human rights analysis by recognising that, although human rights appeal to a universal notion of human dignity, they actually need a social and institutional context in order to be implemented. These proposals therefore go further than either nationalist or postnationalist camps to hold the contradictions between political sovereignty and ethical inclusion. They acknowledge that legal and moral entitlements accrue other than purely on the basis of citizenship. At the same time, in order to implement legal rights, the nation state as a political unit must remain intact. Arguments based on presence and residence, therefore, enlarge the scope of citizenship without

26 Linda Bosniak, 'Persons and Citizens in Constitutional Thought' (2010) 8(1) *International Journal of Constitutional Law* 9, 18. See also Walzer, *Spheres of Justice*, above n. 12, 60–2.

27 Bosniak, 'Being Here', above n. 19, 395.

28 Ibid. 403–4. For instance, in *Plyler v. Doe*, 457 US 202, 211 (1982), the US Supreme Court held that constitutional equal protection applies 'to all within the boundaries of a State'.

29 The Constitution of the United States, Amendment 14.

30 *Australian Citizenship Act 2007* (Cth), s 12.

31 Judy Fudge, 'Making Claims for Migrant Workers: Human Rights and Citizenship' (2014) 18(1) *Citizenship Studies* 29, 29.

making membership entirely universal, arguing that entitlements associated with belonging, while not extending to everyone in the world, must nevertheless be extended to all who are here, or have been here over time.

Yet these approaches ultimately disappoint because, like nationalist and postnationalist theories, they draw definitive lines that include some and exclude others, albeit in relation to time and place rather than legal citizenship or immigration status. They are both inclined to mark the outer circumference of a reasonably 'all-or-nothing' style of membership, viewing the national political community in very fixed terms. Bosniak explicitly acknowledges that her approach treats inclusion as a 'binary', rather than a continuum, with territorial presence as the trigger for full membership.[32] Carens' proposal is more incremental – arguing that 'the longer the stay the stronger the claim'[33] – but nevertheless sets various finite periods of residence as thresholds for bundles of recognition and entitlements.

Also, Bosniak and Carens readily admit that territorial presence and duration of residence are attractive less for their significance in themselves and rather because they are more readily definable attributes than the factors that really animate these ethical distinctions: affective ties and human relationships.[34] For Bosniak, the relevant bonds relate to physical proximity and linkage to place. For Carens, time suggests the degree of imbrication of an individual with the community in which they live. Both acknowledge that co-residence within a territory is a highly imperfect proxy for social attachments.

However, many people reside in a country while distinctly unattached to fellow residents, while many others maintain very close affiliations with a country and its institutions, even though they are present only for a brief time. What is needed is a notion of inclusion that does not rely on an all-or-nothing form of membership. The following section proposes an ethical approach that is able to see citizens and non-citizens alike as sustaining multiple ties to a country's localities, workplaces, laws and national institutions. This lens, which I call 'relational impact', centres the inter-relationships between citizens and migrants within local communities, labour markets and legal structures. I will argue that a range of legal protections should flow from these, rather than from legal citizenship or residence.

32 Bosniak, 'Being Here', above n. 19, 391.

33 Joseph Carens, 'On Belonging: What We Owe People Who Stay' (2005) 30 (3-4) *Boston Review* 16, 18.

34 Linda Bosniak, 'Citizenship Denationalised' (2000) 7 *Indiana Journal of Global Legal Studies* 447, 470–88; Carens 'Citizenship and Civil Society', above n. 22, 109. Hiroshi Motomura does this more explicitly, using the term 'immigration by affiliation' to convey the idea that immigrants gain certain rights as a result of 'leading a common life within a single territorial space': Hiroshi Motomura, 'Immigration Outside The Law' (2008) 108 *Columbia Law Review* 2038.

Relational impact

This section introduces a very different notion of inclusion than the vision of membership that seems to lie at the heart of much nationalist or postnationalist writing. I argue here that migrants' interests matter not merely because they are physically present. It is not just the fact that workers occupy the same territory as their employers that makes their exploitative working conditions troubling. It is because of the profound impact on them of the actions of their employers, and of the collective decisions of government authorities that provide the lawful basis for employer conduct and police it. Migrant workers, resident workers and employers participate together in shared activity that makes their mutual impact meaningful. In this section, I trace the impulse to anchor collective accountability in the impact of the group on the individual back to a foundational premise of liberal democratic theory.

A key commitment of democratic theory is to accord people the right to participate in the collective determination of the rules to which they are subject and which profoundly shape the world in which they live. Political theorist Robert Dahl coined the 'all affected principle',[35] contending that a law or policy is truly just only if all who are affected by it were involved or consulted in its creation. Many democratic theorists who ascribe to this precept argue that collective deliberation must take place within the bounded nation state because mutual understanding and trust require some underlying commonalities.[36] Others simply assume that the people relevantly affected by local laws can only be nationals within a bounded sovereign state, imagining that local laws have no impact on outsiders or temporary guests.[37]

Only a select few have acknowledged the need to expand the scope of inclusion to voices outside of a national community.[38] This re-orientation is shaped by the postnationalist viewpoint, discussed above, that people come together across boundaries of citizenship and nations, in ways that bring about as much conflict or harmonious shared objectives as collaborations that are wholly within national political communities. So this democratic precept provides a potent argument for including non-citizens' interests in formulating laws and policies. Simply by virtue of participating in economic and social partnerships within a country of employment, migrants are heavily affected by local laws and policies, regardless of duration or legality

35 Robert A. Dahl, *After the Revolution? Authority in a Good Society* (Yale University Press, 1970), 49; Robert A. Dahl, *Democracy and its Critics* (Yale University Press, 1989), 85–6.

36 Wil Kymlicka, 'Citizenship in an Era of Globalization: Commentary on Held' in Ian Shapiro and Casiano Hacker-Cordón (eds), *Democracy's Edges* (Cambridge University Press, 1999), 112, 119.

37 Iris Marion Young, *Inclusion and Democracy* (Oxford University Press, 2002), 23; Ludvig Beckman, 'Democratic Inclusion, Law and Causes' (2008) 21(3) *Ratio Juris* 348.

38 Jürgen Habermas discusses the need and potential for a global public sphere in Ciaran Cronin and Pablo De Greiff (eds), *The Inclusion of the Other: Studies in Political Theory* (MIT Press, 1998), 215.

of presence. If any democratic government is obliged to treat with justice all those who are affected by its policies, temporary and unauthorised migrants must be counted within the interests and voices that must be considered in creating them.

It is possible, though, that this principle of relational impact may be unworkable on a globalised scale. It may not be feasible to determine precisely who is 'affected' by any country's laws or decisions. The ranks of these clearly run beyond a country's citizens and those resident non-citizens. They also include aspiring entrants as well as a wide array of other people around the world who may also stand to gain or lose as a result of a government's policy settings. Critics charge that this standard may lead to an impossible conclusion that would give 'virtually everyone everywhere a vote on virtually everything decided anywhere'.[39] Promoting a democratic approach to global decision-making, Carol Gould has suggested instead that consideration be given to everyone 'significantly' or 'fundamentally' affected.[40] Of course, even this broader formulation might still produce a universal franchise.

These implications extend well beyond the scope of this book. It is not argued here for a globalised right of equal participation in government decision making that affects us all. Sarah Song has observed that, while many foreigners beyond the territorial boundaries of a powerful state are impacted by it, territorial inhabitants (however short-term) are more profoundly affected by the state's legal system and coercive power.[41] Thus, in the context of non-citizen workers in a liberal democratic state, a core impulse towards inclusion flows from this democratic precept that those who live under the greatest influence of state authority must, as a matter of justice, play a role in shaping its terms and conditions. To focus only on the effect of laws, policies and institutions on citizens would create what Ayelet Shachar has described as an 'asymmetry between the power to make decisions and the actual responsibility of living through their consequences'.[42]

This insight shifts our focus from who *consented* to laws to who are *affected* by them. This distinction is vital since legal protections are often withheld from migrants on the basis that immigration is a 'privilege'. As a result, temporary entrants are taken to consent to whatever terms or conditions

39 Robert E. Goodin, 'Enfranchising All Affected Interests, and Its Alternatives' (2007) 35(1) *Philosophy and Public Affairs* 40, 68.

40 Carol Gould, 'Envisioning Transnational Democracy: Cross-Border Communities and Regional Human Rights Frameworks' in Heather Gautney, Omar Dabour, Ashley Dawson and Neil Smith (eds), *Democracy, States and the Struggle for Global Justice* (Taylor and Francis, 2009), 63, 68; Carol Gould, *Globalizing Democracy and Human Rights* (Cambridge University Press, 2004), ch. 7.

41 Sarah Song, 'The Significance of Territorial Presence and the Rights of Immigrants' in Sarah Fine and Lea Ypi (eds), *Migration in Legal and Political Theory* (Oxford University Press, forthcoming).

42 Ayelet Shachar, *The Birthright Lottery: Citizenship and Global Inequality* (Harvard University Press, 2009), 112.

attach to their stay, even if these are unilaterally changed over time. Similarly, unauthorised migrants, such as Jin Woog Kim, frequently are taken to have 'chosen' to stay in Australia, working without authorisation and therefore to have consented to whatever legal consequences result from work or injury. This book argues that a national political community cannot, however, be delimited by legal citizenship or residence alone. Migrant workers, such as Kim, must play some role in determining how Australian regulatory power is exercised.

This central argument embraces a profound paradox. The suggestion that laws should reflect a nation's commitments to people beyond the immediate circle of nationals challenges the traditional view that citizens, and only citizens, may ethically come together to design laws to suit only their needs. The national community cannot be the sole basis for inclusion, and a national mandate or border security cannot be the sole source of legitimacy of laws that affect non-nationals. At the same time, I have already acknowledged that laws and government institutions require a stable structure of citizenship in order to be created and implemented at all and sovereignty continues to be foundational in the contemporary world. This stance calls attention, all at once, to both the ethical insignificance and the political significance of the Westphalian nation state. It highlights just how profoundly contradictory state sovereignty always is. How can migrants both be included as meaningful participants within a national community but also differentiated as non-citizens (not yet, or perhaps ever)?

One answer may lie in holding in mind at the same time multiple conceptions of communities, multiple forms of political participation and multiple forums of governance. The work of Seyla Benhabib assists in thinking through the implications of democratic theories for a globalised context. She argues that we are witnessing a 'disaggregation' of citizenship where civil, political and social rights traditionally attached to membership in territory-based states are increasingly 'unbundled' from one another.[43] Civil rights, access to political participation and claims upon shared resources need no longer be packaged together as a unit. They need not be associated with a fixed and singular citizen status. Instead, the entitlement to exercise political agency in relation to governmental processes that affect us – including rights of political participation and standing to make legal claims – can be linked to multiple and overlapping regimes of governance. Inclusion of migrants flows from their multiple ties to a local community, a workplace or a legal institution without legal citizenship or any formalised national membership. At the same time, national sovereignty does not

43 Seyla Benhabib, *The Rights of Others* (Cambridge University Press, 2004), 21; Seyla Benhabib, 'Twilight of Sovereignty or the Emergence of Cosmopolitan Norms? Rethinking Citizenship in Volatile Times' in Heather Gautney, Omar Dabour, Ashley Dawson and Neil Smith (eds), *Democracy, States and the Struggle for Global Justice* (Taylor and Francis, 2009), 79, 92–3.

disappear. A nation must retain its ability (to some extent) to regulate admission to its territory. Thus, sovereignty remains a critical institutional force structuring interactions within and across national borders including, frequently, between citizens and non-citizens. There remains a need to delimit the outer boundaries of a national electoral community as well as the overlapping rules of membership at the state and municipal levels.

Nevertheless, migrants' rights to inclusion may exist without formal membership in any sense. Temporary and unauthorised migration are evidence of the fact that attachment to social and political communities is not permanent, but also that citizenship and political communities matter greatly, as a question of law as well as pragmatics. Indeed, the political stability of liberal democracies can be threatened by the presence of people who pay taxes, access certain public benefits and participate in civil society while politically disenfranchised. The inclination in favour of an inclusive approach to non-citizens can be read therefore as much as an attempt to foster stable governance as to problematise it. Inclusion of the voices of all actually strengthens the fabric of a national community.

Participatory inclusion

The lens of 'participatory inclusion' in many ways flows from these, capturing an aspiration that migrant workers be invited and empowered to play an active part in shaping laws and policies that affect them. This idea is becoming far more mainstream in labour migration literature. Martin Ruhs notes that while the logic of nation states implies that countries must prioritise the interests of citizens, labour migration policy should take at least some account of the interests of actual and prospective non-citizens and, indeed, their countries of origin.[44] This section proposes three fundamental forms of migrant agency: (1) migrants' ability to give voice to their perspectives to shape policy formation; (2) access to legal institutions to gain effective redress for grievances (including a right to be present in the country of employment long enough to access legal institutions that are *there*); and (3) recognition of all workers (whether citizen, resident, temporary migrant or unauthorised) as active participants in the domestic labour market, as subjects of employment law as much as objects of immigration law.

The right of consultation on laws and policies flows directly from the demand that a country of employment take seriously the impact of its laws and policies on migrants working there. As long as nationals vote for parliamentarians who enact laws only in the name of their electoral constituents, migrants toil within a 'democratic deficit': unable to contribute to the formation of regulatory structures controlling their employment

44 Martin Ruhs, *The Price of Rights: Regulating International Labor Migration* (Princeton University Press, 2013), 30–1.

relationship.[45] Laws must be created with the input of broader communities, which include migrants and others who have a significant stake in these issues. Non-citizens need to be supported to give voice to their perspectives, and their views must be positively taken into account. This is what Anne McNevin describes as 'new modes of belonging': forms of political practices by actors who are neither monolithically 'illegal' nor full legal citizens but elsewhere along the spectrum of inclusion.[46] This consultation should be both formal, via government or parliamentary processes, and informal, through public debate and membership in social structures which represent worker interests such as unions.

Thus, it is not enough for policymakers simply to consider what the effect of policies on migrants might be. A key insight of theories which stress the deliberative nature of democracy is that humans are notoriously bad at empathising with the specifics of another person's concrete situation and imagining their needs.[47] Policymakers must work hard to listen directly the voices of 'others'. Migrant workers and community groups must be able to express their diverse standpoints in order to provide a truly collective account of the problems that need to be solved and the consequences for policy settings. This exchange is likely to lead to fairer policies which accommodate the vulnerabilities of both local and migrant workers, and is itself a recognition of migrant workers' inclusion in the community of country of employment.

A second form of agency invoked by the concept of 'participatory inclusion' is migrants' ability to participate as full actors in legal institutions that may provide effective redress for grievances. This is a form of Arendt's 'right to have rights' because of her insight that asserting rights is a political action as much as a legal one; it involves claiming a place not wholly outside of sovereign institutions.[48] In so doing, migrant subjects emphasise their relationship with the broader community in which they are living since, as Martha Minow compellingly argues, rights claims must always be made *to* someone: 'a claim of right, made before a judge, [is constituted] as a plea for recognition of membership in a community shared by applicant and judge, much as reader and author share the world of the text'.[49] Writing outside of the context of immigration and citizenship Minow overlooks the fact that assertion of rights does not automatically equate to a recognition of equal membership for non-citizens. Nevertheless, it does constitute, at least, the

45 Ruben Garcia, 'Labor as Property: Guestworkers, International Trade and the Democratic Deficit' (2006) 10 *Journal of Gender, Race and Justice* 27.

46 Anne McNevin, *Contesting Citizenship: Irregular Migrants and the New Frontiers of the Political* (Columbia University Press, 2011), 118.

47 Iris Marion Young, 'Polity and Group Difference: A Critique of the Ideal of Universal Citizenship' (1989) 99(2) *Ethics* 250, 263.

48 Arendt, *The Origins*, above n. 9, 296–7.

49 Martha Minow, 'Interpreting Rights: An Essay for Robert Cover' (1986-7) 96 *Yale Law Journal* 1860, 1879–80.

migrant as a self in relationship with the institutions of the national community in which they live, as a 'jurisdictional subject'.[50]

This book advocates for a more active framing of Arendt's 'right to have rights' as 'the right to *claim* rights', to adopt Engin Isin's phrase.[51] Refocusing migrants' rights as of value not simply when they are held but more so when they can be claimed shifts attention to the logistical barriers that frequently confront temporary and unauthorised workers who are seeking vindication of legal entitlements: language difficulties, inadequate knowledge of the local legal system and fear of removal for calling attention to one's immigration status. The precariousness of the immigration status of unauthorised workers in particular can leave them unable to stay in the country of employment long enough to avail themselves of legal protections. Participatory inclusion therefore requires greater security of presence for migrant workers who fear removal for voicing their claims. Providing immigration-based support to bring legal action without fear of removal does much to alleviate the coercive and uncertain effects of immigration laws.

The final aspect of agency underpinning 'participatory inclusion' is treatment of migrant workers as subjects of employment law rather than as objects of immigration law. In order to take seriously the inclusion of all whose interests are affected, it is necessary to highlight migrants' roles as workers. 'Industrial citizenship', the bundle of entitlements that attach to participation in the labour market including minimum wages and conditions of employment, worker safety, protection from arbitrary management action (including especially unfair, arbitrary and discriminatory terminations), and rights to participate in rule making through collective bargaining,[52] should not just be the purview of legal citizens and residents since migrants too (even those who work without authorisation) are co-participants in domestic labour markets.

When temporary or unauthorised migrant workers are deprived of protections under labour law, they are treated, in effect, as commodified workers in a globalised labour market. As I discuss in more detail in Chapter 6, unauthorised workers in Australia are frequently excluded from employment protections altogether. When this occurs, they are left to receive the impact of the raw power of an unfettered market. Their bargaining position is the sole determinant of their pay and working conditions. The foundation of industrial citizenship is the decommodification of labour, the provision of labour standards by the state that ameliorate the harshness of unchecked market power. This book therefore advocates a change in focus from the enforcement of immigration law against workers and employers (especially

50 Muneer Ahmad, 'Resisting Guantánamo: Rights at the Brink of Dehumanization' (2009) 103(4) *Northwestern University Law Review* 1683, 1748.

51 The term is coined by Engin F. Isin, 'Citizenship in Flux: The Figure of the Activist Citizen' (2009) 29 *Subjectivity* 367, 371 (emphasis added).

52 Harry Arthurs, 'Developing Industrial Citizenship: A Challenge for Canada's Second Century' (1967) 45 *Canadian Bar Review* 786.

urgent given the proliferation of employer sanctions offences in Europe, the USA and Australia in recent years), to enforcing employment law remedies in favour of workers.

In these ways, participatory inclusion assists in evaluating how the interests of migrants and residents are affected by law and policies in the country of employment. However, greater precision is available through the final conceptual lens introduced here: the precariousness of migrant work.

Attending to the precariousness of migrant work

To this point, this chapter has argued that nationals' ethical responsibilities extend to all whose lives are affected by local laws or regulatory initiatives, citizens and non-citizens, migrants and residents. Participatory inclusion provides a set of standards directing governmental policy toward migrant agency and empowerment. But this still leaves unanswered the question of what sort of consideration of non-citizens' interests would be sufficient for laws or workplace policies in a country of employment to be described as fair? How are migrants' and citizens' interests to be evaluated? How are they to be weighed against each other in circumstances where they conflict? This section argues that, while equality may seem a self-evident benchmark in advocating for migrants' rights, it is not so helpful in the context of citizenship and non-citizenship because it can slide too easily into the 'all-or-nothing' tendencies of nationalist and postnationalist theories of membership or citizenship.

Instead, a focus on the 'precariousness' of migrant work, with insights about vulnerability, dependency and precariousness in relationships by the feminist theorists Martha Fineman and Judith Butler, illuminates the ways that immigration status reshapes employment relationships. This lens provides room for reflection on the vulnerabilities of temporary and unauthorised migrants as well as resident workers, and by fixing on insecurity, it unpacks the coercive and uncertain effects of temporary and unauthorised immigration status. The book will proceed to examine how government intervention can create or allay dependencies between employer and worker, and intensify precariousness or alleviate it.

This section begins by considering, and rejecting, equality-based benchmarks as an approach to exploitation of migrant workers, before providing a foundation for the conceptual tool of 'precariousness'. It then introduces perspectives on how immigration law produces basic structures of precariousness in workplaces.

The drawbacks of equality discourse for migrants' rights

Equality may seem a natural benchmark to assess migrant workers' employment experiences. Equal citizenship is the traditional source of normative demands for labour standards,[53] so it is readily understandable that debates over the exploitation of migrant workers are so frequently couched in terms of whether migrants are receiving treatment at work that is equal to locals. However, this section argues that an equality framework breaks down in the context of migrants' rights for two reasons.

First, feminist scholars have critiqued the liberal doctrine of equality because it is too easily reduced to a claim for formal equality only, the desire that all people be treated the same in similar circumstances, without regard for race, gender or other attributes.[54] The 'sameness-of-treatment' version of equality, which is regularly invoked in political and popular language, ignores underlying or institutionalised forms of subordination and privilege and, indeed, may even serve to validate them. Feminist and critical-race scholarship has long highlighted the failure of these thin conceptions of 'equal citizenship' to account for the multiple axes of disadvantage (as women, ethnic or religious minorities, and so on) that can subsist in one person.[55] Substantive equality of outcome often requires different treatment to address existing inequities of circumstance. These limitations in formal equality analysis stand out in the context of first generation migrants' struggles for justice. Studies in Canada have shown that immigrants with temporary or unauthorised migration status may remain in precarious work well after they have acquired residence.[56] Anti-discrimination laws are designed to protect and remedy disempowerment and vulnerability. But by defining only specific aspects of claimants' subjectivities as eligible for protection, such as race and gender, they frequently fail to address broader social and economic injustices that frequently shape the lives of those in cultural, linguistic and ethnic minorities (such as lesser access to education, difficulties in securing recognition for overseas qualifications, limited English language skills, etc.).

The second reason why the equality standard is ill-equipped to tackle the mistreatment of non-citizens turns on the institutionalised position of non-citizenship itself. Linda Bosniak observes that other minority groups' demands for 'equal citizenship' (on the basis of gender, ethnicity or sexuality, for example) frequently fall within a narrative of 'progressive incorporation, with new social classes increasingly demanding, and ultimately achieving, inclusion as citizens over time'.[57] However, complaints by

53 Judy Fudge, 'Precarious Migrant Status and Precarious Employment: The Paradox of International Rights for Migrant Workers' (2012) 34 *Comparative Labour Law and Policy Journal* 95, 122.

54 Rosemary Hunter, 'Alternatives to Equality' in *Rethinking Equality Projects in Law* (Hart Publishing, 2008), 81.

55 Young, *Inclusion and Democracy*, above n. 37, 92.

56 Luin Goldring and Patricia Landolt, 'Caught in the Work-Citizenship Matrix: The Lasting Effects of Precarious Legal Status on Work for Toronto Immigrants' (2011) 8(3) *Globalizations* 325, 328.

57 Linda Bosniak, *The Citizen and the Alien* (Princeton University Press, 2006), 29.

temporary or unauthorised migrants of being treated as second-class citizens are of another order. As Hiroshi Motomura puts it, 'the entire field of immigration and citizenship assumes that it is legitimate to divide human beings into two groups: one consists of citizens, and the other group consists of noncitizens. The difference must mean something'.[58] The equality standard is unhelpful for non-citizens because, within the architecture of national laws themselves, citizens and non-citizens can never be juridical equals across a spectrum of rights and social protections. This difference creates a closure which is necessary in order to constitute liberal democratic communities. Migrants cannot be treated exactly like citizens because political communities (within which questions of distributive justice are resolved) would cease to exist.[59]

The very conceptual apparatus of an egalitarian system breaks down in the face of a claim by someone who is present without full membership rights. As Joo-Cheong Tham and Iain Campbell eloquently argue, while human rights instruments purport to require equal treatment between migrant and national workers, this is typically a minimum standard rather than a substantive requirement for non-discrimination in absolutely every respect: local and migrant workers could enjoy unequal conditions at work as long as they both enjoy equal basic human rights at work.[60] Nor do international human rights and labour frameworks for migrant worker's protection safeguard equality of treatment in all respects: for instance, unlike local workers, they permit migrant workers to be tied to employer sponsors for two years.[61] I have explored elsewhere how stridently article 79 of the United Nations International Convention on Protection of the Rights of All Migrant Workers and Members of their Families protects the position of sovereignty as a limit on equality, providing that '[n]othing in the present Convention shall affect the right of each State Party to establish the criteria governing admission of migrant workers and their families'.[62]

58 Hiroshi Motomura, 'The Rule of Law in Immigration Law' (2008) 15 *Tulsa Journal of Comparative and International Law* 139, 141.

59 Ayelet Shachar, 'Children of a Lesser State: Sustaining Global Inequality through Citizenship Laws' in Stephen Macedo and Iris Marion Young (eds), *Nomos XLIV: Child, Family, and State* (New York University Press, 2003), 345.

60 Joo-Cheong Tham and Iain Campbell, 'Equal Treatment for Temporary Migrant Workers and the Challenge of their Precariousness' (Paper presented at the Australian Labour Law Association Conference, Rydges Hotel, Canberra, 16–17 November 2012), 5.

61 E.g. Migrant Workers Convention art 52.3(a); Migrant Workers (Supplementary Provisions) Convention, 1975 (ILO No 143) opened for signature 24 June 1975, 1120 UNTS 323 (entered into force 9 December 1978) art 14; International Labour Organization (ILO), Multilateral Framework on Labour Migration: Non-Binding Principles and Guidelines for a Rights-Based Approach to Labour Migration (2006) principle 9(b).

62 Laurie Berg, 'At the Border and Between the Cracks: The Precarious Position of Irregular Migrant Workers under International Law' (2007) 8 *Melbourne Journal of International Law* 1, 18.

In arguing for justice in the context of migrant work, I propose instead the conceptual lens of precariousness, because it illuminates assumptions and biases in traditional discussions of poor treatment of migrant workers that are not exposed by equality analysis. Notions of precarious work have arisen in British, Canadian and Australian scholarship to capture insecure working conditions, as well as marginal immigration status. The next section traces their evolution in industrial relations and sociological literature before turning to my use of the term in this work.

Precarious work and immigration status

The expression 'precariousness' in the industrial relations context seeks to capture forms of work characterised by high insecurity and poor conditions.[63] It comprises the antithesis of the 'standard' employment relationship: a stable, socially protected, full-time job for an indefinite duration with a single employer, with basic conditions regulated to a minimum level by collective agreements, labour regulation and social welfare policies such as unemployment benefits. Conversely, 'precariousness' refers to the relentless insecurity that attends most contemporary employment relationships including:

> all possible shapes of unsure, not guaranteed, flexible exploitation: from illegalized, seasonal and temporary employment to homework, flex- and temp-work to subcontractors, freelancers or so-called self-employed persons.[64]

Guy Standing points to the recent normalisation of precariousness in the new 'precariat'.[65] In post-industrial economies, market-oriented approaches have challenged both the primacy of labour regulation and democratic participation of workers, which were designed to protect employees against economic and social risks, reduce social inequality and increase efficiency.[66] Standing suggests that the 'labour market flexibility' increasingly preferred by employers has several dimensions: wage flexibility (adjusting to changes in demand); employment flexibility (the ability of firms to promote casual and fixed-term labour, reducing employment security); job flexibility (moving employees around inside the firm, subcontracting and changing

63 Bureau for Workers' Activities (ACTRAV), *From Precarious Work to Decent Work: Outcome Document to the Workers' Symposium on Policies and Regulations to Combat Precarious Employment* (ILO, 2012), 3.

64 Brett Neilson and Ned Rossiter, 'From Precarity to Precariousness and Back Again: Labour, Life and Unstable Networks' (2005) 5(22) *Fibreculture* 1.

65 Guy Standing, *The Precariat: The New Dangerous Class* (Bloomsbury Academic, 2011), 6.

66 Kerry Rittich, 'Rights, Risk and Reward: Governance Norms in the International Order and the Problem of Precarious Work' in Judy Fudge and Rosemary Owens (eds), *Precarious Work, Women and the New Economy: The Challenge to Legal Norms* (Hart Publishing, 2006), 31.

job structures to minimise non-wage labour costs); and skill flexibility to be able to adjust workers' skills easily.

International scholarship has devised various typologies in relation to precarious work. Gerry Rodgers and Janine Rodgers identify four dimensions of institutional, social and political factors that contribute to precarious employment arrangements:

(1) the degree of security of continuing employment and the risk of job loss;
(2) control over the labour process which is linked to the presence or absence of trade unions and professional associations, and relates to control over working conditions, wages and the pace of work;
(3) the degree of regulatory protection accessible to workers through union representation or the law; and
(4) income level.[67]

Leah Vosko's conception of precarious employment includes social context (including occupation, industry, and geography) and social location (which she defines as the interaction of social relations, such as gender, and legal and political categories, such as citizenship), exposing the broader social processes that make employment precarious.[68]

The lens of 'precariousness' is useful, therefore, because it bridges the individual experience of work and systemic factors that shape working conditions. It depicts a highly personal state of 'being unable to predict one's fate or having some degree of stability on which to construct a life', while also shifting responsibility for exploitation from individual failures, reframing it as a predictable result of systemic processes embedded in government policies.[69]

It is, therefore, unsurprising that the analytical frame of 'precariousness' has been applied to the structural forces affecting non-citizens. Various typologies of precariousness for migrants build upon the multi-dimensional conceptions of precarious employment just introduced. Goldring and Landolt describe as 'precarity' state processes in Canada in which 'complex institutional and geographic pathways' leave migrants vulnerable for increasingly long periods of time during which they must navigate 'insecure

67 Gerry Rodgers, 'Precarious Work in Western Europe: The State of the Debate' in Gerry Rodgers and Janine J. Rodgers (eds), *Precarious Jobs in Labour Market Regulation: The Growth of Atypical Employment in Western Europe* (ILO, 1989), 1.

68 Leah Vosko, *Managing the Margins: Gender, Citizenship and the International Regulation of Precarious Employment* (Oxford University Press, 2010), 102.

69 Neilson and Rossiter, 'From Precarity to Precariousness', above n. 64.

migratory legal status'.[70] Luin Goldring, Carolina Berinstein and Judith Bernhard characterise 'precarious legal status' as the absence of any of the diagnostic elements normally associated with permanent residence and citizenship:

(1) work authorisation;
(2) the right to remain permanently in the country (residency permit);
(3) not depending on a third party for one's right to be in Canada (such as a sponsoring spouse or employer); and
(4) social citizenship rights available to permanent residents (e.g. public education and public health coverage).[71]

Unauthorised workers, in particular, are widely recognised to epitomise precariousness, described by Bridget Anderson as 'emblematic of the "precarious worker"', by Matthew Gibney as the 'archetypal precarious resident' and by Neilson and Rossiter as 'the exemplary precarious worker'.[72] But the broader intersections between the production of precarious migration status and the production of precarious work are only just emerging and, as Judy Fudge rightly observes, the term precariousness can lack precision in this context since some migrant statuses are far more precarious than others.[73]

This book therefore seeks to unpack how immigration rules produce precariousness for migrants in employment, in particular through coercion and uncertainty. Immigration policies become a regulatory labour market tool used both to create a distinctive (non-citizen) labour supply that can be excluded from standard employment entitlements, and to change employment norms more broadly.[74] Anderson has evocatively described immigration controls not only as a tap regulating the flow of labour, but also

70 Luin Goldring and Patricia Landolt, 'Caught in the Work-Citizenship Matrix: The Lasting Effects of Precarious Legal Status on Work for Toronto Immigrants' (2011) 8(3) *Globalizations* 325, 327.

71 Luin Goldring, Carolina Berinstein and Judith K. Bernhard, 'Institutionalizing Precarious Migratory Status in Canada' (2009) 13(3) *Citizenship Studies* 239, 240–1.

72 Bridget Anderson, 'Migration, Immigration Controls and the Fashioning of Precarious Workers' (2010) 24 *Work, Employment and Society* 300, 304; Matthew Gibney, 'Precarious Residents: Migration Control, Membership and the Rights of Non-Citizens' (Human Development Reports Research Paper No 2009/10, United Nations Development Programme, April 2009), 2, 3; Neilson and Rossiter, 'From Precarity to Precariousness', above n. 64.

73 Fudge, 'Making Claims', above n. 31, 38.

74 Judy Fudge and Fiona MacPhail, 'The Temporary Foreign Worker Program in Canada: Low-Skilled Workers as an Extreme Form of Flexible Labor' (2009) 31(1) *Comparative Labor Law and Policy Journal* 5; Linda McDowell, Adina Batnitzky and Sarah Dyer, 'Global Flows and Local Labour Markets: Precarious Employment and Migrant Workers in the UK' in Jacqueline Scott, Shirley Dex and Anke C. Plagnol (eds), *Gendered Lives: Gender Inequalities in Production and Reproduction* (Edward Elgar, 2012), 123, 135ff.

as a mould, helping to form types of labour within the labour market.[75] The International Labour Organization starkly suggests that:

> in some situations, there may be a deliberate link between policies and practices of excluding migrants from legal and social protection while apparently tolerating their presence in precarious situations that ensure they remain low-paid, docile and flexible.[76]

This literature on precariousness in migration and employment is therefore extremely helpful in illuminating some of the formative features of immigration controls and their impact on classes of migrants working under their influence. However, it has limitations. Its structural focus means it has a tendency to generalise across categories of workers and working conditions. It can also be overly deterministic, downplaying the ways in which workers and employers can assert agency and change their circumstances.

My use of the term 'precariousness' in this book builds upon these insights into the labour market effects of immigration status by also drawing on cognate concepts of 'vulnerability' and 'dependency' developed by Martha Fineman, and 'precariousness' in the work of Judith Butler. These permit a more holistic approach to precariousness, recognising that it is inherent in human life (all our bodies and lives are fragile and we are necessarily dependent on others and vulnerable in certain ways). At the same time, precariousness is seen as highly specific, and frequently produced in relationships (with others, with institutions and with laws). I turn now briefly to explore how these contributions sharpen the analytical tool of precariousness.

How vulnerability and precariousness analysis broaden the relational context

Martha Fineman has argued that a complex understanding of social disadvantage requires close attention to people's 'dependency' and 'vulnerability'.[77] This approach accentuates a person's highly particularised social context, elucidating how he or she is located in varying positions of susceptibility to exploitation or harm, which assists in examining hidden assumptions and biases folded into legal and social institutions and the impact of these. Fineman finds dependency and vulnerability instructive not because they are abnormal states indicating deficiency, but rather because they are universal and inevitable aspects of the human condition: as embodied humans we all live with 'the imminent or ever-present possibility of harm, injury or misfortune'.[78] At the same time, though, vulnerability and

75 Anderson, 'Migration, Immigration Controls and the Fashioning of Precarious Workers', above n. 72, 126, 306 and 312.

76 ILO, *International Labour Migration: A Rights-Based Approach* (2010), 213.

77 Martha A. Fineman, 'The Vulnerable Subject: Anchoring Equality in the Human Condition' (2008) 20 *Yale Journal of Law and Feminism* 1, 1.

78 Ibid. 8, 12.

dependency are experienced by individuals differently, since they are mediated by ethnicity, class and gender and each is differently situated in webs of economic and institutional relationships. Some individuals, or groups, are at heightened risk of exploitation because they possess fewer resources or have inherited disadvantages at birth.

Fineman uses the terms vulnerability and dependency rather than precariousness, and her analysis is helpful in the context of this book because she explains how disadvantage and susceptibility to harm develop in relationships rather than from an abstract legal status. This has significant implications for the central questions addressed here of how to craft laws or policies that respond appropriately to precarious living and working conditions. Fineman's premise is not that we should be striving for invulnerability, for that is unattainable, but rather that vulnerability can be lessened by laws or social action, which are more 'responsive to, and responsible for, vulnerability', and which generate greater 'resilience' with which to confront social challenges.[79] Laws, public institutions and relationships (whether at home or at work) can ameliorate vulnerabilities, or create systems of further exclusion, robbing people of dignity and autonomy.

Dependency analysis also works to lay bare a persistent fiction underlying much government intervention. Interdependency is an inescapable aspect of the human condition, and reliance on government support (through tax breaks or social security payments) is universal: through our constant and complex social interactions we are unavoidably dependent on each other.[80] Yet politicians and social commentators hold people to different standards of self-sufficiency in different situations, stigmatising some people (such as 'welfare mums') as dependent, and therefore representing an undesirable social cost, while labelling others (such as corporate beneficiaries of subsidies) autonomous agents deserving of concessions.

Fineman also notes the role that a narrative of 'individual choice' can play in obscuring our collective responsibilities for each other. She offers 'the contract' as a metaphor to encapsulate a prevalent view that society is ostensibly constituted by individuals autonomously managing their resources to achieve self-interested outcomes, negotiating contractual terms, assessing their options and making rational choices.[81] They consent to the relationships they make and then assume individual responsibility for the consequences. Invoking individual choice in this way, therefore, serves to masks society's role in perpetuating inequality or vulnerability.[82] It ignores the fact that choice occurs within the constraints of social conditions, which 'funnel individual decision making into prescribed

79 Ibid. 13, 19–20.

80 Martha A. Fineman, 'Dependency and Social Debt' in David B. Grushky (ed.), *Poverty and Inequality* (Stanford University Press, 2005), 133, 135–6.

81 Fineman, 'The Vulnerable Subject', above n. 77, 10.

82 Martha A. Fineman, *The Autonomy Myth: A Theory of Dependency* (The New Press, 2004), 40.

channels, often operating along practical and symbolic lines to limit and close down options'.[83]

Thus, invoking choice as an explanation for individual conduct actually works to limit that person's choices. The individual is vested with total responsibility for the costs of their action. This fails to recognise that 'choices' are inevitably structured by social context, including social expectations, and that decisions often carry unanticipated consequences. Fineman uses the example of the woman 'choosing' to be a mother, but this analysis is just as applicable to the migrant worker who is constructed as 'choosing' economic opportunities overseas.[84] Individual choice, in these examples, conceals the question of whether some conditions are simply too oppressive to be imposed by a society even if an individual openly agrees to them.

Like Fineman, Judith Butler takes as her starting point, in two of her works *Precarious Life* and *Frames of War*, the fragility of human existence, and our inevitable dependencies on each other, to argue for a new responsiveness to suffering in others. Butler also notes that our capacity to be easily injured or harmed creates inevitable dependencies on others:

> Precariousness implies living socially, that is, the fact that one's life is always in some sense in the hands of the other. It implies exposure both to those we know and to those we do not know; a dependency on people we know or know not at all.[85]

'Dependency' and 'precariousness' remind us how much our fate depends on the actions of others, so that we may better evaluate our impact on others. Butler intimates that this awareness can form the basis for new ethical responsibilities based on our interconnectedness both with loved ones and strangers, and new forms of political community based on common experiences of suffering within a diversity of individual identities.

She observes that, when confronted with someone else's suffering, people are regularly provoked into responding either empathetically with care, or defensively as to a threat.[86] The ethical challenge is to attend at once to the

83 Fineman, 'Dependency and Social Debt', above n. 80, 141.

84 Fineman herself does not squarely take on the question about the legal or ethical positions of a non-citizen. Instead, she notes in passing, in a footnote:

> I do not want to engage in a debate about the limits of the notions of citizenship here. Certainly, noncitizens should be afforded equality on the same terms as citizens if they are residents of the state or long-term visitors or have some other connection that would make placing state responsibility for them and their situation appropriate.
>
> (Fineman, 'The Responsive State', above n. 8, 256).

I read Fineman against herself here, exposing the difficulties with equal treatment of citizens and more squarely raising the question of precisely what sort of reciprocal ethical relations between citizens and non-citizens are appropriate.

85 Butler, *Frames of War*, above n. 8, 14.

86 Butler, *Precarious Life*, above n. 8, 131–40.

other person's vulnerability as well as recognising one's own. Butler suggests that this is crucial because we are all inescapably vulnerable ourselves. Butler probes the processes that might drive individuals or societies to care or not care for others. Governments (like individuals) can react to suffering in various ways: regulatory action can be deployed protectively to ameliorate an individual's vulnerability or defensively to exploit this vulnerability, mobilising fear of vulnerability as a political instrument. Ordinarily, Butler notes, individuals and states respond most empathically for those who are familiar to them, or with whom they have a kinship (founded on family or nation), rather than those who are strangers. But drawing attention to mutual dependencies has the powerful potential to allow people to overcome their fear of others' extreme vulnerability and respond compassionately, or at least with humility, to those with whom they have little shared understanding. Acknowledging that precariousness is universal may also overcome humans' persistent difficulties in comprehending and responding compassionately to their impact on others.

It is, indeed, striking that a lexicon around 'precariousness', 'precarity', 'vulnerability' and 'dependency' has arisen in these diverse fields: in industrial relations literature and government policy, as well as in apparently unrelated academic theories of social movements and feminist legal philosophy. The meanings of these terms differ depending on the context of their usage, yet there is also a great deal of overlap here. For instance, while precariousness seems currently the preferred expression to describe marginal employment, many employee advocates, scholars and governments in Canada, Australia and the UK also refer to 'vulnerable workers' and 'vulnerable work' to describe extremely poor working conditions and social exclusion.[87] Vulnerability and resilience frameworks in a human rights context capture populations which are particularly at risk, especially migrants and asylum seekers.[88]

I generally prefer the term 'precariousness' to avoid the risk that 'vulnerability' or 'dependency' may emphasise an individual worker and naturalise their lack of capacity.[89] 'Vulnerability' may be misunderstood to suggest an absence of agency, confining the vulnerable subject to a victimised role. Precariousness, on the other hand, tends to reframe responsibility for disempowerment away from individual failure to the terrain of government, pointing to the political, institutional structures within which relations are

87 For example, Law Commission of Ontario, 'Vulnerable Workers and Precarious Work: Interim Report' (2012); Commission on Vulnerable Employment, 'Hard Work, Hidden Lives: The Full Report on the Commission on Vulnerable Employment' (Trades Union Congress, 2008); Alexander Reilly, 'Protecting Vulnerable Migrant Workers: The Case of International Students' (2012) 25 *Australian Journal of Labour Law* 181.

88 For example, David Weissbrodt and Mary Rumsey (eds), *Vulnerable and Marginalised Groups and Human Rights* (Edward Elgar Publishing, 2011); Bryan S. Turner, *Vulnerability and Human Rights* (Pennsylvania State University Press, 2006).

89 Anderson, 'Migration, Immigration Controls', above n. 72, 303.

forged. Precariousness evokes a weakening of social relations and suggests degrees of instability both in employment and in a broader social context. At the same time, there are obviously close linkages between these frames since precarious conditions frequently make someone vulnerable to harm, as does having a high state of dependency on the will of another for one's ongoing employment and residence.

Labour migration and law's precariousness: coercion and uncertainty

This chapter has argued that governments must treat with justice all those who are affected by their laws and policies. The contours of this requirement within the dilemmas of transnational labour migration are moulded by two conflicting imperatives: first, that residents and migrants impact upon one another producing harm or benefit, and second, that strong social welfare commitments are only achievable within a bounded political community.

To take these ideas of justice seriously means according significance to the relationships between migrants and residents (and the harms or benefits flowing from them) as much as to migrants' non-citizenship status. To do so undermines the idea that the 'national interest' inevitably trumps migrant workers' interests. This approach challenges rhetoric which sees these interests as ordinarily in contest along with a frequent, although unspoken, presumption that migrants must be placed in a precarious legal position in order to fortify the position of residents. For instance, the requirement that temporary migrant workers obtain employer sponsorship, which is frequently connected to their right to enter and work in a foreign country, is widely acknowledged to curb their labour market mobility. But this is often seen as a necessary disability to safeguard the employment conditions of resident workers. The chequered denial of workplace protections to unauthorised workers is justified as properly elevating the bargaining position of residents.

Attending to precariousness allows us to look beyond these assumptions and explore the real impact of immigration controls and employer practices on migrant workers. Analysis that fixes on precariousness, vulnerability and dependency illuminates how the employment relationships of temporary and unauthorised migrant workers are re-constituted by immigration law and by immigration enforcement as these interact with other fields of government regulation. Within the industrial relations field, theories of precariousness are often preoccupied with uncertainty,[90] and coercion.[91] When the lens of precariousness is trained on migrant labour, these same elements loom even larger.

90 ACTRAV, *Policies and Regulations to Combat Precarious Employment* (ILO, 2011), 5.

91 Report I(B) of the Director-General of the ILO, *The Cost of Coercion: Global Report under the Follow-Up to the ILO Declaration on Fundamental Principles and Rights at Work* (International Labour Conference, 98th Session, 2009).

The coercive force of immigration law is inherent to non-citizenship status. A great deal of international scholarship has begun to chart specific ways that immigration regulation can intersect with employment laws to mould a migrant labour force.[92] Immigration regulations in the national contexts under consideration in this book frequently require particular categories of entrants to have certain skills or experience. While some, like tourists, are excluded from the formal labour market altogether, others may remain only if they are working, such as those on temporary work visas whose licence to stay may require them to hold a specified position for a sponsoring employer. Still others, such as international students, are frequently subject to temporal or sectoral limitations on their labour market activities.

Precariousness is further engendered by the highly uncertain operation of immigration law and its enforcement. Temporary migrant workers are socially insecure in that they have little certainty about their future and they have no access to social support provided to permanent residents. They are politically insecure because they lack official political status as voters. These forms of insecurity are compounded by legal uncertainty. De Genova refers to the ever-present state of 'deportability' of migrants whose unauthorised status may be detected at any time.[93] Even greater uncertainty derives from the fluidity and indeterminacy of unauthorised migration status itself. The insight that migration status is often imprecise and unable to be defined is taken for granted in much of the literature on immigration controls.[94] However, this view is still highly controversial and confronting in some contexts, such as Australia, where it is assumed that immigration rules are fully codified and predictable and border enforcement generally lacking in discretionary. Non-residents, of course, are also regularly precluded from substantive legal and social welfare protections far beyond the realm of immigration law. When deprived of the legislative protections of employment-related entitlements, migrant workers are left more exposed to the raw power of an unfettered market.

In many cases, the coercive and uncertain effects of immigration controls are structurally connected to temporary residence and non-citizenship and unlikely to disappear. Nevertheless, precariousness analysis takes as its

92 Mary Crock, Sean Howe and Ron McCallum, 'Conflicted Priorities? Enforcing Fairness for Temporary Migrant Workers in Australia' in Cathryn Costello and Mark Freedland (eds), *Migrants at Work: Immigration and Vulnerability in Labour Law* (Oxford University Press, 2014), 422; Bridget Anderson, 'What's in a Name? Immigration Controls and Subjectivities: The Case of Au Pairs and Domestic Worker Visa Holders in the UK' (2009) 29 *Subjectivity* 407, 407; Audrey Macklin, 'Freeing Migration from the State: Michael Trebilcock on Migration Policy' (2010) 60 *University of Toronto Law Journal* 315, 332.

93 Nicholas De Genova, 'Migrant "Illegality" and Deportability in Everyday Life' (2002) 31 *Annual Review of Anthropology* 419.

94 Susan Bibler Coutin, 'Legal Exclusion and Dislocated Subjectivities: The Deportation of Salvadoran Youth from the United States' in Vicki Squire (ed.), *The Contested Politics of Mobility: Borderzones and Irregularity* (Routledge, 2011), 169; Kitty Calavita, 'Immigration, Law, and Marginalization: Notes from Spain' (1998) 32 *Law & Society Review* 529.

premise that regulatory intervention can exacerbate and exploit the vulnerabilities of those it regulates, or it can work protectively to support their resilience and agency. Thus, this book takes as its core case study a decade of immigration-based reforms in Australia. Some are highly responsive to the specific ways in which temporary migrants experience coercion and uncertainty at work, such as a series of adjustments to the temporary skilled work visa scheme. However, others have intensified surveillance of migrant workers' lives without immigration-specific protections, which simply leaves in place, or exacerbates, the underlying power differential in migrants' precarious employment. The idea of participatory inclusion provides an alternative aspiration for policies which enhance the resiliency of migrants, acknowledging migrants as legal subjects who have claims upon the law and perspectives which should shape the law, rather than simply as objects of immigration regulation.

Conclusion

This chapter presented conceptual perspectives to unpack the relationships of justice and law between longer-term and temporary residents of a workplace, neighbourhood or national polity. It argued that instead of ethical frameworks centred on nationality or post-nationality, time or place, and citizenship or equality, the idea of relational impact is a more helpful starting point for theorising how and why justice for non-citizens matters. Participatory inclusion captures a model of engagement between migrant workers, the broader national community and legal institutional structures. This chapter then argued that law's impact on migrant workers should be understood in terms of precariousness, foreshadowing how precariousness is engendered by the coercion and uncertainty that inheres in immigration regulation and enforcement.

This book now turns to the Australian case study. In each of the three parts that follow (Part I on temporary migrant labour, Part II on unauthorised migrant labour, and Part III on forced migrant labour) it is argued that better mechanisms are needed in this country to empower migrants to feed into consultation processes on laws and policies that shape their lives. Part I, which follows, focuses on the precarious working conditions for migrants working in Australia on lawful temporary visas. Chapter 3 explains the recent arrival of temporary labour migration on the Australian policy landscape and examines how precariousness has been built into the work and working conditions of temporary migrant workers.

Part I

Temporary migrant labour

3 Keeping up the 'Australian standard'

The regulation of temporary migrant workers in Australia

Mikko Siikaluoma, a 43-year-old Finnish construction worker, arrived in Newcastle, two hours north of Sydney, in June 2005 on an employer sponsored subclass 457 temporary skilled work visa.[1] He alleged that he severely injured his shoulder in February 2006 after falling through an un-barricaded hole on a building site. His employer failed to report the incident to the New South Wales (NSW) state workers compensation authority (WorkCover NSW) and, apparently to avoid workers compensation liability, advised Siikaluoma to attend a doctor and say that he was injured while playing golf. Siikaluoma subsequently sought the assistance of the Construction Forestry Mining and Energy Union (CFMEU) and lodged a workers compensation claim. Surgery was unsuccessful and, unable to perform his usual employment duties, Siikaluoma received workers compensation payments from the employer's insurer.[2]

However, after 26 weeks of physical incapacity to work, further compensation is payable only if the injured worker actively seeks alternative employment for which they are physically capable (usually lighter duties with the same employer or a different job with another employer altogether).[3] Siikaluoma was unable to satisfy these requirements because they conflicted with condition 8107 of his visa, which at that time required the visa-holder not to cease work in the nominated position for the sponsoring employer for more than 28 days.[4] He was not legally permitted to change employers or work in a different

1 This narrative has been distilled from testimony given by union organiser Peter Harris, CFMEU, 'Transcript of Evidence to the Joint Standing Committee on Migration (JSCM) 2007', 16 May 2007, 86–91; the employer's submission to this inquiry: TK Building Pty Ltd, Submission No 89 to the JSCM, Parliament of Australia, 'Inquiry into Temporary Business Visas', 7 August 2007; Stephanie Toh and Michael Quinlan, 'Safeguarding the Global Contingent Workforce? Guestworkers in Australia' (2009) 30(5) *International Journal of Manpower* 453, 466; author's conversation with Peter Harris, organiser, CFMEU, 20 February 2013.

2 *Workers Compensation Act 1987* (NSW), s 36 (*Workers Compensation Act*).

3 Ibid. ss 38(2) and (4).

4 *Migration Regulations 1994* (Cth), sch 8 cl 8107(3) (*Migration Regulations*). This period has since been extended to 90 days.

> position unless a new nomination was approved by the Department of Immigration and Citizenship (DIAC).
>
> When the CFMEU secured a new employer sponsor, Siikaluoma found himself ineligible to apply for a new 457 visa because he no longer met the minimum health requirements due to his injury.[5] Indeed, it seems that even if he had been in a position to negotiate a graduated return to work for his employer in the same position, this may have contravened condition 8107 at that time. (It was possible for a 457 visa worker to work part-time but only where the nominated position was part-time and met the minimum salary level.)
>
> 26 weeks after his compensation claim was accepted, Siikaluoma's employer terminated his employment.[6] No longer in compliance with his visa conditions, Siikaluoma's only option to avoid the cancellation of his visa after 28 days, was to notify DIAC to explain his position and seek a dispensation. The Immigration Department is under no obligation to accept a reasonable excuse and may exercise its discretion to cancel the visa and order immediate removal. At the same time, the insurer curtailed the worker's weekly compensation payments as it was legally entitled to do. By the end of 2007, Siikaluoma remained in Australia on a medical treatment visa awaiting further surgery and pursuing further arbitration. Later, with the support of his union, Siikaluoma was granted a permanent visa, affording him security of residence unfortunately too late to affect his compensation payout.

Siikaluoma's experience illustrates the constitutive role played by government regulation in creating precariousness directly through restrictions attached to temporary visas, as well as the complex interaction of immigration regulation with broader employment and social welfare protections, which is often obscured.

This chapter examines in detail how the coerciveness and uncertainty of temporary immigration status can reconstitute visa workers' employment relationships in ways that create or perpetuate their susceptibility to poor working conditions. Each temporary migrant worker experiences this coercion and uncertainty uniquely, and to vastly varying degrees. Nevertheless, I suggest that there are four major ways in which these effects can occur. First, eligibility requirements of the visa and the conditions of stay can constrain temporary migrants' options and entrench dependencies on ongoing employment. Second, temporary migrants' efforts to enforce employment protections can be severely hampered by immigration enforcement. Third, immigration law can interact with other fields of government

5 Ibid. sch 2 cl 457.224. Note that, since 2009, visa-holders may change their nominated position and employer sponsor without lodging a fresh visa application (as long as the Immigration Department has approved the new position and sponsorship).

6 It is an offence for an employer to terminate a compensated worker's employment within six months of sustaining injury: *Workers Compensation Act* s 248.

regulation to leave temporary migrant workers with weaker (and unpredictable) substantive protections under law. Fourth, a migrant worker's highly particularised transnational social context is also an essential determinant of precariousness or resilience.

While these elements arise in temporary labour programmes across most OECD countries, Australia provides a significant case study of the ways uncertainty and coercion can be folded into temporary migrants' employment relationships. While Australia has followed international trends embracing the use of temporary visas to address labour market demands, attitudes towards temporary migrant labour remain markedly ambivalent. The 'Australian standard' in the title to this chapter refers to the newly federated nation's aspirations in 1901 for egalitarian industrial citizenship. At that time, protectionist commitments to robust and centralised industrial arrangements coincided with hard-line immigration restrictions on non-Anglo Saxon labour (in the form of the notorious 'White Australia' policy) and rejection of temporary migrant labour whether from Britain or elsewhere. It was only in the 1980s and 1990s that moves to deregulate the economy and national labour market set the scene for normalised temporary migrant labour in Australia, through the 457 visa scheme. This streamlined approach to temporary entry, designed for high-skilled professionals, was established as recently as 1996. Furthermore, unlike most countries in the OECD, Australia continues to have no dedicated low-skill migrant labour programme (other than a very small seasonal worker programme first piloted in 2008). At the same time, since the mid 2000s hundreds of thousands of international students and working holiday makers, ostensibly on 'cultural exchange', have proliferated in highly insecure and low-paid jobs. This contradiction appears to be driven by successive governments' desire to embrace this highly flexible labour for its perceived high economic value, without openly endorsing a segmented low-waged migrant labour force. Because the presence of temporary migrant workers is so recent and runs counter to decades of national consensus favouring permanent settlement in a culturally homogeneous frame, mainstream policy debates about exploitation of migrant labour in Australia are novel and still undeveloped with little awareness of the coercion and uncertainty generated by temporary immigration status.

This chapter provides an introduction to this case study, which comprises the bulk of this book. It commences with a brief historical account of Australia's traditional aversion to temporary labour migration. In telling the story of over a century of labour migration policy, there are two narratives that need to be unpacked. The first concerns the close relationship between immigration and industrial relations policies from the earliest days of federation, which were driven, initially, to maintain a racially homogeneous national labour force protected by strong and fair labour standards. The second narrative tells a very different story, challenging the prevailing view that colonial Australia always eschewed temporary, non-White or indentured labour. In fact, forced labour of Pacific Islanders in Queensland and Chinese migration during the gold rush were pointed exceptions to this trend. These important counterpoints may in fact have shored up later cultural resistance to so-called guestworker programmes. Contemporary debates still resonate with anxieties about the dangers of migrant labour schemes for both vulnerable migrants and local workers. The chapter then sketches the recent evolution of temporary labour migration policies in contemporary Australia.

The remainder of the chapter is dedicated to detailed analysis of the forms of precariousness engendered by law at the intersection of immigration and labour regulation in the context of the three major temporary visa schemes that facilitate labour in Australia: the 457 visa, student visas and working holiday visas. Each section briefly explains how each visa category works and the demographics of visa-holders. The contours of Australian policies in each scheme are set against temporary labour schemes in comparable English-speaking Western countries. Each section then exposes how, despite the applicability of general labour protections, migrant workers in each visa category have become susceptible to exploitative employment relationships. This analysis also tracks where Australian government interventions have been pleasingly responsive to workers' precariousness, for instance through the work of the Fair Work Ombudsman. Australia's labour controller has made significant efforts to monitor industries in which temporary workers are prevalent, and vigorously prosecute labour violations. Courts have also advanced workers' resilience by being willing to name the vulnerabilities fashioned by temporary immigration status and provide redress. The results, however, are at times confusingly contradictory.

Historical aversions to temporary labour migration

In Australia, the presence of significant numbers of temporary workers is often described as a very recent phenomenon, given Australia's profound historical antipathy to temporary labour migration.[7] This section traces the evolution of policy settings that initially eschewed but now have come to embrace temporary migrant labour. It explores two interconnected narratives. First, historic resistance to temporary migrant labour appears to have been driven by interrelated concerns to maintain an egalitarian and also racially pure nation state. Temporary and non-British workers alike were generally viewed as anathema to decent working conditions buttressed by a homogeneous society and vigorous collective bargaining. This speaks to just how inter-linked Australia's immigration policies and industrial relations arrangements have been from colonial days.

Second, this section challenges the prevailing narrative that all migration until the 1970s fitted the pattern of permanent white settlement. Although temporary migration was generally shunned, moments in nineteenth-century Australia have cut against this trend. Two distinct forms of

7 Mary Crock, 'Contract or Compact' in Mary Crock (ed.), *Nation Skilling: Migration Labour and the Law* (Desert Pea Press, 2002), 55.

temporary labour migration were striking exceptions to this norm, both associated with indenture: forced labour of Pacific Islanders in the Queensland sugar industry, and Chinese migration precipitated by the gold rush. Tracing these counter-narratives of temporary labour migration assists in understanding the dynamics of contemporary governance of temporary migrant labour and the anxieties these produce, which are explored throughout the book. It explains, for instance, what is meant and seen to be at stake in a claim that 'the backpacker is the new Kanaka', or why some suggest that union opposition to current policies to encourage temporary labour migration may recall past racist attempts by unions to maintain a closed shop for Australian workers.[8]

Temporary servitude in the colonies

The colonies that would later become Australia were largely built on immigrant labour: first convicts and then, from the early 1800s, free British, Irish and North American settlers who were courted with 'assisted passage' subsidy schemes. Both forms of migration were overwhelmingly permanent: Australia was far from Europe and there was no assisted passage home. Nevertheless, focusing on settlement schemes alone overlooks two non-British labour forces in the colonies at that time: Pacific Islander and Chinese workers.

Between 1863 and 1904 over 62,000 Pacific Islander men, mainly from New Hebrides and the Solomon Islands, laboured in the Queensland sugar industry.[9] While some came willingly, most were abducted or enslaved through contracts of indenture and treated with 'ferocious barbarity'.[10] Living and working conditions were extraordinarily harsh with annual mortality rates as high as 147 for every 1000 workers. The *Polynesian Labourers Act 1868* (Qld) made desultory moves to regulate this exploitation by formalising three-year indentures and requiring masters to fund repatriation of the Islanders at the end of their term. Apparently, after this, many ships that were supposed to return Islanders to their homes simply dumped people in the Torres Strait islands not far from Queensland.[11] Slightly stronger protections were introduced in the *Pacific Island Labourers Act 1880* (Qld), which required employers to obtain a licence to bring in labourers, pay wages biannually in the presence of an inspector, provide minimum living standards and post a bond against kidnapping. But these laws also formally enshrined Islanders' inferior employment status. This servitude

8 Damien Murphy, 'Apply Within', *Sydney Morning Herald*, 6 May 2006, 28; Joel Butler, 'Reviving the White Australia Policy: The Labour Movement Returns to its Roots', *Quadrant*, March 2007, 26.

9 Tracey Banivanua-Mar, *Violence and Colonial Dialogue: The Australian Pacific Indentured Labor Trade* (University of Hawaii Press, 2007), 104.

10 Kay Saunders, *Indentured Labour in the British Empire, 1834–1920* (Croom Helm, 1984), 226.

11 Tracey Flanagan, Meredith Wilkie and Susanna Iuliano, *A History of South Sea Islanders in Australia* (Human Rights and Equal Opportunity Commission, 2003).

never held a sense of permanence: very few men were ever permitted to remain in Australia long term, and the scheme itself was never envisaged to last. At Federation, in 1901, the *Pacific Islander Labourers Act 1901* (Cth) prohibited further recruitment of Islanders and ordered the deportation of almost all Islanders found in Australia from 1907 who had arrived after 1880.[12]

The experience of Chinese migration was very different. They initially entered NSW as indentured labourers when convict labour declined in the 1830s, and were generally contracted for work with a specific employer in mining, pastoral, construction, trade and manufacturing for a fixed number of years at low rates of pay.[13] Because Chinese migrants were not eligible for 'assisted passage', by the 1850s gold rushes, informal agreements within local Chinese communities emerged instead to advance credit to intending migrants for their travel, repaid with interest from their earnings over time.[14] Hostility towards Chinese migrants quickly manifested politically and through physical violence, such as the notorious Lambing Flat Riot on the Burrangong Goldfield in 1860. The tendency of Chinese men to leave their families in the relative safety of China was used to portray them as opportunistic sojourners with no intention of settling in the colonies.[15] These views were also driven by racialised perceptions of Chinese workers as members of an inherently servile labour force, culturally at odds with the colonies' aspiration of egalitarianism, freedom of labour and permanent community membership.

Victoria introduced the first statutory immigration restrictions against Chinese immigrants in 1855, and then differential taxation targeting Chinese residents.[16] Thousands of Chinese people were fined or imprisoned in Victoria for tax evasion, and tens of thousands returned to China or moved to NSW.[17] In 1862, NSW passed comparable laws and other colonies followed.[18] By 1888 all Australian colonies had committed to new legislation banning the entry of 'coloured races'.

12 See *Robtelmes v. Brenan* (1906) 4 CLR 395.

13 Alexander Turnbull Yarwood, *Race Relations in Australia* (Methuen Australia, 1982), 167.

14 John Fitzgerald, *Big White Lie: Chinese Australians in White Australia* (UNSW Press, 2007), 47–51.

15 John Rourke, 'White Australia: Origins' (1957) 20 *Current Affairs Bulletin* 170.

16 The *Act to make Provisions for Certain Immigrants (Chinese) 1855* (Vic) and the *Act to Regulate the Residence of Chinese Population 1857* (Vic) limited the number of Chinese passengers on arriving vessels to one for every 10 tonnes of shipping.

17 Alexander Turnbull Yarwood, *Asian Migration to Australia: The Background to Exclusion 1896–1923* (Melbourne University Press, 1964), ch. 4, fn 51.

18 E.g. *An Act to Regulate and Restrict the Immigration of Chinese 1861* (NSW); *Act to Regulate the Immigration of Chinese and to Make Provisions Against Their Becoming a Charge upon Colony 1877* (Qld); *Act to Regulate and Restrict Chinese Immigration 1881* (SA); *Coloured Races Restriction and Regulation Act 1896* (NSW).

Federation: freedom of labour and White Australia

Federation of the colonies in 1901 marked the creation of Australia, a sovereign state deliberately constituted as homogeneous and egalitarian. The earliest legislation established a system of compulsory conciliation and arbitration for resolving industrial disputes, along with protective trade tariffs and a racially restrictive immigration system. As Crock, Howe and McCallum observe, this protectionist agenda was enshrined on three planes: labour, economic and racial.[19]

To avoid industrial conflict, Australia developed a unique centralised system of resolving workplace disputes through legally enforceable sets of wages and conditions, known as awards. Trade unions, government and employer associations each participated in determining the content of awards through a process of arbitration and conciliation.[20] This industrial framework preserved a fundamental role for trade unions and union density in Australia was among the highest in the world.[21] At the same time, national immigration was unashamedly controlled.[22] Under the 'White Australia policy', entrants were welcomed only if they were British and intended to settle permanently. Two categories of immigration were prohibited almost entirely: temporary migration under labour contract and immigration from Asia. The first was mainly eschewed on economic grounds, the second principally due to racism.[23] But hostilities to both were clearly linked. As Lenore Layman argues, both were seen as threats to the 'Australian standard': the Federation's aspirations for universal citizenship and dignity of labour, and its determination to differentiate itself from class-based Britain, and the racial divisions around slavery in the post-Civil War United States.[24] From the earliest days of convict transportation, colonists had

19 Mary Crock, Sean Howe and Ron McCallum, 'Conflicted Priorities? Enforcing Fairness for Temporary Migrant Workers in Australia' in Cathryn Costello and Mark Freedland (eds), *Migrants at Work: Immigration and Vulnerability in Labour Law* (Oxford University Press, 2014), 422, 430.

20 *Constitution of the Commonwealth of Australia* s 51(xxxv) grants parliament power to make laws with respect to 'conciliation and arbitration for the prevention and settlement of industrial disputes extending beyond the limits of any one state'.

21 Michael Quinlan and Constance Lever-Tracy, 'From Labour Market Exclusion to Industrial Solidarity: Australian Trade Union Responses to Asian Workers, 1830–1988' (1990) 14 *Cambridge Journal of Economics* 159, 169.

22 Kathryn Cronin, 'A Culture of Control: An Overview of Immigration Policy-Making' in James Jupp and Marie Kabala (eds), *The Politics of Australian Immigration* (Australian Government Publishing Service, 1993), 83.

23 There is much contestation among historians about whether these restrictive immigration policies were motivated by fears about race or class. See Myra Willard on the economic imperative: *History of the White Australia Policy* (Melbourne University Press, 1923); and for the argument that ethnic fears dominated: Quinlan and Lever-Tracy, 'From Labour Market Exclusion', above n. 21, 167; Andrew Markus, *Fear and Hatred: Purifying Australia and California 1850–1901* (Hale and Iremonger, 1979), 256.

24 Lenore Layman, '"To Keep Up the Australian Standard": Regulating Contract Labour Migration 1901–50' (1996) 70 *Labour History* 25, 26.

engaged in a 'self-consciously Australian struggle against servitude', carefully distinguishing convict labour from slavery.[25] By Federation this sensibility had evolved into a generalised antipathy to any legally differentiated forms of labour. Therefore, as Robin Archer writes, '[f]reedom was intimately connected to whiteness'.[26] Egalitarian social welfare was assumed to be dependent on racial homogeneity and a local labour market insulated from any forces that might segment it, or interfere with worker solidarity (including temporary migrant workers).

To achieve this racial exclusion the 'dictation test', introduced by the *Immigration Restriction Act 1901* (Cth), granted the government unfettered discretion to exclude any immigrant it wished until its abolition in 1958.[27] Customs officials or police could administer the test in any European language whatsoever, within one year (and later five years) of a migrant's entry. Failing the test rendered one a prohibited immigrant subject to six months' imprisonment and deportation. The dictation test was frankly acknowledged by government to be an all-encompassing mechanism for exclusion of Asians. Consequently, the already low levels of non-European settlement in Australia declined further from 1.25 per cent of the population in 1901 to 0.21 per cent by 1947.[28] Even long-time residents from China lived with intense uncertainty. Their families were prohibited from entering Australia to disincentivise permanent settlement. Chinese residents could not leave Australia and return without extensive documentation and 'Certificates of Exemption from the Dictation Test', which, once granted, could be cancelled at any time.[29] As noted earlier, Melanesian workers were barred even more explicitly from 1904 and all Islander residents were subject to deportation after 1907, with very few exceptions. Labour restrictions were added to these immigration restrictions and initially non-Anglo workers were also barred from union membership. Given the compulsory unionism within many industries in which foreign labourers sought work, these racially discriminatory union membership rules deprived workers not only of the protections and solidarity of union membership but also the opportunity to

25 Markus, *Fear and Hatred*, above n. 23. The state owned the labour services of transported felons for the duration of their punishment, but not 'property in the person': *Transportation Acts* of 1717 and 1824. Aborigines, on the other hand, were forced to work in conditions much more akin to slavery. Unlike the convicts, they were not granted any remissions of their 'sentence' and, unlike migrant workers, were not subject to the contractual rights or obligations of their indenture: Saunders, *Indentured Labour*, above n. 10, 214.

26 Robin Archer, *Why is There No Labor Party in the United States?* (Princeton University Press, 2010), 54.

27 Sections 3 and 5; *Chia Gee v. Martin* (1905) 3 CLR 648.

28 Gwenda Tavan, *Long, Slow Death of White Australia* (Scribe Publications, 2005).

29 *Immigration Restriction Act* ss 3(h) and 4.

work in their chosen profession or at all.[30] They were later courted as members so as not to be used as strike-breakers.[31]

The *Immigration Restriction Act* also prohibited temporary migration under labour contracts.[32] While the perceived threat was likely partly racial (given the pervasive assumption that contract labour usually involved indentured Asian migrants), there was also a broader concern that even British contract workers would depress wages or be used as strike-breakers to drive down working conditions.[33] The *Contract Immigrants Act 1905* (Cth) relaxed this broad ban slightly, permitting limited contract labour as long as it would not affect an industrial dispute, where wages and conditions matched those of Australian 'workers of the same class at the place where the contract is to be performed', and no labour of 'equal skill and ability' was available in Australia.[34]

With strong economic growth in the 1940s and 1950s, Australia's ambitious labour needs could no longer be met by Britain alone. This generated bipartisan support for mass migration with little concern for skills or qualifications. 160,000 displaced Eastern Europeans were assisted to migrate between 1948 and 1952, rapidly joined by Italians, Maltese, Dutch, Germans, Greeks and Yugoslavs. These settlers were called 'New Australians' by Immigration Minister Arthur Calwell, underscoring Australia's assimilationist aspirations for them. The new *Migration Act 1958* (Cth) abolished the dictation test and all references to race, but government policy continued to restrict entry of temporary workers and non-Caucasians, with full discretion to grant entry permits still vested in the minister.[35] On arrival, migrants (still overwhelmingly from the UK) were granted full permanent residence, which carried entitlement to family reunion, full labour market mobility, access to unemployment benefits and an easy pathway to citizenship.

30 These rules were upheld in *AWU v. Machine Shearers' and Shed Employees' Union* [1902] AR 16, 2; *United Furniture Trade Society v. Hordern* [1905] AR 125, 133.

31 Anthony O'Donnell and Richard Mitchell, 'Immigrant Labour in Australia: The Regulatory Framework' (2001) 14 *Australian Journal of Labour Law* 269, 291.

32 Section 3(g).

33 As Lenore Layman recounts, six skilled British hatters were denied entry because they were under three-year contracts to a Sydney manufacturer. Amidst outrage that Britons could be classified as prohibited immigrants, the government required the workers to formally apply for a certificate of exemption on the grounds that they possessed 'a special skill not available to meet demand in Australia': Layman, '"To Keep Up the Australian Standard"', above n. 24, 29–31.

34 *Contract Immigrants Act 1905* (Cth), s 5. British subjects born in Britain were exempted from the last requirement. Prime Minister Deakin accepted this concession as a compromise between keeping labour market protections intact while making a 'distinction in favour of persons of our own blood and race, as against the rest of the world': quoted ibid. 36.

35 Sections 6(2) and 6B.

Throughout this period, Australia's centralised award system provided for near-universal coverage of minimum wages and entitlements (at least for full-time workers, who tended to be men). The pervasive coverage of this system meant that the presence of non-Anglophone workers did not depress wages, reduce union membership or create local unemployment. If trade unions were indifferent to the specific needs of migrants, who were often given the least attractive and most hazardous jobs, they were sufficiently organised to enforce these universal entitlements.[36]

1970s: in the wake of White Australia

I have sought to show how protectionist economic and labour market regulation at Federation coincided with racially exclusionary migration policies and a preference for permanent migration. From the 1970s, Australia (like other Western countries) saw widespread economic and labour market deregulation, decline of union membership and more widespread flexible employment. Both centrist Labor and conservative Coalition governments came to the view that opening Australia to global markets served the economic well-being of Australia. In the 1980s, the Labor government entered into an 'Accord' with the Australian Council of Trade Unions to restrict wage demands on the understanding that the government would use fiscal policy to minimise inflation. The Australian dollar was floated, financial markets were liberalised and tariff walls were dropped.

Once again, parallel changes occurred in migration policy: the White Australia policy officially ended in 1973, giving way to higher skilled migration and temporary entrants.[37] The introduction in 1979 of the 'points test' for permanent visas was the first of ever stronger moves to emphasise skilled immigration as a proportion of the total annual settlement intake. The points test replaced racial criteria and bureaucratic discretion with codified assessments on the basis of formal skills, relevant work experience, English language ability and age.[38] As Australia sought to restructure its economy around high-technology goods and services, highly skilled professionals from Asia were preferred in order to foster these industries and enlarge the Australian domestic market for services.

After decades of exclusively permanent migration, this period heralded the rise of temporary residency status. In the late 1970s approximately 17,000 temporary employment visas were issued annually.[39] The 1980s saw

36 Michael Quinlan and Constance Lever-Tracy 'Immigrant Workers, Trade Unions and Industrial Struggle: An Overview of the Australian Experience, 1945–85' (1988) 9(1) *Economic and Industrial Democracy* 7, 26–8.

37 Commonwealth, *Parliamentary Debates*, House of Representatives, 24 May 1973, 2649 (Edward Gough Whitlam, Prime Minister).

38 Laurie Berg, '"Mate, Speak English, You're in Australia Now": English Language Requirements in Skilled Migration' (2011) 36(2) *Alternative Law Journal* 110, 111.

39 Arthur Faulkner and Des Storer, 'Hunting for Witches' (1982) 1(6) *Australian Society* 16, 17.

growing numbers of backpackers (mostly from Europe and North America) and foreign students (largely from Asia). But there remained few pathways from temporary visas (whether tourists or students) to permanent residence other than by marriage or for very wealthy highly-skilled applicants.[40]

1990s: labour market deregulation and temporary skilled migration

The concept of 'precarious work' emerged in Australian labour law policy and scholarship in the late 1990s to describe the effects of radical changes to the centralised system of conciliation and arbitration of working conditions enshrined at Federation.[41] The centrist Keating Labor government legislated in 1993 to decentralise this framework, emphasising collective bargaining at the level of business enterprises to enhance the flexibility of the terms and conditions under which Australians worked.[42] 'Enterprise bargaining' progressively replaced industry-wide arbitration as the determinant of terms and conditions of employment, leading to increasingly diverse employment forms and entitlements. This has seen new forms of employment (casual, contract-based or informal employment) that leave many workers outside of the protected minimum industry standards stipulated in awards.

Consequently, one of the most striking features of contemporary employment in Australia is the degree of casualisation. In Australia, casual employees are not necessarily employed under short-term contracts. Rather, 'casual' is a designation that provides higher rates of pay but deprives workers of a range of statutory entitlements.[43] Australia has one of the highest rates of casual and non-standard work in the OECD: 23.9 per cent of employees were casuals in 2010.[44] Union density continued its marked decline from a high of 57 per cent in the 1950s to 20 per cent in 2006.[45] Migrants have been especially affected by these trends.[46]

40 *Migration Act 1958* (Cth), s 6A(1)(d) (*Migration Act*); *Migration Regulations* reg 1.28.

41 John Burgess and Iain Campbell, 'The Nature and Dimensions of Precarious Employment in Australia' (1998) 8 *Labour and Industry* 5; Judy Fudge, 'Precarious Employment in Australia and Canada: The Road to Labour Law Reform' (2006) 19 *Australian Journal of Labour Law* 105.

42 *Industrial Relations Act 1988* (Cth) as amended by *Industrial Relations Legislation Amendment Act 1992* (Cth).

43 Rosemary Owens, 'Decent Work for the Contingent Workforce in the New Economy' (2002) 15 *Australian Journal of Labour Law* 209, 230–1.

44 Richard Johnstone *et al.*, *Beyond Employment: The Legal Regulation of Work Relationships* (Federation Press, 2012), 34.

45 Santina Bertone, *From Factory Fodder to Multicultural Mediators: A New Typology of Immigrant Work Experiences in Australia* (VDM Verlag, 2008).

46 Caroline Alcorso and Ghassan Hage, *Bargained Away? Enterprise Bargaining and Non-English Speaking Background Women in the Australian Labour Force* (Australian Government Publishing Service, 1994).

The election of the conservative Coalition government in 1996, led by Prime Minister John Howard, signalled a stronger emphasis on individual bargaining. The *Workplace Relations Act 1996* (Cth) (*WR Act*) weakened workers' institutional power to bargain and the strength of independent industrial supervision. The *WR Act* transformed Commonwealth industrial awards from all-encompassing regulatory instruments into mere safety nets of minimum entitlements, and provided for two forms of statutory agreements: collective enterprise agreements (between an employer and employees, which could, but need not, involve unions) and individual 'Australian Workplace Agreements' (AWAs) (between employer and an individual employee).

Also in 1996, its first year in government, the Howard government introduced the subclass 457 (Business–Long Stay) visa scheme (as it was then called) to streamline employer recruitment of skilled temporary workers from overseas.[47] The 457 visa permits employers to sponsor foreign skilled employees to work in Australia in a specific position for up to four years. Although this visa category has become highly politicised over time, it initially enjoyed bipartisan support. It had been developed under the Keating Labor government, in an effort to liberalise cross-border admission procedures of business personnel to fulfil Australia's international obligations under the General Agreement on Trade in Services (GATS).[48] While designed to fill temporary skills gaps in the Australian labour market, this visa rapidly normalised temporary labour migration in the Australian labour market in what has been described as a 'permanent shift to temporary migration'.[49] By 2008, the annual temporary skilled migration intake under the 457 visa scheme had overtaken the annual permanent skilled migration intake.[50] This trend was particularly sharp since, over the lifespan of the Howard government (1996–2007), the permanent migration programme itself came to be dominated by skills over family ties.[51]

47 *Migration Regulations (Amendment) 1996 No 76* (Cth).

48 Neville Roach, *Business Temporary Entry: Future Directions, Report by the Committee of Inquiry into the Temporary Entry of Business People and Highly Skilled Specialists* (Department of Immigration and Ethnic Affairs, August 1995); Marrakesh Agreement Establishing the World Trade Organization, opened for signature 15 April 1994, 1867 UNTS 154 (entered into force 1 January 1995) annex 1B, GATS/SC/6/Suppl.1AUSTRALIA – Schedule of Specific Commitments.

49 Peter Mares, 'The Permanent Shift to Temporary Migration' in Suvendrini Perera, Graeme Seal and Sue Summers (eds), *Enter At Own Risk? Australia's Population Questions for the 21st Century* (Black Swan Press, 2010), 65; Graeme Hugo, 'A New Paradigm of International Migration in Australia' (1999) 25(1) *New Zealand Population Review* 1.

50 30,880 457 visa grants in 1997–8 grew to 110,570 in 2007–8: DIAC, *Subclass 457 State-Territory Summary Report 1 July 2007–30 June 2008* (2008), 2.

51 The percentage of settlers in the skill categories increased from 29.1 per cent in 1993–4 to 69.6 per cent in 2005–6: Graeme Hugo, 'Flows of Immigrants 1993-2008: Australia' in John Higley, John Nieuwenhuysen and Stine Neerup (eds), *Nations of Immigrants: Australia and the USA Compared* (Edward Elgar, 2009), 22, 25.

The Howard government's most dramatic industrial relations reforms were passed in 2005 in the WorkChoices legislation.[52] Under WorkChoices, individual bargaining between an employee and employer in AWAs became the primary determinant of employment terms and conditions. This was achieved by removing the 'no disadvantage test' which had ensured that any collective agreement or AWA, on balance, could not leave an employee worse off than the underpinning award, thus depriving awards of any general 'safety net' function.[53] The WorkChoices amendments also exempted business with up to 100 employees from unfair dismissal laws.[54] Numerous studies were conducted into the impact of the short-lived WorkChoices legislation, although none focused specifically on the experiences of migrant workers. It is clear that the largest increases in the uptake of 457 visas coincided with this industrial policy, and scholars have pointed out that both the 457 visa scheme and WorkChoices privileged 'employer prerogative and self-regulation'.[55]

When the Labor party came to power in 2007 under Prime Minister Kevin Rudd, it quickly dismantled most aspects of the WorkChoices regime. The *Fair Work Act 2009* (Cth) (*FW Act*) removed the ability to certify individual agreements in favour of boosting collective bargaining at the enterprise level.[56] It retained the structural feature of ten national minimum legislative standards in the form of National Employment Standards (the NES), supported by a new system of 'modern awards'.[57] The Fair Work regime also created the Fair Work Ombudsman (FWO), an industrial inspectorate vested with power to pursue its own investigations and audits or act at the request of employees who believe they are being exploited.[58] It enforces compliance with the *FW Act* and employment instruments by referring a matter to relevant authorities, or commencing legal proceedings in a court or an industrial tribunal, initially called Fair Work Australia and since 2013 known as the Fair Work Commission.[59] It also has statutory power to issue compliance notices and to accept written undertakings from employers suspected of contravening the *FW Act*, which are enforceable by courts.[60]

52 *Workplace Relations Amendment (Work Choices) Act 2005* (Cth), amending the *WR Act*.

53 *WR Act* s 348(2) provided that an AWA would prevail over any collective agreement.

54 Ibid. s 643(10).

55 Crock, Howe and McCallum, 'Conflicted Priorities?', above n. 19, 440.

56 *FW Act* s 3(f) gave statutory force to collective bargaining at the level of enterprise through the certification of Enterprise Agreements.

57 Modern awards set a minimum safety net of terms and conditions by industry and occupation that cannot be lower than the NES: ibid. ss 55–56. Unlike awards of the past, modern awards are not created through arbitration but rather through an inquisitorial process of rationalisation of the terms and conditions of numerous state and Commonwealth awards: s 134.

58 Section 682(1).

59 Sections 682(1)(d), 682(1)(e).

60 Section 715.

As I explore in the remainder of this chapter and the next, the Labor government from 2007 also made significant reforms to temporary labour migration in Australia, strengthening safeguards in the 457 visa programme, addressing integrity concerns in the international student programme and significantly expanding the working holiday visa programme through the global financial crisis. In these ways, the evolution of temporary migration policy settings continues to disclose intimate connections with the governance of employment in Australia. Before turning to these categories of temporary migrant workers in Australia later in the chapter, the next section provides a brief overview of the contemporary immigration framework governing temporary migrants who may lawfully work here and applicable federal labour regulations.

Regulating temporary labour migration in contemporary Australia

In 2013 there were over 1.33 million temporary visa-holders with permission to work in Australia.[61] Aside from New Zealanders (who are granted full work rights in Australia), temporary migrants with permission to work generally fall into three visa categories: 457 visa workers, young working holiday makers (WHMs) and international students, among other smaller visa categories. One of these small categories of temporary workers is the Seasonal Migration Scheme (visa subclass 416), which was introduced as a small-scale pilot scheme in 2008 and was made permanent in July 2012. Workers from East Timor, Kiribati, Nauru, Papua New Guinea, Samoa, Solomon Islands, Tonga, Tuvalu and Vanuatu may work for up to six months with a sponsoring recruiter in low-skilled agricultural positions, with additional trials in the cotton, cane, aquaculture and accommodation industries. The quotas for workers in the scheme are low, for instance 2,500 in 2012–13, however, take-up has been even lower, with only 1,492 visa grants in 2012–13 and 2,014 in 2013–14, overwhelmingly Tongans working in horticulture.[62] It is broadly agreed that the scheme has enjoyed strong compliance and it was structured from the beginning to support the workers' rights, with the FWO actively monitoring arrangements. However, some argue that the dense web of regulatory safeguards has hampered its development.[63] Because of its size, this programme is not given detailed treatment in this book.

Another visa scheme not considered in detail here are temporary visas for asylum seekers, which the conservative government under Prime Minster Tony Abbott introduced in late 2014. From this date, asylum seekers who arrive irregularly by boat who were found to be genuine refugees were to be

61 DIAC, *Temporary Entrants and New Zealand Citizens in Australia as at 30 June 2013* (2013), 3.
62 DIBP, *Annual Report 2013–14* (2014), 73.
63 Alexander Reilly, 'The Ethics of Seasonal Labour Migration' (2011) 20(1) *Griffith Law Review* 127; Therese MacDermott and Brian Opeskin, 'Regulating Pacific Seasonal Labour in Australia' (2010) 83(2) *Pacific Affairs* 283.

granted a Temporary Protection visa for up to three years, with the possibility of transfer onto a Safe Haven Enterprise visa, which permits work or study in regional areas for five years.[64] At the time of publication, the regulatory framework for this scheme was not available. Considerable criticism has been levelled at the downgrading of refugee protection to temporary visas that require new protection applications every three years, and the conflation of humanitarian protection, which is obligatory under international law, with discretionary skilled migration.[65] From the perspective of creating precarious labour, the scheme is deeply troubling because it will create a temporary workforce with extreme anxieties about being returned to persecution in their home countries. Significant concerns also arise in relation to the limited geographic mobility of visa-holders and lack of availability of family reunion.

As this indicates, Australia is perhaps unique among similar countries in that (other than the tiny Seasonal Migration Scheme) it has no dedicated low-skilled migration programme. By contrast, the USA admits lower-skilled workers under the H-1A visa for agricultural workers and the H-2B visa for non-agricultural workers, with a long and notorious history of low-skilled admissions through the Bracero programme in the mid twentieth century. Canada has also seen a marked increase in the composition of its temporary migration programme, with the proportion of lower-skilled workers shifting from 26 per cent to almost 60 per cent between 2002 and 2010, predominantly comprising live-in caregivers and agricultural workers.[66] In Britain, foreign workers have been admitted under the Seasonal Agricultural Workers Scheme since 1945 and in recent years full-time agricultural students from Eastern European countries may enter the UK for up to six months to work on farms.

In Australia, the absence of a dedicated visa for the admission of low-waged migrant workers belies their presence in the Australian labour market. The Australian case study in this book focuses on the three visa programmes that, although not explicitly geared toward the entry of low-waged workers, have been instrumentalised to meet Australia's tacit labour shortages in less skilled occupations. The 457 visa attracts professionals, managers and tradespersons; international students are permitted to work up to 40 hours per fortnight; and WHMs, young travellers from a specified list of industrialised nations, are permitted to live and work in Australia for 12 months. All three programmes have experienced significant growth since 2004.

64 *Migration and Maritime Powers Amendment (Resolving the Asylum Legacy Caseload) Act 2014* (Cth), schs 2 and 3.

65 Jane McAdam *et al.*, Submission to the Senate Legal and Constitutional Affairs Legislation Committee, Parliament of Australia, 'Inquiry into the Migration and Maritime Powers Legislation Amendment (Resolving the Asylum Legacy Caseload) Bill 2014 (Cth)', 31 October 2014, 8.

66 Delphine Nakache and Paula J Kinoshita, *The Canadian Temporary Foreign Worker Program: Do Short-Term Economic Needs Prevail over Human Rights Concerns?* (Institute for Research on Public Policy, 2010), 5.

Literature on temporary skilled workers and international students has largely concentrated on their labour market integration and transition to residence.[67] In 2006, a leading demographer estimated that temporary migrant workers may have comprised around 4 per cent of the workforce at that time, although their impact may have been amplified because of concentration in particular professional occupations and urban areas.[68] The labour market impact of temporary migrants is likely to have increased to around 6 to 8 per cent of the labour market since then because of ongoing increases in temporary migration.

There has been less attention on the working conditions that temporary migrants find on arrival. Indeed, understanding exactly how employment regulation maps onto categories of migrant workers is especially challenging because of the complexity of Australian labour laws. The complexity of the labour regulation system can inhibit complaints even by resident workers. The federal industrial statute, the *FW Act*, is extensive, applying to all employees in the national workplace relations system (including citizens, permanent residents and temporary visa-holders).[69] As mentioned above, the Fair Work regime provides a 'safety net' that includes ten legislative minimum entitlements (the NES) and 122 modern awards specifying minimum standards in specific industries and occupations. Collective bargaining at the level of business enterprises is given statutory force through the certification of enterprise agreements.[70] Common law employment contracts sit alongside these. Additional complications arise because the statutes and industrial instruments accord different entitlements depending on the status of employment (continuing, fixed-term or casual) and working-time arrangements (full-time or part-time), even where workers are performing the same work. However, there is a basic minimum rate of pay for unskilled work not covered by an award, whether permanent or casual, part-time or full-time, which is set annually by the Fair Work Commission.[71] Temporary migrant workers are covered by this minimum wage rate,[72] as they are by other areas of employment laws and occupational health and safety laws, which oblige employers to provide a safe working environment for all workers. The federal industrial controller, the FWO, serves an increasingly prominent role as a front-line aid to migrant workers who believe they are

67 Lesleyanne Hawthorne, 'The Impact of Economic Selection Policy on Labor Market Outcomes for Degree-Qualified Migrants in Canada and Australia' (2008) 14(5) *Choices* 1; Bob Birrell, Lesleyanne Hawthorne and Sue Richardson, *Evaluation of the General Skilled Migration Categories* (Cth of Australia, 2006).

68 Graeme Hugo, 'Temporary Migration and the Labour Market in Australia' (2006) 37 *Australian Geographer* 211, 211.

69 *FW Act* ss 3(f), 13–14.

70 Ibid. pt 2–4. An Enterprise Agreement must satisfy a Better-Off Overall Test where a modern award is operative (s 193).

71 Section 287.

72 See *FWO v. Kingsford Carwash Pty Ltd (No 2)* [2012] FMCA 1210, [37].

being exploited at work. The FWO estimates that Fair Work inspectors provide advice, education and workplace compliance to more than 90 per cent of employees in Australia.[73]

However, despite the applicability of general labour protections, temporary migrant workers are nonetheless susceptible to precarious work as a result of the impact of immigration controls. The following sections turn to how precariousness can flow from temporary immigration status through the three major temporary visa schemes (the 457 visa, student visas and working holiday visas) that facilitate low-waged labour in Australia, along with comparative perspectives on schemes in similar Western countries.

Temporary skilled workers

Most temporary migrants in Australia whose entry is explicitly linked to their employment hold the subclass 457 Temporary Work (Skilled) visa. Designed primarily to address skills shortages, the scheme permits visa workers and their dependents to work in Australia for up to four years.[74] Visa workers must work for a specified employer-sponsor, in a specified occupation, but may transfer employers if the new employer meets the sponsorship requirements. Visa workers may transition to permanent residency if eligible. After a peak of 58,050 primary 457 visa grants in 2007–8 (i.e. excluding family members who held secondary visas), numbers fell to 34,790 during the global economic downturn, although they subsequently reached as high as 68,480 in 2012–13.[75] The stock of primary 457 visa workers in Australia reached 100,000 for the first time in September 2012.[76]

The hallmark of this visa category has been deference to employer demand, although the eligibility criteria have evolved over time.[77] This section tracks some of these iterations with comparisons to temporary skilled work schemes in Britain, the USA and Canada. The first decade of the 457 visa programme, under the conservative Howard government from 1996, saw a trajectory towards ever-increasing levels of flexibility, before the framework was significantly tightened under Labor governments in 2009 and 2013. The core structure of the scheme, however, has remained constant

73 Michael Campbell, 'Perspectives on Working Conditions of Temporary Migrant Workers in Australia' (2010) 18(2) *People and Place* 51, 51.

74 *Migration Regulations* sch 2 cl 457.511; Department of Immigration and Multicultural and Indigenous Affairs (DIMIA), *In Australia's Interests: A Review of the Temporary Residence Program* (2002), 23–24.

75 DIAC, *Subclass 457 State-Territory Summary Report 1 July 2007–30 June 2008* (2008), 2; DIAC, *Subclass 457 State-Territory Summary Report 1 July 2009 to 30 June 2010* (2010), 3; DIBP, *Annual Report 2013–14* (2014), 69.

76 DIAC, *Strengthening the Integrity of the Subclass 457 Program* (Discussion Paper prepared for the Ministerial Advisory Council on Skilled Migration, December 2012), 1.

77 For more detail on the technical requirements see Mary Crock and Laurie Berg, *Immigration, Refugees and Forced Migration: Law, Policy and Practice in Australia* (Federation Press, 2011), 270–85.

throughout, with three stages of processing: approval of the employer as a sponsor; nomination of the job position; and application by the proposed visa-holder. As at January 2015, the requirements for the predominant pathway, the Standard Business Sponsorship scheme, were as follows. (A second pathway, through labour agreements, which allow for recruitment of 457 visa workers outside of the usual parameters of the scheme through negotiated arrangements with the government, is discussed in more detail in Chapter 4.)

To obtain employer sponsorship, the employer must demonstrate a lawfully operating business (in Australia or overseas).[78] An Australian business must meet certain training benchmarks,[79] and must attest in writing that it has a strong record of, or demonstrated commitment to, employing local labour and non-discriminatory employment practices. Overseas-based businesses must instead evidence an auditable plan to meet training benchmarks.[80]

Second, the nominated occupation must be specified in a legislative instrument, known as the Consolidated Sponsored Occupation List, which includes managerial, professional and trade occupations.[81] Terms and conditions of employment of the nominated position must be no less favourable than those provided to a citizen or resident performing equivalent work in the same location (unless the position exceeds a specified annual income, currently A$250,000).[82] In any event, the salary rate must be greater than a baseline amount known as the Temporary Skilled Migration Income Threshold (TSMIT), currently A$53,900. The nominating employer must certify that the nominated occupation is a genuine position in its business,[83] and, for certain positions, conduct 'labour market testing' to demonstrate that residents could not be found to fill the nominated position.[84]

Third, the Department of Immigration and Border Protection (DIBP) considers the application for the visa itself. Here, the visa applicant must demonstrate their genuine intention to perform the occupation and be the direct employee of the sponsor.[85] Applicants nominated for trades

78 *Migration Regulations* reg 2.59.

79 Two alternatives are offered. The sponsoring business must maintain throughout the sponsorship payments of the equivalent of either at least 2 per cent of its payroll to an industry training fund, or at least 1 per cent of its payroll on training to its employees. If the business has been trading for less than 12 months, it must provide an auditable plan to meet such benchmarks. See *Specification of Training Benchmarks and Training Requirements* (IMMI 13/030, F2013L01236) (Cth).

80 Reg 2.59(f).

81 *Specification of Occupations, a Person or Body, a Country or Countries* (IMMI 14/048, F2014L00749) (Cth).

82 *Specification of Income Threshold and Annual Earnings* (IMMI 13/028, F2013L01231) (Cth).

83 *Migration Regulations* reg 2.72(10)(f).

84 *Migration Act* s 140GBA.

85 *Migration Regulations* sch 2 cl 457.223(4). The visa-holder must be an employee at law of the sponsoring business, engaged under a contract of service: *CHA Agencies v. Minister for Immigration* [2004] FMCA 279, [21].

occupations must demonstrate a level of English language competency unless certain exemptions apply.[86] Applicants are required to obtain any relevant licence, registration or membership, and may need to establish additional English proficiency for that purpose.[87]

This scheme is in many ways typical of the various iterations of temporary migrant labour programmes in Western countries that have markedly proliferated since the early days of 'guestworker' programmes in the mid twentieth century. While there are now many streams in each country with specific rules governing recruitment, employment, conditions of stay and returns,[88] they tend to share a devolving to employers of control over admissions (and determination of labour force needs). In the USA, entry of skilled temporary workers is facilitated primarily through the H-1B visa, permitting workers to remain in the USA for up to six years. Introduced shortly before the 457 visa scheme in 1990, as in Australia this visa category went undiscovered by employers for several years before employers became aware of it and its use exponentially increased, quickly hitting the annual ceiling of 65,000 admissions a year.[89] Visa-holders are required to work in a specialty occupation, generally requiring at least bachelor's degree qualifications and relevant work experience, and must be paid the prevailing wage.[90] Another scheme, the Intercompany Transfer L-1 visa, allows multinationals to transfer workers with 'specialised knowledge' to their US operations for up to five years. Here, there is no requirement to pay the prevailing wage and the main criterion for admission is that the employee has worked at least one year in the foreign company.[91] Between 124,000 and 155,000 of these visas were issued each year from 2007 to 2011.[92]

Canada's Temporary Foreign Worker Program was first introduced in 1973, and entry of temporary workers over time has grown to 83,740 in 2013 (as in Australia, this scheme is uncapped).[93] Employers are authorised to hire a skilled temporary worker for four years if they receive a validated labour market opinion issued by the government. Foreign workers may also be

86 *Tests, Scores, Period, Level of Salary and Exemptions to the English Language Requirement for Subclass 457 (Temporary Work (Skilled)) Visas* (IMMI 14/009, F2014L00327) (Cth).

87 Condition 8107(3)(c).

88 Philip Martin, *Towards Effective Temporary Worker Programs: Issues and Challenges in Industrial Countries* (International Migration Papers No 89, International Migration Programme, ILO, 2007), 12.

89 Philip Martin, Manolo Abella and Christiane Kuptsch, *Managing Labor Migration in the Twenty-First Century* (Yale University Press, 2006), 65.

90 Ruth Ellen Wasem, 'Immigration of Foreign Workers: Labor Market Tests and Protections' in Benjamin J. Ruiz (ed.), *Foreign and Guest Workers: Immigration and Admission Issues* (Nova, 2011), 1, 12ff.

91 Martin, Abella and Kuptsch, *Managing Labor Migration*, above n. 89, 68.

92 Rey Koslowski, 'Selective Migration Policy Models and Changing Realities of Implementation' (2014) 52(3) *International Migration* 26, 33.

93 Citizenship and Immigration Canada, *Facts and Figures 2013: Immigration Overview: Permanent and Temporary Residents* (2013).

admitted pursuant to international agreements such as the North American Free Trade Agreement where work permits are tied to a single position and employer, and require labour market justification based on employer demand.

Temporary labour migration policy in Britain is quite different because nationals from selected European Economic Area states (comprised of the European Union as well as Iceland, Lichtenstein and Norway) have unrestricted access to the British labour market. Since 2008, temporary migrant workers from elsewhere have been classified under tiers to simplify and centralise the admission system. Tier 1 visas are issued to very highly-skilled independent workers untied to an employer for up to five years and 14 days. Tier 2 visa-holders are skilled migrants sponsored by an employer, in various streams. Under Tier 2 (General), applicants may enter for up to three years and one month, and must demonstrate appropriate English language skills, receive a salary 'appropriate for the position' and least £20,300, and either the sponsor must satisfy a labour market test, or the position must be on a list of occupations in shortage (with some exceptions). Tier 2 (Intra-Company Transfer – Short Term Staff) permits skilled employees of multinationals to work in the UK branch for up to 12 months if they have worked for the employer outside of Britain for at least a year, with no English language requirements and a minimum annual salary of £24,300. Tier 2 (Intra-Company Transfer – Long-Term Staff) permits skilled employees of multinationals to work for up to three years and a month in the UK branch in a position commanding a salary of at least £40,600.

Clearly, with very few exceptions, employer demand is the mainstay of these programmes that require sponsorship. Scholars in Australia have pointed to the 'deregulatory thrust' of the 457 visa scheme, which has never been subject to a numerical cap.[94] The deepest structural source of deference to employers (and of visa-holders' vulnerability to abuse) lies in the fact that the visa's validity depends on ongoing employer sponsorship. It is granted on the condition that visa-holders work only for the sponsoring employer in the occupation listed in the most recently approved nomination (condition 8107).[95] This condition may be breached 90 days after any of the following occur: the worker ceases work in that position for their sponsor; the worker moves to a lower position with the same sponsoring employer; the worker terminates their employment; the employer withdraws their sponsorship; or the business sponsorship or nomination itself is cancelled because of an employer's non-compliance with sponsorship requirements.[96]

94 Iain Campbell and Joo-Cheong Tham, 'Labour Market Deregulation and Temporary Migrant Labour Schemes: An Analysis of the 457 Visa Program' (2013) 26 *Australian Journal of Labour Law* 239, 241; Mary Crock, 'Immigration and Labour Law: Targeting the Nation's Skills Needs' in Andrew Frazer, Ron McCallum and Paul Ronfeldt (eds), *Individual Contracts and Workplace Relations* (1997), 140.

95 *Migration Regulations* sch 2 cl 457.611 and sch 8 cl 8107.

96 Ibid. reg 2.43(1)(l). For an interpretation of some of the rigid requirements involved in sponsorship, see *Sam v. Minister for Immigration* [2007] FMCA 1217.

Upon breach of this condition the visa may be cancelled, which may then render the visa-holder an unlawful non-citizen liable to mandatory detention and immediate removal.[97] Between 2004 and July 2013, the time period in condition 8107 was 28 days. The extension to 90 days in 2013 was a major reprieve from what had been an extremely small window following termination of employment for a visa-holder to find an alternative sponsor, depart Australia voluntarily or be removed. Still, regardless of this time period, making workers' visas conditional on the ongoing support of employers leaves employers with a great deal of control over their presence in Australia.

When the framework was significantly reformed in 2009, to offset this employer prerogative, stronger sponsorship sanctions were introduced along with a requirement that visa-holders be offered conditions no less favourable than resident workers.[98] Prior to this, there were three weaker safeguards against employer abuse. First, the nominated position had to meet mandatory minimum occupational thresholds (requiring professional or trade skills) as specified in a list of occupations deemed by the government to be subject to labour shortages. Second, employer sponsors were required to pay a minimum salary requirement (previously known as the Minimum Salary Level (MSL)) of the higher of either the minimum wage rate in an applicable award or a minimum threshold salary gazetted by the department, which was initially set at A$34,075. This was designed to provide a price signal to employers to encourage the hiring and training of residents, to ensure employers gained no benefit from inflating the skill descriptions of positions they wished filled by foreign workers, and to protect migrant workers' livelihoods as well as local labour standards.[99] Third, employers were required to abide by sponsorship undertakings as to training of residents and other matters of bona fides.

In 2006, commentators began to criticise these checks on employer freedom as weak, charging the government with allowing the scheme to inflate far beyond its initial purpose as a short-term response to acute skills shortages.[100] It was argued, first, that the range of gazetted occupations extended far beyond typically high-waged professional or technical roles, and included 'hairdressers, sales assistants, transport and dispatch clerks, cooks, bakers and pastry cooks'.[101] A significant minority of 457 visas were

97 *Migration Act* ss 189(1), 198, 200–206.

98 *Migration Regulations* regs 2.72(1)(10)(c), 2.79.

99 Barbara Deegan, *Visa Subclass 457 Integrity Review: Final Report* (Cth of Australia, 2008), 11 (*Deegan Report*).

100 E.g. Bob Birrell, Ernest Healy and Bob Kinnaird, 'Cooks Galore and Hairdressers Aplenty' (2007) 15(1) *People and Place* 30.

101 Siew-Ean Khoo, Peter McDonald and Graeme Hugo, *Temporary Skilled Migrants in Australia: Employment Circumstances and Migration Outcomes* (DIMIA, 2005), 6.

(and continue to be) granted in trades occupations and industries marked by less secure working conditions.[102] Initially, temporary work agencies (called 'labour-hire' firms in Australia) could also be standard business sponsors and use the scheme to employ workers, who would then be placed in third-party workplaces. Although this route was prohibited in 2007,[103] labour-hire agencies can still access the 457 visa scheme through the labour agreements pathway. Also the MSL came to be seen as an illusory constraint on the sponsorship of foreign workers. As a baseline, it was inadequate in safeguarding local working conditions because it fell far short of prevailing market salaries in many professions and trades. Further, concessional arrangements for regional employers had been progressively introduced that permitted them to nominate a broader range of lesser-skilled occupations, at salaries discounted by 10 per cent of the MSL.[104] The uptake of these was such that almost a third of all 457 visas granted onshore between 2003 and 2006 were approved at or below the then MSL.[105]

Responding to this criticism, the Howard Coalition government introduced stronger compliance measures to compel sponsoring businesses to fulfil their formal obligations under the scheme. From 2004, an employer's breach of sponsorship undertakings could result in cancellation of sponsorship or future bars from the programme. In 2007, an English language requirement was put in place for 457 visa applicants in trade occupations. The government also introduced, but did not pass, the Migration Amendment (Sponsorship Obligations) Bill 2007 (Cth), designed to further strengthen sponsors' undertakings and increase the severity of sanctions.

Nevertheless, these changes did not significantly overcome the weakness in the scheme. Reports of mistreatment of workers on 457 visas proliferated in 2005, reaching their height by 2008, and included: gross underpayments, unlawful deductions from wages, excessive hours, arbitrary terminations, harassment, forcing workers to sign unlawful employment contracts purporting to bar union membership, preventing workers from bringing their immediate dependents to Australia (to which they were lawfully entitled under the visa) and injuries and fatalities due to manifestly unsafe work practices (such as that of Guo Jiandong described at the opening of Chapter

102 In 2012–13, 27.5 per cent of 457 primary visa grants were to technicians and trades workers. Applications for these occupations increased by 20.8 per cent on the 2011–12 figures: DIBP, *Subclass 457 State/Territory Summary Report 2012–13 to June 2013* (2013), 1, 7, 8.

103 *Migration Amendment Regulations 2007 (No 11)* (Cth). See currently *Migration Regulations* sch 2 cl 457.223(4) (ba).

104 Originally reg 1.20GA(2). All of Australia was declared 'regional' except Brisbane, Gold Coast, Newcastle, Central Coast, Sydney, Wollongong, Melbourne and Perth.

105 Bob Kinnaird, 'Current Issues in the Skilled Temporary Subclass 457 Visa' (2006) 14 *People and Place* 59, 59.

1 and Mikko Siikaluoma in this chapter).[106] The sudden and dramatic nature of this rise (in media reports, academic literature and the courts) may have been attributable to the exponential growth in 457 visa grants during that period, from 40,124 in 2003–4, to 110,570 in 2007–8.[107] They were arguably also fuelled by the Howard government's efforts to deregulate the Australian labour market further under the WorkChoices legislation it introduced in 2005.

After a national election in 2007, the incoming Rudd Labor government launched several reviews of the scheme, including one by industrial relations expert Barbara Deegan focusing on worker exploitation.[108] In 2009 and again in 2013, the scheme was considerably remodelled;[109] these reforms are the subject of detailed analysis in Chapter 4. Briefly, the 2009 changes included a new framework of sponsorship obligations, civil penalties for breach and greater powers for immigration officials to investigate and police them. The MSL was renamed the TSMIT and new provisions required sponsoring employers to observe not only this baseline salary but also the 'market rate' of pay and conditions for workers in that position and industry. Further wholesale revisions were made by the Labor government under Prime Minister Julia Gillard in 2013, including extending the 28-day period in condition 8107 to 90 days, and introducing labour market testing to discourage employers from hiring 457 visa workers over resident workers.

Significant scholarship has been directed at the 457 visa scheme, comprising economic analysis of visa-holders' labour market outcomes,[110] detailed critique of the scheme from the perspective of its regulatory objectives (especially by Joo-Cheong Tham, Iain Campbell and Joanna

106 E.g. Barbara Deegan, *Response to Issues Paper 3: Integrity/Exploitation* (2008); JSCM, Parliament of Australia, *Temporary Entry … Permanent Benefits: Ensuring the Effectiveness, Fairness and Integrity of the Temporary Business Visa Program* (2007), 112–14; Australian Manufacturing Workers Union, *Temporary Skilled Migration: A New Form of Servitude* (Australian Expert Group in Industry Studies, University of Western Sydney and the AMWU, July 2006).

107 DIMIA, *Population Flows: Immigration Aspects 2003–04* (Cth of Australia, 2005); DIAC, *Population Flows: Immigration Aspects 2007–08* (Cth of Australia, 2009).

108 Visa Subclass 457 External Reference Group, *Final Report to the Minister for Immigration and Citizenship* (2008); *Deegan Report*, above n. 99; DIAC, *Discussion Paper: Business (Long Stay) Subclass 457 and Related Temporary Visa Reforms* (2008).

109 The reforms were largely contained in *Migration Legislation Amendment (Worker Protection) Act 2008* (Cth); *Migration Amendment Regulations 2009 (No 5)* (Cth); the *Migration Amendment Regulations 2009 (No 9)* (Cth); *Migration Amendment (Temporary Sponsored Visas) Act 2013* (Cth).

110 Siew-Ean Khoo, Peter McDonald and Graeme Hugo, *Temporary Skilled Migrants in Australia: Employment Circumstances and Migration Outcomes* (DIMIA, 2005); Siew-Ean Khoo, Graeme Hugo and Peter McDonald, *Temporary Skilled Migrants' Employment and Residence Outcomes: Findings from the Follow-Up Survey of 457 Visa Holders* (DIMA, 2006); Siew-Ean Khoo, Graeme Hugo and Peter McDonald, 'Which Skilled Temporary Migrants Become Permanent Residents and Why' (2008) 42 *International Migration Review* 193.

Howe),[111] and some critical socio-legal scholarship.[112] The following section adds to this literature by exploring the pattern of employer mistreatment that materialised in the final years of the Howard government and tracing this back to key sources of precariousness for workers on this visa. My approach explores this exploitation through case law that has ordered sanctions against employers for underpayment of entitlements, building on scholarly analysis of this case law that is only just emerging.[113] This study explores the rise of judicial attentiveness to the particular vulnerabilities of 457 visa workers but also charts inconsistencies within this jurisprudence as well as blind spots where courts underestimate the potent coercion and uncertainty which this visa can introduce into employment relationships.

Jurisprudence on exploitation

In a variety of instances, the Australian courts have ordered penalties and back payments against employers for failing to pay 457 visa workers correct minimum wage rates under awards, overtime, leave entitlements and penalty rates for evening, weekend and public holiday work.[114] In 2009, one sponsoring employer was fined A$183,400 after paying a Malaysian chef just A$9,650 for 18 months' work, less than 12 per cent of his minimum entitlements.[115] Frequently employers' failures to keep records prevent

111 Campbell and Tham, 'Labour Market Deregulation', above n. 94; Joanna Howe, 'Is the Net Cast Too Wide? An Assessment of Whether the Regulatory Design of the 457 Visa Meets Australia's Skill Needs' (2013) 41 *Federal Law Review* 443; Joo-Cheong Tham and Iain Campbell, 'Temporary Migrant Labour in Australia: The 457 Visa Scheme and Challenges for Labour Regulation' (Working Paper No 50, Centre for Employment and Labour Relations Law, University of Melbourne, March 2011); Joanna Howe, 'The *Migration Legislation Amendment (Worker Protection) Act 2008*: Long Overdue Reform, But Have Migrant Workers Been Sold Short?' (2010) 24 *Australian Journal of Labour Law* 251; Hitoshi Nasu, 'Reform of Subclass 457 Visa Scheme: Proposal of Three Models' (2008) 33(3) *Alternative Law Journal* 147.

112 Martina Boese *et al.*, 'Temporary Migrant Nurses in Australia: Sites and Sources of Precariousness' (2013) 24(3) *The Economic and Labour Relations Review* 316; Selvaraj Velayutham, 'Precarious Experiences of Indians in Australia on 457 Temporary Work Visas' (2013) 24(3) *The Economic and Labour Relations Review* 340; Santina Bertone, 'Precarious Bystanders: Temporary Migrants and Multiculturalism' in Andrew Jakubowicz and Christina Ho (eds), *For Those Who've Come Across the Seas: Australian Multicultural Theory, Policy and Practice* (Australian Scholarly Publishing, 2013), 171.

113 Crock, Howe and McCallum, 'Conflicted Priorities?', above n. 19; Michelle Bissett and Ingrid Landau, 'Australia's 457 Visa Scheme and the Rights of Migrant Workers' (2008) 33 *Alternative Law Journal* 142; Miriam Cullen and Bernadette McSherry, 'Without Sex: Slavery, Trafficking in Persons and the Exploitation of Labour in Australia' (2009) 34(1) *Alternative Law Journal* 4.

114 E.g. *Flattery v. Zeffirelli's Pizza Restaurant* [2007] FMCA 9; *Workplace Ombudsman v. KSN Engineering* [2009] FMCA 538; *FWO v. Ultra Tune Australia Pty Ltd* [2012] FMCA 560.

115 *Iser v. Penang Kayu Nasi Kandar Pty Ltd* (Unreported, Magistrates' Court of Victoria, Industrial Division, Magistrate Hawkins, 13 May 2009).

courts from determining the true extent of the underpayments. In one matter, the Federal Magistrates Court of Australia concluded that a café owner in Perth, Western Australia, had failed to pay three Chinese workers at all for 'at least 3 months, and more likely 5 months', while failing to keep any records or issue any payslips.[116] The court imposed a total fine of A$28,820, observing that '[r]ecord-keeping is particularly important in this context as a way for the authorities to monitor government programmes such as a sponsored business visa scheme'. Another employer, this time of a Chinese chef, was fined A$100,000 in late 2014 after underpaying their employee A$86,118.[117] The Chinese man worked 60 hours each week between 2008 and 2011 in a fast food restaurant in Tasmania although he was paid for a 38-hour week, underpayments that were facilitated and aggravated by the employer providing false time-and-wages records to Fair Work inspectors.

Numerous cases document employers who have made unlawful deductions from the minimum wage rates under awards or the 457 visa scheme to satisfy debts.[118] Workers frequently assumed these debts prior to their arrival in Australia for travel, visa expenses or accommodation in Australia, which were owed either to the employer, or a migration or employment agent associate of the employer. One Chinese acupuncturist had been making weekly cash repayments to his employer from his formal salary, which the South Australian Industrial Relations Court found 'were not voluntary and certainly formed no part of his employment agreement'.[119]

Another series of cases involved employers offering AWAs to 457 visa workers in circumstances which contravened the industrial laws,[120] illustrating the acute vulnerabilities of 457 visa workers under the short life of the WorkChoices legislation. In *Jones v. Hanssen Pty Ltd*,[121] Hanssen had committed numerous breaches of the AWA requirements in relation to fifteen Filipino and Irish 457 visa workers including: lodging AWAs that were purportedly signed and dated on a date that was later than the day they were lodged with the Office of the Employment Advocate; failing to lodge an AWA within the required 14-day period; failing to ensure that employees had access to the AWA within the mandated seven-day bargaining period before it was approved; and failing to ensure that each employee was given an

116 *FWO v. Orwill Pty Ltd* [2011] FMCA 730, [7], [29]. Failing to comply with obligations to keep employee records attracts higher penalties: *FW Act* ss 535, 536, 539 and 546.

117 *FWO v. ECFF Pty Ltd* [2014] FCCA 2996.

118 See, for example, *FWO v. Taj Palace Tandoori Indian Restaurant Pty Ltd* [2012] FMCA 258, [44] (*Taj Palace*), where an Indian chef was underpaid A$24,217.90. In *Hortle v. Aprint (Aust) Pty Ltd* [2007] FMCA 1547, a worker was required under his employment contract to accrue a debt of A$5,000 (out of a larger debt of A$10,000) as 'a bond repayable to the Employee on completion of his employment under the visa': [49].

119 *Han v. Mt Gambier Chinese Medical Centre* [2007] SAIRC 75, [51].

120 See e.g. *Lawlor v. Dartbridge Welding Pty Ltd* [2007] FMCA 2119, [7]–[9] (*Dartbridge Welding*); *Wilson v. Nicholson* [2009] FMCA 923.

121 [2008] FMCA 291 and *Hanssen Pty Ltd v. Jones* [2009] FCA 192 (*Hanssen* appeal).

information statement at least seven days prior to the approval of the AWA.[122] The Federal Magistrates Court found that Hanssen had engaged in a 'deliberate strategy … to create the impression that each of the employees in question had had access to the AWA for at least seven days after the employer had signed the AWA, whether or not that had been the case'.[123] Aware that his company had not complied with the AWA approval process, Hanssen had instructed his employees not to date their agreements when they signed them, or they would lose their jobs and be sent back overseas. In Hanssen's own words, 'I told them they had 7 days to think about it, but they didn't have anything to think about. The one thing they are frightened of is being sent back. They are only too eager to please'.[124] Federal Magistrate Lucev considered these contraventions to 'strike at the essence of the scheme' to have time to consider AWAs and 'the trust invested in employers by the Parliament when providing for greater self-regulation in the AWA approval process' and issued a penalty of A$173,250.[125] This penalty was reduced on appeal by the Federal Court in circumstances that are discussed below.

Judicial acknowledgement of 457 visa workers' vulnerability in employer penalties

Much of this case law recognises the precarious situation of temporary migrant workers and treats it as a relevant factor in determining the appropriate penalty. Courts frequently mention the 'vulnerability' of 457 workers, applying precedent from a 2007 case, *Mason v. Harrington*, which sets out a list of matters to be considered in fixing sanctions for employers' contraventions of federal awards.[126] It is striking that *Mason v. Harrington* itself involved the exploitation of Filipino 457 visa workers in two Canberra restaurants. Arguably, the exploitation of 457 visa workers has shaped the jurisprudence on penalties for award contraventions more generally.

In *Mason v. Harrington*, Margarito Sorrosa and Rosanna Cabisidan were employed as chefs in a restaurant called Pangaea in Canberra, working 51 hours per week for seven weeks from August to October 2005. They were not paid the correct hourly rate under the award nor anything at all for overtime. The court found that Sorrosa and Cabisidan were paid A$4,263.56 and A$3,603.93 respectively, only half the income to which they were entitled over this time. In determining the employer's penalty, Federal Magistrate

122 Contrary to *WR Act* ss 341, 342, 337(1), 337(2), 337(8) and 337(9).

123 [2009] FCA 192, [51].

124 Ibid. [45].

125 [2008] FMCA 291, [21].

126 *Mason v. Harrington* [2007] FMCA 7, approved by the Federal Court of Australia in *Kelly v. Fitzpatrick* [2007] FCA 1080, [14] and by the Full Court of the Federal Court in *Australian Ophthalmic Supplies Pty Ltd v. McAlary-Smith* [2008] FCAFC 8, [46]. These judgments considered penalties awarded under the now repealed *WR Act* s 719, but this case is now cited as authority for the awarding of penalties under *FW Act* s 546.

Mowbray set out a non-exhaustive list of considerations including: the nature and extent of the conduct that led to the breaches; the circumstances in which that conduct took place; the nature and extent of any loss or damage sustained as a result of the breaches and other matters. In this context, the court then noted that 'the workers being from overseas under subclass 457 visas were very vulnerable, their tenure in Australia being in effect dependent on their remaining on good terms with the [employer]'.[127] Since then, the Federal Magistrate Court (and, now, the re-named Federal Circuit Court) have regularly accorded judicial recognition to the fact that 457 visa workers can be vulnerable because of the sponsorship requirements, their lack of knowledge of Australian employment protections and their foreign background 'where wages and working conditions are very poor.'[128]

However, this approach to the vulnerability of 457 visa workers is not uniform. In a judgment later in 2007, involving alleged employer abuse, which had attracted a great deal of publicity, the court downplays the significance of employees' immigration status, stating:

> It is probably as well to say a few words about what this case is not about ... It is not about the use of 457A [sic] long-stay visas for the importation into Australia of foreign labour. It is not about using foreign labour that might or might not bring economic advantages to the particular employer concerned.
>
> This case is not about any of those things, but rather a relatively simple matter – the failure by the first respondent and the second respondent to lodge Australian Workplace Agreements in accordance with the provisions of the Workplace Relations Act 1996 in respect of a number of worker's [sic] recruited from the Philippines and Malaysia to work in the first respondent's business in Brisbane.[129]

In *Jones v. Hanssen*, where the employer had boasted that the workers would 'sign anything' because they were 'frightened of being sent back', the Federal Magistrates Court at first instance imposed civil penalties at the higher end of the scale for this reason, among others.[130] However, on appeal, the Federal Court reduced the employer's penalty, finding the Magistrate placed too much emphasis on the vulnerable position of the migrant workers, rather than articulating their actual detriment, which, it found, was no greater than, nor different to, that of any other employee.[131] Other cases follow this approach over *Mason v. Harrington*, finding that a worker's immigration status alone is not sufficient evidence of their vulnerability or that,

127 [2007] FMCA 7, [59].
128 E.g. *Taj Palace* [2012] FMCA 258, [40].
129 *Dartbridge Welding* [2007] FMCA 2119, [4]–[5].
130 [2008] FMCA 291, [7] and [38]–[47].
131 *Hanssen* appeal [2009] FCA 192, [59]–[62] and [99].

even if vulnerable, a temporary migrant worker suffers no unique detriment because of employer misconduct.[132]

Uncertainty and coercion generated by the 457 visa

With reasoning like this, Australian courts frequently underestimate the particular precariousness that can arise within temporary migrant labour. Coercion inheres in temporary non-citizenship status itself by placing constraints on the duration of a migrant's stay in Australia (457 visas are valid for up to four years). The International Labour Organization (ILO) has observed that temporariness of a worker's licence to stay in a country of employment alone can create vulnerability.[133] To this is added the sponsorship mechanism, which contains many of the hallmarks of existential insecurities of non-citizens that have been mapped out in theories of precarious immigration status in Anglo-American scholarship.[134]

Of course, condition 8107, mandating employer sponsorship, may well have been intended to afford temporary migrant workers greater security, by requiring evidence of the demand for this migrant's work in a particular position. Apparently, the 28-day limit on the visa's validity in the absence of sponsorship was introduced in 2004 to prevent labour-hire companies leaving 457 visa workers for periods without employment between placements.[135] However, to view sponsorship as an indicator of security is to assume a generally equal bargaining relationship between employer and employee. When, frequently, this is not the case, constraining migrants' access to the Australian labour market can reshape visa-holders' employment relationships along more rather than less coercive lines. Coercion occurs, first, by circumscribing workers' mobility (some scholars have used the term 'unfree labour' to capture this dynamic) and, second, by amplifying pre-existing dependencies in the work relationship. This section considers these in turn.

The heuristic of 'unfree labour' was developed by Robert Steinfeld to describe restraints on a worker's rights to leave an employer and to work for whom one wishes.[136] Judy Fudge has applied this concept to migrant workers

132 *Alcantara v. Buildpower Pty Ltd (No 2)* [2010] FMCA 763, [21]; *Workplace Ombudsman v. Golden Maple Pty Ltd* [2009] FMCA 664, [15]–[16] (*Golden Maple*).

133 ILO, *Towards a Fair Deal for Migrant Workers in the Global Economy* (2004), 89–90; ILO, *International Labour Migration: A Rights-Based Approach* (2010), 168–9.

134 Matthew Gibney, 'Precarious Residents: Migration Control, Membership and the Rights of Non-Citizens' (Human Development Reports Research Paper No 2009/10, United Nations Development Programme, April 2009), 10; Audrey Goldring, Carolina Berinstein and Judith K. Bernhard, 'Institutionalizing Precarious Migratory Status in Canada' (2009) 13(3) *Citizenship Studies* 239, 240–1; Martin, *Towards Effective Temporary Worker Programs*, above n. 88, 12.

135 Kinnaird, 'Current Issues', above n. 105, 53.

136 Robert J. Steinfeld, *Coercion, Contract and Free Labor in the Nineteenth Century* (Cambridge University Press, 2001), 4.

whose visas restrict them from circulating in the labour markets of the host countries in which they are working.[137] Employer sponsorship limits the mobility of visa-holders within the domestic labour market and, indeed, their geographical mobility. Of course, 457 visa workers formally have the option to change jobs within Australia by finding a new sponsor or applying for an alternative visa. They may freely exit employment as long as they are willing to depart Australia. However, in practice, the risk of losing sponsorship and facing removal, which some have termed 'deportability',[138] can seriously undermine visa-holders' ability to leave a workplace at will.

As a result, in addition to their role as employer, sponsors play a role in a worker's continued right to be present in Australia, intensifying a worker's dependency on them. This is not to say that condition 8107 creates dependency where none previously existed. As Martha Fineman observes in *The Autonomy Myth*, workplace relationships already tend towards subordination because they frequently lack real reciprocity between the needs of employers and workers.[139] Of course, this is not always the case. An employer may keenly need the particular talents of a sponsored employee where skills shortages affect the position to be filled. However, once in Australia, the mutual needs between employer (of labour) and employee (of the job and livelihood) can be overshadowed by a larger lack of parity: the employee depends on the employer not only for this job, but also access to the Australian labour market and their ongoing legal presence in Australia (as well as that of their family).[140]

It is not surprising, then, that this structural advantage can be seized upon by employees as a dramatic coercive power personally vested in an employer. Employers easily exploit the perception of many 457 visa workers that their employer could cancel their visas, although in fact it is DIBP that formally holds this power. The manager of Hanssen Construction, Dick Smith, perpetuated this perception, observing in a radio interview:

> if they want to change employer they then have to go back home … I suppose, you know it's not such a captured market but you know where

137 Judy Fudge, 'Precarious Migrant Status and Precarious Employment: The Paradox of International Rights for Migrant Workers' (2012) 34 *Comparative Labour Law and Policy Journal* 95, 95.

138 Nicholas De Genova, 'Migrant "Illegality" and Deportability in Everyday Life' (2002) 31 *Annual Review of Anthropology* 419.

139 Martha A. Fineman, *The Autonomy Myth: A Theory of Dependency* (The New Press, 2004), 241ff.

140 In fact, sponsors in Australia are actually authorised to advise migrant workers about their entitlements under migration law. Although the *Migration Act* generally prohibits anyone other than a registered migration agent from giving advice about migration rules, one of the few exceptions is someone who is sponsoring a visa applicant for a visa application: *Migration Act* ss 280(1), 280(4) and 280(5).

you are with them. You know that they're going to turn up and you know that they're not going to swap employers.[141]

Precariousness is further heightened where a migrant worker is hopeful of attaining permanent residence. Not only can migrants experience profound uncertainty as the requirements for permanent skilled visas perpetually change. In addition, application criteria valorise Australian work experience and, increasingly, employer sponsorship itself, which powerfully intensifies the incentives to stay in exploitative workplace relationships. The implications of these pathways from 457 visas to residence for worker precariousness are addressed in more detail in the following chapter.

One of the cruellest consequences of this dependency dynamic is that it can be intensified by employer misconduct. Numerous court proceedings record circumstances in which workers were not paid at all for weeks or months at a time,[142] and therefore become more reliant on employers for the provision of accommodation, food and transportation. Also, as I will explore in more detail in the following chapter, because of the requirement for employer sponsorship, an employer's violation of labour laws or immigration rules frequently has legal consequences that are far graver for the worker than the employer. These circumstances offer no incentives for a visa-holder to call attention to their employer's contraventions.

Barriers to enforcement

Furthermore, a temporary visa can inject uncertainty into otherwise robust employment entitlements through the logistical hurdles that frequently confront temporary workers attempting to pursue claims after departing Australia. Little dispensation is offered to claimants who fall foul of rigid time periods in which to commence proceedings, and lack of familiarity with Australian employment laws or the need to arrange one's affairs for a precipitous departure are typically not accepted by tribunals as compelling justifications for delay.

Even sharper impediments are faced by 457 visa workers in obtaining legal redress as a result of the strictures of employer sponsorship. Condition 8107 is breached automatically 90 days after a 457 visa worker's employment ends. Termination enlivens the statutory visa cancellation power regardless of whether the employment was terminated by the employee or by employer dismissal.[143] Of course, employers are legally prohibited from dismissing an

141 ABC Radio National, 'Australian Workers Passed Over for Improved Labour', *PM*, 12 May 2006.

142 *FWO v. Kentwood Industries Pty Ltd (No 2)* [2010] FCA 1156, [165]; *Freya v. Yoga Tandoori House Pty Ltd* [2008] FMCA 288, [13]; *Kumar v. Rahul Chauhan (t/as Swaad of India)* [2008] SAIRComm 46, [74]–[76].

143 *Migration Regulations* reg 1.20E; *Migration Act* s 116(1)(b).

employee in an effort to retaliate against their lawful complaint.[144] Australia also prohibits unfair dismissal, that is, termination at the initiative of the employer that is harsh, unjust or unreasonable.[145] However, there is no formal channel through which DIBP may suspend cancellation where the dismissal may have been unlawful or unfair. Consequently, in practice, a 457 visa may be cancelled for lack of sponsorship, leading to the worker's removal, well before any claim for the original unlawful employer conduct has been ventilated, much less a claim for improper dismissal. In addition, during the period March 2006 to July 2009, the conservative Howard government's WorkChoices legislation compounded the coerciveness of employer sponsorship by abolishing unfair dismissal protections for employees in businesses with 100 employees or fewer.[146] This further exacerbated the difficulties faced by 457 visa workers in seeking redress for abuses of their rights, since an arbitrary termination was no longer even open to legal challenge.

Of course, a determined worker may find ways to remain in Australia to pursue an employment-related claim. A 457 visa worker may transfer employment as long as the new employer is recognised as a sponsor and DIBP has accepted the nomination of the new occupation.[147] Alternatively, the migrant may, if eligible, apply for a different temporary visa. Furthermore, the section 116 visa cancellation power is discretionary rather than mandatory so a 457 visa worker who has lost their sponsorship may persuade DIBP to leave the visa on foot long enough to seek redress. After the visa is cancelled, the worker may remain in Australia on a bridging visa by seeking a review of the cancellation decision in the Migration Review Tribunal.[148] If this application for review is rejected, a migrant may request the minister to exercise his or her personal and non-reviewable discretion to grant a visa.[149] However, these avenues are extremely costly and speculative. Migrant workers are surely entitled to a far more certain and rights-based mechanism to allow them to regularise their immigration status for a period of time in order to pursue industrial claims. This argument is made in Chapter 9, which also explores possible models for this proposal. But even with such a dispensation, 457 visa workers face strong disincentives to complain about employer misconduct and risk destabilising the employment/sponsorship relationship.

144 It is a civil penalty offence for a person to 'organise or take, or threaten to organise or take, any action against another person with intent to coerce the other person, or a third person' to exercise or not exercise a 'workplace right': *FW Act* s 343. 'Workplace right' is defined in s 341 to protect persons who are entitled to a workplace instrument or law, or able to make a complaint or inquiry to a person or body having the capacity under a workplace law to seek compliance.

145 *FW Act* s 385(b).

146 Former *WR Act* ss 634(10)-(11), before this was repealed by *FW Act*.

147 *Migration Regulations* sch 8 cl 8107(3)(a)(i).

148 *Migration Act* s 338(3).

149 Ibid, s 351.

Alternatively, some employment proceedings can be brought in the absence of the impacted worker. Considerable research in countries with long-standing temporary labour schemes indicates that the characteristics that contribute to their precariousness – including language and cultural barriers, lack of awareness of work rights and distrust of government officials – also make them less likely to complain.[150] Indeed, union representatives have posited that most 457 visa workers approaching unions had been advised to do so through informal employee or community networks.[151] The *FW Act* removes from the shoulders of workers the burden of bringing court proceedings (and exposure to costs), by empowering the FWO to enforce workplace entitlements. On top of orders to reimburse unpaid wages, courts may award penalties of up to A$33,000 per contravention. The FWO publicly acknowledges its particular role in protecting temporary migrant workers because of their vulnerability. Its decisions to initiate proceedings are made in accordance with a Guidance Note on Litigation Policy, which provides that an employee's status as a 'vulnerable worker' may be considered when deciding whether to commence proceedings.[152] Among those considered vulnerable are young people, people with literacy difficulties, recent immigrants and people from non-English speaking backgrounds. Temporary workers almost certainly will fall into one or more of these categories. In 2010 the FWO launched an array of protective measures targeting foreign workers, including translation services, information sheets on employment and other legal protections in 27 languages and broadcasting its services through non-English speaking radio programmes. This is a substantial improvement on DIBP efforts in this field, which include far more limited publications in only six foreign languages.[153] FWO has also developed linkages with community organisations and runs confidential investigations where the complainant is not identified.

The FWO has made great strides in targeting the exploitation of temporary migrant workers, with a noticeable spike in activity since 2011. In 2011 the FWO National Overseas Workers initiative was established, which monitors compliance with labour laws in industries that employ high numbers of migrant workers. Campaigns have focused on the cleaning services sector, for example, revealing high levels of non-compliance.[154] The South Australian office of the industrial controller in the construction industry, Fair Work Building and Construction, launched a pilot programme in 2013 targeting exploitation of 457 visa workers involving an educational

150 David Weil and Amanda Pyles, 'Why Complain? Complaints, Compliance and the Problem of Enforcement in the US Workplace' (2005) 27 *Comparative Labour Law and Policy Journal* 59, 64–5.

151 Toh and Quinlan, 'Safeguarding the Global Contingent Workforce?', above n. 1, 463.

152 FWO, *Guidance Note 1: Litigation Policy of the Office of the Fair Work Ombudsman* (4th edn, 3 December 2013), [11.6].

153 DIBP, *Your Rights and Obligations: Immigration Facts for Workers*.

154 FWO Targeted Campaigns Unit, *National Cleaning Services Campaign 2010–11* (2011), 4.

campaign and information-sharing with DIBP and FWO. This is significant because these inspectorates have historically relied heavily on complaints-based inspection strategies. Between 27 March 2006 and 31 December 2010, the FWO finalised 2,308 complaints in relation to temporary migrant workers on a range of visas, recovering A$3,226,837 in unpaid entitlements including through 26 court proceedings.[155] In the two years between July 2012 and June 2014 the FWO completed more than double this figure, 4,643 complaints, recovering A$2.4 million for temporary migrant workers on a range of visas.[156] Even so, these statistics (like those published by DIBP on the prevalence of employer breaches of 457 visa sponsorship obligations) may considerably understate the true extent of employer non-compliance.

Differential protection in workers compensation, unfair dismissal and leave entitlements

To this point, this chapter has looked at how the 457 visa can inject precariousness into visa-holders' employment relationships both directly, through visa conditions that constrict workers' options, and more indirectly through barriers to enforcement of employment rights. This section explores how 457 visa status can work at a deeper level, to undermine substantive workplace protections which seem, on their face, applicable to all workers in Australia, including those holding 457 visas. Their differential treatment in the legal domains of workers compensation laws, unfair dismissal and leave entitlements are examined in turn. This jurisprudence both illustrates and contributes to the precariousness of temporary migrant workers, who are left with industrial protections weaker than those enjoyed by residents, and far more uncertain.

The experiences of Finnish worker Mikko Siikaluoma, discussed at the opening of this chapter, vividly illustrate how the structure of 457 visas can alter workers compensation protections, which would otherwise appear to be generally applicable to workers regardless of immigration status. Recall that Siikaluoma injured his back while working on a building site and, with union assistance, received standard workers compensation payments. Under NSW legislation, six months after a compensable work injury, a worker continues to be entitled to ongoing workers compensation payments only if they can demonstrate that they are seeking suitable alternative employment either with the same or different employer.[157] However, for Siikaluoma, condition 8107 on his 457 visa at that time prevented him from doing either: case law confirms that a 457 visa may be cancelled where a worker undertakes duties

155 Senate Standing Committee on Education Employment and Workplace Relations, Parliament of Australia, 'Question Taken on Notice EW0766-11, Additional Estimates Hearing: 13 April 2011, Education Employment and Workplace Relations Portfolio' (2011).

156 FWO, *Annual Report 2013–14* (2014), 30.

157 *Workers Compensation Act* ss 38(2) and (4).

different to those of the nominated occupation during a workers compensation rehabilitation programme.[158] He was also prevented from applying for a fresh 457 visa with a different occupation nomination because his injuries meant that he was unable to satisfy the health requirements in a fresh visa application.

NSW workers compensation jurisprudence also downgrades the quantum of compensation for overseas-based workers. Under NSW law, a worker's entitlement to weekly payments ceases once they no longer reside in Australia, unless their incapacity from the injury is 'likely to be of a permanent nature'.[159] If they satisfy this test, workers are entitled to an amount equivalent to their lost ability to earn as a result of the injury. This is calculated by subtracting their average actual earning capacity since the injury, from their average probable earnings but for the injury.[160] With this starting point, the NSW Workers Compensation Commission (WCC) may then exercise discretion in fixing a final amount. For overseas workers, the initial calculation of lost earning capacity is done on the basis of hypothetical earnings in the Australian labour market.[161] However, in exercising its discretion, the WCC will reduce this amount where a migrant worker's country of nationality enjoys far lower wages that Australia. This seems logical, of course, because '[m]oney which was not likely to be earned cannot be regarded as lost earnings for that purpose'.[162]

However, it results in detriment to temporary migrant workers since it can wrongly assume that a worker would always have relocated to her country of origin. Simply taking for granted that the worker had a temporary licence to work in Australia and has returned home since the injury fails to take into account that the injury might have interfered with a worker's visa status to cause an early departure. This is illustrated by a claim brought by an Indian temporary worker, Sasibhooshanan Nair Raghavadev.[163] Raghavadev worked as a labourer on a mushroom farm from 2005, and on 5 November 2006 he injured his back while lifting mushroom boxes and then continued to work on restricted duties until February 2009 when his employment was terminated. His entitlement to work apparently expired on 15 July 2009, and he returned to India. He claimed ongoing compensation for his permanent injury. In assessing the quantum of these weekly payments, the WCC exercised discretion to reduce the amount by one half, given the 'economic differences between Australia and India'. But this did not consider the reasons for Raghavadev's departure. He had testified that 'if not for his injury, he would have returned to Australia to work so he could

158 *Rahhal v. Minister for Immigration (No 2)* [2008] FMCA 935.

159 *Workers Compensation Act* s 53.

160 Ibid. s 40(2).

161 *Taufia v. Nonferral (NSW) Pty Ltd* (1995) 12 NSWCCR 431; *Singh v. TAJ (Sydney) Pty Ltd* [2007] NSWWCCPD 152.

162 *Australian Wire Industries Pty Ltd v. Nicholson* (1985) 1 NSWCCR 50, 57G.

163 *Raghavadev v. Moonlight Mushrooms Pty Ltd* [2010] NSWWCCPD 120.

continue to send money to his family in India'.[164] However, the WCC finds this evidence 'of limited relevance', concluding that he left Australia because he lost the 'right to work in Australia'.[165] This reasoning fails to grapple with the possibility that Raghavadev's injury (and his loss of earnings) may have prevented him from extending his visa or work entitlements, or indeed seeking permanent residency. Raghavadev was arguably left uncompensated for the actual cost of his injury to him, including its impact on his precarious immigration status.

Another important feature of Australian employment laws are statutory entitlements against arbitrary dismissal. The *FW Act* provides relief against unfair dismissal, that is, termination at the initiative of the employer that is harsh, unjust or unreasonable.[166] Broadly, unfair dismissals involve dismissals that have a disproportionate effect on the employee (balanced against the gravity of the misconduct triggering the termination), which are not based on a 'valid reason' or which do not show sufficient procedural fairness (for example, failure to notify the worker of that reason or to give a warning).[167] An industrial tribunal (currently the Fair Work Commission) may order reinstatement or compensation.[168]

As long as they meet the general eligibility requirements, 457 visa workers are protected by unfair dismissal laws. For instance, to qualify, workers must have been continuously employed for at least six months (or twelve months for small businesses).[169] In one case, where a 457 visa worker had not been in Australia for six months, the tribunal held that he nevertheless did qualify, counting towards this period of employment the additional time he worked overseas for the Australian employer.[170] Having satisfied that hurdle, helpfully for 457 visa workers, tribunals have confirmed that an employer's unilateral withdrawal of visa sponsorship can amount to an unfair dismissal if it contains an element of harshness, unjustness or unreasonableness.[171] However, acute enforcement barriers arise here, with countless reports of

164 Ibid. [47].

165 Ibid. [48]. For a different approach see *Crowhurst v. North Sydney City Council* (Unreported, No 35179 of 1998, 26 July 1999) where a New Zealander injured his back in Australia and was paid weekly compensation until he returned to New Zealand 'where there was "much unemployment"'. The WCC in that case declined to reduce the weekly entitlement, finding that 'had Mr Crowhurst not been injured, he would probably have continued to work for the employer in Sydney' so there was no reason to reduce the award: [52]. In *Ahmed and Kaka Enterprises Pty Ltd t/as Desi Hut* [2012] NSWWCC 65, the WCC also determined not to reduce a worker's weekly payment after returning to Pakistan.

166 *FW Act* s 385(b).

167 Ibid. ss 387(a)-387(g).

168 Sections 390(1) and (2).

169 Sections 382(a), 383.

170 *Usman Ali v. Industries Services Training Pty Ltd* [2011] FWA 9177.

171 *L and the Employer* [2007] AIRC 457, [22] (*L*); *Daniel Coppard and Australian Cable & Telephony Pty Ltd* (Unreported, AIRC, 14 January 2005), [24].

457 visa workers who may have been unfairly dismissed and removed before having the opportunity to press their claims. For instance, Zi Hong Fun was allegedly forced to work after breaking a wrist falling from a ladder and was dismissed for taking sick leave; another 457 visa worker was given four weeks' notice after informing his employer that he had been diagnosed with cancer, his employer explaining that the conditions of the 457 visa did not require the employer to assume a financial burden if the employee became ill.[172]

As in the domain of workers compensation, beyond enforcement barriers, unfair dismissal jurisprudence itself also indicates an uneven responsiveness to the particularly precarious circumstances of temporary migrant workers. A critical issue arises because of the finite duration of the 457 visa. Workers are excluded from unfair dismissal protection where they are terminated at the conclusion of their fixed-term contract since no dismissal takes place in these circumstances.[173] This has serious implications for temporary migrant workers since, in some cases, the presence of the 457 visa is frequently taken to imply that the employment contract was of fixed duration, terminating automatically on the expiry of the visa.[174] However, other cases downplay the significance of the visa and take a broader approach to the availability of unfair dismissal for workers at the expiry of their visa, especially where the visa-holder was not clearly aware of the implications of the visa duration or assumed the visa would be extended upon its expiry.[175]

Some tribunals have been attentive to another area of significant vulnerability in 457 visa workers: the fact that, because of employer sponsorship, dismissal before the expiry of the visa can trigger the loss of immigration status and forced relocation overseas. This issue was particularly acute before 2013 when the grace period between employment termination and visa cancellation was 28 days. One dismissal was determined to be 'harsh' because 'of the serious financial consequences to [the 457 visa worker] and the social dislocation which was clearly inevitable on summary termination of his employment'.[176] Another dismissal was deemed 'unfair' due to an insufficient period of notice before the dismissal since the temporary worker had been encouraged by her employer to move to Australia for this position and on termination would be forced to return to China.[177] Thus, 457 visa workers may in principle have been entitled to additional notice of dismissal

172 Natalie Sikora, 'Men Forced to Work with Broken Hands, Arm', *Herald Sun*, 18 June 2008; Australian Council of Trade Unions (ACTU), *Response to Discussion Paper: Business (Long Stay) Subclass 457 and Related Temporary Visa Reforms* (2008), 8–9

173 *FW Act* s 386(2)(a).

174 E.g. *Motomu Izawa and Ocean Spirit Dive Pty Ltd* (Unreported, AIRC, 2 February 2001).

175 E.g. *McNally v. Neale Taylor Plumbing Pty Ltd* [2014] FWC 5226; *Dillon v. Knight Chiropractic Pty Ltd* [2014] FWC 2244.

176 *Luke Webster v. Mercury Colleges Pty Limited* [2011] FWA 1807, [45] (*Webster*).

177 *Su Hong and Rainbow (Australia) Pty Ltd* (Unreported, AIRC, 10 November 1997); *Hong Su* [1998] IRTA 11373. The plaintiff here held a subclass 456 Business (Short Stay) visa, which, before it was discontinued in March 2013, permitted entry for up to three months for short-term business purposes.

when they had only 28 days after termination to regularise their immigration status or relocate overseas. Even after the extension of time in condition 8107 to 90 days, tribunals have found that a termination with little warning was harsh because its impact on the employee's immigration status was 'to him devastating'.[178]

The primary remedy for unfair dismissal, reinstatement, is not available to 457 visa workers where employer sponsorship has ended.[179] Indeed, the limited labour mobility of 457 visa workers can also be problematic in calculating compensation awards, since employees are typically required to mitigate their loss by finding alternative employment. At times, tribunals have waived this rule where visa restrictions prevent temporary workers from working except in the sponsored position, or when non-citizens are unable to work while preparing to depart Australia.[180] However, in one matter, a tribunal reduced a compensation award because a 457 visa worker failed to mitigate his loss by leaving Australia immediately.[181] The South Australian Industrial Relations Commission noted that the temporary migrant worker remained in Australia on a tourist visa for two months after his dismissal. His compensation was reduced because he 'knew that for so long as he remained in this country he would be unable to mitigate his loss, unless he obtained another working visa'.

A final area where 457 visa workers' precariousness is sometimes given voice relates to tribunals' discretion to accept applications for unfair dismissal that are lodged out of time. At the federal level, such applications are currently required to be made to the Fair Work Commission within 21 days from termination (previous federal statutory schemes set deadlines of 14 or 21 days).[182] Tribunals may accept late applications in exceptional circumstances, which are now enumerated in an exhaustive statutory list.[183] Case law is extremely inconsistent as to whether temporary immigration status (or loss of employer sponsorship) suffice as acceptable reasons for delay.

In *Eugene Magoo*, a Western Australian tribunal with a 28-day application deadline accepted a South African welder's application eight days out of time, since he was unaware of the statutory timeframe and when 'terminated he was mainly concerned about obtaining alternative employment in order to remain in Australia'.[184] In *Anthony Emurugat*, the tribunal also took a

178 *Pope v. D & E Air Conditioning Pty Ltd* [2014] FWC 1149, [10].

179 *L* [2007] AIRC 457, [23]; *Webster* [2011] FWA 1807, [47]. Although in one 457 visa worker's claim for reinstatement, the industrial tribunal conceded that '[t]he obtaining of a work visa may be within the bounds of possibility, making re-employment possible': *Cunningham v. Bensons Building Services Pty Ltd* [1998] SAIRComm 26 (*Cunningham*).

180 *Richard Paternella v. Electroboard Solutions Pty Ltd* [2011] FWA 3323, [96]; *Webster* [2011] FWA 4772, [12].

181 *Cunningham* [1998] SAIRComm 26.

182 *FW Act* s 394(2)(b).

183 Section 394(3).

permissive approach to the time limits, given that the employer had led the applicant to believe that he had no avenue to challenge the termination of employment decision.[185] The tribunal in *S Liu* took into account the difficulties of reliable communication between a 457 visa worker and her legal representative because of her 'hasty departure from Australia' following the termination of her employment and (presumed) cancellation of her visa.[186] In *Vadhan*, the Fair Work Commission accepted a late application where the employee delayed lodgement in an effort to preserve a positive relationship with his employer in the hopes of maintaining employment and retaining his visa.[187]

Several other decisions have rejected applications out of time where 457 visa workers have pointed to language difficulties or unfamiliarity with Australian industrial protections, frequently also ordering these workers to pay their employers' costs.[188] One Filipino worker, Robert Lim, lodged his application two days late. He said that he was unaware of his right to apply for unfair dismissal until he sought assistance from the Philippines Consulate the day before his lodgement. The federal tribunal held that this:

> is not an unusual situation regardless of an applicant's place of birth. Many applicants are unaware of their rights and become aware of them only after the statutory time period for lodging applications has passed.[189]

The tribunal rejected Lim's suggestion that he would 'suffer prejudice compared to other employees in a similar position of greater magnitude':

> The particular prejudice the applicant will suffer in terms of being deported [sic] is not relevant in regard to this factor [of fairness as between the person and other persons in a similar position] nor more broadly in deciding the question of whether a further period to apply should be allowed … the fairness referred to in s. 394(3)(f) does not relate to the consequences of not being able to pursue an application for a particular applicant.[190]

It is positively confounding that other decisions have permitted late applications in comparable circumstances. In *Usman Ali*, the 457 visa worker's late

184 *Eugene Magoo v. Dwyer Engineering & Construction Pty Ltd* [2006] WAIRComm 4244, [26].
185 *Anthony Emurugat and Utilities Management Pty Ltd* [2008] AIRC 247.
186 *S Liu v. Sinotrans Group Australia Pty Ltd* (Unreported, AIRC, 15 February 2000).
187 *Vadhan v. Night Owls Pty Ltd T/A Ferntree Print* [2014] FWC 5329.
188 *Mrs Q, Mr J and Mr S and the Employer* [2007] AIRC 695; [2007] AIRC 457; *Purvi Sudani and Ashishkumar Sudani v. HealthWise Management (Aust) Pty Ltd T/A HealthWise Pharmacies Group* [2011] FWAFB 1022; *Raymond Cordero Pagkaliwangan v. Siganto & Stacey Pty Limited* [2010] FWA 9104; *Rajeev Prasad v. Alcatel-Lucent Australia Ltd* [2011] FWAFB 1515.
189 *Robert Lim v. Downer EDI Mining* [2009] FWA 457, [29].
190 Ibid. [36].

application was accepted in light of the 'significantly greater adverse impact [of the dismissal] on Mr Ali than the dismissal of a citizen or permanent resident'.[191]

In a final domain of employment law, the provision of extended leave (including parental leave, leave following a workplace injury or leave without pay) under the NES and modern awards, condition 8107 interferes with 457 visa workers' entitlements.[192] As mentioned earlier, since 2009, sponsors are required to accord 457 visa-holders terms and conditions of employment that are no less favourable than those that are or would be offered to residents. Reading this together with condition 8107 requiring visa-holders to work only in the nominated position, DIBP policy permits 457 visa workers to undertake lower level duties for up to two months if necessary to comply with occupational health and safety requirements without a new nomination.[193] However, policy stipulates that leave longer than 12 months may trigger visa cancellation if this causes a visa-holder to earn less than the TSMIT.[194] It is possible that where an employer withdraws visa sponsorship in these circumstances, this would not amount to wrongful dismissal. This issue has been raised but not resolved in the industrial tribunals.[195]

The precariousness of workers' social context

The preceding sections have argued that the precariousness wrought by 457 visa conditions is by no means uniform. The uncertainty and coercion that inhere in temporary migration status and employer sponsorship themselves create vulnerability, can also hamper enforcement of workers' entitlements and can even reshape substantive labour law protections and remedies. All of this, of course, varies greatly according to a migrant worker's social context. This section briefly considers the array of circumstances personal to temporary migrant workers, which may foster resiliency or intensify vulnerabilities.

Temporary migrant workers are frequently denied social and economic rights in their countries of employment. Non-residents in Australia are excluded from Medicare (publicly-funded healthcare),[196] unemployment benefits through the Newstart Allowance (although migrants who have lived in Australia for more than 10 years after 2001 may receive the allowance for

191 *Usman Ali v. Industries Services Training Pty Ltd* [2011] FWA 9177.

192 *FW Act* pt 2-2, divs 5-9.

193 DIBP, *Procedures Advice Manual 3* sch 8/8107, [7.1].

194 Ibid. [11].

195 *Young Sim Lee v. Jimmy's on the Mall Pty Ltd* [2011] FWA 3386; *LL Baker and Flight Centre Limited* [2007] AIRC 281.

196 *Health Insurance Act 1973* (Cth), ss 3(1) and 10(1). Nationals of countries with Reciprocal Health Care Agreements with Australia may be eligible for limited Medicare benefits, for 'immediately necessary treatment' only. These countries include Britain, New Zealand, Sweden, Finland, Netherlands, Malta, Italy, Belgium, Slovenia, Norway and Ireland.

six months),[197] state-provided health services and public housing, free public education for their children (in NSW, the Australian Capital Territory and, from 2015, Western Australia, although exceptions for hardship may apply), federally funded rebates for the costs of childcare, tax concessions for families (including a federal 'bonus' for school-aged children), rent assistance, and the National Disability Insurance Scheme. International students receive the same public transport concessions available to local secondary and tertiary students, except only recently in the two states with the greatest number of international students: Victoria offered concessions in 2015 and NSW has granted only highly circumscribed concessions since 2012. Non-residents are excluded from the Commonwealth financial assistance scheme for employees whose employer becomes insolvent or bankrupt and unable to pay their entitlements for work done.[198] This was brought into strong relief when, in June 2013, approximately 300 international students who worked as cleaners could not recoup unpaid wages, leave and entitlements when their employer, Swan Services, one of Australia's largest cleaning companies, went into liquidation.[199] However, a comparative perspective demonstrates that excluding temporary residents from publicly funded benefits is not inevitable. In Canada, temporary workers have access to provincial health insurance and schooling for their children and in the USA the Supreme Court has ruled that even undocumented children must be given access to public education.[200]

Various government and non-government agencies have suggested alternative mechanisms that might provide a temporary safety net for visa-holders who become redundant or unemployed due to circumstances beyond their control. One suggestion is to include an additional obligation on sponsors to pay premiums on income protection insurance;[201] another is to permit 457 visa workers to access accumulated superannuation at the termination of their employment rather than on departure, to provide a temporary income in Australia in the event of unemployment.

In the absence of social benefits, the personal circumstances and attributes of migrant workers take on heightened significance. Selvaraj Velayutham's qualitative study of Indian 457 visa workers in Australia illuminates how diverse are the experiences of visa-holders who may be white-collar professionals, blue-collar unionised workers in large- and mid-size workplaces or workers in non-unionised, subcontracting or small businesses.[202] Complex and intersecting contexts can create compelling

197 *Social Security Act 1991* (Cth), ss 7(7)(b) and 593(g)(ii).

198 *Fair Entitlement Guarantee Act 2012* (Cth), s 10(1)(g).

199 Joanna Howe, 'Foreign Workers Excluded from the Aussie Fair Go', *Sydney Morning Herald*, 4 June 2013.

200 Sandra Algersma, *Temporary Foreign Workers* (Political and Social Affairs Division, Library of Parliament, Canada 2007), 4; *Plyler v. Doe*, 457 US 202 (1982).

201 DIAC, *Discussion Paper: Business (Long Stay) Subclass 457 and Related Temporary Visa Reforms* (2008), 11; *Deegan Report*, above n. 99, 31; ACTU, 'Submission to Visa Subclass 457 Integrity Review', *Response to Issues Paper 3: Integrity/Exploitation* (2008), 23.

incentives for some temporary migrant workers more than others to accept extremely poor working conditions in a job in Australia that a resident worker would leave. These include features of their country of nationality such as the availability of welfare protections and labour market prospects there. They also include workers' personal characteristics: age, family or other financial obligations, familiarity with the legal system and the existence of social support networks in Australia. The security of a worker's Australian job is also significant here, and this in turn can depend on their skills, the strength of the Australian labour market in that industry and whether their qualifications are recognised.[203] Indeed, most reports of exploitation involving 457 visa workers have arisen at the lower end of the occupational skill spectrum.[204] Residential segregation, social exclusion and immigrant saturation of particular occupations or areas can also diminish employment prospects and the accessibility of assistance from authorities and unions.[205]

There is particularly strong evidence of systemic disadvantage in the Australian labour market for immigrants from a non-English speaking background.[206] Weak English skills can prevent employees from communicating effectively with employers, and from accessing regulatory agencies or information.[207] Indeed, the government-sponsored Deegan inquiry into the 457 visa programme in 2008 found a prevalent lack of awareness among temporary workers of workplace rights under Australian laws.[208] Employment discrimination based on cross-cultural differences or speaking English with a foreign accent can compound disadvantage. A comprehensive 2013 study commissioned by the Immigration Department

202 Velayutham, 'Precarious Experiences of Indians', above n. 112.

203 Regine Wagner and Merilyn Childs, 'Exclusionary Narratives as Barriers to the Recognition of Qualifications, Skills and Experience: A Case of Skilled Migrants in Australia' (2006) 28(1) *Studies in Continuing Education* 49.

204 In 2008, the primary industries to receive sanctions for abuses were hospitality (43%), construction (20%) and manufacturing (19%): Barbara Deegan, *Visa Subclass 457 Integrity Review: Issues Paper 1: Minimum Salary Levels and Labour Agreements* (2008), 17.

205 Stephen Castles and Mark J. Miller, *The Age of Migration: International Population Movement in the Modern World* (Macmillan, 2nd edn, 1998); Julia Connell and John Burgess, 'Migrant Workers, Migrant Work, Public Policy and Human Resource Management' (2009) 30(5) *International Journal of Manpower* 412, 416; Pramod N. (Raja) Junankar and Stéphane Mahuteau, 'Do Migrants Get Good Jobs? New Migrant Settlement in Australia' (2005) 81(255) *Economic Record* S34, S40.

206 Val Colic-Peisker, 'A New Era in Australian Multiculturalism? From Working-Class "Ethnics" to a "Multicultural Middle-Class"' (2011) 45(3) *International Migration Review* 562, 579; Prem Jung Thapa, 'On the Risk of Unemployment: A Comparative Assessment of the Labour Market Success of Migrants in Australia' (2004) 7(2) *Australian Journal of Labour Economics* 199, 202; Christina Ho and Caroline Alcorso, 'Migrants and Employment: Challenging the Success Story' (2004) 40(3) *Journal of Sociology* 237.

207 Jawad Syed and Peter Murray, 'Combating the English Language Deficit: The Labour Market Experiences of Migrant Women in Australia' (2009) 19(4) *Human Resource Management Journal* 413.

208 *Deegan Report*, above n. 99, 31 and 52.

found that 18.4 per cent of 457 visa workers from non-English speaking backgrounds had experienced discrimination 'because of their skin colour, ethnic origin or religious beliefs'.[209] A 2012 survey on international students in the cleaning industry found that 40 per cent suffered rude or abusive behaviour by a supervisor, which was almost twice as many as cleaners who were not international students.[210] A three-year study by Deakin University in 2014 reported that academics, peak bodies and international students viewed a key reason most international student graduates were unable to secure employment in their field in Australia without permanent residency lay in endemic racism amongst middle management.[211] Indeed, a Federal Court decision, which ordered a significant civil penalty, quoted a company manager espousing the view that foreign workers, especially from Asia, have a higher tolerance for poor working conditions, stating, 'I suppose from the Philippines side of things, I'm not saying that they're of a lower intelligence or anything like that, it just seemed that they can do one task and not want to do something different until they're told to do something different.'[212]

The aspirations for temporary migrant workers are also highly relevant: those wishing to gain permanent residency may be particularly dependent on Australian work experience and employer sponsorship, as explored in more detail in the next chapter. Pre-existing debts taken on by workers (for travel and visa costs, or to foreign recruiters) in the expectation of acquitting these through deductions from their Australian wages also clearly produce intense vulnerabilities. Any of these circumstances can enhance the superior bargaining strength of employers and enable them to exploit a migrant worker's structural disadvantage, including vulnerabilities which the employer played no part in creating.

These characteristics comprise what some have called a 'dual frame of reference',[213] where workplace experiences in the country of employment are assessed against the backdrop of wages, working conditions and opportunities in workers' home countries. Michael Piore has argued that new migrants frequently imagine their stay to be temporary, and therefore may view their work more instrumentally than do residents, possibly with shorter-term expectations.[214] This may lead some 457 visa workers to choose to

209 Migration Council of Australia, *More Than Temporary: Australia's 457 Visa Program* (Cth of Australia, 2013), 5.

210 Victorian TAFE International and United Voice, *Taken to the Cleaners: Experiences of International Students Working in the Australian Retail Cleaning Industry* (2012), 5.

211 Jill Blackmore *et al.*, *Australian International Graduates and the Transition to Employment* (Deakin University, 2014), 23.

212 Dick Smith, quoted in ABC Radio National, 'Employers Abusing Migrant Workers System: CFMEU', *AM*, 13 May 2006 (Josie Taylor).

213 Roger Waldinger and Michael I. Lichter, *How the Other Half Works: Immigration and the Social Organization of Labor* (University of California Press, 2003), 9.

maximise earnings over career progression, or to accept less than equal treatment in the Australian labour market balanced against the opportunity to gain non-pecuniary returns, such as English language capabilities or an entrée into the labour market. These may be some of the reasons why, even in times of alleged skill shortages in advanced OECD economies, migrants continue to flow into low-skilled, low paid and poorly protected jobs.[215]

In summary, this section has examined how 457 visa status can tend to create or perpetuate visa-holders' susceptibility to precarious work, injecting coercive and uncertain dynamics into employment relationships. I have suggested that there are four major ways in which these effects can occur. Eligibility requirements of the visa and the conditions of stay can constrain temporary migrants' work options or intensify dependency on employer-sponsors. Immigration controls can create barriers to enforcement of employment law protections. In some circumstances, immigration regulation can even vary the substance of those protections. Finally, a range of other characteristics of individual migrant workers, their background and their current social context can worsen or ameliorate this precariousness.

The next section turns to a second category of temporary migrant workers, international students. Naturally, I will not reiterate those issues already discussed in relation to temporary work status that also apply to international students. Instead, the next section commences with a brief description of international student migration in Australia, its economic ascendancy and the characteristics of the international student workforce, noting comparisons with other countries, before turning to issues peculiar to student visa workers that increase precariousness in their working lives.

International student workers

Over roughly the same period as the expansion of the 457 visa category the international student sector in Australia also grew dramatically. This coincided with the escalating number of foreign students in OECD countries: this doubled to 1.8 million between 1980 and 2000 and is expected to quadruple again by 2025. In Australia, this increase was driven by the Howard government's deliberate interlinkages between education and skilled migration policy through schemes from around 1999 that favoured international students as skilled migrants.[216] Although many of these concessions for international student graduates of Australian education providers have since been removed, Australia still has the highest proportion of students

214 Michael J. Piore, *Birds of Passage: Migrant Labour and Industrial Societies* (Cambridge University Press, 1979).
215 Patrick Taran and Eduardo Geronomi, 'Globalization, Labor and Migration: Protection is Paramount' (Paper No 3E, ILO Perspectives on Labour Migration Program, 2003).
216 Martin, Abella and Kuptsch, *Managing Labor Migration*, above n. 89, 63.

on student visas of all OECD countries.[217] As of 30 September 2014, there were 387,799 international students in Australia, down from a peak of 491,565 in 2009.[218] By comparison, in 2012, 764,495 international students were enrolled in the USA and 488,000 in the UK, both significantly more populous countries.[219]

In Australia, students are permitted to work part-time during their studies (as are their partners on secondary visas) and comprise a significant part of the low-skilled casual workforce. One expert has estimated that more than 200,000 international students work in casual part-time or full-time paid employment in Australia at any one time, which is equivalent to 6 per cent of the part-time workforce of 3.4 million people.[220] Therefore, in a reversal of historical trends, non-English speaking migrants are now predominantly entering employment in Australia on a part-time basis.

The rise and fall of the international student sector

The surge in the number of international students in Australia in the 2000s was reflected in sharp increases in student visa grant rates, which climbed from 171,778 in 2003–4, to a record high of 319,600 in 2008–9, before falling again in 2011–12.[221] While coinciding with the global economic boom and then downturn, the steep rise and sudden decline were likely just as attributable to policy settings that first linked, and then de-linked, the international student visa programme and the general skilled migration programme granting permanent residence.[222]

In the words of a leading demographer, '[f]rom 1999–2009, Australia experimented with two-step student migration'.[223] This began when the Howard government in 2001 created a direct pathway for international students to apply for residency onshore. The number of permanent visas issued to overseas students in Australia quickly outnumbered those who

217 Australian Education International, *Research Snapshot: The Global Context of Tertiary Student Mobility* (September 2012).

218 DIBP, *Student Visa and Temporary Graduate Visa Programme Quarterly Report: Quarter Ending at 30 September 2014* (2014), 7; Michael Knight, *Strategic Review of the Student Visa Program 2011: Report* (Cth of Australia, 2011), vii.

219 Institute of International Education, *International Students in the United States* (Open Doors Report, 2013); Higher Education Statistics Agency, *Statistics: Students and Qualifiers at UK HE Institutions* (2013).

220 Alexander Reilly, 'Protecting Vulnerable Migrant Workers: The Case of International Students' (2012) 25 *Australian Journal of Labour Law* 181, 185.

221 DIAC, *Trends in Migration: Australia 2010–11: Annual Submission to the OECD's Continuous Reporting System on Migration* (2012), 38.

222 For a more detailed account of the reform agenda that dramatically reshaped student visas and the evolution of student visa criteria see Crock and Berg, *Immigration, Refugees and Forced Migration*, above n. 77, 298–318.

223 Lesleyanne Hawthorne, 'How Valuable is "Two-Step Migration"? Labor Market Outcomes for International Student Migrants to Australia' (2010) 19 *Asian and Pacific Migration Journal* 5, 25.

applied from offshore. By 2006 eligibility criteria for skilled residence visas included elaborate concessions for applicants with Australian qualifications and work experience. In 2008 a new 18-month temporary work visa, the subclass 485 Skilled Graduate visa, allowed international students who were not yet eligible for residency upon graduation to gain work experience or English language skills to increase their chances.

These measures rapidly inflated the numbers of temporary resident students living (and working) in Australia. At around this time, various vocations were accorded additional points in applications for points-tested permanent skilled visas because they were listed as 'in demand'. This created 'perverse incentives' for international students to enrol in short courses in these fields (notably cookery, hairdressing and accountancy), and an industry quickly developed in cheap, low quality courses in these areas by private education providers, with lower fees and entry requirements in terms of previous study and English-language capabilities. The emergence of these pathways to residence for Australian graduates with vocational qualifications, therefore, fundamentally altered the demographics of international students who came, increasingly, from lower socio-economic backgrounds. Many students enrolling from 2005 onwards had less financial security, had accrued personal or family debt in order to cover the costs of their study and were by necessity more engaged in the casual workforce than previous cohorts.[224] Reports soon emerged of poor labour market outcomes for newly resident former international students.[225] And international student lobbies also began to vocalise concerns about the quality of their courses, poor treatment at work and in the rental housing market, and lack of police protection from a spate of violent physical attacks on international students in Melbourne and Sydney.[226]

In 2010, amidst wholesale reforms to the permanent skilled visa programme, the Rudd Labor government resolved to break the nexus between international students and residency pathways and address vulnerabilities in the international student population. Students from lower socio-economic backgrounds were discouraged from studying in Australia at all when the government increased the amount of savings required per year of study to obtain a student visa from around A$12,000 to more than A$18,000. New regulations restricted permanent residency for applicants with lower-skilled vocational qualifications and decreased the rewards for Australian qualifi-

224 Shanthi Robertson, *Transnational Student-Migrants and the State: The Education-Migration Nexus* (Palgrave Macmillan, 2013), 52.

225 Bob Birrell, 'Implications of Low English Standards Among Overseas Students at Australian Universities' (2006) 14(4) *People and Place* 53; Birrell, Healy and Kinnaird, 'Cooks Galore', above n. 100.

226 Kevin Dunn *et al.*, 'Racism in the Tertiary Education Sector: A Case of Indian Student Attacks in Australia' (2011) 43(3) *Geography Bulletin* 7; Jacqueline Joudo Larsen, Jason Payne and Adam Tomison, *Crimes against International Students in Australia: 2005–09* (Australian Institute of Criminology, 2011).

cations and work experience in points-tested visas. They did this by abolishing the list of so-called 'in demand' occupations and recalibrating the points test. Also in 2010, new policies prioritised the granting of residence through employer-sponsorship over independent skilled points-tested visas. This worked to advantage 457 visa workers over international students in gaining permanent residence via employment (since the former were, of necessity, already in full-time jobs with pre-existing employer-sponsorship). This encouraged students to transition into sponsored employment relationships via a 457 visa with a view to gaining sponsored residence.

As a result of these changes, the number of new offshore applications for international student visas plummeted.[227] Alarmed by this fall, in 2011 the Gillard Labor government initiated a more comprehensive inquiry by Michael Knight of the integrity and competitiveness of the student migration programme. Responding to Knight's recommendations, in 2013 the government oversaw the liberalisation of post-study temporary residence and work rights for graduating students, explicitly designed to give Australian universities an advantage over competitor countries where work rights either do not exist or are not as generous. In the USA, for example, the student F-1 visa programme allows students to work only on campus on a part-time basis during the school year, as well as the possibility of working after graduation for up to one year. In the UK, work rights for students were tightened in 2011: students taking a bachelors degree programme or higher are permitted to work 20 hours per week while classes are in session and full-time during vacations, while work during term time for students taking a qualification below this level is limited to 10 hours per week. Many student visa-holders may not bring a partner or dependents at all and dependents' work rights are more restricted. Indeed, Australia's decision to decouple education and migration was closely followed by UK government efforts to tighten post-study work opportunities for international graduates.[228] The two-year post-study work visa in Britain for non-EU students was discontinued in 2012. Instead, only 1500 employer-sponsored permanent visas are available for international graduates with skill and salary prescriptions through Tier 2.

In Australia, by contrast, the subclass 485 Temporary Graduate visa, renamed and redesigned in 2013, now includes two streams.[229] The 'Graduate Work stream' reflects the original visa that has been in place since

227 Of course, a range of other factors may well have also precipitated the fall in numbers, including the high Australian dollar, media reports of several violent assaults upon international students (mainly from South Asia) in 2008 and 2009, and the global economic downturn: see Simon Marginson *et al.*, *International Student Security* (Cambridge University Press, 2010), 50ff; Lesleyanne Hawthorne, 'Indian Students and the Evolution of the Study-Migration Pathway in Australia' (2014) 52(2) *International Migration* 3.

228 C. Gribble and J. Blackmore, 'Re-positioning Australia's International Education in Global Knowledge Economies: Implications of Shifts in Skilled Migration Policies for Universities' (2012) 34(4) *Journal of Higher Education Policy and Management* 341.

229 *Migration Legislation Amendment Regulation 2013 (No 1)* (Cth).

2008, granting graduated students with Australian qualifications less than a bachelor degree 18 months of work rights. Applicants must be qualified in an occupation on the government gazetted Skilled Occupation List and undertake a skills assessment. The 'Post-Study Work stream' grants graduates of Australian bachelor or master's by coursework degrees a two-year work visa; graduates with Australian master's by research or doctoral degrees are eligible for a 3- or 4-year work visa respectively. Work rights in this stream are unlimited, irrespective of occupation. This scheme both increased the attractiveness of studying in Australia and significantly enlarged the number of temporary workers in the Australian labour market.

The international student workforce

Currently, most student visas contain a mandatory limit on work of 40 hours per fortnight while their course is in session, with unlimited work permitted during course breaks.[230] However, there is no comprehensive information on the number of international students engaged in paid work or the types of jobs in which they are employed. An Australian Education International Survey in 2007 found 56 per cent of international students in the previous year in paid employment during session, and up to 70 per cent during holiday periods.[231] This has led one expert to conclude that there are likely more than 200,000 international students in casual or part-time employment in Australia at any one time, which is equivalent to 6 per cent of the part-time workforce of 3.4 million people.[232]

But there are also three additional categories of education-related temporary visa-holders who are permitted to work in Australia who must be added to this figure. First, international students' partners may hold secondary visas with work rights identical to students'.[233] As of September 2014, there were 49,454 secondary student visa-holders in Australia.[234] Second, as mentioned above, international students have been eligible since 2008 for temporary 485 visas on graduation. In 2013–14 122,334 students stayed in Australia on other visas after graduation, including 20,870 on a Temporary Graduate (subclass 485) visa with at least eighteen months work rights. The numbers of these visa-holders in Australia are likely only to increase, since this visa has been extended to two to four years for graduates of a bachelor degree or higher and internal DIBP modelling indicates that 485 visa-holders could exceed 200,000 by 2017–18. In fact, if processing times are slow, a two year post-study entitlement may actually

230 Condition 8105 attaches to a variety of different visas available to international students, other than postgraduate research students who have unlimited work rights.

231 Chris Nyland *et al.*, 'International Student-Workers in Australia: A New Vulnerable Workforce' (2009) 22(1) *Journal of Education and Work* 1, 4.

232 Reilly, 'Protecting Vulnerable Migrant Workers', above n. 220, 185.

233 Condition 8104.

234 DIBP, *Student Visa Quarterly Report*, above n. 218, 63.

grant around three years of work rights since graduates are entitled to live and work in Australia on a bridging visa, which regularises their status while the 485 visa application is being processed.

A third cohort of former students entitled to work in Australia arose when 'two-step student migration' hit its peak in 2009. In the face of a substantial backlog of tens of thousands of valid applications for residence by international students at that time, processing priorities were introduced so as to leave those with Australian vocational qualifications at the back of a very long queue. Waiting multiple years for their applications to be processed, these former international students were granted Bridging A visas with full work rights (but no right to sponsor immediate family to join them in Australia and restricted ability to travel overseas). Although the government may have been hoping that these former students would abandon their aspirations for residence and return to their countries of origin, by mid 2014 this group still contained 10,361 people. As a result, in addition to current international students and their partners, there are large numbers of former international students in Australia on temporary visas with permission to work.

International students and precarious work

Scholars and policy analysts have only very recently considered the vulnerabilities of international students as workers. For some time, research primarily addressed students' 'welfare' within the international student industry and, less frequently, their ability to access social services.[235] This changed dramatically when a group of researchers from Monash University in Melbourne undertook a multi-year study involving interviews of 200 international students at nine Australian educational institutions in 2005.[236] They argued that attention to students' rights as consumers of education services should be refocused on international students' rights to security, both physical and financial.[237] Investigating the particular vulnerabilities of international students as a workforce, Christopher Nyland and his partners found that illegal underpayment of wages was prevalent. Over half (58 per

235 Council of Australian Governments, *International Students Strategy for Australia* (2010); Bruce Baird, *Stronger, Simpler, Smarter ESOS: Supporting International Students. Final Report on the Review of the Education Services for Overseas Students Act 2000* (Department of Employment and Workplace Relations, 2010), v–vii, 39–43; Senate Education, Employment and Workplace Relations References Committee, *Welfare of International Students* (2009).

236 Ana Deumert *et al.*, *The Social and Economic Security of International Students in Australia: A Study of 200 Student Cases* (Monash Centre for Research in International Education, 2005).

237 Christopher Nyland, Helen Forbes-Mewett and Simon Marginson, 'The International Student Safety Debate: Moving Beyond Denial' (2010) 29(1) *Higher Education Research and Development* 89. See also Australian Human Rights Commission, *Principles to Promote the Rights of International Students* (Cth of Australia, 2012).

cent) of working students they interviewed were earning less than the legal minimum wage and one third as little as A$7–8 per hour.[238] Research undertaken in Victoria in 2012 and 2013 by hospitality union United Voice supports these findings, noting that over a third of international students in their study reported working additional time without pay and some were systematically underpaid by up to A$15,000 a year.[239]

International students are also highly susceptible to 'sham contracting' arrangements whereby workers are illegally classified as self-employed 'independent contractors' to avoid statutory employment protections and minimum wage rates.[240] This particular vulnerability of international students has been recognised by reported case law, the United Voice study and Fair Work Building and Construction,[241] and was noted, but not considered in detail, by a 2011 government inquiry into sham contracting.[242]

The reasons for these forms of precariousness are varied, and relate to the demographic profile of international students (which flow from visa eligibility requirements), visa conditions and aspirations for permanent residency. These factors work potently to insert uncertainty into students' working lives, constraining employment options and workforce mobility. Clearly, international students' youth and limited employment experience (like that of resident students) can exacerbate the power differential in their employment relationships. But international students tend to be more vulnerable than resident students because they lack support structures available to resident students including social security benefits, knowledge of where to seek external help in managing the employment relationship and a cultural awareness of what are deemed acceptable employment standards. Unlike the information available for 457 visa workers and working holiday makers, the international student section of the Immigration Department website contains no information about employment under Australian law or accessing help in relation to employment disputes. Social isolation and lack of English language ability likely also play a role here, especially since international students overwhelmingly come from non-English speaking countries and study in Australia to improve their English, as I discuss in more detail below.

238 Christopher Nyland *et al.*, 'International Students: A Segregated and Vulnerable Workforce' (Working Paper No 24/07, Business Department of Management, Monash University, September 2007), 6.

239 United Voice, *A Dirty Business: The Exploitation of International Students in Melbourne's Office Cleaning Industry* (2013), 3.

240 *FW Act* s 357.

241 E.g. *FWO v. Bedington* [2012] FMCA 1133, involving sham-contracting with a Pakistani man on a 485 visa; *Director of the Fair Work Building Industry Inspectorate v. Tunc* [2013] FCCA 438, where eight workers on student visas and working holiday visas were engaged on sham contracts in the construction industry.

242 Office of the Australia Building and Construction Commissioner, *Sham Contracting Inquiry Report 2011* (2011).

Although conclusive data is unavailable, international students seem to be concentrated in low status, casual work due to their limited work experience, qualifications and English language ability. They populate industries in Australia's service economy: retail, cleaning, taxi-driving, and staffing late night convenience stores, restaurants and petrol stations.[243] This, of course, is also a result of current students' limited work rights, which (in the absence of widely available standard part-time positions) virtually compel them into casual, insecure work. Nyland and his partners also note that because large numbers of international student job seekers are restricted to a small range of occupations and geographical location, they 'are crowded into a limited market', driving down employment standards.[244] Discriminatory employer practices and uncertainties about temporary visa status also play a role here, concerning both students and graduates on 485 visas, since research indicates that many employers in professional fields have a blanket rule precluding international graduates from applying for positions unless they have permanent residency status.[245]

The FWO, therefore, has brought legal proceedings focusing in industries where international students are prevalent. As a result of one prosecution, operators of two 7–Eleven stores in Victoria were fined A$150,000 for underpaying six international students (four of them teenagers and all from Zimbabwe and India) almost A$90,000 (one student was underpaid A$40,583).[246] In another investigation, 32 cleaners (many of them international students) working in office buildings in Sydney were underpaid a total of A$133,845. Their employer deliberately entered into an elaborate subcontracting arrangement, requiring the cleaners to work three hours in a night shift and outsourcing their employment for a fourth hour to another company, in order to prevent them from receiving their full statutory entitlements for this last hour of each shift.[247]

International student visas require applicants to evidence their ability to fund their tuition fees, airfare and A$18,610 per year for living expenses for themselves.[248] Commentators have pointed out that these funding requirements are well below the poverty line threshold (which was, for instance, A$21,484.32 for a single person in 2014).[249] The resultant vulnerability is

243 Peter Mares, 'Fear and Instrumentalism: Australian Policy Responses to Migration from the Global South' (2011) 100(415) *The Round Table: The Commonwealth Journal of International Affairs* 407, 417; Victorian Immigrant and Refugee Women's Coalition, *Heart Break Hotels: The Crisis Inside Melbourne's Luxury Hotels* (2010).

244 Nyland *et al.*, 'The International Student Safety Debate', above n. 237, 8.

245 Blackmore *et al.*, *Australian International Graduates*, above n. 211, 18.

246 *FWO v. Bosen Pty Ltd* (Unreported, Magistrates Court of Victoria, Industrial Division, Magistrate Hawkins, 21 April 2011), [28], [30].

247 *FWO v. Glad Group Pty Ltd* [2012] FMCA 731, [17]. See also *FWO v. Kingsford Carwash Pty Ltd (No 2)* [2012] FMCA 1210, where a Sydney car wash business underpaid 62 casual young international students a total of A$99,646.74

248 *Evidence of Further Funds and Living Costs* (IMMI 14/004, F2014L00316) (Cth).

249 Marginson *et al.*, *International Student Security*, above n. 227; Reilly, 'Protecting Vulnerable Migrant Workers', above n. 220, 186.

even more acute since, as Danny Ong and Gaby Ramia point out, unlike residents, international students generally have no entitlement to government-funded financial support while studying nor concessions on the full cost of their studies.[250] Given that, in Nyland's study, one third of interviewees said paid employment was their main source of income,[251] the 'study-work-life-balance' is exceedingly more precarious for international students than for resident students.

Clearly, international students from lower socio-economic backgrounds are more likely to be working, and to be working more heavily. The international student programme draws greatly from countries in the Global South. As at September 2014, China and India were the two largest source countries of international students, accounting for 25 per cent and 12 per cent of the total, followed by Vietnam, South Korea, Malaysia, Nepal, Thailand and Indonesia.[252] The home nations of the highest number of 485 visa-holders in 2013–14 were China (31 per cent), India (17 per cent) and Nepal (10 per cent).[253] Students from lower socio-economic backgrounds are not only likely to be fully supporting themselves, but may also be repaying loans accrued at home for the initial student fees and travel.

In addition, students are pressed into casualised and uncertain work by their visa condition limiting them to a maximum of 40 hours of work per fortnight during session. Violating this condition, even inadvertently, can trigger visa cancellation, mandatory detention and removal from Australia.[254] Undertaking unauthorised work can also leave students with significantly weaker protections under employment law, as discussed in Part II of this book on 'Unauthorised Workers'. A further complexity that flows from this work limitation relates to course-related work. Course-related work is exempt from the limitation of 40 hours per fortnight but only where this work is specified as a 'requirement of the course'.[255] Labour law experts have pointed out that an unpaid internship as part of an elective subject is unlikely to come within this exemption, much less volunteer work more broadly.[256] This leaves international students with significantly less opportunity to undertake internships than resident students. It also has the potential to create uncertainty for international students as to the legality of

250 Danny Ong and Gaby Ramia, 'Study-Work-Life Balance and the Welfare of International Students' (2009) 20(2) *Labour and Industry* 181, 186.

251 Nyland *et al.*, 'International Student-Workers', above n. 231, 5.

252 DIBP, *Student Visa Quarterly Report*, above n. 218, 65.

253 DIBP, *Student Visa Quarterly Report: Quarter Ending at 30 June 2014* (2014), 8, 68.

254 *Migration Act* s 116(3) and *Migration Regulations* reg 2.43(2).

255 Under *Migration Regulations* sch 8 cl 8105(2)(a) the limitation of 40 hours per fortnight does not apply to work that 'was specified as a requirement of the course when the course particulars were entered into the Commonwealth Register of Institutions and Courses for Overseas Students'.

256 Andrew Stewart and Rosemary Owens, *Experience or Exploitation? The Nature, Prevalence and Regulation of Unpaid Work Experience, Internships and Trial Periods in Australia* (University of Adelaide, Report for the FWO, January 2013), 171.

their paid work if undertaken in addition to voluntary course-related placements.[257]

Precariousness attends students even while working in compliance with immigration limitations. As with 457 visa workers, insecurity stems from the temporary nature of the student visa itself. But, unlike for 457 visa workers, permanent residence has become less attainable for international students. Instead, pathways to residency have effectively been replaced with more ready access to temporary work visas upon graduation. The 2010 reforms were explicitly designed to re-establish 'the "temporary nature" of Australia's temporary visa program'.[258] Shanthi Robertson has pointed out that by reinforcing the 'temporariness' of the international student visa programme, these policies have positioned students as 'having little ongoing relationship to the national community'.[259] Permission to work in Australia for two or three years may be highly attractive, especially to students from developing countries with poorer labour market conditions, but it leaves them working in extended liminality.

Relatedly, residence aspirations play a crucial role in students' precariousness. Many students consciously submit to the constraints of temporary student visas with a view towards permanent residence. Numerous studies record a clear majority of international students intending to apply for permanent residence and suggest that international students' identities in Australia are anchored as much in their desire to immigrate and work as study.[260] Work in Australia, therefore, becomes desirable not only for the income it generates but as a strategy to gain permanent residence in the future, because an employer may agree to sponsor a permanent visa (such as the subclass 186 Employer Nomination Scheme visa) or Australian work experience may provide additional points for independent points-tested skilled permanent visa applications. An expert report commissioned by the FWO on unpaid work notes that international students may face strong pressure to take on unpaid 'training programs', providing free labour in an

257 See, for example, *Kamely v. MIAC* [2011] FCA 1071, where an international student's visa was cancelled after she worked more than the 20 hours per week then permitted in condition 8105. She asserted this work was part of an industry placement for her course, although evidence from her educational facility contradicted this.

258 Kruno Kukoc, DIAC, 'Key Issues in Skilled Migration to Australia' (Speech delivered at the Australia–Canada Roundtable on Foreign Qualifications Recognition, University of Melbourne, 13 April 2011), 13.

259 Shanthi Robertson, 'Time and Temporary Migration: The Case of Temporary Graduate Workers and Working Holiday Makers in Australia' (2014) 40(12) *Journal of Ethnic and Migration Studies* 1915, 1923.

260 Bilal Rafi and Phil Lewis, 'Indian Higher Education Students in Australia: Their Patterns and Motivations' (2013) 57 *Australian Journal of Education* 157, 168; Michiel Baas, 'Students of Migration: Indian Overseas Students and the Question of Permanent Residency' (2006) 14(1) *People and Place* 9, 13; Shanthi K. Robertson, 'Residency, Citizenship and Belonging: Choice and Uncertainty for Students-Turned-Migrants in Australia' (2008) 4(1) *International Journal of Asia Pacific Studies* 97.

effort to gain an entrée into the Australian labour market and gain valuable local work experience for a future permanent residence application.[261] Of course, alongside these coercive elements, students' hopes for permanent residency cause great uncertainty, especially in the context of the dramatic policy changes in this area. Ethnographic research has revealed that international students see immigration authorities as capricious and unpredictable.[262]

The FWO, on the other hand, has sought pro-actively to engage international students via the internet and at educational institutions and to target industries that tend to attract international students.[263] This is far from straightforward: it is considerably easier for the FWO (in collaboration with DIBP) to monitor the working conditions of 457 visa workers than of international students since all workplaces employing 457 visa workers are traceable through DIBP. There is no way to identify and track employers of international students. For this reason, I disagree with a statement by the Federal Magistrates Court that '[a]n employee on a working holiday or student visa might also be vulnerable, and open to exploitation by reason of their migratory status, but not as vulnerable as an employee whose migration status was dependent upon the ongoing support of their employer'.[264] Instead, international students are differently vulnerable.

Working holiday maker workers

The final section of this chapter turns briefly to the third major category of temporary migrant workers, young WHMs. Two visa subclasses permit 'cultural exchange' for young travellers aged 18–30 including short-term work during a 12-month holiday in Australia.[265] Visa-holders must be nationals of specified countries with which Australia has a reciprocal relationship.[266] WHMs are permitted to do any kind of work during their 12-month stay, as long as they spend no more than six months with any

261 Stewart and Owens, *Experience or Exploitation?*, above n. 256, 68.

262 Shanthi Robertson and Anjena Runganaikaloo, 'Lives in Limbo: Migration Experiences in Australia's Education-Migration Nexus' (2014) 14(2) *Ethnicities* 208.

263 FWO, *International Students: Study Your Workplace Rights!* (2013).

264 *Golden Maple* [2009] FMCA 664, [14].

265 The subclass 417 Working Holiday visa (WHV) and the subclass 462 Work and Holiday visa. Unlike the WHV, the Work and Holiday visa is subject to numerical caps on visas granted and requires applicants to have the support of their government, hold or be studying for tertiary qualifications and speak functional English: *Migration Regulations* sch 2 cll 462.213-462.215.

266 Nineteen countries qualify for the WHV: Belgium, Canada, Cyprus, Denmark, Estonia, Finland, France, Germany, Hong Kong, Ireland, Italy, Japan, South Korea, Malta, the Netherlands, Norway, Sweden, Taiwan and the UK; and thirteen for the Work and Holiday visa: Argentina, Bangladesh, Chile, Indonesia, Malaysia, Papua New Guinea, Poland, Portugal, Spain, Thailand, Turkey, Uruguay and the USA. See *Specification under Subparagraph 1225(3)(b)(i) – Class of Persons* (IMMI 09/008, F2009L01343) (Cth); *Specification of Arrangements for Work and Holiday Visa Applicants* (IMMI 14/098, F2014L01498) (Cth).

one employer.[267] Under the scheme 239,592 visas were issued in 2013–14, more than double the figure of nine years earlier.[268] The largest two source countries in 2014 were the UK and Germany (which together made up 33 per cent of the visas issued), followed by France, South Korea and Taiwan.[269]

The scheme was designed to allow genuine tourists to supplement their holiday finances. A Commonwealth Senate inquiry into the scheme was conducted in 1997 amidst concerns about the impact of WHMs on the job prospects of Australian residents, and allegations that WHMs were being paid under-award wages. It recommended that it remain:

> a program which provides an opportunity for an extended holiday with incidental work and is not used to solve labour market programs in Australia or as a mechanism by which people can circumvent normal migration processes in order to remain in Australia, particularly in employment related categories.[270]

Nevertheless, the scheme is deployed by government to address specific labour shortages by providing short-term casual employment to regional industries. This was evident when, in 2006, the permitted duration of work with a single employer was increased from three to six months.[271] In 2005, holders of a Working Holiday visa (WHV) became eligible to apply for a second 12-month visa if they have done at least 88 days of 'specified work in regional Australia'.[272] The 'specified' industries extended from first agriculture and mining, to later fishing, pearling, tree felling and construction.[273] This extension is highly popular: in 2013–14 approximately one in four WHV-holders acquired a second WHV, of which 25 per cent were issued to Taiwanese nationals.[274]

In many Western countries, young people on a 'cultural exchange' are often there to work and visas tend to facilitate this. In the UK, Tier 5 (Youth Mobility Scheme) permits people aged 17–30 from various Commonwealth

267 Condition 8547 attaches to each visa: *Migration Regulations* sch 2 cll 417.611 and 462.611.

268 By comparison, 104,605 visas were issued in 2005: Productivity Commission, *Economic Impacts of Migration and Population Growth: Final Report* (Cth of Australia, 2006), 229; DIBP, *WHM Visa Programme Report* (30 June 2014), 7 (*WHM Report 2014*).

269 *WHM Report 2014*, above n. 268, 7.

270 JSCM, Parliament of Australia, *Working Holiday Makers: More than Just Tourists* (1997), xvii.

271 Condition 8547.

272 *Migration Regulations* sch 2 cl 417.211(5).

273 See now *Specification under Subitem 1225(5) – Working Holiday Visa – Definitions of 'Seasonal Work' and 'Regional Australia'* (IMMI 08/048, F2008L02264) (Cth). The list of regional areas presently covers all of Australia excluding only the Australian Capital Territory and eight urban centres (Sydney, Wollongong, Newcastle, the Central Coast, Melbourne, Brisbane, the Gold Coast and Perth).

274 *WHM Report 2014*, above n. 268, 4.

and South East Asian countries to work in non-professional jobs for up to two years. The J-1 programme in the USA permits a 'cultural exchange' visa that can involve employment; there is evidence that the 100,000 J-1 visa-holders who participate annually in the 'Summer Work Travel program' work in 'largely unskilled positions' including at resorts and amusement parks.[275] In response to complaints about working conditions by J-1 visa-holders, a 2011 State Department rule required sponsors in this programme to pay at least the prevailing wage rate.[276]

The Australian case study is striking in that the programme is so much larger. In 2011, 16,100 young people were admitted under Tier 5 in the UK, and 54,900 WHMs were in Canada that year.[277] By contrast, there were 107,978 WHMs in Australia as at 30 June 2011.[278] Furthermore, WHMs in Australia may be particularly motivated to work. According to an extensive survey of WHMs conducted in 2008, 69 per cent of respondents worked during their time in Australia, and 48 per cent said that 'work in Australia' was a principal reason for their trip.[279] The relative economic stability in Australia since 2010 compared with the global economy was an even greater attraction, with the scheme numbers increasing by 23.2 per cent between 2011 and 2012.[280] Numbers of Irish WHMs alone increased from 2010 by almost 60 per cent to 25,827 in 2012.[281] The Australian government frankly acknowledged that this increase was associated with 'uncertain' labour market opportunities 'in some partner countries'.[282] By 2014, Spain and Portugal had been added to the list of nationalities for Work and Holiday visas and the Immigration Minister had signed a reciprocal agreement with Greece that was yet to enter into effect. Furthermore, many WHMs are clearly motivated to continue to work in Australia after the expiry of their initial visa: in 2013–14, 10,157 457 visas were granted to former WHMs.[283]

Research on WHMs has focused on their labour market effects which go some way to illuminating their workplace experiences.[284] Two major surveys of WHMs were undertaken in 2000 and 2008 (although for methodological

275 US Department of State, 'Exchange Visitor Program: Cap on Current Participant Levels and Moratorium on New Sponsor Applications for Summer Work Travel Program' Notice, 76 *Federal Register* 68808-68809, 7 November 2011.

276 US Department of State, 'Exchange Visitor Program: Summer Work Travel' 76 *Federal Register* 23177-23185, 26 April 2011.

277 OECD, *Immigration Outlook 2013* (2013), 240, 304.

278 DIAC, *WHM Visa Programme Report* (30 June 2011), 7.

279 Yan Tan *et al.*, *Evaluation of Australia's Working Holiday Maker Program* (Flinders University, 2009), 13.

280 DIAC, *WHM Visa Programme Report* (30 June 2012), 7.

281 Ibid. 12.

282 Ibid. 7.

283 DIBP and Australian Customs and Border Protection, *Proposal Paper: Simplification of the Skilled Migration and Temporary Activity Visa Programmes* (December 2014), 9.

284 Yan Tan and Laurence Lester, 'Labour Market and Economic Impacts of International Working Holiday Temporary Migrants to Australia' (2012) 18 *Population, Space and Place* 359, 359.

reasons their results are not strictly comparable).[285] According to the 2008 study, the occupations of 'farm hand' (including 'fruit/vegetable picker') and 'waiter' together accounted for 40 per cent of WHMs' jobs followed by 'cleaner' (8 per cent) and kitchen hand (5 per cent).[286] Unsurprisingly, because of the eligibility criteria for a second visa, jobs in agriculture increased as a proportion of total jobs of WHMs from 10 per cent in 2000 to 23 per cent in 2008. Internal DIBP research in 2014 indicated that one third of WHMs worked in tourism and hospitality and 25 per cent in agricultural industries at that time.[287] Emerging studies suggest that WHMs are the major supplier of seasonal harvest labour in Australia, and an important source of labour in the residential construction sector, both industries marked by more precarious working conditions.[288]

However, there has been less interrogation of WHMs' working conditions or job security. For instance, reflecting on the results of the 2008 survey, the researchers state in passing, '[a]bout 10% of WHMs dislike their job, which is probably higher than the general population or recent immigrants. Nonetheless, given the proportion that are in low-skilled and relatively low paid employment, this is not surprising.'[289] And they conclude that 'WHMs are more flexible, and less concerned with longer-term labour market issues, such as career development or advancement, than the regular Australian workforce.'[290] It is uncertain whether these attitudes result from a laid back attitude during a vacation, or are a coercive product of poor labour market opportunities and visa restrictions. While WHMs have been found to be better educated, on average, than Australians,[291] they have a vulnerable labour market profile. Their age, temporary visa status and the limited duration of permitted employment with a single employer create a bias

285 The 2000 survey involved face-to-face interviews of 1,001 WHV-holders in airport departure lounges, 1 per cent of arrivals in that year: Glenys Harding and Elizabeth Webster, *The Working Holiday Maker Scheme and the Australian Labour Market* (University of Melbourne, 2002), 12, 58. The 2008 study involved an internet survey of 19,888 WHMs, 14.8 per cent of arrivals in that year: Tan *et al.*, *Evaluation of Australia's Working Holiday Maker Program*, above n. 279, 6.

286 Tan and Lester, 'Labour Market and Economic Impacts', above n. 283, 373.

287 DIBP and Australian Customs and Border Protection, *Proposal Paper*, above n. 283, 9.

288 Jayde Hanson and Martin Bell, 'Harvest Trails in Australia: Patterns of Seasonal Migration in the Fruit and Vegetable Industry' (2007) 23 *Journal of Rural Studies* 101, 103, 110; Susan McGrath-Champ, Stuart Rosewarne and Yasmin Rittau, 'From One Skill Shortage to the Next: The Australian Construction Industry and Geographies of a Global Labour Market' (2011) 53 *Journal of Industrial Relations* 467, 479.

289 Tan *et al.*, *Evaluation of Australia's Working Holiday Maker Program*, above n. 279, 25.

290 Ibid. 23.

291 Harding and Webster, *The Working Holiday Maker Scheme*, above n. 284, 5–6.

292 The 2000 survey recorded 78 per cent of WHMs employed in lower-skilled occupations, while WHMs in the 2008 survey were even more likely to work in lower-skilled occupations: Tan *et al.*, *Evaluation of Australia's Working Holiday Maker Program*, above n. 279, VII.

towards short-term, casualised and lesser-skilled jobs.[292] WHMs in the 2008 survey averaged 2.3 jobs per person during their stay, working for an average of 52 days in each job. Rotating quickly through a variety of jobs, WHMs may be more exposed to dangerous work (including because they lack experience) than workers in more permanent work arrangements.

These relatively highly educated young workers accept low wage rates. The 2008 survey found that, overall, the average hourly wage for WHMs was A$16.20, low compared with the average hourly wage of Australian private sector workers (A$29 in 2008).[293] Wage rates varied significantly by national origin: UK nationals were paid the highest average wage (A$19.40) whereas Japanese and Korean nationals were paid the lowest (A$13.60 and A$13.90 respectively). Most strikingly, more than one third of respondents reported wage rates below the federal minimum (which was A$13.74 in 2007).[294] Between 2012 and 2014, the FWO received about 2000 requests for assistance from WHMs (primarily in the accommodation, food and agriculture industries) and, between 2011 and 2014 recouped A$673,000 in unpaid entitlements for this workforce.[295] A series of judgments have also found significant underpayments of large numbers of WHMs.[296]

As with students, WHMs are vulnerable to employers' convoluted tactics to reduce their liabilities, such as through sham contracting.[297] In 2010 the Federal Magistrates Court penalised a Queensland cucumber farm for underpaying seven Japanese WHMs working as casual vegetable pickers half their wages, a total of A$28,028 between May and September 2008.[298] The employer argued that these workers were not employees but rather were in 'partnership' with the employer, sharing both the risk and the reward of the farm crop. There was no evidence of a 'partnership' agreement in writing; the employer argued that it was a verbal agreement. The employer submitted that the farm ultimately made a loss rather than the anticipated profit and the small payments to the workers were 'advances' or a loan rather than wages. The Magistrate noted that employees were vulnerable because they were non-citizens on WHVs, were in transient employment and had limited knowledge of English, concluding that this arrangement was 'at best ill-

293 Tan and Lester, 'Labour Market and Economic Impacts', above n. 283, 367.

294 Ibid. 368.

295 FWO, 'FWO to Review Entitlements of Overseas Visa-Holders on Working Holidays' (media release, 4 August 2014).

296 E.g. 181 staff, mainly Japanese and South Korean WHMs, in a Sushi Train restaurant in Cairns in Far North Queensland, were underpaid their basic wage, overtime rates and allowances to a total of A$119,760.92: *FWO v. Sanada Investments Pty Ltd* [2010] FMCA 401. *FWO v. Australian Sales and Promotions Pty Ltd* [2013] FCCA 1502 records that an employer paid five young people, three of whom were WHMs, A$50 between them for a combined total of 426 hours of door-to-door sales work and 25.5 hours on a Saturday.

297 E.g. a Sydney cleaning operator hired a South Korean WHM under a sham contract, underpaid him and threatened to sack him unless he lied to the FWO about the arrangement: *FWO v. Jooine (Investment) Pty Ltd* [2013] FCCA 2144.

298 *FWO v. Nu Life Organic Farms Pty Ltd* [2010] FMCA 694.

conceived and poorly executed and at worst a deliberate attempt to avoid the industrial relations system in this country'.[299] In September 2013, the FWO secured a record A$343,860 in court-ordered penalties against a Perth company who underpaid six domestic cleaners, including WHMs from Taiwan, Hong Kong and Ireland.[300]

These judgments, like other case law considered in this chapter, are evidence both of temporary migrant workers' vulnerability and of law's responsiveness to this. Not only does much of this jurisprudence restore these workers their full entitlements, it articulates the particular pressures wrought by temporary visas. In August 2014, the FWO announced an inquiry into whether employers are exploiting the 88-day regional work requirement by requesting WHMs undertake free labour to qualify for the second year of their visa.

Conclusion

Focusing on the precarious working conditions for migrants working on lawful temporary visas in Australia, this chapter has primarily been diagnostic, exploring how the coerciveness and uncertainty of temporary immigration status can reconstitute visa workers' employment relationships in ways that create or perpetuate precarious poor working conditions. Each temporary migrant worker experiences this coercion and uncertainty uniquely and to vastly varying degrees depending on their highly particularised transnational social context. Nevertheless, eligibility requirements of the visa, conditions of stay and immigration enforcement can constrain temporary migrants' options and entrench dependencies on ongoing employment. Furthermore, immigration law can interact with other fields of government regulation to leave temporary migrant workers with weak and uncertain substantive protections under law.

This chapter explored these sources of precariousness in the context of an introduction to the Australian case study that is the focus of this book. Contrasting with similar English-speaking countries, the recent arrival of temporary labour migration on the Australian policy landscape and distinctly ambivalent attitudes towards temporary migrant labour have produced policies that facilitate low-waged migrant labour through three major temporary migration schemes (the temporary skilled 457 visa and international student and working holiday maker programmes) while simultaneously denying the presence of a segmented labour market for low-skilled temporary workers. The next chapter turns to the 457 visa in detail, evaluating a range of immigration-related regulatory measures introduced since 2008.

299 Ibid. [60].

300 *FWO v. ACN 146435118 Pty Ltd (No 2)* [2013] FCCA 1270.

4 Worker protection for which workers?

Successive reforms to the temporary skilled 457 visa programme

In 2012, Radovan Laski, owner of Clinica International, convinced up to 100 Indian students and workers – some with master's degrees – to pay between A$5,000 and A$40,000 to middlemen in return for promising to sponsor them for residency through Australia's Regional Sponsored Migration Scheme (RSMS).[1] Other workers were charged A$3,950 to do a A$1,300 cleaning course that was sold to them as part of a pathway towards permanent residency. Failing to provide the promised jobs and visa sponsorship, Laski sent some of the workers to unskilled jobs with employers in abattoirs where they complained that Laski had misled them about their residence status. Laski threatened one worker in an email that 'I will be down on you like a ton of bricks' if they complained. One 27-year-old woman, Bhawna Verma, was pregnant and desperate to stay in Australia when Laski promised her in writing to find employment and 'regional sponsorship' for an upfront fee. After paying A$5,000, she was sent to work for Laski's associate near Geelong in Victoria where she did odd jobs, receiving only money for groceries but no wages. A former subcontractor for Laski reported him to immigration officials.

Chapter 3 provided an overview of the immigration framework governing temporary migrant labour in Australia. It sought to lay bare the constitutive role played by various regulatory processes in creating precariousness directly through restrictions attaching to temporary visas and the complex interaction of these with broader employment and social welfare regulation.

This chapter examines four clusters of reforms to the dominant vehicle for temporary migrant labour in Australia, the 457 visa scheme, and pathways from it to residence, starting in 2008. Many elements of these have done much to foster the resilience of 457 visa workers in Australian workplaces. However, the central argument of this chapter is that these reforms

1 Details of this narrative are drawn from Nick McKenzie and Ben Schneiders, 'Visa Scheme Rorting Leaves Foreigners in Debt Bondage', *Sydney Morning Herald*, 6 June 2013; Ben Schneiders, Nick McKenzie and Daniel Hurst, 'Abbott Defends 457 Visas, as Government Plans Crackdown', *Canberra Times*, 6 June 2013; '80 Indians Duped to Pay Excessive Fee for Australia Work Visa: Report', *Press Trust of India*, 6 June 2013.

have located the problem in unscrupulous employers and vulnerable migrant workers, overlooking the role of the regulatory environment of immigration controls in intensifying pre-existing power differentials in migrant workers' employment relationships. Integrity measures have been introduced in the name of protecting vulnerable migrants, without appreciating how these can actually close down options for temporary migrant workers and worsen their insecurity. More sophisticated attention is needed to unpack how policing workers' immigration status in Australia can result in greater precariousness of labour.

Indeed, some of these measures have also set up a contest between foreign workers and local workers, impliedly opting to keep migrant workers precarious in the name of shoring up locals' conditions and opportunities. Others may have improved security for 457 visa workers at the expense of other temporary workers, especially international students. For instance, new eligibility criteria for the 457 visa were introduced in 2008 and in 2013. Because these affect 'not yet' 457 visa workers, public debate has assumed that the most vulnerable foreigners are simply denied access to the Australian labour market altogether, therefore leaving actual 457 visa workers in Australia more resilient. But this view obscures the fact that aspiring 457 visa applicants include not just foreigners outside of Australia but also various categories of temporary migrant workers in Australia. The increased precariousness of such workers cannot be simply externalised outside Australia's territorial borders.

Indeed, at the same time, other significant reforms have accelerated pathways to permanent residence for some 457 visa workers while impeding the progression to residence for other temporary migrant workers, especially international students. These changes have exacerbated two dependencies: the reliance of 457 visa workers on ongoing employer sponsorship, and also the stimulus for other temporary visa-holders to use the 457 visa pathway to residence. By prioritising employer sponsorship so heavily, the refashioned nexus between temporary and permanent labour migration in Australia has arguably structurally embedded precariousness in temporary migrants across the spectrum of visa categories as well as redrawn the demographic profile of the 457 visa category. This chapter closes by considering alternative adjustments to immigration regulation that might better empower temporary migrants at work.

This chapter is structured around four phases of regulatory reforms. The first dramatic reconfiguration of the scheme considered here came into force in 2009 with the *Migration Legislation Amendment (Worker Protection) Act 2008* (Cth) (*Worker Protection Act*), which sought to address the extreme exploitation of 457 visa workers that emerged in the final years of the conservative Howard government. Two features of these amendments, in particular, did much to strengthen 457 visa workers' bargaining power: first, visa-holders were accorded more flexibility in transferring their sponsorship to an alternative employer; second, sponsors were required to offer 457 visa workers salary and working conditions no less favourable than those provided to resident workers in the same position. Two other major elements centred on the scheme's integrity: employers' obligations as sponsors were clarified and made more robust, with stronger penalties for non-compliance, and the threshold criteria for 457 visa applicants rose significantly. This statutory framework (along with the replacement of the WorkChoices industrial relations framework by the Labor government's *Fair Work Act 2009* (Cth) (*FW Act*)) clearly lessened 457 visa workers' precariousness, with some of the worst excesses of underpayment of entitlements between 2004 and 2008 falling away. However, these amendments increased compliance costs on employers with insufficient safeguards to ensure that these are not passed onto workers. The new penalties imposed on employers may have resulted in greater detriment to migrant workers who frequently have more to lose than employers when employer misconduct is detected.

Although workers in so-called 'semi-skilled' occupations and with weaker English language skills were excluded from the programme in 2009, the impact of these reforms on the demographics of the 457 visa programme overall were short-lived. The second cluster of reforms tracks the dramatic rise of labour agreements, exceptional arrangements negotiated between employers and government that allow employers to sponsor 457 visa workers while bypassing some of the core stipulations of the scheme. This secondary pathway in the 457 visa scheme was emphasised shortly after the 2009 reforms and again later by the conservative Abbott Coalition government from 2013. The ambiguities and lack of transparency in this framework has intensified the need for structural or institutional safeguards for vulnerable migrant workers.

A third cluster of sweeping changes, this time to permanent skilled migration, increasingly prioritised employer sponsorship over independent migration as the dominant pathway to residence. While these moves were expressly designed to facilitate 457 visa workers' transition to permanent residence, they have given even greater significance to what the earlier 457 visa reforms kept in place: workers' dependency on their employer-sponsor.

A fourth cluster of amendments followed heated debate in 2013 over the scheme's ongoing integrity. Peaks in application numbers within certain occupations were portrayed as compliance failures, the result of employer 'rorts' and workers' misuse of the scheme as a 'backdoor' to settlement. Arguments surfaced that a degree of vulnerability in 'guest workers' may be the necessary cost of better protection for Australian workers. The antidote was found in the reintroduction of labour market testing (which had been abandoned in 2001), obscuring the far more likely cause of these short-term distortions in the programme: a predictable response by international students and working holiday makers (WHMs) resorting to the 457 visa as an avenue towards residence when previous options were closed.

This chapter examines these four areas of regulatory reform (the legislative amendments of 2009, enhanced use of labour agreements, background changes to the permanent skilled migration programme and the adjustments to the integrity of the scheme in 2013). The principal argument throughout is that these policy responses to precarious work overlook the agency of the migrant workers themselves and their access to support structures to empower decision making within the limited industrial options available to them. To address this, the chapter concludes with suggestions for regulatory adjustments that may achieve greater labour market mobility, empower workers to give voice to concerns and recast exploitation as a labour law abuse rather than an immigration law violation.

The *Worker Protection Act:* building resilience in 457 visa workers

The first major revamp of the 457 visa scheme took place between 2007 and 2009, when innovative safeguards were introduced in order to 'improve community confidence in the temporary working visa scheme, to protect overseas workers from exploitation and to address chronic skill shortages in the Australian economy'.[2] The centrepiece of these reforms was the *Worker Protection Act*, which came into force in September 2009 with accompanying regulations.[3] While policy settings regarding skilled migration had traditionally enjoyed bipartisan support, these initiatives marked a new divide between the major parties' approach to the precariousness of temporary migrant workers.[4]

The legislative package (which I will call the Worker Protection reforms) included several major features, of which four are explored in turn below. First, it permitted 457 visa workers to transition to alternative employer sponsorship more easily. Second, the statutory Minimum Salary Level (MSL) was replaced with a new requirement that, over a legislative baseline, an employer provide sponsored workers with terms and conditions of employment no less favourable than those of residents in that workplace. Third, a range of more stringent sponsorship obligations were introduced along with additional penalties for employers' non-compliance and stronger investigatory powers for immigration officers. Fourth, the scheme's entry criteria rose in relation to eligible skilled occupations and the English language ability of applicants.

Unquestionably these measures improved 457 visa workers' disadvantaged position in the Australian labour market. Labour law scholars, in particular Joo-Cheong Tham, Iain Campbell and Joanna Howe, have paid careful

2 Commonwealth, *Parliamentary Debates*, Senate, 24 September 2009, 5419-21 (Senator Joe Ludwig, Second Reading Speech on Migration Legislation Amendment (Worker Protection) Bill 2008).

3 *Migration Amendment Regulations 2009 (No 5)* (Cth), *Migration Amendment Regulations 2009 (No 9)* (Cth) and *Migration Amendment Regulations 2009 (No 5) Amendment Regulations 2009 (No 1)* (Cth).

4 Mary Crock, Sean Howe and Ron McCallum, 'Conflicted Priorities? Enforcing Fairness for Temporary Migrant Workers in Australia' in Cathryn Costello and Mark Freedland (eds), *Migrants at Work: Immigration and Vulnerability in Labour Law* (Oxford University Press, 2014), 422, 427.

attention to the 457 visa scheme, commending the 2009 reforms for improving safeguards for visa workers.[5] Each also offers critiques of the scheme, as I explain below, but their overall positive assessments appear to be borne out. Although causal connections are difficult to substantiate, 457 visa workers' average nominated base salaries increased from A$77,500 in 2008–9 to A$96,800 in mid 2011,[6] a 117 per cent rise beyond inflation, pointing to greater bargaining capacity among these workers.

Despite these gains, this section argues that considerable precariousness remains because, in seeking to 'protect' migrant workers from exploitative employers (note that the legislation was called the *'Worker Protection' Act*), this cluster of reforms located the problem in vulnerable migrant workers and in employer malfeasance. It overlooked the role played by Australian immigration and labour regulations themselves in intensifying relationships of dependency in which labour exploitation can flourish.

Easing the transition to alternative employer sponsorship

Employer sponsorship in condition 8107 has been a mandatory component of 457 visas since their inception. Until 2002, this condition provided that '[t]he holder must not change employer or occupation without the permission in writing of the Secretary' of the Immigration Department.[7] In 2002, the condition was amended so that the visa worker must not:

(i) cease to be employed by the employer in relation to which the visa was granted; or
(ii) work in a position or occupation inconsistent with the position or occupation in relation to which the visa was granted; or
(iii) engage in work for another person or on the holder's own account while undertaking the employment in relation to which the visa was granted.[8]

This version, which was effective until 2009, not only tied each 457 visa to continued employment with the sponsoring employer in the nominated position, it also limited workers' ability to exercise other employment choices open to residents, such as taking unpaid leave or undertaking lighter duties as residents are entitled to do under workers compensation legislation.

5 Joo-Cheong Tham and Iain Campbell, 'Temporary Migrant Labour in Australia: The 457 Visa Scheme and Challenges for Labour Regulation' (Working Paper No 50, Centre for Employment and Labour Relations Law, University of Melbourne, 2011), 18; Joanna Howe, 'The *Migration Legislation Amendment (Worker Protection) Act 2008*: Long Overdue Reform, But Have Migrant Workers Been Sold Short?' (2010) 23 *Australian Journal of Labour Law* 251.

6 Department of Immigration and Citizenship (DIAC), *Population Flows: Immigration Aspects 2010–11* (2012), 66.

7 *Migration Regulations 1994* (Cth), sch 8 condition 8107 (as at 1996) (*Migration Regulations*).

8 *Migration Amendment Regulations 2002 (No 2)* (Cth).

The Worker Protection reforms in 2009 revised condition 8107 to read:

(3) (a) the holder must:
(i) work only in the occupation listed in the most recently approved nomination for the holder; and
(ii) unless the circumstances in subclause (3A) apply – work only for:
(A) the standard business sponsor, former standard business sponsor, party to a labour agreement or former party to a labour agreement (the sponsor) who nominated the holder in the most recently approved nomination; or
(B) … an associated entity of the sponsor; and
(b) if the holder ceases employment – the period during which the holder ceases employment must not exceed 28 consecutive days.

(3A) for subparagraph (3) (a) (ii), the circumstances are that: …
(b) the holder is continuing to work for the sponsor, or the associated entity of the sponsor, for the purpose of fulfilling a requirement under a law relating to industrial relations and relating to the giving of notice.[9]

This involved two key changes. First, 457 visa workers were freed from the restriction of working only for the employer identified at the outset, and allowed to transition smoothly to a new employer identified in a more recently approved nomination, without lodging a fresh application. Second, 457 visa workers were now permitted to work for an entity other than their sponsor where necessary under industrial laws. This amendment meant workers no longer breached condition 8107 while taking leave or undertaking rehabilitation activities following a workplace injury (as had occurred with Mikko Siikaluoma, whose ordeals were described in Chapter 3).[10]

These amendments are a welcome expansion in labour mobility of 457 visa workers. At the same time, their impact ought not to be overstated since they did not seriously reduce the ongoing dependency of 457 visa workers on retaining employer sponsorship for their continued lawful residence, as discussed in more detail below.

Equity of wages and conditions

Arguably the strongest protective feature of the Worker Protection reforms for migrant workers was their reappraisal of salary requirements. The amendments required sponsors to provide migrant workers with terms and

9 *Migration Amendment Regulations 2009 (No 5) Amendment Regulations 2009 (No 1)* (Cth), amending *Migration Regulations* sch 8 condition 8107.

10 Under the pre-2009 scheme, in *Rahhal v. Minister for Immigration* [2008] FMCA 933, [58], the Federal Magistrates Court upheld a decision of the Migration Review Tribunal finding that engaging in rehabilitative activities for an entity other than their sponsor could amount to a breach of condition 8107, triggering possible visa cancellation.

conditions of employment no less favourable than those for a resident performing equivalent work in the same workplace.[11] Ordinarily, this is set by the enterprise agreement or award governing the sponsor's workplace, though a baseline salary still applies and was renamed the Temporary Skilled Migration Income Threshold (TSMIT), currently A$53,900.[12]

As explained in Chapter 2, the equality principle decreeing equivalent treatment between temporary migrants and residents seems an obvious yardstick. A well-established norm in various international labour conventions,[13] the critique of unequal treatment has frequently been invoked against 457 visa exploitation.[14] Equality of treatment is particularly appealing because it explicitly protects the rights and entitlements of all workers: migrants and residents alike. In their meticulous analysis of the 457 visa scheme, Joo-Cheong Tham and Iain Campbell address the importance of equality:

> There is also a close relationship between protecting local workers and protecting the working conditions of migrant workers. Migrant workers will be employed in the same labour market as local workers ... If the working conditions of migrant workers are inferior to those of local workers there is again a risk that migrant workers will underprice local workers. Whether this risk eventuates depends on the extent to which the working conditions of migrant workers are adequately protected so as to be on par with working conditions of comparable local workers.[15]

Clearly this salary requirement is designed as a price signal to remove financial incentives to employ 457 visa workers ahead of residents. Restrictions on the wages and other employment conditions at which migrants must be employed are, therefore, typical features in temporary labour migration programs. In Sweden, employers wishing to employ migrant workers must

11 *Migration Regulations* regs 2.72(10)(c) and 2.79. An exemption from this requirement is currently provided where the visa worker's salary exceeds A$250,000: *Specification of Income Threshold and Annual Earnings* (IMMI 13/028, F2013L01231) (Cth).

12 *Migration Regulations* reg 2.72(10)(cc).

13 E.g. International Convention on Protection of the Rights of All Migrant Workers and Members of their Families, adopted by GA Res 45/158, UN GAOR, 45th sess, UN Doc A/RES/45/158, 18 December 1990 (entered into force 1 July 2003) art 25.2 (Migrant Workers Convention); Migration for Employment Recommendation (Revised), 1949 (ILO No 86), International Labour Conference, 32nd sess (1 July 1949) art 17.1; Migration for Employment Convention (Revised), 1949 (ILO No 97), 20 UNTS 79 (entered into force 22 January 1952) art 6; Migrant Workers (Supplementary Provisions) Convention, 1975 (ILO No 143), 1120 UNTS 323 (entered into force 9 December 1978) (ILO Convention 143) art 8.2; Migrant Workers Recommendation, 1975 (ILO No 151), International Labour Conference, 60th sess (24 July 1975) art 2.

14 E.g. Michelle Bissett and Ingrid Landau, 'Australia's 457 Visa Scheme and the Rights of Migrant Workers' (2008) 33(3) *Alternative Law Journal* 142, 144.

15 Tham and Campbell, 'Temporary Migrant Labour in Australia', above n. 5, 10.

comply with prevailing industrial standards in collective agreements.[16] The USA and UK take similar approaches to Australia, requiring employers to pay migrants the average or prevailing wage in the relevant occupation or sector.

However, this 'no less favourable' standard for working conditions requirement contains certain shortcomings. First, resident workers are themselves frequently subject to unequal industrial treatment and are differentially situated within legal and institutional protections. Thus, it is often impossible to find a basis for comparison to assess equal treatment. Further, prior to 2013, the scope of the requirement was limited to a single workplace (in 2013 it was expanded to the same 'location' or region). Apparently, at that time, the Department of Immigration and Citizenship (DIAC) required a sponsor, if they employed no resident workers, to demonstrate they provided wages and conditions equivalent to those prevailing in their industry. However, it is not clear to what extent sponsors were practically put to this proof. More significantly, this 'no less favourable' requirement settles for a somewhat superficial equivalence between 457 visa workers and residents. It seeks to elevate 457 visa workers' bargaining power and offset the dependencies wrought by employer sponsorship. However, its focus on conditions of employment alone risks obscuring underlying legal and social structures that often leave 457 visa workers with differentiated living costs and social entitlements, as discussed in detail in the previous chapter.

Indeed, in at least one respect, the Worker Protection reforms further deprived 457 visa workers of certain institutionalised social protections. Prior to 2009, sponsors were required to meet any outstanding medical or hospital expenses arising from treatment of the worker in a public hospital.[17] To better insulate taxpayers from unpaid medical costs, a major inquiry into the scheme conducted by Barbara Deegan in 2008 recommended permitting 457 visa workers to access Medicare public health care through a levy on sponsoring employers.[18] Alternatively, Deegan suggested, if workers are required to pay their own health care fees, their salary rates should include a premium to account for the fact that they are not entitled to access publicly funded health care.[19] A DIAC discussion paper in 2008 proposed a further possibility of requiring sponsors to pay for visa workers' private health insurance.[20] Rejecting these recommendations, as part of the Worker Protection reforms, the Labor government shifted the burden for healthcare

16 Martin Ruhs, *The Price of Rights: Regulating International Labor Migration* (Princeton University Press, 2013), 62.

17 *Migration Regulations* reg 1.20CB(1)(k) (as at 2008).

18 Barbara Deegan, *Visa Subclass 457 Integrity Review: Final Report* (Cth of Australia, 2008), 69 and 73 (*Deegan Report*).

19 Barbara Deegan, *Visa Subclass 457 Integrity Review: Issues Paper 3* (2008), 16.

20 DIAC, *Discussion Paper: Business (Long Stay) Subclass 457 and Related Temporary Visa Reforms* (2008), 14.

away from sponsors altogether, inserting a new 457 visa condition that workers maintain private health insurance at their own expense for the duration of their stay.[21]

This was represented as for the workers' benefit, to prevent 'employers from pressuring [workers] not to access health care ... [and give] visa holders a greater ability to change employer, again reducing their risk of exploitation'.[22] However, this amendment externalised workers' medical costs onto the worker themselves, just as the sponsorship mechanism shifts the risk of unemployment onto migrant workers, insulating Australia from related costs. The 457 visa worker became even more, in Fineman's terms, the archetypal 'self-sufficient subject'.[23] Any possible dependency of 457 visa workers is directed away from public organs and onto private actors: any burden on the domestic labour market is contained by employer sponsorship; any burden on the public health sector is mediated by insurance. Governments may deploy this strategy to enhance the attractiveness of the scheme to the public but these burdens can belie the promised equality of working conditions.

Policing sponsor compliance

A third significant element of the Worker Protection reforms was the monitoring and enforcement of employers' obligations under the scheme. At its inception in 1996, very little was done to ensure that sponsors conformed to the scheme's basic regulatory objectives. Only later, in 2003, did the Howard government strengthen sponsorship compliance measures, requiring employers to make various sponsorship attestations or 'undertakings', with sanctions for breach including warnings, cancellation of sponsorship and bars on future sponsorship.[24] This framework was intended to enhance the integrity of employers' participation as well as transfer any costs generated by 457 visa workers to sponsors rather than the Australian community.[25]

However, between 2003 and 2006, immigration compliance checks on 457 visa sponsors dropped by more than one third even as the scheme rapidly grew.[26] The Immigration Department 'usually' gave employers advance warning of monitoring site visits.[27] Sanctions were rarely enforced, the

21 *Migration Regulations* sch 2 cl 457.228B and sch 8 condition 8501.

22 DIAC, *Population Flows*, above n. 6, 66.

23 Martha A. Fineman, 'Dependency and Social Debt' in David B. Grushky (ed.), *Poverty and Inequality* (Stanford University Press, 2005), 133, 135–6.

24 As introduced by the *Migration Legislation Amendment (Sponsorship Measures) Act 2003* (Cth) and now reflected in *Migration Regulations* Div 2.20; *Migration Act 1958* (Cth), s 140K (*Migration Act*).

25 As expressed by the Migration Review Tribunal in *0806368* [2009] MRTA 803, [34].

26 Department of Immigration, Multicultural and Indigenous Affairs (DIMIA), *Annual Report 2005–06* (2006), 84.

27 Information provided by DIMIA to Senate Estimates questioning in May 2006: Bob Kinnaird, 'Current Issues in the Skilled Temporary Subclass 457 Visa' (2006) 14 *People and Place* 49, 54.

sponsorship of only three employers was cancelled in 2005–6, increasing to 95 employers the following year.[28] It may be recalled that sanctions against the employer of Guo Jiandong – the Mongolian wood machinist whose death was recounted in the opening of Chapter 1 – were overturned by the Migration Review Tribunal on review.[29] Indeed, of the four other 457 visa workers who died in workplace accidents between 2004 and 2008 (Wilfredo Navales, Petro Balading, Rey Garcia Jardinel and Antonio Julio Guerrero Pili), only Balading's employer, Panoy Pty Ltd, received a three year ban from sponsorship in September 2007.[30] Even when imposed, these sanctions (the most serious of which barred current or future sponsorship) were not perceived as serious deterrents against employer misconduct.[31] This perception still appears to hold. In 2014, the FWO brought legal action against operators of Chinese noodle takeaway shops for underpaying six Chinese cooks and kitchen supervisors on 457 visas collectively a full A$642,311, five years after the same employer was barred from sponsorship for eighteen months because of failing to pay the minimum salary to nine 457 visa workers in around 2007.[32]

The Worker Protection reforms introduced stronger investigative powers and took a more comprehensive approach to 'sponsorship obligations', elevating these from bilateral commitments with each employer to overarching regulatory requirements.[33] Currently, grouped thematically, these are:

Guarantee the integrity of the sponsorship arrangement

- Ensure that 457 visa workers only work in nominated occupations and are a direct employee of the sponsor (reg 2.86);
- Ensure that workers receive the market rate for terms and conditions of employment (reg 2.79);

Support or protect sponsored workers

- Pay the travel costs for workers to leave Australia if they have requested these costs in writing (reg 2.80);

28 Matthew Moore and Malcolm Knox, 'Exploitation of Skilled Migrants Exposed', *Sydney Morning Herald*, 28 August 2007.

29 *071776514* [2007] MRTA 809.

30 Senate Legal and Constitutional Affairs Legislation Committee, Parliament of Australia, 'Question Taken on Notice 21, Budget Estimates Hearing: 28–29 May 2008, Immigration and Citizenship Portfolio' (2008).

31 Joint Standing Committee on Migration (JSCM), Parliament of Australia, *Temporary Visas … Permanent Benefits: Ensuring the Effectiveness, Fairness and Integrity of the Temporary Business Visa Program* (2007), 107–24 (*Permanent Benefits Report*).

32 Esther Han, 'Noodle Business Operators Underpaid 457 Visa Workers Almost $650,000', *Sydney Morning Herald*, 21 January 2014; *0806368* [2009] MRTA 803.

33 *Migration Amendment Regulations 2009* (No 5) (Cth); *Migration Act* s 140H.

- Not recover recruitment or sponsorship costs from workers or a third party, regardless of worker consent (regs 2.60S and 2.87);

Protect local labour market conditions

- Meet training benchmarks for the benefit of local employees throughout the sponsorship (regs 2.59(j), 2.82 and 2.87B);

Assist with compliance activities

- Keep records of their compliance with sponsorship obligations (reg 2.82);
- Provide information to the DIBP when certain events occur, such as any change in circumstances related to the business' approval as a sponsor, and within five days after a worker ceases employment (reg 2.84);
- Provide records and information to the minister which they are required to keep (ie under tax laws, sponsorship obligations or the terms of a government-negotiated labour agreement) (reg 2.83);
- Cooperate with DIBP inspectors (reg 2.78);

Indemnify the government

- Pay costs incurred by the Commonwealth to locate and remove the worker if they become an unlawful non-citizen (reg 2.81).

In addition to warnings, cancellation of sponsorship and bars on future sponsorship, infringement notices were introduced (up to A$10,200), along with quite substantial civil penalties (up to A$33,000 per breach for a corporation and A$6,600 for an individual), enforceable in Federal Circuit Court proceedings.[34] These sanctions could be ordered for breach of sponsorship obligation, failure to continue to meet criteria for approval as sponsor, provision of false or misleading information to the immigration department and contravention of the law.[35]

The Department's monitoring capacity was also augmented, with the right of compliance inspectors to enter the sponsor's business premises, inspect any aspect of the business, interview anyone associated with the business and require the sponsor to produce documents.[36] The reforms also created a legislative framework for immigration officers to exchange information with other commonwealth, state and territory agencies more freely.[37] The Immigration Department was, therefore, no longer required to enter into

34 Now set out in *Migration Act* s 140Q and regulations prescribed under s 506A.

35 *Migration Act* s 140L; *Migration Regulations* regs 2.89-2.94B. E.g. *Minister for Immigration v. Roberts* [2011] FMCA 77; *1008556* [2013] MRTA 444; *1113002* [2013] MRTA 517.

36 *Migration Act* ss 140V-140XJ; *Migration Regulations* reg 2.102C.

37 *Migration Act* ss 140ZA and 140ZH.

Memoranda of Understanding with other government bodies to facilitate interdepartmental liaison and joint operations. These arrangements were introduced at least in part in the name of safeguarding migrant workers' entitlements. Justifying the amendments, the Minister cited the Immigration Department's need to access information from the Australian Taxation Office to ensure visa workers were being paid correct salary levels.[38] This goal was also evident in DIAC's agreement in 2008 with WorkCover NSW (an occupational health and safety body) to exchange names and addresses of businesses employing 457 visa holders and details of any work-related fatalities or workplace safety incidents (unfortunately, it appears this and similar arrangements in other states were abandoned in around 2012).[39] In 2011, the Australian Building and Construction Commission (which later became Fair Work Building and Construction) agreed to provide DIAC with information to assist it in considering whether to grant or cancel applications for sponsorships or visas in relation to labour agreements and the 457 visa program,[40] and the Immigration Department has had interdepartmental arrangements with the Fair Work Ombudsman (FWO) for the benefit of workers' rights, referring 24 matters to the FWO in 2010–11 and 13 matters in 2012–13.[41]

However, other integrity measures seem primarily driven by concerns of other agencies to protect Australia from temporary migrant workers. The Australian Taxation Office, for example, instigated a data-matching project with the Immigration Department in 2013 to pursue fraud and tax evasion by temporary visa workers.[42] Industrial tribunals have referred evidence of immigration fraud from several unfair dismissal proceedings before them to immigration officials. In one matter, Fair Work Australia directed that a transcript of a decision be sent to DIAC disclosing allegations including falsification of skills assessments for the purpose of permanent residence applications by overseas students.[43] In another matter, recalling the experience of Bhawna Verma in the narrative opening this chapter, Commissioner Cambridge directed that evidence be forwarded to immigration officials that an employer had requested A$30,000 to sponsor a temporary migrant worker for permanent residence.[44]

38 Chris Evans, Minister for Immigration and Citizenship (MIAC), 'Joint Agreement to Protect Overseas Workers in NSW' (media release, 30 September 2008).

39 *Memorandum of Understanding between WorkCover Authority of New South Wales and DIAC*, 16 September 2008.

40 *Memorandum of Understanding between DIAC and Australian Building and Construction Commission*, 6 April 2011, cl 6.3.

41 Katie Malyon, 'Employment Related Visas, Compliance and Prosecutions' (Paper presented at Immigration Lawyers Association of Australasia Conference, Sydney, 10 March 2012), 25; email from Michele Schiller, Monitoring and Free Trade Agreements Policy Section, DIAC to author, 9 August 2013.

42 Commonwealth Treasury, 'Notice of a Data Matching Program: DIAC Temporary Working Visas Data Matching Program' in Commonwealth, *Gazette Notice*, No 15 of 2013 (C2013G00598), 17 April 2013, 1044.

43 *Kirshnakanth v. Saai Bose Pty Limited* [2010] FWA 4578, [69].

44 *Shim v. JMNE Pty Limited t/as Wooden Bowl Restaurant* [2010] FWA 8230.

Nevertheless, these new sanctions and additional investigatory powers have seen 457 visa program compliance activities become considerably more targeted over time, as demonstrated in Table 4.1.

Table 4.1 Immigration department monitoring activities and sanctions

	2006–2007	*2007–2008*	*2008–2009*	*2009–2010*	*2010–2011*	*2011–2012*	*2012–2013*	*2013–2014*
Active sponsors (at end of financial year)	15,410	18,750	19,610	18,270	18,520	22,450	30,090	35,285
Sponsors monitored	6,463	5,293	4,438	2,546	2,091	1,754	1,857	2,223
Site visits conducted	1,553	1,759	1,752	1,245	814	856	1,238	1,278
Sponsors formally warned	313	1,353	941	510	453	449	302	350
Sanction imposed (bar or cancellation of sponsorship)	95	192	190	164	140	125	217	365
Infringement notice issued by DIAC/DIBP	n/a	n/a	n/a	0	9	49	68	28
Civil penalty issued by judiciary	n/a	n/a	n/a	0	0	1	0	0

Data produced from DIBP, *Annual Report 2013–14* (2014), 72; DIAC, *Annual Report 2011–12* (2012), 86; DIAC, *Annual Report 2008–09* (2009), 72.

These figures indicate the Immigration Department's evolving approach to compliance oversight over time, from attempting to monitor a large number of sponsors (around 47 per cent in 2007) to targeting sponsors thought to be high risk (around 11 per cent in 2013).[45] In accordance with this approach, sanctions as a percentage of monitoring have demonstrably increased during this period, along with sanctions and infringement notices. Nevertheless, finding non-compliance in roughly 40 per cent of workplaces monitored,[46] even if based on risk factors, seems somewhat alarming. Enforcement concerns appear to be ongoing, as highlighted by a major independent review of the 457 visa programme in 2014 conducted by a team led by John Azarias and commissioned by the Abbott Coalition government,

45 DIAC, Department of Education, Employment and Workplace Relations, Department of Industry, Innovation, Climate Change, Science, Research and Tertiary Education and the Department of Resources, Energy and Tourism, Submission No 24 to the Senate Legal and Constitutional Affairs References Committee, Parliament of Australia, 'Inquiry into the Framework and Operation of Subclass 457 Visas, Enterprise Migration Agreements and Regional Migration Agreements', May 2013, 18.

46 Letter from Chris Bowen, MIAC to Andrew Naylor, Chair of the Human Rights Council of Australia, 9 August 2012.

which recommended DIBP coordinate with the Australian Taxation Office to develop a better risk matrix to target compliance activities.[47]

Further concerns relate to the severity of penalties. From 2013–14, infringement notices appear to have been replaced with lesser sanctions such as sponsorship cancellation or bars, and it took more than two years for the first (and to date only) employer sponsor to face the Federal Magistrates Court of Australia, which issued a civil penalty order of A$35,000 in June 2012.[48] A St Kilda restaurant in Victoria had underpaid the visa worker A$14,796 (including five weeks when the employee was not paid at all), breaching the sponsorship obligations to accord sponsored workers terms and conditions of employment equivalent to residents and to keep appropriate pay records. The employer had been barred from the scheme for four years in 2011 and had failed to pay the A$6,600 infringement notice issued in April that year.

Enforcement concerns aside, while sponsorship obligations and sanctions compliance mechanisms support the integrity of the 457 visa programme, they are not especially well adapted to ameliorating the precariousness of visa workers because they do not significantly restructure dependencies in the employment relationship. Employers can devise ways of passing on costs imposed by sponsorship obligations to 457 visa workers. For instance, reg. 2.87 specifies that sponsors 'must not recover ... certain costs' from the sponsored worker but does not prohibit a sponsor from requiring a worker to pay certain costs (for instance related to their own travel) up front. Similarly, reg. 2.81 provides that sponsors must pay costs incurred by the commonwealth in locating or removing unlawful non-citizens. Evidence in court judgments suggests that employers regularly specify in employment contracts that workers will be liable to reimburse the sponsor for such costs. For instance, one contract stated 'Please note: if you breach your Visa condition while in Australia, you will reimburse the employer for any debts incurred by the Department ... in locating and detaining you, while you are sponsored by the employer in a sub class 457 Visa.'[49] There have been efforts to build mechanisms to provide redress for workers' grievances into the compliance framework itself. For example, since 2003, the *Migration Act* allows a worker to recover a debt in civil penalty proceedings owed by their sponsor as a result of breach of sponsorship obligations. However, while monetary payments have been recovered from sponsors under these provisions (currently *Migration Act* s. 486S(4)), it is not clear how frequently

47 John Azarias *et al.*, *Robust New Foundations: A Streamlined, Transparent and Responsive System for the 457 Programme* (September 2014), 18.

48 *Minister for Immigration v. Sahan Enterprises Pty Ltd* [2012] FMCA 619.

49 *Flattery v. Zeffirelli's Pizza Restaurant* [2007] FMCA 9, Annexure 1, Agreed Statement of Facts, [3]; *Mason v. Harrington Corporation Pty Ltd* [2007] FMCA 7, Annexure 1, Agreed Statement of Facts, [9].

this has occurred and they appear to have remained underused.[50] More often employment enforcement agencies pursue entitlements on behalf of 457 visa workers, entirely separate from immigration compliance, as explained in the previous chapter.

The difficulty with viewing compliance efforts as empowering of workers is that an employer's violation of labour laws and immigration rules may have far graver consequences for workers than employers. The coerciveness of condition 8107 means that enforcement activities directed at both 457 visa workers and sponsors frequently shift disproportionate risk onto workers. This is vividly illustrated where the 457 visa worker is doing work other than in accordance with the nomination (for instance in a less skilled position than approved). Such conduct, of course, amounts to a breach of sponsorship obligation, for which the employer may be penalised.[51] However, the worker, even if not voluntarily colluding in this arrangement, will have also breached their visa condition 8107, which may trigger visa cancellation.[52] This infraction may jeopardise a future application for a further 457 or permanent visa.[53] These circumstances offer no incentives for a visa worker to call attention to their employer's contraventions. This was precisely the situation faced by South Korean Jeong Dae Kim, whose 457 visa was cancelled when an immigration compliance site visit revealed the business was no longer operating.[54] Kim testified that he had reported to work, was (under-)paid A$3,000 for three months' work, had become depressed and was advised to take sick leave. When he returned to work, he found the corporate office empty and was unable to contact his employer. The Migration Review Tribunal accepted that Kim 'may not have intended to breach the visa condition' but nevertheless cancelled his visa because he had not in fact been working for his sponsor as required by condition 8107.[55]

Indeed, even if the sponsor's breach is theirs alone (for instance, failure to comply with DIBP's requests for information or pay the TSMIT), whatever penalties may or may not be ordered against the sponsor, the 457 visa may still be cancelled since one of the grounds for cancellation of the 457 visa is a sponsor's failure to satisfy a sponsorship obligation.[56] This occurred to Bao Ping Bian, who challenged the cancellation of her 457 visa before the Migration Review Tribunal because she had instituted proceedings against

50 Email from Jeanie Bruce, Director, National Employer Sanctions Support Team, DIAC to author, 19 July 2013.

51 *Migration Regulations* reg 2.86.

52 See *Yan v. MIMIA* [2002] FCA 1404 where Yan's visa was cancelled under s 116(1)(b) for breach of condition 8107 as he was working in a position other than that nominated.

53 Visa applications can be refused on the basis of a prior breach of immigration rules: *Migration Regulations* sch 2 cl 457.221. See *Poskus v. MIMIA* [2005] FCA 118 where a 457 visa was refused because the applicant had failed to substantially comply with conditions applying to his last substantive visa (in this case the 8101 No Work condition).

54 *Kim v. Minister for Immigration* [2007] FMCA 1580.

55 Ibid. [35].

56 Reg 2.43(1) and s 116.

her employer Shanghai Garden Chinese Restaurant alleging unfair dismissal, underpayment of the hourly rate and absence of annual leave. The Tribunal noted that the FWO had confirmed it would progress 'a full investigation of her allegations' but nevertheless let the visa cancellation stand.[57]

Even where the worker and employer persuade the Immigration Department to leave their current sponsorship and 457 visa in place, a ban on future sponsorship can deprive the 457 visa worker of sponsorship for permanent residence. In one matter, the Tribunal accepted 'that it is relevant to take into account potential implications regarding' the worker's application for a permanent employer sponsored visa.[58] However, it nevertheless concluded that 'under Australian migration legislation there is no automatic right to permanent residence for the holder of a temporary subclass 457 visa merely because they have worked or received an education in Australia'. In affirming the sponsorship ban, the Tribunal determined to give 'lesser weight' to the consequences for the migrant worker. In several published cases, 457 visa workers' aspirations for sponsored permanent residence have been denied because of bans on their sponsors.[59] Indeed, the dependency of hopeful visa applicants on their sponsors is underscored by Full Federal Court case law precluding visa applicants from legally challenging the department's refusal or cancellation of sponsorship unless the sponsor participates in the proceedings.[60] Furthermore, a 457 visa sponsorship ban can preclude an employer from sponsoring a worker for permanent residence even after the period of the ban has expired because regulations require a prospective sponsor to show that they are 'an employer of good standing',[61] and previous failures to comply with immigration law (including past sponsorship bars) may disqualify a potential sponsor from making this requirement out. Sadly there are international precedents here: Canada for instance recently moved to deny work permits to employees on the basis of the employer's previous lack of compliance or discrepancies with the original job offer.[62]

In Australia, this uneven impact of compliance is rarely explicitly acknowledged – much less taken into account – by decision makers in sanctioning employers. Only one publicly available Migration Review Tribunal decision appears to have accorded importance to the possible impact on the 457 visa worker in deciding whether to issue a sponsorship ban. In 2010, the sponsor, a steel fabrication business in Revesby, challenged before the Tribunal a 14-month bar from future sponsorship. The sponsor had breached its sponsorship undertaking by underpaying the employee, Weili Zhang,

57 *1001499* [2010] MRTA 1541, [20]. For a similar outcome see *Hong v. MIMIA* [2004] FCA 1308.

58 *1008125* [2011] MRTA 1096, [28].

59 *0902056* [2010] MRTA 1010; *1008125* [2011] MRTA 1096; *Radeshar Pty Ltd v. Minister for Immigration* [2011] FMCA 560.

60 *Lee v. MIAC* [2007] FCAFC 62.

61 Reg 5.19(2).

62 Sarah Marsden, 'The New Precariousness: Temporary Migrants and the Law in Canada' (2012) 27(2) *Canadian Journal of Law and Society* 209, 225.

A$3,762 because it had paid his salary based on a 40-hour week rather than a 38 hour week. The Tribunal overturned the departmental bar and decided to issue no sanction, due to the inadvertent nature of the breach, the fact that the employer had quickly rectified the mistake and that Zhang would be eligible to apply for a permanent visa sponsored by this employer within the following year.[63] Arguably, this decision gives more appropriate weight to the significance of the breach and the severity of penalty from the worker's perspective rather than, as many other decisions do, assuming that the only relevant relationship is between the sponsor and DIBP.

Increased barriers to eligibility

The final element of the 2009 Worker Protection reforms considered here is the increased thresholds of skills and English language ability for visa applicants. Greater barriers to entry sought to reduce exploitation of semi-skilled workers or those with weaker English skills by limiting their ability to participate under the scheme at all. This allowed the government to claim to have addressed concerns about worker precariousness without addressing its structural causes. However, in this section, I take issue with these claims, suggesting instead that aspiring 457 visa workers may simply continue to endure precarious work either outside Australia's borders or in Australia on other visas or indeed on 457 visas obtained through concessional arrangements under labour agreements negotiated with the government (and which are discussed in more detail in the following section).

First some background to these amendments. The demographic profile of 457 visa workers had changed dramatically as the scheme was made more flexible during the mid 2000s. At its inception in 1996, the programme was small and favoured managerial and professional workers, often from industrialised countries such as the UK, Japan and USA.[64] During years of economic boom and as employers gained greater awareness of the scheme, more visas were granted for trade occupations and to applicants from developing countries. By 2006, 24 per cent of all 457 visa grants were for trades and other so-called 'semi-skilled' occupations (such as cook, welder metal fabricator and motor mechanic).[65] European and North American source countries were matched or outpaced by increasing applicants from India, the Philippines and China.[66] Numerous assessments of the 457 visa programme saw these changes as key sources of migrant worker exploitation. In particular, weak English language skills, and 'semi-skilled' occupations,

63 *1006146* [2010] MRTA 2294.

64 Siew-Ean Khoo *et al.*, 'Temporary Skilled Migration to Australia: The 457 Visa Sub-Class' (2003) 11(4) *People and Place* 27, 38.

65 Department of Immigration and Multicultural Affairs, *Population Flows: Immigration Aspects 2005–06* (2007), 70.

66 DIAC, *Subclass 457 Business (Long Stay): Subclass 457 State-Territory Summary Report 1 July 2007–30 June 2008* (2008).

were seen to make migrant workers especially vulnerable to mistreatment.[67] Not only were these workers more likely to work in industries marked by greater physical safety hazards and receive lower pay rates, demographers also suggested that trades workers were highly invested in future residence and therefore particularly dependent on their employer sponsors.[68]

Responding to these findings, the Worker Protection reforms pared back the semi-skilled occupations eligible for nomination under the scheme. Skills assessments were introduced for the first time for migrants applying from designated high immigration risk countries (in the Global South) in certain occupations. Legislative amendments also raised the English language thresholds for 457 visa applicants working as chefs or in trade occupations (although these were later slightly relaxed by the Coalition government in 2014). By increasing the skills and English language criteria for visa applicants, the government sought to reduce harm to vulnerable workers, restore the integrity of the visa programme and insulate the Australian labour market from the most egregious abuses. This was achieved by excluding a specific profile of worker. As eminent demographers have observed, '[f]ew applicants with trade skills were likely to achieve [this increased English language requirement], especially on the reading and writing modules, if they originated from non-English-language-speaking countries like China'.[69] Such temporary workers were 'protected' from falling prey to employer misconduct by being refused entry to the Australian labour market altogether.

In the face of vulnerability the government moved to exclude and it seems difficult to maintain that vulnerable workers were left better off. Bridget Anderson has noted that prevention of harm is frequently invoked to justify immigration enforcement in the UK.[70] A similar stance is visible here, recasting exclusion as protective of rights. Locating the problem (and the source of vulnerability) in the attributes of the workers themselves erases the complex combination of labour market pressures, social disadvantage and immigration controls, which produce relations of coercion and control. Instead, in the name of protection, stricter entry criteria restrict workers' choice to work in Australia under the scheme. While professional 457 visa workers with strong English language skills may also be subject to oppressive working conditions as a result of their precarious temporary immigration status, these workers are considered sufficiently capable of appraising their

67 *Deegan Report*, above n. 18, 23, 52–3. In July–December 2007, the main industries to receive sanctions for abuses were those primarily reliant on so-called 'semi-skilled work' such as hospitality (43 per cent), construction (20 per cent) and manufacturing (19 per cent): Barbara Deegan, *Visa Subclass 457 Integrity Review: Issues Paper 1* (2008), 17.

68 Siew-Ean Khoo, Graeme Hugo and Peter McDonald, 'Which Skilled Temporary Migrants Become Permanent Residents and Why' (2008) 42 *International Migration Review* 193, 205.

69 Bob Birrell and Ernest Healy, 'Immigration Overshoot' (Research Report, Centre for Population and Urban Research, Monash University, November 2012), 11.

70 Bridget Anderson, 'Where's the Harm in That? Immigration Enforcement, Trafficking and the Protection of Migrants' Rights' (2012) 56 *American Behavioral Scientist* 1241, 1242.

circumstances and deciding for themselves whether to engage in such work. Migrant workers with weaker English and lesser qualifications are treated as less autonomous subjects, less capable of rejecting substandard working conditions. While these workers may indeed experience greater dependency in their employment, these reforms further shut down their options rather than enhanced their agency.

Excluding the more vulnerable from participating in the 457 visa scheme may indeed have improved the precarious working conditions of 457 visa workers to some extent. However, it is unlikely to have ameliorated the position of those potential migrant workers no longer eligible for 457 visas whether they remained in foreign labour markets or indeed in the Australian labour market on other temporary visas. The image of failed visa applicant, denied the opportunity to enter the Australian labour market, is typically that of a foreigner overseas, but up to half of all 457 visa applications are in fact made by non-citizens in Australia.[71] Indeed, as I argue below, this cohort increased sharply as a result of concurrent reforms which took permanent residence out of the reach of most international students graduating from Australian educational facilities. Exploitation frequently flows from structural forces which constrain the options for decent work available to workers and raising 457 visa application thresholds tightened those options further for other temporary migrant workers.

Changing the eligibility criteria allowed the government to claim it addressed conditions that foster exploitation without tackling the central features of the 457 visa that breed uncertainty and choicelessness. It is a cause for considerable concern that a government-commissioned comprehensive survey of 457 visa workers in June 2012 indicated that 2 per cent of respondents' earnings were less than A$40,000 and 11 per cent were at or below A$50,000, right at the edge or below the TSMIT of A$49,330 at that time.[72] Of those who earned under A$50,000, 55 per cent had not received any pay increase after working for a year. Indeed, frozen or low wage rates are likely to be more prevalent after the Coalition government in 2014 declined to index the TSMIT (which had been indexed annually under successive Labor governments), essentially cutting the wage threshold compared to inflation.

Furthermore, it appears the impact of these reforms on the demographics of the 457 visa programme overall were short-lived. Although the modified entry criteria initially halved the numbers of 457 visa grants for trades and technician occupations, their share increased from 14 per cent to 28 per cent of the programme over the following four years.[73] This could occur, in

71 Azarias *et al.*, *Robust New Foundations* above n. 47, 36.

72 Migration Council of Australia, *More Than Temporary: Australia's 457 Visa Program* (Cth of Australia, 2013), 14 (*More than Temporary Report*). This survey did not include 457 visa workers on labour agreements who may be earning less than the TSMIT with departmental approval.

73 Migration Council of Australia, Submission to the 'Independent Review of Integrity in the 457 Visa Subclass' (2014), 11; DIAC, *Subclass 457 Business (Long Stay): State and Territory Summary Report 2009–10* (2010), Table 1.12, 8.

part, because avenues to bypass the English language, skills and salary requirements are available through an alternative labour agreements pathway, which allows for recruitment of 457 visa workers outside of the usual parameters of the scheme through negotiated arrangements with the government. Labour agreements gained increased significance following the Worker Protection reforms in 2009 and then again under the Coalition government from 2013.

The rise of labour agreements

Labour agreements comprise a second major 457 visa pathway for businesses to bypass the standard business sponsorship scheme.[74] They facilitate sponsorship of workers across a business or an entire industry through specialised agreements brokered between employers and DIBP. Labour agreements stipulate the minimum skill levels of nominated workers, English language requirements, salary levels, length of stay of workers in Australia and how compliance shall be monitored, unbound by the regulatory strictures that underpin the core 457 visa programme. The legislative labour market testing requirements, which hopeful sponsors must currently meet, do not apply. Instead, according to departmental guidelines, employers seeking a labour agreement must provide evidence of a genuine labour market need to recruit workers from overseas, and must first demonstrate their efforts to recruit locally.[75] However, importantly, employer parties to labour agreements are bound by sponsorship obligations, including the obligation to accord workers 'no less favourable' wages and conditions than residents.[76]

This section tracks the dramatic rise of labour agreements in the years following the Worker Protection reforms and the emphasis placed on this pathway by the Abbott Coalition government from 2013, and the implications for precarious visa-holders. In 2010–11, 2,510 457 visas were granted under labour agreements, an increase of 25.1 per cent on 2009–10.[77] The number of labour agreements in effect then grew from 129 in 2011 to 190 by October 2014, with 39 further requests under consideration at that time. These cover the on-hire, aged care, agriculture, meat processing, transport, specialist construction and engineering recruitment industries. Some of these are the result of agreements between individual employers and the government while others are template agreements negotiated at an industry-wide level. Since labour agreements facilitate the entry of lower-skilled workers, and if this cohort is more likely to be exposed to employer mistreatment, the need for structural or institutional safeguards for vulnerable migrant workers seems likely to intensify.

74 *Migration Regulations* sch 2 cl 457.223(2).
75 Reg 2.76.
76 Reg 2.79.
77 DIAC, *Population Flows: Immigration Aspects 2010–11* (2012), 19.

In addition, in 2010 the Labor government introduced two further meta-structures for labour agreements, which the Coalition government renamed and began promoting in 2014. The first, Designated Area Migration Agreements enable regional areas, states and territories to negotiate an umbrella framework agreement which may contain English language and salary (up to 10 per cent below the TSMIT) concessions, although there may be no derogation from the prescribed occupations in the standard 457 visa scheme nor from the requirement to pay market rates at the enterprise level as introduced in 2009 Worker Protection reforms.[78] Within this umbrella framework, individual labour agreements may be made between employers and the DIBP (and requests for further concessions may be agreed on a case-by-case basis). The second, known as Project Agreements, build on the Enterprise Migration Agreements scheme, introduced by the Labor government during a resources boom driven by high commodities prices. These, in principle, permitted an umbrella sponsorship agreement with a project owner or prime contractor of a resources sector project, with a capital expenditure of over A$2 billion.[79] However, following what Tham called a 'storm of controversy',[80] no such arrangement was ever finalised.

As an alternative to the access of lower-skilled workers to the standard 457 visa programme, the use of labour agreements appears to provide fewer safeguards against precariousness. While the sanctions scheme governing employer sponsors applies, it was not until 15 February 2012 that the Immigration Minister announced the first ever termination of a labour agreement when a Victorian on-hire company breached its sponsorship obligations by employing its 457 visa workers on a casual basis, underpaying them and providing false and misleading information to the Immigration Department.[81] Furthermore, Howe and Tham have each highlighted acute transparency concerns connected to the criteria and standards relating to labour agreements, which, as executive arrangements rather than creatures of statute, can be easily altered through changes to departmental policy without public or parliamentary consultation.[82] In general, little is known about the content of labour agreements as 'all information from the employer is treated as Commercial-in-Confidence'.[83] Early promises by the Abbott government to reduce the processing times of labour agreements

78 DIBP, *Designated Area Migration Agreements* (2014), 9–10.

79 DIAC, 'Employer Sponsored Workers: Enterprise Migration Agreements' (2011).

80 Joo-Cheong Tham, '457 Reasons for Reform', *Sydney Morning Herald*, 29 May 2012.

81 Chris Bowen, MIAC, 'First Ever Termination of a Labour Agreement' (media release, 15 February 2012).

82 Iain Campbell and Joo-Cheong Tham, 'Labour Market Deregulation and Temporary Migrant Labour Schemes: An Analysis of the 457 Visa Program' (2013) 26 *Australian Journal of Labour Law* 239, 241; Joanna Howe, 'Enterprise Migration Agreements under the Subclass 457 Visa: Much Ado about Nothing?' (2014) 27 *Australian Journal of Labour Law* 86.

83 DIAC, *Labour Agreement Information Pack* (2012), 1.

raise questions about what procedures are followed in negotiations and how exhaustive are checks on sponsors' record of compliance with immigration and labour laws.

The redirecting of lower skilled migrant workers from the standard 457 visa programme into labour agreements is further evidence of an institutionalised conception of exploitation in terms of employer malfeasance, while regulatory structures intensifying migrant worker precariousness (creating lack of transparency or relationships of dependency) are left intact. The next section argues that another key element of this regulatory context is the pathways to residency for temporary visa workers, which in recent years have favoured employer sponsorship even more strongly and, in so doing, some temporary workers over others.

The carrot of permanent residence

As the opening narrative poignantly depicted, 457 visa workers' aspirations for permanent residence can amplify further their reliance on employer sponsors.[84] The number of 457 visa workers granted permanent skilled visas can be well over 40 per cent of new 457 visas issued in a year.[85] Of course, the number of visa workers who aim for permanent residence is likely to be higher still, since these include those whose applications were rejected or who did not apply because they were clearly ineligible. A wide-scale government survey in 2012 found that 71 per cent of 457 visa workers intended to apply for residence after their visa expired.[86] At the same time, it should not be assumed that temporary migrant workers are always hoping to immigrate permanently, nor that aspirations for residence apply evenly. A recent global Gallop poll found that, worldwide, twice as many people would move for temporary work than would move permanently.[87] Nevertheless, sweeping changes to the permanent skilled migration programmes in 2011 and 2012 ensured that this dependency, where it exists, became more pronounced.

By way of background, there are two broad skilled-based routes to residence in Australia: the General Skilled Migration programme (GSM) and Employer Nomination Scheme (ENS) (which includes the Regional Sponsored Migration Scheme (RSMS), which Radovan Laski referred to in his promise to Bhawna Verma in the opening narrative).[88] GSM visas are points-tested visas open to independent applicants, applicants sponsored by

84 Philip Martin, *Managing Labor Migration: Temporary Worker Programs for the 21st Century* (International Institute for Labour Studies, 2003), 4–5.

85 In 2013–14, 43,170 permanent skilled visas were granted to 457 visa workers, while 98,570 457 visas were granted: DIBP, *Subclass 457 Quarterly Report at 30 June 2014* (2014), Tables 1.04 and 1.27.

86 *More Than Temporary Report*, above n. 72, 4.

87 Julie Ray and Neli Esipova, 'More Adults Would Move for Temporary Work than Permanently', *Gallup World*, 9 March 2012.

88 Subclass 186 Employer Nomination Scheme visa; subclass 187 Regional Skilled Migration Scheme visa.

a family member in a regional area and applicants nominated by a state or territory government.[89] The GSM program borrowed policy settings from Canada, focussed on independent points-tested admissions, which are still dominant in that country today. ENS visas, on the other hand, closely reflect the structure of 457 visas, requiring employer sponsorship in a nominated occupation, which must be gazetted and subject to market-based salaries. RSMS visa requirements are similar, although nominated occupations are not restricted by a gazetted list. The ENS/RSMS model is more like permanent skilled migration pathways in the USA (E-1, E-2 and E-3 categories), which are employer-sponsored and highly skilled. In Australia, while the support of an employer is a pre-requisite for ENS applicants, it can also benefit applicants for points-tested visas, who receive additional points when they have at least 12 months of local work experience in a relevant skilled occupation.[90]

In Australia, sponsored skilled migration has become the dominant pathway to permanent residency. After the points test was first introduced in 1979, points tested pathways to residence for skilled migrants quickly prevailed, especially under the conservative Howard Coalition government, which strongly emphasised skilled over family-based settlers from the late 1990s. However, by the mid 2000s, policy analysts criticised the employment outcomes of these skilled residents (including particularly former international students who often chose qualifications on the basis of the potential occupational points they would accrue).[91] The incoming Labor government in 2007 moved quickly to tighten the points-tested GSM program and make the employer sponsored ENS programme more generous.[92] Prioritising 'demand-driven' over 'supply-driven' skilled pathways to residence has been the mainstay in the USA and is now increasingly evident in Australia (and to a lesser extent Canada).[93]

This deliberate shift was achieved in Australia in July 2011 by dramatically narrowing the eligibility criteria for independent points-tested visas under the GSM programme. The government shrank the gazetted list of occupations for permanent residency through GSM (known as the Skilled Occupation List (SOL)), excluding many trades or low-skilled qualifications and abolished the availability of extra points that had been available for certain occupations deemed in demand. Furthermore, the allocation of points on the points test itself was significantly reconfigured: fewer points

89 The GSM visas include subclass 189 Skilled – Independent visa, subclass 190 Skilled – Sponsored visa and subclass 489 Skilled – Nominated or Sponsored (Provisional) visa.

90 The points test is set out at *Migration Regulations* sch 6C.

91 Bob Birrell, Lesleyanne Hawthorne and Sue Richardson, *Evaluation of the General Skilled Migration Categories* (Cth of Australia, 2006), 168ff.

92 Grants of employer sponsored visas rose from 16,585 in 2006–7 to 44,345 in 2010–11, while Skilled–Independent visa grants fell from 54,179 to 36,167 in the same period: DIAC, *Population Flows: Immigration Aspects 2010–11* (2012), 5.

93 Rey Koslowski, 'Selective Migration Policy Models and Changing Realities of Implementation' (2014) 52(3) *International Migration* 26.

were available for Australian work experience and qualifications, while additional points were available for higher degree qualifications and extensive work experience (whether in Australia or overseas) and superior English competency. A new method of applying for GSM visas through a selection register was introduced in 2012. 'SkillSelect' requires prospective applicants to express interest in skilled migration before they are invited to lodge a visa application. Hopeful applicants who are not immediately invited to apply remain in a pool that may be used by employers to initiate conversations regarding sponsorship to Australia. GSM occupations, which were previously uncapped, are now subject to application ceilings that limit the pools of applicants from particular occupational fields.[94] All of these changes were squarely addressed at restricting access to points-tested residence for graduating international students in Australia and directing hopeful residents towards sponsorship through the ENS programme or as pooled applicants in SkillSelect.

Concurrently, in July 2012, the ENS sponsored permanent visa category was also radically simplified and given priority in processing. Visa applicants must be nominated by an approved Australian employer sponsor for an occupation on a list, the Consolidated Sponsored Occupation List (CSOL), which governs ENS, 457 and state/territory sponsored GSM visas, stipulates managerial, professional, associate professional and trade occupations, and is far more expansive than the SOL for the GSM.[95] The ENS scheme, unlike the GSM, contains no occupational caps. The scheme is divided into three streams. The Direct Entry stream, for people who have never or only briefly worked in Australia, requires the visa applicant to demonstrate three years' work experience in their field, and moderate English language ability and to undertake a skills assessment in their occupation (unless exceptions apply). A separate Temporary Residence Transition Stream was created for applicants currently holding 457 visas, who were granted considerable concessions, including lesser English language skills, no skills assessment and two years of work experience rather than three. A third stream provides for ENS visas negotiated as part of a labour agreement, with negotiated age, skills and English language requirements as set out in the agreement.

To the extent that these changes reserved residence for 'more highly skilled' workers who are already in Australia over 'lesser skilled' and offshore applicants, they reflect approaches increasingly taken elsewhere. In Canada, the Canadian Experience Class visa, established in 2008, gives priority for points-tested residence to highly skilled workers who have been in Canada for at least two years.[96] Of the 862,500 permanent residents admitted to the

94 *Migration Regulations* sch 2 cl 189.211.

95 Both the CSOL and SOL are currently gazetted in the *Specification of Occupations, a Person or Body, a Country or Countries* (IMMI 14/048, F2014L00749) (Cth).

96 Canada, *Immigration and Refugee Protection Regulations*, SOR/2002-227, s 87.1(1).

USA on the basis of their skills between 1995 and 2010, 88 per cent were temporary residents just prior to being granted their green card.[97]

However, by linking permanent residence so strongly to sponsorship (both on the 457 and ENS visa), a significant effect of the reforms in Australia was demonstrably to enhance the dependency of all temporary workers who aspire to stay. In 2014, the FWO reported that a Chinese man performed unpaid worked for 12 months in Adelaide, South Australia, as an accountant under what was termed work experience, although his services were charged out to clients. Genuinely fearful that he would not secure his RSMS visa, he refused to cooperate with the investigation or any litigation and the FWO achieved only a modest A$9,000 back payment for him. In 2015, the FWO alleged that an Indian couple working in Indian restaurants in regional Victoria were reluctant to complain about being paid no wages for 14 months because they were reliant on their employer for sponsorship of an RSMS visa. In fact, relationships of dependency can continue for two years after the grant of the permanent visa, since an RSMS visa may be cancelled if employment is terminated in that time and DIBP is not satisfied that the visa-holder has made a genuine effort to be engaged in that employment for two years.[98]

But there is more specific precariousness here, for 457 visa-holders in particular. This may seem paradoxical since 457 visa workers are so strongly privileged as future settlers by these policy settings: in 2013–14, 457 visa-holders comprised 77 per cent of ENS grants.[99] The difficulty arises because the concessions for 457 visa workers are only available to those who have worked two years full-time with the employer who is sponsoring the ENS.[100] If the worker changes employers under the 457 visa, they must accrue another two years before applying for an ENS visa with that employer. This was a significant modification to earlier versions of the ENS. Previously, certain concessions were available to ENS applicants based on the length of time working in Australia, rather than time on the 457 visa in particular and time working for this sponsor. These revisions considerably increase incentives for 457 visa workers to stay in unhappy employment relationships, with substandard entitlements, to take advantage of this pathway, which promises fully equal benefits, residence and later citizenship. While these changes more readily facilitate the transition from 457 visa to residence, they also accord greater significance to what the earlier *Worker Protection Act* reforms kept in place: visa workers' dependence on their employer sponsor. Cognisant of the propensity of this pathway to create a bonded employment relationship, the Azarias review recommended changing the threshold requirement for the Temporary Residence Transition Stream to two years of work on a 457 visa but only one year with the nominating employer.[101] I

97 Monica Boyd, 'Recruiting High Skill Labour in North America: Policies, Outcomes and utures' (2014) 52(3) *International Migration* 40, 43.

98 *Migration Act* s 137Q.

99 DIBP, *Annual Report 2013–14* (2014), 51.

100 *Migration Regulations* reg 5.19(3)(c).

101 Azarias *et al.*, *Robust New Foundations*, above n. 47, 82.

suggest, instead, liberalising the requirement simply to two years on a 457 visa with any employer.

But other temporary migrant workers arguably fare worse than 457 visa-holders as a result of these reforms. Emphasising pathways from the 457 visa to employer sponsorship residence correspondingly weakened pathways from student and working holiday visas. Without 457 visas, applicants for an ENS visa are eligible only through the Direct Entry Scheme, which requires three years' full-time work experience, creating virtually insuperable obstacles to graduating students (who in most cases are restricted to 40 hours work per fortnight) or WHMs who are restricted to a maximum of six months' work with any one employer. In any event, a 2014 study of international student graduates in Australia noted that many despaired at obtaining employer sponsorship at all because of poor employer attitudes towards them.[102] While in theory employer-sponsored residence through the ENS is available for 457 visa-holders on labour agreements, in practice this pathway is also virtually non-existent. In 2013–14, of the 47,450 permanent places given to ENS applicants, only nine were under the labour agreement stream.[103]

A significant unintended consequence of these changes, therefore, has been to create incentives for all these temporary residents to seek standard 457 visas as the favoured pathway to residence, keeping temporary migrant workers in prolonged temporariness. This likely reshaped the 457 visa programme itself and reintroduced a more highly vulnerable profile of 457 visa worker without addressing the structural sources of their precariousness. In 2012–13, 49 per cent of 457 visas applications were lodged onshore by people who held a temporary visa, 17 per cent more than in the previous year.[104] That year also saw a significant increase in 457 visa workers with no family dependents and from South Asia, a major source region of the surge in international students in the late 2000s.[105] Furthermore, the accommodation and food services industry comprised a record share of the programme (9.4 per cent of grants, quadrupling between 2010–11 and 2012–13), with the average salary among 457 visa workers in this industry of A$55,000 compared to A$83,000 for the programme overall.[106] Several hundred international students and other temporary residents quickly fell prey to various employment/migration agents who began illegally charging up to A$70,000 for a job placement and visa, no longer promising permanent residence (like Radovan Laski in the opening narrative) but now 457 visas.[107]

102 Jill Blackmore *et al.*, *Australian International Graduates and the Transition to Employment* (Deakin University, 2014), 18.

103 DIBP, *Annual Report 2013–14*, above n. 99, 51.

104 Azarias *et al.*, *Robust New Foundations*, above n. 47, 36.

105 Ibid. 28, 43.

106 *More Than Temporary Report*, above n. 72, 17.

107 SBS News, 'Dodgy Employers Investigated Over "Exploitation" of 457 Visa Holders', 8 October 2014 (Abby Dinham and Manpreet Singh); ABC News, 'Sydney Businessman Eddie Kang Accused of Ripping Off Foreign Students Over 457 Visa Contracts', *Lateline*, 15 October 2013 (Steve Cannane).

The final major phase of reforms considered in this chapter was devised in the wake of these demographic changes to the 457 visa programme. In 2013, the Labor government introduced adjustments to strengthen the scheme's integrity amidst a shrill public debate for stronger protections for resident employees. The next section analyses these regulatory modifications as well as proposals made by sectors of the union movement defending against the spectre of a globalised labour market manifest in the 457 visa. It argues that, on top of restrictions to residence for unsponsored workers, these protections for locals often took an even heavier toll on the precariousness of temporary residents not (yet) on 457 visas.

Protecting local jobs

In early 2013, a federal election year, Labor Prime Minister Julia Gillard expressed concerns that work was being made available to 457 visa workers at the expense of residents. This rapidly expanded into a wholesale (and, frankly, inflammatory) critique of the entire visa scheme. She pronounced, 'We all have a fight to win. A fight … to stop foreign workers being put at the front of the queue, with Australian workers at the back.'[108] The Immigration Minister declared that some employers 'are using 457 visas to discriminate against locals'.[109] This rhetoric drew from Australia's historical suspicion of temporary migration, which is periodically challenged as a 'backdoor immigration scheme'.[110] The perceived threat posed by temporary migrants to the domestic labour force seems especially potent in relation to lower skilled occupations.[111] As mentioned above, such anxieties lent support to the higher skills and English language requirements introduced by the 2009 Worker Protection reforms.

Of course, social objections to temporary labour schemes are not uniquely Australian. Philosopher Michael Walzer memorably likened them to a 'family with live-in servants', rejecting temporary migration as morally suspect in a liberal democracy.[112] In Australian debates, though, questions are raised less about the structural sources of precariousness embedded in temporary immigration status than the legitimacy of temporary workers' presence in the Australian labour market itself. Peter Mares has observed that the combination of these workers' 'foreignness' along with their

108 Phillip Coorey, 'Whatever It Takes', *Australian Financial Review*, 9 March 2013.

109 Brendan O'Connor, MIAC, 'Reforms to the Temporary Work (Skilled) (Subclass 457) Program' (media release, 23 February 2013).

110 E.g. Stephanie Toh and Michael Quinlan, 'Safeguarding the Global Contingent Workforce? Guestworkers in Australia' (2009) 30(5) *International Journal of Manpower* 453, 455; Bob Birrell and Ernest Healy, 'Globalisation and Temporary Entry' (1997) 5(4) *People and Place* 43.

111 Alexander Reilly, 'The Ethics of Seasonal Labour Migration' (2011) 20(1) *Griffith Law Review* 127, 130.

112 Michael Walzer, *Spheres of Justice* (Basic Books, 1983), 52.

temporary presence contributes to a view that they 'disrupt the normal Australian order'.[113] At Federation, threats to the 'Australian standard' of industrial protections and threats to Australia's cultural homogeneity were easily conflated. This is arguably evident still in the statement by Construction Forestry Mining and Energy Union (CFMEU) National Secretary John Sutton in 2008:

> Make no mistake, the large movement of guest workers from the Asia/Pacific into our small labour market would have profound effects on the ability of governments or unions to uphold standards. It is no exaggeration to warn that an open-door approach could lead to the Mexicanisation of our job market where lower skilled jobs would be performed almost exclusively by guest workers.[114]

Government alarm about perceived employer abuse of the scheme centred on statistics showing a record number of primary 457 visa grants outstripping the national employment growth rate.[115] Average wages for 457 visa workers fell from A$96,800 in mid 2011 to A$89,900 in 2013.[116] Pointing to these trends, the government concluded that employers were using the scheme outside of 'a demonstrated genuine labour shortage'.[117]

However, portraying these peaks in application numbers as integrity failures or rorts may have obscured the role of the wholesale reforms to the permanent skilled migration programme in restructuring incentives for hopeful applicants. After 2012, most graduating international students and WHMs found themselves no longer eligible for either independent GSM visas or employer sponsored ENS visas. It is readily understandable that both cohorts would turn to 457 visas as an avenue towards residence when other options were foreclosed. The presence of these groups arguably expanded the proportion of 457 visa-holders in occupations in those industries with lower average salaries. And these new 457 visa workers were delegitimated in policy commentary and the media as either temporary migrants exploiting the system as a 'backdoor' to residence or evidence of visa 'churn', temporary migrants instrumentalising the ability to transfer from one temporary visa to another to remain in Australia in the medium term.[118] This rhetoric

113 Peter Mares, 'The Permanent Shift to Temporary Migration', *Inside Story*, 16 June 2009.

114 John Sutton, 'Asia-Pacific Labour Mobility and the Two Track Labour Market' (2008) 16 *People and Place* 85, 89.

115 There were 68,310 457 visa grants in 2011–12: DIAC, *Subclass 457 State-Territory Summary Report 1 July 2011 to 30 June 2012* (2012), 3.

116 Tim Colebatch, 'The Books are Being Cooked on 457 Visas', *Sydney Morning Herald*, 19 March 2013.

117 Senate Legal and Constitutional Affairs Committee, Parliament of Australia, 'Inquiry into the Migration Amendment (Temporary Sponsored Visas) Bill 2013', June 2013, 16.

118 Bob Birrell and Ernest Healy, *Immigration and Unemployment in 2014* (Centre for Population and Urban Research, Monash University, 2014), 4.

obscures the fact that making the strategic choice to apply for a temporary visa for which one is eligible is a right of any non-citizen.

In an effort to address what the government portrayed as either employer or migrant worker manipulation of the programme, the final cluster of amendments assessed in this chapter was passed by the Labor government in 2013. The *Migration Amendment (Temporary Sponsored Visas) Act 2013* (Cth) (*457 Amendment Act*), effecting substantial changes to the 457 visa, was the very last piece of legislation passed before a federal election. It included important mechanisms to bolster visa workers' working conditions, which are considered below. But these were overshadowed in public debate by the incorporation of labour market testing in the employer nomination process in a form that garnered a mixed reception. It is to this element that this section next turns.

Labour market testing

In two respects, the *457 Amendment Act* transformed the intersection between the 457 visa and prevailing labour market conditions. First, the requirement that a sponsor provide conditions of employment no less favourable than residents performing equivalent work 'in the person's workplace' was expanded to residents' work 'at the same location', enlarging the assessment of market wage rates and conditions to a regional locality.[119] Exemptions from this requirement were also narrowed from positions attracting an annual salary of A$180,000 to A$250,000.[120]

More dramatically, it introduced mandatory labour market testing for many occupations.[121] Prior to approving a nomination, the minister must be satisfied that, in light of evidence of labour market testing, a suitably qualified and experienced citizen or resident is not readily available to fill the nominated position, nor, in the agricultural sector, is a WHM eligible to be employed.[122] Employers are required to provide evidence of their attempts to recruit suitable residents prior to making a sponsorship application. Possible exemptions are available, however, for professional and paraprofessional occupations (except engineering and nursing occupations, which cannot be exempt from labour market testing under the Act) as well as occupations and nationalities that give rise to international obligations under trade agreements.[123] Employers must also stipulate whether any redundancies of Australian workers have been made in the four months prior to the sponsorship application.[124] A federal election and change of

119 Reg 2.72(10).
120 *Specification of Income Threshold and Annual Earnings* (IMMI 13/028, F2013L01231) (Cth).
121 *Migration Act* s 140GBA.
122 Ibid. ss 140GBA(3) and 140GBA(7).
123 Section 140GBC(2)(a).
124 Section 140GBA(4A).

government took place before these reforms came into effect and the incoming Abbott Coalition government in 2013 immediately diluted the impact of these requirements. Labour market testing was limited to 35 per cent of occupations, with all professional and paraprofessional occupations exempt, other than nursing and engineering.[125] The permitted timeframe for advertising a vacancy prior to lodging a sponsorship application was increased from four to twelve months.[126]

The introduction of labour market testing was also immediately subject to incisive analysis by legal scholars. Joo-Cheong Tham broadly endorsed it, finding the controversy surrounding it 'puzzling' since it simply requires employers to 'demonstrate a labour shortage', which is after all the premise of their use of the scheme.[127] Joanna Howe, joined by Andrew Stewart and Alex Reilly, on the other hand, approved of labour market testing in principle but rejected this model.[128] They pointed out that, originally a minor component of the scheme,[129] labour market testing was abandoned in 2001 in favour of objective standards such as a minimum salary threshold and occupation list. Experts had advised that labour market testing had imposed a heavy bureaucratic burden on conscientious employers since evidence was onerous to gather and difficult to verify while unscrupulous employers can evade the stipulations by advertising jobs in a way that elicited minimal local candidate response.[130] Thus, Howe, Stewart and Reilly recommended that labour market testing be done largely 'independently of employers', by a government agency independent of the immigration department, and be fed into a shorter list of occupations eligible for 457 visas that were truly in demand. They proposed that employers recruiting for occupations on this revised list not be required to adduce any additional proof of labour market shortage. However, they allowed that employers

125 See *Specification of Occupations Exempt from Labour Market Testing* (IMMI 13/137, F2013L01952) (Cth); *Determination of International Trade Obligations Relating to Labour Market Testing* (IMMI 14/107, F2014L01510) (Cth); Senate Legal and Constitutional Affairs Legislation Committee, Parliament of Australia, 'Question Taken on Notice, Supplementary Budget Estimates Hearing: 19 November 2013, Immigration and Border Protection Portfolio' (SE13/0310).

126 *Determination of Specified Period in Which Labour Market Testing Must be Undertaken* (IMMI 13/136, F2013L01953) (Cth).

127 Joo-Cheong Tham, Submission No 22 to the Senate Committee on Legal and Constitutional Affairs, Parliament of Australia, 'Inquiry into the Migration Amendment (Temporary Sponsored Visas) Bill 2013', 21 June 2013, 14.

128 Joanna Howe, Alexander Reilly and Andrew Stewart, Submission No 8 to the Senate Committee on Legal and Constitutional Affairs, Parliament of Australia, 'Inquiry into the Migration Amendment (Temporary Sponsored Visas) Bill 2013', 20 June 2013, [8].

129 *Migration Regulations* regs 1.20H(2) and 1.20B as at 1 August 1996 required labour market testing only for positions lasting more than 12 months and involving 'non-key activities', which were positions not essential to the business operations of the employer or requiring specialist skills or knowledge.

130 External Reference Group, *In Australia's Interests: A Review of the Temporary Residence Program* (June 2002), 18.

could nominate positions in occupations outside of this list, including semi-skilled occupations, on the condition that they conduct labour market testing themselves. (This model is similar to those in the UK and New Zealand where employer labour market testing is required only if the job is not on the occupational shortage list.) An independent review led by John Azarias into the integrity of the 457 visa scheme in 2014 broadly accepted Howe's recommendation, as have other inquiries.[131] Azarias suggested that a tripartite ministerial advisory council make evidence-based recommendations on eligible occupations, replacing both the overbroad and rigid CSOL and employer-reliant labour market testing with more a transparent, efficient and flexible process.

These nascent debates about labour market testing in Australia mirror policy challenges confronting other Western states. For instance, countries throughout the European Economic Area (EEA), which includes European Union countries and Liechtenstein, Norway and Iceland, require labour market tests to ensure that no EEA workers are available before a non-EEA national is admitted to fill the vacancy. Globally, policy analysts delineate weak labour market tests based on employer 'attestation' from stronger tests based on 'certification'.[132] Attestation, the historically dominant approach in Australia, simply requires employers to state that they have unsuccessfully searched for local workers without government scrutiny into their recruitment efforts. The H-1B visa scheme in the USA takes this approach, which has been shown to be easy for employers to manipulate or circumnavigate. Employers must simply state that they are offering genuine jobs, pay the prevailing wage and there is no strike in progress, all via an internet application; the Department of Labor does not verify the information provided except through irregular audits and routinely approves almost all applications.[133] Indeed, the OECD has concluded that employers' identification of skills shortages through attestation is widely considered unreliable in the absence of certification, or testing that requires independent verification by public authorities to confirm actual labour needs.[134] In Ireland, for instance, the public employment service must certify that employers have advertised the vacancy and found no local workers before applying for a work permit. Australia's requirement to notify DIBP of any recent redundancies prior to applying for sponsorship has fewer precedents than other

131 Senate Legal and Constitutional Affairs References Committee, Parliament of Australia, 'Inquiry into the Framework and Operation of Subclass 457 Visa, Enterprise Migration Agreements and Regional Migration Agreements' (June 2013); Azarias *et al.*, *Robust New Foundations*, above n. 47, 14.

132 Philip Martin and Martin Ruhs, 'Independent Commissions and Labour Migration: The British MAC' (2014) 11(1) *Migration Letters* 23.

133 Ibid. 25; Joanna Howe, 'Is the Net Cast Too Wide? An Assessment of Whether the Regulatory Design of the 457 Visa Meets Australia's Skill Needs' (2013) 41 *Federal Law Review* 443, 456.

134 OECD, *International Migration Outlook: Sopemi 2009* (2009), 134.

elements of its labour market testing, although in the USA employers with more than 15 per cent of H-1B workers must certify they did not lay off locals prior to hiring H-1B workers.[135]

The reintroduction of labour market testing was broadly welcomed by the union movement in Australia, which had advocated for legislative guarantees enshrining employment preferences for locals over 457 visa workers for several years. In 2012 the federal construction union, the CFMEU, campaigned (unsuccessfully) for exemptions from anti-discrimination laws permitting employers to preference residents over temporary workers in recruitment and redundancies.[136] In 2013 the CFMEU went further, advocating (again unsuccessfully) for a legislated 'right of appeal for Australian workers' assessed by employers as unsuitable for positions filled by 457 visa workers.[137] Various unions have sought assurances in industrial enterprise agreements that employers would refrain from using the 457 visa scheme. These perspectives are founded on a clear logic. If residents are being made redundant, or overlooked for vacancies, migrant workers can no longer be said to be filling labour market gaps. The *457 Amendment Act* sees labour market testing as a means of avoiding such scenarios, articulating its objective as to 'balance the interests of Australian workers with the need to strengthen protections for overseas workers'.[138] In essence, these interventions imply that adequate protection for resident workers demands, to some extent, higher levels of vulnerability in, or exclusion of, migrant workers. If more precarious working conditions for migrant workers result from a marginal immigration status voluntarily acquired, this is seen as a necessary evil.

But Tham has argued against union proposals that employers be required to accord preference to residents in retrenchment on the basis that employers could then threaten migrant employees with termination in order to force their acceptance of inferior working conditions.[139] Even beyond their security of tenure, this would inject further precariousness into migrant workers' conditions of labour. Although Tham has supported labour market testing, I suggest that Tham's argument on preferential retrenchment applies also, although perhaps less obviously, to the preferential hiring in a

135 Philip Martin, Manolo Abella and Christiane Kuptsch, *Managing Labor Migration in the Twenty-First Century* (Yale University Press, 2006), 67.

136 CFMEU, Submission No 382 to the Senate Standing Committee on Legal and Constitutional Affairs, Parliament of Australia, 'Inquiry into the Exposure Draft of Human Rights and Anti-Discrimination Bill 2012', 21 December 2012, 3ff.

137 CFMEU, Submission No 41 to the Senate Legal and Constitutional Affairs References Committee, Parliament of Australia, 'Inquiry into the Framework and Operation of Subclass 457 Visas, Enterprise Migration Agreements and Regional Migration Agreements', May 2013, 7.

138 Supplementary Explanatory Memorandum, Migration Amendment (Temporary Sponsored Visas) Bill 2013 (Cth), 1.

139 Joo-Cheong Tham, 'Multiculturalism and Temporary Migration: Where Does Justice Fit?' (Paper presented to the Australian Multicultural Council, draft on file with author), 8.

scheme unpinned by labour market testing. It might be imagined that excluding 457 visa applicants from job opportunities protects them from precarious work simply by preventing them from working in Australia at all (after all, this was the rationale asserted in relation to the higher application thresholds around language and skills imposed in 2009). However, again, this is only true if we imagine applicants for 457 visas on foreign shores, thereby assuming that if restricting employment opportunities breeds precarity, at least it does not do so here.

In fact, we know that applications for 457 visas are increasingly made onshore, by people already working in Australia as international students and WHMs. Permitting recruitment that discriminates on the basis of immigration status, as labour market testing does, can further limit the labour market mobility of these temporary migrant workers, and thereby further intensify the precariousness of their work. Changes to pathways towards residence for international students have left ever greater numbers of job seekers on temporary post-study visas in the Australian labour market. Aside from WHMs in the agricultural sector (for whom an exception was made in the labour market testing provisions), all international students and WHMs must now be passed over in favour of resident job applicants before a 457 visa in certain occupations will be issued. The introduction of labour market testing leaves these temporary workers with far less secure prospects for transitioning to 457 visas after their temporary visa expires. Insofar as these migrants are already working for the employers who wish to retain them through the 457 visa scheme, the 2013 reforms place little value on employment relationships they have already established during their time in Australia.

It is, of course, hardly surprising that Australian labour immigration policies are driven by the national interest. In Tham and Leigh Hubbard's words, '[t]here is nothing necessarily xenophobic in emphasising that the government's primary duty in relation to job creation is to the citizens and permanent residents'.[140] The need to strengthen the integrity of the immigration programme, safeguard national borders or protect the domestic labour force are regularly invoked to justify laws and policies that create precarious living and working conditions for migrant workers. However, this chapter has argued that more robust protections for temporary migrants can coincide with these interests. Far from minimising migrant precariousness, exclusion and immigration enforcement sustain it, and in so doing, they compromise the working conditions of residents. Indeed, allegations that temporary labour migration in itself constitutes a threat to residents simply divert attention from considering the quality and security of work for migrants and residents alike.

140 Leigh Hubbard and Joo-Cheong Tham, '457 Visa Scheme: Time for a Proper Debate', *The Guardian*, 17 June 2013.

Strengthening visa workers' employment conditions

Along with a range of other adjustments to the programme beyond the scope of this chapter,[141] the *457 Amendment Act* entailed two further substantial reforms that may go further in strengthening 457 visa workers' labour market position.

The most significant was to extend the period between cessation of employment of visa cancellation from 28 days to 90 days in condition 8107.[142] Although numerous inquiries and advocates had urged this change, without explanation it was not included in the Worker Protection reforms in 2009.[143] As Peter Mares points out, in practice, immigration officials often 'extended the grace period, but bureaucratic discretion is no replacement for a legislated right'.[144] As argued in this and the previous chapters, the effect of this modification on 457 visa workers' bargaining power cannot be understated. With 90 days now to seek access to welfare support, employment placement services or simply to make alternative arrangements to leave Australia, 457 visa workers can be more assertive in resisting exploitation.

The final element of reforms discussed in this chapter is less unequivocally supportive of workers' rights. This was the move to vest legislative powers in Fair Work Inspectors (appointed under the *FW Act*) to monitor employers' compliance with three 457 visa sponsorship obligations: ensuring that workers are paid market rates, that they are working in the position approved in their nomination and that employers cooperate with inspectors.[145] This marked the first time that the FWO was authorised to investigate immigration compliance, supplementing the 32 DIBP inspectors policing sponsor compliance with the 300 Fair Work Inspectors already monitoring workplaces across Australia.[146] This initiative was welcomed by unions and employer representatives alike. Giving effect to this scheme, random audits by the FWO in 2013–14 assessed 1,029 employers (of 1,902 457 visa workers), finding 18 per cent of workers underpaid or not working in their nominated

141 These include: a sponsorship obligation not to recover costs associated with sponsorship or recruitment from the employee or third parties regardless of the worker's consent (reg 2.87); a sponsorship obligation to meet training benchmarks for the duration of the sponsorship (regs 2.59(j), 2.82 and 2.87B); mandatory licencing and registration of sponsored workers (condition 8107(3)(c)); a clearer prohibition of on-hiring arrangements except through labour agreements (sch 2 cl 457.223(4)(ba)); and fewer exemptions for the English language requirement. A nomination ceiling of a 'reasonable' number of sponsored workers was introduced by the Labor government in 2013 and then abolished in the early months of the Abbott Coalition government in 2014.

142 Conditions 8107(3)(b) and 8107(3B)(b).

143 Evidence to JSCM, Parliament of Australia, 'Inquiry into Temporary Business Visas', 14 March 2007, 8 and 22 (Michelle Bissett, ACTU); *Deegan Report*, above n. 18, 68; *More Than Temporary Report*, above n. 72, 14.

144 Peter Mares, 'Fixing and Fiddling on 457s', *Inside Story*, 7 June 2013.

145 *Memorandum of Understanding between DIAC and FWO*, 3 July 2013.

146 DIAC *et al.*, Submission No 24 to the Senate Legal and Constitutional Affairs References Committee, above n. 45, 17.

position.[147] In one case, a 457 visa worker recruited as a customer service manager was found working as a cleaner and being paid just A$28,000.[148]

While it is extremely positive that this monitoring function has directed crucial resources toward employer non-compliance, optimism may be misplaced because of conflicts of interest that may arise between Fair Work Inspectors' oversight of 457 visa workers' compliance with visa conditions and their policing of labour conditions. Rosemary Owens and Andrew Stewart pointed out, in an expert report by prepared for the FWO in 2013, that entrusting labour inspectors with immigration compliance can undermine labour rights enforcement under an international labour convention to which Australia is a party.[149] It is unclear for example, what the outcome has been for the 338 457 visa workers whose sponsors were detected by the FWO as possibly non-compliant. If this placed their sponsorship arrangements at risk in any way, other 457 visa workers could well be far more reluctant to lodge complaints with the FWO or indeed cooperate with their investigation knowing FWO staff immediately refer suspicious activity to DIBP. The complex implications of the coordination between DIBP and FWO for the precariousness of migrant labour are considered in more detail in Chapter 9.

Returning agency to 457 visa workers

This chapter has reviewed major reforms introduced to the 457 visa program between 2009 and 2014, concluding that, on the whole, they have not adequately attended to the uniquely precarious situations in which many 457 visa workers work. Naturally, disadvantages created through temporariness and lack of formal citizenship or residence can never be completely dissolved. However, what has been overlooked in these reforms is the agency of the migrant workers themselves. More could be done to foreground participatory inclusion to promote migrant workers' resiliency in relationships with their employers, in particular to support temporary migrant workers to make empowering decisions within the limited industrial options available to them. This final section, therefore, develops proposals along a number of lines: first to extend 457 visa workers' labour market mobility through a redesigned visa structure, second to reduce dependencies on

147 FWO, *Annual Report 2013–14* (2014), 30.

148 FWO, *457 Visa Monitoring – Detail Report 2013–14* (2014).

149 Andrew Stewart and Rosemary Owens, *Experience or Exploitation? The Nature, Prevalence and Regulation of Unpaid Work Experience, Internships and Trial Periods in Australia* (University of Adelaide, Report for the Fair Work Ombudsman, January 2013), 182ff, citing Labour Inspection Convention, 1947 (ILO No 81), International Labour Conference, 30th sess, opened for signature 11 July 1947 (entered into force 7 April 1950). Art 3(2) provides: 'Any further duties which may be entrusted to labour inspectors shall not be such as to interfere with the effective discharge of their primary duties or to prejudice in any way the authority and impartiality which are necessary to inspectors in their relations with employers and workers.'

sponsors through reformed pathways to permanent residence, and third to empower workers to give voice to concerns and participate in institutional structures delivering concrete redress.

One possible mechanism to reduce dependency on employers and enlarge 457 visa workers' mobility would be to abolish employer sponsorship for this visa subclass altogether. Indeed, such a proposal has been made in a joint report by the Organization for Security and Cooperation in Europe, the International Organization for Migration and the ILO, which recommends that migrant workers be given 'an unlimited right to change employment and occupation after a short period of, for example, three months'.[150] The UK's Tier 1 programme admits highly skilled migrants without a prior job offer.

However, at no point in the fifteen-year life of the scheme have Australian governments given serious consideration to crafting a temporary skilled migration programme without employer sponsorship. Sponsorship is widely viewed as a mechanism to protect visa workers. A recent study comparing sponsored with unsponsored skilled residents in Australia found that 92 per cent of the former were fully employed after six months with 90 per cent of those in professional or managerial positions.[151] Conversely, only 82 per cent of unsponsored residents who had applied from abroad were in full-time employment, with 75 per cent of these were using their skills. Sponsored migrants reported median salaries of A$75,000 at 12 months compared with just A$47,000 for those who were not sponsored.

Sponsorship is also appealing for protectionist reasons. By ensuring that migrant workers' access to the national labour market is temporary and highly circumscribed, employer sponsorship seems designed to protect residents from the downgrading of employment standards feared to occur if migrants were free to seek work across the labour market. The 457 visa scheme is directed at addressing skills shortages and its effectiveness in accomplishing this goal is ensured, at least in part, by regulating the eligibility of the various labour sectors to employ visa workers and restricting migrant workers to occupations in which those shortages are perceived to exist. As Tham and Campbell have argued, constraints on labour market mobility are inherent in such schemes.[152] Recent evidence from the USA indicates that labour mobility for temporary skilled (H-1B) workers there disappears entirely when the unemployment rate is high, arguably achieving

150 Organization for Security and Cooperation in Europe, International Organization for Migration and International Labour Organisation, *Handbook on Establishing Effective Labour Migration Policies in Countries of Origin and Destination* (2006), 115.

151 Lesleyanne Hawthorne and Anna To, 'Australian Employer Response to the Study-Migration Pathway: The Quantative Evidence 2007–2011' (2014) 52(3) *International Migration* 99, 110.

152 Joo-Cheong Tham and Iain Campbell, 'Equal Treatment for Temporary Migrant Workers and the Challenge of their Precariousness' (Paper presented at the Australian Labour Law Association Conference, Rydges Hotel, Canberra, 16–17 November 2012), 12.

a key goal of the programme.[153] Indeed, even international labour rights standards articulated in ILO and UN Conventions permit 'employer bonding' of temporary migrant workers for limited periods of time,[154] and many countries, such as Austria, Denmark and the UK only allow migrants on temporary permits to remain in the country for a certain period without a job after they have lost their employment.[155]

However, this chapter has sought to illustrate that insisting on precarious working conditions as a means of safeguarding residents' conditions does not work. The vulnerabilities that result from employer sponsorship risk degrading migrants' working conditions and thereby undercutting residents' entitlements as well. The intensity of the restriction in condition 8107 is so extreme that modifications short of outright abolition of sponsorship would still be desirable beyond the extension of period between cessation of employment and cancellation to 90 days. For instance, as Martin Ruhs has argued in his global survey of temporary labour migration, restricting migrant workers to a particular occupation or industry sector rather than a specific employer might adequately achieve the objectives of addressing labour shortages in particular industries with less coercive effects.[156] Indeed, such an industry restraint would be more analogous to the practical restrictions on residents' change of careers. Furthermore, while the 457 visa scheme remains subject to occupational limitations and employer sponsorship, the Australian labour market now contains tens of thousands of graduated international students on 485 visas (discussed in more detail in Chapter 3) who may remain in Australia for eighteen months to four years on visas with completely unrestricted work rights. Driven by Australia's historical ambivalence toward the presence of a temporary migrant workforce, this contradiction is rarely explicitly acknowledged much less confronted head on.

As well as modifying sponsorship, the pathways to residence must be adjusted. As long as the employer-sponsored ENS visa is accorded priority over independent skilled migration channels, temporary migrant workers may tend to remain in employment relationships marked by pronounced dependency. Conversely, if GSM visas accorded more points to applicants who have spent a significant period of time in Australia, this would better acknowledge the significance of the bonds and relationships that migrants develop by working in Australia, without exacerbating power disparities in the employment/sponsorship relationship. Alternatively, concessions in the

153 Hiroshi Motomura, 'Designing Temporary Worker Programs' (2013) 80 *The University of Chicago Law Review* 263, 272.

154 Migrant Workers Convention, above n. 13, art 52 permits member states to restrict free choice of employment for lawfully resident migrant workers to a maximum of two years, as does ILO Convention 143, above n. 13, art 14[a] (Australia is not a party to either Convention).

155 Ruhs, *The Price of Rights*, above n. 16, 70.

156 Ibid. 174–5.

ENS scheme could be based on the length of time working in Australia, rather than time on the 457 visa or time working for the sponsoring employer. This would improve the portability of 457 visa workers and reduce the incentives for international students to obtain 457 visas or stay in employment purely out of hope for future residency. Such a model resembles the Canadian Experience Class visa, which provides a pathway to residency to international students and temporary workers on the basis of work experience in particular skilled occupations in Canada over a specified time.

Beyond the visa framework itself, temporary migrant workers also require better assistance to pursue their employment entitlements without prejudicing their right to remain in Australia in the short term. Positive steps have been made in recent years towards disseminating information to migrant workers. The Australian Council of Trade Unions for instance has established a dedicated confidential phone line for 457 visa workers to seek assistance. An information booklet for migrant workers on employers' key sponsorship obligations, and basic *FW Act* entitlements, including the National Employment Standards, developed by DIBP with the Australian Council of Trade Unions, Department of Employment and the FWO is available through departmental websites. However, it is extraordinary that as recently as 2014, the Azarias inquiry still needed to recommend that 457 visa-holders be given a copy of their signed contract together with information on employment entitlements from the FWO and DIBP with their initial visa grant.[157]

Other proposals for facilitating workers' complaints or supporting workers to more fully participate in institutional structures that offer tangible redress remain unexplored. For instance, a 2007 parliamentary inquiry into the 457 visa programme recommended the introduction of a comprehensive confidential complaints mechanism, allowing workers to report abuses without provoking retaliatory action.[158] Such a facility seems particularly pressing given a 2012 study showing that only 8 per cent of 457 visa workers surveyed indicated that they were union members (compared to 18 per cent of residents).[159] Additionally, a more developed proposal is made in Chapter 9 for a new visa to allow any migrant worker to regularise their immigration status pending labour enforcement processes, which would greatly assist 457 visa workers fearing the cancellation of their visas consequent on the withdrawal of sponsorship by an employer. Furthermore, other transparency measures are lacking, as pointed out in numerous inquiries.[160] Unlike the FWO, DIBP does not publish detailed information about firms, industries, occupations or locations of 457 visa workers. Conversely in the UK and USA, information related to all sponsors is publicly accessible on a register or online database, in the case of the USA with information on how many

157 Azarias *et al.*, *Robust New Foundations*, above n. 47, 17.
158 *Permanent Benefits Report*, above n. 31, rec 19.
159 *More Than Temporary Report*, above n. 72, 18.
160 Azarias *et al.*, *Robust New Foundations*, above n. 47, 98.

migrants work for each sponsor and their wage rates. At present the only public disclosure of sanctions in Australia beyond overall statistics occurs if the sponsor challenges the sanction in a court or MRT. Comprehensive reporting of sponsorship sanctions or the results of monitoring, as occurs in other jurisdictions such as Canada, where Employment and Social Development Canada maintains a list of employers who have breached the rules or been suspended from their temporary labour scheme, would assist deterrence of employer misconduct and protect applicants for 457 visas. But, short of this, a list of 457 visa sponsors would enable migrant advocates and unions to scrutinise labour conditions, monitor visa compliance and aid vulnerable employees.

Conclusion

In many ways the various iterations of reforms to the 457 visa scheme and pathways to permanent residence have strengthened the hand of 457 visa workers in workplaces across Australia, when compared with the operation of the scheme in its earlier years. However, this chapter has argued that individualising the problem of exploitation as located in rogue employers and vulnerable migrants leaves unaddressed more enduring ways in which immigration controls can intensify pre-existing power differentials in migrant workers' employment relationships. In particular, a number of measures introduced in the name of protecting against exploitation or bolstering the integrity of the immigration programme simply increase insecurity for 457 visa-holders and other temporary workers alike. This chapter therefore closed by considering possible regulatory adjustments to the 457 visa scheme that might better empower temporary migrants at work. Part III turns to the precariousness of unauthorised migrant workers.

Part II

Unauthorised migrant labour

5 How immigration controls produce unauthorised migrant workers

> Mahabub Alam's visa was cancelled in December 2002 after he worked 22.25 hours in one week to help his employer who was temporarily short-staffed: more than the 20 hours per week permitted at that time.[1] Immigration compliance officers discovered the breach during a raid of Alam's house while looking for his friend. Without an authorised warrant, they searched his room and found a payslip documenting the 22.25 hours. Upon being immediately apprehended, his visa was cancelled at 11.00pm and he was detained at Villawood detention centre for three weeks over the Christmas–New Year period: he was unable to pay the A$10,000 bond required for his release because he was refused a phone call to ask his sister to arrange payment. The Full Federal Court overturned the cancellation in 2005 on the basis that evidence of the breach was illegally obtained.

De Genova has described the ever-present state of 'deportability' of migrants whose unauthorised status may be detected at any time.[2] The world over, unauthorised workers are notoriously vulnerable to exploitation because the costs associated with complaining about abusive treatment are dramatically higher for them than for others in the local labour market. Uneven immigration law enforcement, ubiquitous throughout the developed world, adds uncertainty to these coercive effects, as does the marginality of unauthorised status, which may or may not become known to authorities or even to the worker over time, as Alam's experiences suggest.

In the Australian context, the coercive experience of unauthorised workers is particularly acute because a highly codified legislative scheme constructs rigid binarisms between lawful and unlawful immigration status. Exacerbating the coercive consequences that can follow detection of unauthorised work status, unlawful status in Australia automatically triggers mandatory detention and summary removal without much of the judicial

1 *Minister for Immigration and Multicultural and Indigenous Affairs (MIMIA) v. Alam* (2005) 145 FCR 345, 349, 354 and 361.

2 Nicholas De Genova, 'Migrant "Illegality" and Deportability in Everyday Life' (2002) 31 *Annual Review of Anthropology* 419.

oversight or bureaucratic discretion that exist in other legal contexts or other Western countries. At the same time, belying its inflexible, codified appearance, the actual indeterminacy of the legal category of 'unauthorised work' in Australia injects uncertainty into the precariousness of unauthorised migrant labour.

This chapter explains how immigration rules in Australia constitute unauthorised migrant labour and govern its enforcement, explaining some significant points of contrast with like countries such as Canada or the USA. It commences with a brief overview of the profile of unauthorised workers in Australia, before turning to the factors that breed precariousness; from the marginal industries towards which unauthorised workers tend to gravitate, to the coercive consequences of unauthorised work under immigration law and enforcement. Australian case law preventing former unauthorised workers from regularising their status illustrates an unyielding approach to immigration violations by centring analysis on the damaged relationship between unauthorised workers and the Australian state, ignoring entirely the workers' other social ties in the Australian community. Belying this rigid approach, however, the chapter concludes by exploring the deeper insecurity that can arise from the fluidity of unauthorised migration status itself.

Forms of unauthorised migrant labour in Australia

While detailed information on the demographic contours of unauthorised labour migration may be scarce, Australia is uniquely placed to gather precise data about the number of people unlawfully present in the country at any time. This population is extremely small by global standards because Australia's geographic isolation and lack of contiguous land borders prevent clandestine entry. With a highly effective universal visa system, the Immigration Department uses a Movements Reconstruction database to track the personal details of all international arrivals and departures, estimating that there were around 62,700 visa-overstayers in Australia as of 30 June 2013.[3] This produces a ratio of unlawful non-citizens to total population of about 1:375, very small compared to the ratio of 1:29 in the USA, with approximately 11 million undocumented migrants in 2011,[4] or 1:100 in Britain and in the wider European Union, where the number of unauthorised residents was estimated at, respectively, 618,000 in 2009 and between 1.8 to 3.3 million in 2013.[5] As Leanne Weber (who has undertaken a detailed empirical study

3 DIBP, *Australia's Migration Trends 2012–13* (2014), 77.

4 Jeffrey S. Passel and D'Vera Cohn, 'Unauthorised Immigrants: 11.1 Million in 2011' (Pew Hispanic Centre, December 2012).

5 Ian Gordon *et al.*, *Economic Impact on the London and UK Economy of an Earned Regularisation of Irregular Migrants to the UK* (GLA Economics, Greater London Authority, 2009), 48; Stephen Castles, 'International Migration at a Crossroads' (2014) 18(2) *Citizenship Studies* 190, 192.

of the detection of unlawful non-citizens in Australia) and Catherine Dauvergne each observe, Australia's confidence in its ability to monitor and tally unauthorised migration strongly contrasts with British officials who have admitted they had not the 'faintest idea' how many people are present illegally and to US media reports that approximate the undocumented population not in hundreds of thousands but millions.[6] The Canadian House of Commons estimates the number of undocumented workers in Canada with a range as wide as 80,000–500,000.[7] Perhaps this bears out the conclusion of Australia's own Auditor-General that Australia's immigration compliance arrangements are 'arguably the most effective of any country in the world',[8] although the number of overstayers has significantly increased in recent years from 53,900 in 2010.[9] This rise is likely attributable to an increase in temporary visa-holders in Australia overall, especially young working holiday makers (WHMs) from European countries that were particularly affected by the global financial downturn.

A 2011 government-commissioned review into unauthorised migrant labour estimated that 50,000–100,000 people may be working in Australia without authority at any one time.[10] This includes workers who have overstayed their valid visa; workers holding visas that prohibit work entirely; and those who are working contrary to limited work entitlements (such as international students). Since they are ineligible for services and supports, government experts estimate that half of overstayers in Australia work.[11] However, this estimate is difficult to substantiate since compliance statistics indicate that only roughly 10 per cent of detected unlawful non-citizens are positively identified as working without permission.[12] 100,000 unauthorised workers would account for 0.8 per cent of the Australian workforce, as opposed to the 8 million unauthorised workers in the USA who comprise 5.2 per cent of that country's labour market.[13]

The Immigration Department provides snapshots on the demographic profile of overstayers. As of June 2013, the top five nationalities of visa-over-

6 Leanne Weber, *Policing Non-Citizens* (Routledge, 2013), 23; Catherine Dauvergne, *Making People Illegal: What Globalization Means for Migration and Law* (Cambridge University Press, 2008), 13.

7 David Tilson, *Temporary Foreign Workers and Nonstatus Workers* (Report of the Standing Committee on Citizenship and Immigration) (Library of Parliament, 2009), 65.

8 Australian National Audit Office (ANAO), *Onshore Compliance – Visa Overstayers and Non-Citizens Working Illegally: Department of Immigration and Multicultural and Indigenous Affairs (DIMIA)* (the Auditor-General Audit Report No 2 2004–05 Performance Audit, 2004), 20.

9 DIAC, *Population Flows: Immigration Aspects 2010–11* (2012), 71.

10 Stephen Howells, *Report of the 2010 Review of the* Migration Amendment (Employer Sanctions) Act 2007 (Cth of Australia, 2011), 12.

11 Department of Immigration and Multicultural Affairs, *Review of Illegal Workers in Australia: Improving Immigration Compliance in the Workplace* (1999), 18.

12 DIAC, *Annual Report 2009–10* (2010), 2.

13 Jeffrey S. Passel and D'Vera Cohn, 'Unauthorised Immigrant Population: National and State Trends, 2010' (Pew Hispanic Centre, February 2011).

stayers in purely numerical terms were: Chinese, Malaysian, US, British and Indian, of which Malaysia had by far the highest overstayer rate.[14] Of these, 71.5 per cent had previously held visitor visas, 17 per cent student visas, 3 per cent working holiday visas with the rest on other temporary visas; Table 5.1 indicates their age.

Table 5.1 Age profile of overstayers as at 30 June 2013

Age (years)	*Percentage*
0–20	5
21–30	23
31–40	19
41–50	21
51–60	15
61–70	9
71+	8

Testimony to parliament in 2009 recorded the durations of stay of overstayers at that time, which is shown in Table 5.2.[15]

Table 5.2 Duration of stay of overstayers as at 30 June 2009

Age (years)	*Percentage*
Less than 1	19
1–2	9
2–3	6
3–4	5
4–5	4
5–10	19
10–15	13
More than 15	25

These two tables suggest that almost 40 per cent of overstayers had been living in Australia for at least ten years and a sizeable majority are over forty years old. This tends to dispel the suggestion that overstayers are young tourists whose presence after visa expiry is simply an oversight, a view expressed by the Immigration Minister during a 2009 Senate Committee hearing:

> Senator Evans: The other point I would make about overstayers – for instance visitor overstayers – is that they are often young Englishman

14 DIBP, *Migration Trends*, above n. 3, 78.

15 Senate Legal and Constitutional Affairs Legislation Committee, Parliament of Australia, 'Question Taken On Notice 51, Supplementary Budget Estimates Hearing: 20 October 2009, Immigration and Citizenship Portfolio' (2009).

	[sic] who have gone to a party and are a few days late because they are having such a good time in Sydney.
Senator Fierravanti-Wells:	That is right. They are drunk on a beach or something!
Senator Evans:	Or they have met a young lady and are having a good time, but often they go home within a week of the visa.[16]

There is less data available on the profile of people working while holding otherwise valid visas, which would shed light on their susceptibility to precarious working conditions. These unauthorised workers may also hold current visas prohibiting work entirely (such as tourists on subclass 600 Visitor, subclass 651 eVisitor or subclass 601 Electronic Travel Authority visas), or limiting the amount or place they may work (such as WHMs, international students, and 457 visa workers). Excluding New Zealanders who have unlimited permission to work, there were approximately 1,017,440 temporary visa-holders in Australia in September 2014 with limited or no permission to work.[17] Publicly, the government has postulated that a 'significant number' of these are working contrary to visa conditions,[18] but it is impossible to quantify this figure since much of this work is hidden to avoid detection. Added complexity arises because the line between authorised and unauthorised work can be less clear than one may imagine.

Two groups of visa-holders may be particularly susceptible to engaging in unauthorised work. Most students and their family members hold visas permitting a mandatory maximum of 40 hours' work per fortnight during semester (as Alam's story indicates, this condition was previously 20 hours per week).[19] This limited work entitlement is justified as assisting international students to meet the costs of their studies without over-committing to work that would jeopardise their studies. However, the line between compliant and non-compliant work is a particularly fine one for students who may overshoot their work cap by a small amount, on isolated occasions, or even without realising it has happened.[20] Such subtleties leave student visa-holders teetering on the edges of legality.[21] Because the ever-present

16 Commonwealth, *Parliamentary Debates*, Senate Legal and Constitutional Affairs Legislation Committee, 20 October 2009, 69.

17 DIBP, *Temporary Entrants and New Zealand Citizens in Australia at 30 September* (2014).

18 Howells, *Report of the 2010 Review*, above n. 10, 22.

19 Condition 8105 attaches to most visas available to international students, except for postgraduate research students. Condition 8104 attaches to secondary visas for family members.

20 In several reported cases, the breaches are extremely marginal. In *090314* [2010] MRTA 522 the visa-holder breached condition 8105 on only one instance, which involved a choice between covering an absent employee's shift or losing his job.

21 Brett Neilson, 'The World Seen from a Taxi: Students-Migrants-Workers in the Global Multiplication of Labour' (2009) 29 *Subjectivity* 425, 432.

threat of detention and removal can prevent students from reporting violations of employment standards for fear of detection by immigration authorities, many have called for this limitation on students' work rights to be removed.[22]

The second group is even more vulnerable.[23] While unauthorised workers tend worldwide to be envisioned primarily as people who have entered clandestinely, in Australia there is no evidence to date of any person working illegally immediately after entering without permission. Instead, migrants who travel to Australia by boat without documentation are almost inevitably identified upon arrival and held in detention. Until recently, those subsequently released into the community were granted a Bridging Visa E (BVE) which usually carried permission to work pending determination of their application for asylum.[24] However, since August 2012 governments have released asylum seekers who had arrived by boat after this date into the community on BVEs lacking work entitlements. As of February 2014, 19,353 asylum seekers were living in the community on BVEs with no entitlement to work.[25] Deprivation of work rights has been trenchantly criticised by parliamentary inquiries and marked a return to the conservative Howard government policies prior to 2007.[26] A rare judicial insight on the effect of these laws emerges from a judgment in 2001 of Merkel J, a Federal Court judge, determining the legality of refusal of a further BVE to a Sri Lankan asylum seeker who was placed in detention after engaging in unauthorised work on a previous BVE in order to support his wife and young children. Commencing with an observation that 'the law can be used as an instrument of injustice', his Honour observed:

> It is difficult to understand why any person entitled to remain in Australia to await the outcome of an application for a visa permitting residence in Australia should be absolutely prohibited from seeking work when work is available to that person … It is a matter of some concern that the current regulatory environment can operate to require that persons employing proper procedures to remain in Australia be

22 Senate Education, Employment and Workplace Relations Committee, Parliament of Australia, *Welfare of International Students* (2009), [3.87]ff.

23 See Lisa Hartley and Caroline Fleay, *Policy as Punishment: Asylum Seekers in the Community Without the Right to Work* (Curtin University Centre for Human Rights Education, 2014); Michael Grewcock, 'Back to the Future: Australian Border Policing Under Labor, 2007–2013' (2014) 3(1) *State Crime* 102; Penelope Mathew, *Reworking the Relationship between Asylum and Employment* (Routledge, 2012).

24 *Migration Regulations 1994* (Cth), sch 2 cl 051 (*Migration Regulations*).

25 Senate Legal and Constitutional Affairs Legislation Committee, Parliament of Australia, 'Question Taken On Notice AE14/122, Additional Budget Estimates Hearing: 25 February 2014, Immigration and Citizenship Portfolio' (2014).

26 Parliamentary Joint Committee on Human Rights, Parliament of Australia, 'Examination of Legislation in Accordance with the *Human Rights (Parliamentary Scrutiny) Act 2011*: *Migration Legislation Amendment (Regional Processing and Other Measures) Act 2012* and Related Legislation' (2013), [2.197].

> required to live off such charity as may be available or to beg to make up the shortfall to enable their sustenance.[27]

By forcing people to subsist in the Australian community with minimal financial support but no permission to work, the return to BVEs with conditions precluding lawful work is likely to see thousands of asylum seekers in unauthorised work. This strongly exemplifies the observations of Anderson and Dauvergne that immigration laws create 'illegal workers', rather than simply classifying them.[28]

Unauthorised workers and precarious work

In the sociological literature, unauthorised migrant workers are recognised as quintessentially precarious workers, notoriously susceptible to labour exploitation.[29] Surprisingly, Australia has seen negligible empirical research on this workforce, despite Australian newspapers reporting sporadic incidents of exploitation as early as the 1980s,[30] and case law and parliamentary debates documenting sexual exploitation,[31] illegally unsafe work practices,[32] kidnapping,[33] unpaid compensation, such as to Jin Woog Kim (see Chapter 2), and deaths, such as of Myung Yeol Hwang (see Chapter 10). Barrister Stephen Howells noted in a far-ranging 2011 government-commissioned inquiry on employer sanctions laws that:

> DIAC officers have encountered dozens of [unauthorised] workers in single rooms and [busloads] of workers who do not appear to know who is employing them, where they are working or staying, who will pay them, whether they are actually entitled to work and what is the proper rate of pay ... These workers are particularly vulnerable. They may be underpaid, mislead [sic] about what they are doing, undernourished, beaten and threatened.[34]

27 *De Silva v. MIMA* [2001] FCA 962, [1], [4] and [11].

28 Bridget Anderson, 'Migration, Immigration Controls and the Fashioning of Precarious Workers' (2010) 24(2) *Work, Employment and Society* 300, 304; Dauvergne, *Making People Illegal*, above n. 6.

29 Matthew Gibney, 'Precarious Residents: Migration Control, Membership and the Rights of Non-Citizens' (Human Development Reports Research Paper No 2009/10, United Nations Development Programme, April 2009); Institute for Public Policy Research, *Irregular Migration in the UK: An IPPR Fact File* (2006), 11.

30 Jock Collins, *Migrant Hands in a Distant Land: Australia's Post-War Immigration* (Pluto Press, 2nd edn, 1991), 255.

31 *R v. Kovacs* [2007] QCA 143; [2008] QCA 417; and [2009] 2 Qd R 51.

32 Commonwealth, *Parliamentary Debates*, House of Representatives, 6 February 2007, 96 (Laurie Ferguson, ALP, Second Reading Speech for the Migration Amendment (Employer Sanctions) Bill 2006).

33 'Foreign Worker Awarded $96k Kidnapping Compensation', *ABC News* (online), 21 September 2007.

34 Howells, *Report of the 2010 Review*, above n. 10, 56.

A key source of precariousness stems from the fact that unauthorised work frequently takes place in marginally viable industries where employment protections are underdeveloped and informal work practices widespread. Chronic labour shortages in the agricultural sector, for example, have led government inquiries to remark upon its undue dependence on unauthorised migrant labour.[35] A surveyed conducted in the Murray Valley horticultural area in 2005 found one in four growers admitting to employing unauthorised workers.[36] That migrant workforce is thought to comprise visa-overstayers (primarily from Pacific Islander, South East Asian and Chinese backgrounds), international students working in excess of visa restrictions, tourists working without authorisation, as well as some WHMs working lawfully. Unions report that many of these workers can earn as little as A$3 per hour.[37] Immigration department research suggests that construction is the second-largest employer of unauthorised workers in Australia.[38] Other industries frequently associated with unauthorised work in Australia include sex and manufacturing, and to a lesser degree retail and accommodation.[39]

Coercion and unauthorised work

Undoubtedly the far greater cause of the precariousness of unauthorised workers lies in the extremely harsh consequences following detection of unauthorised status in Australia.[40] Unauthorised workers are so highly vulnerable to exploitation because the costs of complaining about abusive treatment can be dramatically higher for them than other workers. This section explores the coercive effects of immigration enforcement, commencing with the rigid binary constructions of illegality on which it depends.

The law governing unlawful migration status appears on its face transparent and conceptually simple. The *Migration Act* defines an 'unlawful non-citizen' as 'a non-citizen in the migration zone who is not a lawful

35 Employment, Workplace Relations and Education Committee, Parliament of Australia, *Perspectives on the Future of the Harvest Labour Force* (2006).

36 Peter Mares, *Labour Shortages in Murray Valley Horticulture: A Survey of Growers Needs and Attitudes* (Swinburne Institute for Social Research, 2006).

37 Australian Workers' Union, Submission to the Senate Employment, Workplace Relations and Education Reference Committee, Parliament of Australia, 'Inquiry into Pacific Region Seasonal Contract Labour, 2006'.

38 Bodean Hedwards, Hannah Andrevski and Sarah Gosper, *Trafficking in Persons in the Australian Construction Industry: Risks and Protections for Migrant Workers* (Australian Institute of Criminology, forthcoming).

39 DIAC, 'Illegal Workers Located by Industry: 1 July 2009 to 31 March 2010' (Tabled Document No 6, Senate Legal and Constitutional Affairs Committee (Budget Estimates, Parliament of Australia, 24–27 May 2010)); Hall & Partners Open Mind, *Engagement Strategies Associated with Deterring Illegal Workers* (research report submitted to DIAC, 11 October 2012), 14.

40 Sharon Pickering *et al.*, 'Migration Control and Human Security' in Satvinder S. Juss (ed.), *The Ashgate Research Companion to Migration Law, Theory and Policy* (Ashgate, 2013), 535, 545.

non-citizen'; a lawful non-citizen is, in turn, 'a non-citizen in the migration zone who holds a visa that is in effect'.[41] 'Unlawful non-citizens', therefore, include unauthorised entrants, people who have stayed beyond the expiry date of their visa and people whose visa was cancelled for breach of a condition. Working contrary to a visa condition can lead to visa cancellation at the Immigration Department's discretion under the general visa cancellation framework in the *Migration Act*.[42]

The predictability encapsulated in this approach to unauthorised migrants sharpens the coercive effects of detention and removal. Under Australia's mandatory detention policy, in effect since 1992, anyone reasonably suspected of being an unlawful non-citizen, once apprehended, *must* be detained.[43] Officers may also, at their discretion, detain a non-citizen whom the officer knows or reasonably suspects holds a visa that may be cancelled because of work done in contravention of visa restrictions.[44] Although broad oversight is offered by the Commonwealth Ombudsman, detention and arrest are subject to no curial supervision and factors that militate against the denial of liberty of an unauthorised migrant in other countries, such as their low risk of absconding, are irrelevant under Australian law. Limited qualitative research suggests that fear of exposing themselves to detention is even stronger for unauthorised employees than contemplating removal.[45] The climate of intimidation in which unauthorised workers live is also compounded by the criminalisation of working without authorisation,[46] which is explored in detail in the following chapter.

Unauthorised migrants are also susceptible to deportation or removal, which Matthew Gibney describes as representing the epitome of forced migration since it is 'all push and no pull', although it is rarely conceptualised as such because it works with rather than against the grain of state sovereignty.[47] In the Australian context, this coercion is particularly acute because any unlawful non-citizen, unless granted a visa, *must* be removed from Australia as soon as practicable by force of law; no specific order is required provided that legal conditions for removal have been met.[48] This is quite different from the Canadian federal immigration law regime, for example, where there are different types of removal, with enforcement prioritised on the basis of security threat or serious criminality. For instance, departure orders may require the person to leave Canada but are issued on

41 *Migration Act* ss 13 and 14.
42 Section 116 contains the power to cancel visas because of a breach of visa conditions including where non-citizens work contrary to visa restrictions.
43 Section 189(1).
44 Section 192(1).
45 Hall & Partners Open Mind, *Engagement Strategies*, above n. 39, 17.
46 *Migration Act* ss 235(1) and 235(3).
47 Matthew J. Gibney, 'Is Deportation a Form of Forced Migration?' (2013) 32(2) *Refugee Survey Quarterly* 116, 118.
48 *Migration Act* ss 198, 200–206

a conditional basis and are not immediately enforceable.[49] To be sure, in Australia, the government has sought to soften the harshness of the legal framework by promoting 'voluntary compliance'.[50] For instance, a Community Status Resolution Service encourages overstayers to come forward and leave Australia voluntarily by granting short-term bridging visas. The government reports that 81 per cent of all unauthorised migrants located in the community in 2013–14 were voluntary (a total of 13,875 people).[51] However, as Weber points out, such representations mask the ways in which law and government practices produce voluntariness through more subtle forms of coercion, including monitoring of unauthorised migrants, requiring people to report to immigration authorities after being detected by compliance field operations and creating a network of exclusion that makes it almost untenable for unauthorised migrants to sustain their existence such that seemingly voluntary presentation becomes the only viable possibility.[52] Furthermore, the forcefulness of removal is consolidated by the extremely limited options for unauthorised migrants to regularise their status. Even applicants for partner visas issued on the basis of a spousal relationship with an Australian citizen or resident are generally not permitted to apply from within Australia if they are unlawful or on a bridging visa.[53]

Naturally, the threat that an employer may notify authorities allows employers to insist upon employment terms favourable to them. As Linda Bosniak has observed in the US context, 'employers and their undocumented employees usually share … an interest in avoiding enforcement of the immigration law. But some employers deploy … that same law against undocumented workers when their interests diverge'.[54] That this occurs in Australia is borne out by one extraordinary observation by Howells in his inquiry into unauthorised work. He noted that the Immigration Department is actually aware of at least one case where a labour hirer withheld payments from unauthorised workers and then reported them to enforcement officers whereupon they were rapidly removed without legal redress.[55]

There is also evidence of even more orchestrated exploitation by employers of lawfully working temporary visa-holders. The hospitality union, United Voice, has observed that contractors in the cleaning industry commonly 'push a student to work over their [maximum] … or risk losing their job or hours. Once they have done so, the contractor can use the threat

49 *Immigration and Refugee Protection Regulations*, SOR/2002-227, s 226.
50 DIBP, *Annual Report 2013–2014* (2014), 168.
51 Ibid. 169.
52 Weber, *Policing Non-Citizens*, above n. 6, 47 and 143.
53 By operation of *Migration Regulations* sch 3.
54 Linda Bosniak, 'Exclusion and Membership: The Dual Identity of the Undocumented Worker Under United States Law' (1988) *Wisconsin Law Review* 955, 994.
55 Howells, *Report of the 2010 Review*, above n. 10, 57. This is also evidenced in government-commissioned research on unauthorised workers: Hall & Partners Open Mind, *Engagement Strategies*, above n. 39, 15.

of reporting students to immigration officials if they do not accept the conditions of employment the contractor sets.'[56] Michael Knight's 2011 review of the student visa programme, commissioned by the government, similarly notes anecdotal evidence of employers pressuring international students into breaching their work restrictions, then 'blackmailing' them with demands for 'work at reduced wages, breaches of occupational health and safety conditions, even sexual favours'.[57] And, as a matter of either employment or immigration law, unauthorised workers have no protections against an employer who reports a worker's unauthorised status to the authorities to prevent or retaliate against workers seeking to exercise workplace rights.[58] Practically, an employer could contact the Department anonymously in any event.

Even in the absence of employer tip-offs, the efficiency of departmental detection of unauthorised migrants is fierce. The number of unlawful non-citizens located by compliance officers each year has risen from roughly 4,500 in 1994–5 to 17,185 in 2013–14.[59] Officers are empowered to enter and search premises at any time where they have reason to believe they may locate an unlawful non-citizen upon authorisation of the Department Secretary or their delegate.[60] Officers' capacity to conduct on-the-spot checks has been greatly enhanced in recent years by a 24-hour telephone system that provides immediate information on legal status to migration policing partner agencies.[61] Mahabub Alam's experience, described at the top of this chapter, illustrates the ruthlessness of immigration surveillance practices. Community surveillance also serves a crucial role. Even before launching the 'Dob-In Line' in February 2004 (a phone line for reporting – or 'dob-bing in' in the Australian vernacular – suspected unauthorised migrants), community tip-offs led to a fifth of the department's 'priority locations' of unauthorised migrants.[62] This is so, even though police officers report that such informing can occur by local members of migrant communities to pursue personal vendettas or maintain control over migrants with unauthorised or uncertain immigration status.[63]

56 Jacqui Mills and Lily Zhang (United Voice), Submission No 163 to DIAC, *Strategic Review of the Student Visa Program*, 2011, 5.

57 Michael Knight, *Strategic Review of the Student Visa Program 2011: Report* (Cth of Australia, 2011) (*Knight Review*), 85.

58 *FW Act* s 342.

59 Senate Legal and Constitutional Affairs Legislation Committee, Parliament of Australia, 'Question Taken On Notice SE11/0266, Supplementary Budget Estimates Hearing: 17 October 2011, Immigration and Citizenship Portfolio' (2012); DIBP, *Annual Report 2013–14*, above n. 50, 161.

60 *Migration Act* ss 251(5) and 251(6).

61 Leanne Weber, 'It Sounds Like They Shouldn't Be Here: Immigration Checks on the Streets of Sydney' (2011) 21(4) *Policing and Society* 456, 457.

62 Peter Mares, 'A Routine Removal' (2007) 18 *Griffith Review* 207.

63 Weber, *Policing Non-Citizens*, above n. 6, 136.

Nor is the precariousness ameliorated by the prospect of regularisation of status, which is curtailed by the character test and bleak Administrative Appeal Tribunal jurisprudence on the exercise of the discretion to grant visas to people with a prior history of unauthorised employment. A visa may be refused if an applicant fails the 'character test', which may occur in a range of circumstances including where an applicant has a substantial criminal record, or is determined by the Minister not to be of good character, having regard to their 'past and present criminal conduct' or even their 'past and present *general* conduct'.[64] Tribunal decisions applying the character test do not deal with the precariousness of unauthorised work directly, but they nevertheless illuminate how uncompromising immigration exclusions are, and the precariousness that can result. A strong theme that emerges from this jurisprudence is the way that unauthorised workers' agency in violating immigration rules is constructed as indicative of bad character. In one decision, by way of example, a Malaysian man, Peng Soon Yoong, overstayed his visitor's visa for a decade, during which time he had an unblemished record as a taxpayer and resident, working his way up from KFC to restaurants before being sponsored for residence by a major hotel in an attempt to regularise his status. The Tribunal held that, far from integration into the Australian community being a point in his favour, the length of his unauthorised employment was evidence of his riding 'roughshod' over migration rules.[65] By focussing on immigration violations, the character test structures an inquiry into the wrongs done by the migrant worker to the national community. This preoccupation downplays the significance of many other interactions between an immigrant and the Australian government, employers or individual residents, including their contributions to Australian society, through productivity, taxation or social ties. This case law enhances unauthorised workers' precariousness not just because it denies them an opportunity to regularise their immigration status but also because it considers legally irrelevant the community ties that would, in fact, provide practical support.

The uncertainty of unauthorised work

In addition to the coercive consequences that can follow detection of unauthorised migration status, precariousness is compounded by how indeterminate that status actually is. The suggestion that migration status is often fluid or imprecise is highly controversial in an Australian context. It is frequently assumed in Australia that immigration rules are far more predictable, and border enforcement far less discretionary, than elsewhere in the world. Consequently, Australian scholarship has frequently overlooked

64 This may occur by exercise of the general power in s 501(1) or the Public Interest Criteria which include good character as a criterion of visa eligibility: *Migration Regulations* sch 4 cl 4001 (emphasis added). The character test is set out in s 501(6).

65 *Re Tan and MIMA* [2001] AATA 308, [9]–[11].

the uncertainties of the effects of breach of visa conditions, visa cancellation and the unevenness with which immigration rules are enforced. These in themselves produce precariousness for temporary and unauthorised migrants, and those on the boundaries between the two.

Although 'illegal' status is often referred to as if it were a natural characteristic attributable to individuals, migrants become 'illegal' only by operation of national immigration laws. Unauthorised status is therefore inevitably uncertain, since it depends upon the application of immigration rules. Frequently, it flows from migrants' relationships with residents (for instance employers or universities) and can involve varying levels of awareness of breaking the rules, from complete inadvertence to considered intention to manipulate. Consequently, unauthorised worker status is fluid since it is assigned (or left behind) when a visa-holder adjusts their visa status under law,[66] from legislative changes, novel judicial interpretations of the regulations and the discretion of immigration officials.[67] The term 'semi-compliance' has arisen in sociological immigration literature, especially in Europe, to capture the ambiguities and variations in migrants' lived experiences that are obscured by the unsatisfactory dichotomy of legality and illegality.[68]

By contrast, Australian immigration policies have generally been presumed to be highly routinised, memorably described as a 'culture of control'.[69] The Australian *Migration Act* is predicated on binarisms: a visa is either in effect or not. Indeed, in 2012, Hayne J on the High Court described the *Migration Act* as leaving:

> no middle ground between being a lawful non-citizen (entitled to remain in Australia in accordance with any applicable visa requirements) and being an unlawful non-citizen, who may, usually must, be detained and who ... must be removed from Australia as soon as reasonably practicable.[70]

Nevertheless, this chapter concludes by suggesting that subtleties surrounding unauthorised work in other jurisdictions are indeed also manifest in the Australian context. An illustrative example arises in *Johnson v. Minister for*

66 Bridget Anderson and Ben Rogaly, *Forced Labour and Migration* (Trades Union Congress, 2005).

67 Elspeth Guild, 'Who is an Irregular Migrant' in Barbara Bogusz (ed.), *Irregular Migration and Human Rights: Theoretical, European and International Perspectives* (Martinus Nijhoff Publishers, 2004), 3.

68 Martin Ruhs and Bridget Anderson, 'Semi-Compliance and Illegality in Migrant Labour Markets: An Analysis of Migrants, Employers and the State in the UK' (2010) 16(3) *Population, Space and Place* 195.

69 Kathryn Cronin, 'A Culture of Control: An Overview of Immigration Policy-Making' in James Jupp and Marie Kabala (eds), *The Politics of Australian Immigration* (Australian Government Publishing Service, 1993), 83.

70 *Plaintiff M47-2012 v. Director General of Security* [2012] HCA 46, [178].

Immigration and Multicultural and Indigenous Affairs, where Silas Johnson sought clarification on whether he was permitted to work.[71] His circumstances were unusual. A New Zealand citizen, his residence visa was cancelled after a long history of criminal conduct. With his deportation pending, Johnson challenged the cancellation decision on the ground that he was neither immigrant nor alien, but rather 'absorbed' into the Australian community and therefore outside the constitutional limits of the *Migration Act* insofar as it relates to the cancellation of visas and removal from Australia. He sought review of his deportation order after two High Court judgments had delivered complex and conflicting views suggesting that British subjects who had migrated to Australia before 1987 may not be 'aliens' for constitutional purposes or therefore liable to deportation.[72] At the time of his hearing before the Federal Court, the High Court had reserved judgment in a matter that was slated to resolve the uncertainties.[73] In relation to the legality of his taking up employment, French J concluded that, given the uncertainty as to his lawfulness, Johnson should refrain from working pending the outcome of this matter since he would be at risk of committing an offence under s. 235 if his visa was ultimately found to have been validly cancelled.

More prosaic uncertainty arises because of complexities around the interpretation of visa conditions. For instance, it is relatively clear that 457 visa workers breach visa condition 8107 (permitting work only for the sponsoring employer in the nominated position) and risk visa cancellation by working for another employer, on their own account, or for the sponsor in a different job. But it is far less obvious what actually constitutes work, legislatively defined as an activity that in Australia normally attracts remuneration.[74] This suggests that unpaid activities can fall within the *Migration Act's* definition of 'work'. In *Braun v. Minister of Immigration, Local Government and Ethnic Affairs*, a young German woman was staying at a cattle station in Western Australia on a tourist visa, which prohibited work.[75] She offered to cook from time to time for no pay after the cook resigned and, when immigration officers visited the property, argued that she was not working but undertaking 'work experience'. French J disagreed, finding that the assessment of a work-like activity as purely domestic or social is a matter of degree and the fact that the work was unpaid was not determinative. A quite different result emerged in *Dib v. Minister of Immigration and Multicultural Affairs*, where Dib was visiting his sister on a visitor visa without work rights.[76] Dib frequently drove his brother-in-law to his tyre business since he was

71 *Johnson v. MIMIA* [2003] FCA 758, [32].

72 *Nolan v. MIEA* (1988) 165 CLR 178; *Re Patterson; Ex parte Taylor* (2001) 207 CLR 391.

73 In *Shaw v. MIMIA* (2003) 218 CLR 28, the High Court concluded that all non-citizens are aliens and subject to the *Migration Act* cancellation, removal and deportation powers.

74 *Migration Regulations* reg 1.03.

75 (1991) 33 FCR 152. See also *Kim v. Witton* (1995) 59 FCR 258.

76 [1998] FCA 415.

struggling with severe health problems, sometimes collecting tyres by himself. When his brother-in-law was hospitalised, Dib spent time at the business which would have suffered without him. Einfeld J held that these circumstances sat in a 'grey area between work done for the purpose of gaining remuneration or a livelihood and activities that are purely in the pursuit of personal satisfaction or compassion'.

Interpreting work restrictions attached to student visas in mandatory condition 8105 has been even more fraught. This condition initially limited work to 20 hours per week while a student's course was in session. Following criticism of the ambiguity of this rule, amendments in 2008 clarified that a week was defined as a seven day period commencing on a Monday.[77] In 2012 the limitation was changed to 40 hours per fortnight, after the Knight Review advocated a softening of the harshness of the rule.[78] More significantly, prior to 2013, the cancellation scheme for breach of student visa conditions was extremely complex: either discretionary, mandatory or automatic depending on which condition was breached.[79] In a move that substantially lessened the precarious circumstances of international student workers, automatic and mandatory student visa cancellations were abolished in 2013. Breach of any student visa condition (including relating to restricted work hours) now only triggers discretionary cancellation (with consideration of the particular case on its merits).[80] Decided cases illustrate the significant injustice that flowed from the inflexibility of this scheme prior to these amendments. For example, international student and taxi driver Faruk Al Ferdous's visa was cancelled when he worked 51 minutes over the 20 hour limit in one week as a result of chasing a fare-evading passenger late in his shift. He argued that the time it took to return to base, log on and off, or hand over to the next driver was not time spent at work. The Migration Review Tribunal and courts denied Al Ferdous' applications for review, although the Federal Magistrate expressed disquiet that this lack of flexibility reflected 'poorly on our self-proclaimed image as an open society committed to the notion of a "fair go"'.[81]

By removing the mandatory cancellation power and changing the work condition to 40 hours per fortnight, these amendments ameliorate the most egregious unfairness in the scheme. However, student visa workers continue

77 *Migration Amendment Regulations 2008 (No 2)* (Cth), pt 3.

78 *Migration Legislation Amendment Regulations 2012 (No 2)* (Cth) sch 5; *Knight Review*, above n. 57, 84.

79 The discretionary cancellation of student visas, where the student was no longer a genuine student or engaged in conduct not contemplated by the visa, was permitted in s 116(1)(fa). Mandatory cancellation for breach of work conditions was prescribed by s 116(3) and reg 2.43(2)(b)(i). Automatic cancellation could occur where a student did not achieve satisfactory course progress, under s 137J.

80 *Migration Regulations* reg 2.34(2)(aa), amended by *Migration Legislation Amendment (Student Visas) Act 2012* (Cth) and *Migration Amendment Regulations 2013 (No 1)* (Cth).

81 *Al Ferdous v. Minister for Immigration* [2010] FMCA 824, [59]; *Al Ferdous v. MIAC* [2011] FCA 1070.

to experience especially precarious work rights. A student who works 40.5 hours in two consecutive weeks will still face discretionary cancellation of their visa, even if they work 39 hours the following fortnight. A study commissioned by the Fair Work Ombudsman on unpaid work recommends that students 'be particularly vigilant in monitoring their hours each week to see that they never exceed 40 hours by the end of the second week in any two week period'.[82] Alex Reilly notes that the increase from 20 to 40 hours constitutes:

> a minimal increase in flexibility in students' work arrangements, and simply delays the possibility of breach by a week. It does not address the core concern that students might, nonetheless, find themselves in circumstances of minor or inadvertent breach.[83]

And, while arguably the abolition of complicated cancellation mechanisms for breach of student visa conditions has created more certainty for international students, this certainty may be undermined by the high rate at which tribunals set aside student visa cancellations on merits review.[84]

Further uncertainty arises for students from changing visa eligibility requirements. In 2011 the government reduced the amount of financial support students need to show when applying to study in Australia by around A$36,000.[85] While this move was celebrated for improving prospective applicants' access to student visas, it may lead students to work even longer hours to finance their studies. Indeed, precarious work can also produce unauthorised work status, since reduced financial resources and insecure work can lead students to work more than they are permitted. As long as visa conditions limit the permissible work of international students, heightened vulnerabilities will remain. While the harshest impacts of these conditions have been softened, further reforms have reduced international students' pathways to permanent residence, which have been acknowledged as likely to lead to higher overstay rates (as discussed in previous chapters).[86] Lacking other avenues, 31,022 international students were permitted to remain in Australia on tourist visas in 2013–14, an increase of 12 per cent on

82 Andrew Stewart and Rosemary Owens, *The Nature, Prevalence and Regulation of Unpaid Work Experience, Internships and Trial Periods in Australia: Experience or Exploitation?* (University of Adelaide, Report for the Fair Work Ombudsman, January 2013), 169.

83 Alexander Reilly, 'Protecting Vulnerable Migrant Workers: The Case of International Students' (2012) 25 *Australian Journal of Labour Law* 181, 200.

84 The Migration Review Tribunal set aside more than one third of student visa cancellations between 2002 and 2005 and 41 per cent in 2009–10, with a recent decrease to 21 per cent in 2011–12 and 17 per cent in 2013–14: Weber, *Policing Non-Citizens*, above n. 6, 32; Migration Review Tribunal, *Annual Report 2013–14* (2014), table 18.

85 *Migration Amendment Regulations 2011 (No 6)* (Cth), sch 2. Further reductions were introduced by *Migration Legislation Amendment Regulations 2012 (No 2)* (Cth), sch 4.

86 DIAC, *Annual Report 2009–10*, above n. 12, 159.

the previous year.[87] International students, therefore, are now perhaps as likely to experience precariousness as unauthorised workers after their expiration of their student visas as they are on otherwise valid student visas.

Additional unpredictability surrounds the selectivity of enforcement. As Weber points out, vagaries around the implementation of the law mean that lawfulness is best understood as dynamic, discretionary and elusive: immigration status might be incorrectly recorded; an unauthorised migrant may have legal avenues about which they are unaware or which they have not pursued; their identity may be in dispute.[88] While immigration enforcement officials should pursue all unauthorised residents equally, the surveillance of unauthorised work has historically been highly uneven. Reportedly, in 1993, compliance officers in one office used a phone book to identify suspect individuals 'selected in part because their names were uncommon in the Australian community'.[89] The department was far more efficient at locating unlawful non-citizens from some countries than others. The National Audit Office found that the overall 'rate of location' of overstayers in 1992–3 was nearly 20 per cent (of an estimated total of 79,755 overstayers, 14,874 were located). However, the 'rate of location' for Brazilians, Tongans, Fijians, Samoans and Thais was closer to 30 per cent, while French, American and Dutch overstayers were rarely found.[90] In somewhat more recent data, in 2003–4 British nationals made up the largest single group of overstayers: more than 10 per cent of the total. Yet their 'rate of location' was 18.5 per cent compared with 64.4 per cent of Fijians, 82.4 per cent for Indians, 69.9 per cent for Chinese, 64.2 per cent for Indonesians, 53 per cent for Thais and 42.8 per cent for South Koreans.[91]

At least at the point of cancellation, the fact that the power to cancel visas for unauthorised work is now discretionary might be thought to soften the hard impact of enforcement, permitting immigration officials to take exceptional, compassionate or compelling circumstances into account.[92] Previously, when student visas were subject to mandatory cancellation, under law 'where a student may have only breached the [then] 20 hour limit by one hour, the delegate would have no option but to decide to cancel'.[93] However, a government report on the administration of student visas in 2011 found that, in practice, immigration officials previously exercised discretion even

87 DIBP, *Student Visa and Temporary Graduate Visa Programme Quarterly Report* (30 June 2014), 68.

88 Weber, *Policing Non-Citizens*, above n. 6, 23.

89 Mares, 'A Routine Removal', above n. 62.

90 ANAO, *The Compliance Function: Department of Immigration and Ethnic Affairs* (the Auditor-General Audit Report No 30 1993–94, 1994) 24–6.

91 DIMIA, *Managing the Border: 2003–04* (2004), 53; DIMIA, *Population Flows: Immigration Aspects 2003–04* (2004) Appendix C, 144.

92 *Migration Act* s 116(1)(b).

93 DIAC, Submission No 111 to the Senate Education, Employment and Workplace Relations Reference Committee, Parliament of Australia, 'Inquiry into the Welfare of International Students', September 2009, 20.

while professing to apply the mandatory provisions absolutely strictly: breaches of only 'one or two hours above the [then] 20 hour limit [were] not given priority' by immigration compliance staff.[94] Indeed, in one industry – the taxi industry – case managers routinely declined to apply the 20 hour limit because a standard shift is 12 hours, and proceeded on the assumption – unwritten because it conflicts with the Regulations – that drivers would take breaks during two shifts otherwise totalling 24 hours.[95] It is unknown what proportion of student visas are typically cancelled for breach of work restrictions in condition 8105 because published cancellation figures are not disaggregated for breach of work-related condition. Figures from 2009–10 (when this cancellation power was mandatory) indicate that only 132 student visas were cancelled on this basis.[96]

But even if rare, this condition generates the fear of cancellation among student workers as much as posing an actual threat of cancellation. Either function organises student workers into precarious employment. It also remains to be seen whether this informally permissive approach will continue. One of the stated purposes of the shift from mandatory to discretionary cancellation powers was to 'allow integrity resources to be more strategically targeted towards risk'.[97] It is possible that these amendments yet presage greater enforcement of breaches of students' work-related conditions, if this is prioritised over other grounds for cancellation which were also previously subject to automatic cancellation, such as failure to make satisfactory course progress.

Conclusion

This chapter has examined the ways that immigration controls produce unauthorised migrant labour, pointing to a central contradiction in this area of regulation in Australia. On the one hand, the coercive effects of enforcement are particularly intense because of the rigid structure of immigration legislation in Australia, and the harshness of mandatory detention and summary removal in particular. At the same time, however, undermining this apparent inflexibility, actual indeterminacy of the category of 'unauthorised work' sharpens uncertainty for migrant workers. The next chapter turns to an additional source of precariousness for unauthorised workers: that which arises from the intersection of the criminalisation of unauthorised work, under the *Migration Act*, with employment protections, including workers compensation, unfair dismissal and restitutionary claims.

94 ANAO, *Management of Student Visas: Department of Immigration and Citizenship* (the Auditor-General Audit Report No 46 2010–11 Performance Audit, 2011), 115.

95 Ibid. 116.

96 Ibid. 114.

97 Explanatory Memorandum, Migration Legislation Amendment (Student Visas) Bill 2012 (Cth), 2.

6 A jurisprudence of unauthorised work

> Ms Masri was 18 years old when Nelly Santoso brought her from Indonesia to Australia to be a 'housemaid' at Santoso's home in southern Sydney in June 1995.[1] Santoso had accompanied Masri, who spoke little English, to the Australian Embassy in Jakarta where she procured Masri a passport and tourist visa under a false name along with a sham sponsorship arrangement, and later retained her passport. Masri signed no forms at the Embassy and spoke to no officials. In Australia, Masri carried out domestic duties for the Santosos and their three children 17 hours each day, seven days a week. Santoso had promised Masri A$62.50 per month: over four years Masri received a total of A$5,190, half of which she sent home to her family, subsistence farmers in Indonesia. When her fraudulently obtained visa expired after three months, Masri became an unlawful non-citizen, although she was unaware of her unauthorised status until Santoso informed her that she was in Australia illegally and would be jailed if discovered.

There are many contextual factors that led Masri to toil for years barely compensated, including the background coercion and uncertainty within the immigration law framework which produces unauthorised work, explored in the previous chapter. This chapter turns to a more specific constitutive role, which Australian government regulation plays in producing precariousness for unauthorised workers, the criminal offence in s. 235 of the *Migration Act 1958* (Cth) (*Migration Act*) for temporary migrants who work in contravention of visa conditions, and unauthorised migrants like Masri who work in Australia at all.

The criminalisation of 'illegal work' in Australia generates precariousness not only through the threat of prosecution. Far more punitively, it can remove substantive protections for unauthorised workers in workers compensation entitlements, unfair dismissal protections and restitution for labour performed, and weaken workers' remedies. Largely as a result of this

1 This account of Masri's story derives from *Masri v. Santoso* [2004] NSWIRComm 108, [1], [3], [26], [171], [181]; Leonie Lamont, 'Silent Shame of our New Slaves', *Sydney Morning Herald*, 10 June 2004.

statutory offence, the ways in which employment laws apply to unauthorised workers are partial and unpredictable, leaving them vulnerable to the raw effect of market forces unmediated by law. Because of the small number of cases on record, Australian law on this point is far less definitive than that in other jurisdictions. However, this does not reduce the importance of this analysis. Rather, this moment provides an opportunity for reform and crucial reflection before particular approaches become firmly entrenched.

What the Australian jurisprudence indicates is that s. 235 can lead courts to fixate on workers' contravention of immigration rules and how this harms the 'relationship' between migrant workers and the state, overshadowing any attention on workers' relationship with their employers. This erases a multitude of realities related to unauthorised workers' presence in the workplace including legal recognition of the work done, or of their injury and any future consequences of it, or indeed the employers' culpability in breaching employment laws. By taking an individualised focus on migrants workers' unauthorised immigration status, judgments withholding labour law protections assume they have willingly chosen precarious conditions when deciding to work without authorisation. Of course, workers do exercise agency in ways that can intensify or ameliorate poor working conditions, but the regulatory structures of immigration law (interacting with other Australian laws and the global economy) also significantly constrain workers' agency.

A related preoccupation in the jurisprudence is to punish workers who have violated Australian sovereignty and immigration rules by denying the law's protection. Here, I suggest, even from the perspective of strengthening law's coherence and authority, this move is counter-productive. Far from restoring the efficacy and authority of the governmental prohibition of unauthorised work, withholding rights arising from unauthorised migrants' work-related relationships and interactions in fact diminishes the scope of governmental regulation of unauthorised work. An important premise of the criminal offence is that lesser protections for migrant workers equate with stronger protections for local workers. Precisely the opposite is true. The best protection of the employment conditions of all workers will occur where the law can acknowledge migrants' membership in the workplace without disavowing the consequences of their unauthorised presence.

This chapter begins by considering the criminalisation of unauthorised work under the *Migration Act*. It then turns to Australian jurisprudence denying workers compensation entitlements to unauthorised workers by virtue of the common law doctrine of illegality of contracts. The analysis traces the origins of this doctrine in British precedent. The effect of s. 235 is then examined in other fields of protection, in particular unfair dismissal and restitution and civil claims. Together, this jurisprudence suggests some of the imagined policy objectives articulated by the courts to justify their approach. Finally, the chapter points to some of the more protective approaches to unauthorised workers' entitlements in the European Union (EU) and USA that acknowledge that positioning unauthorised workers in acutely precarious work does not strengthen the hand of resident workers or strengthen the integrity of the legal system itself, but diminishes the governance of employment for the benefit of the nation. Therefore, the conclusion argues for the repeal of the criminalisation provision in Australia.

The offence of unauthorised work

Working without authorisation has constituted a criminal offence under the *Migration Act* since 1979.[2] Section 235(1) prohibits work done in contravention of a condition on a temporary visa (whether the condition prohibits a non-citizen from doing any work, specified work, or work other than specified work). Section 235(3) proscribes an 'unlawful non-citizen' from working in Australia, 'for reward or otherwise'.[3] With a maximum penalty of A$10,000, these are strict liability offences: fault (including mistakes about visa status, even if caused by a migration agent or departmental official) is irrelevant to the worker's guilt.[4]

Australia's criminal offence specifically proscribing unauthorised work stands in contrast to similarly placed countries, where no specific offence exists. British law prohibits unauthorised work only indirectly by prohibiting unauthorised entry, overstaying and conduct that breaches a visa condition.[5] In the USA, conversely, it is not illegal to work without authorisation at all; indeed, from the inception of contemporary immigration legislation in that country in 1952 until 1986, when sanctions against *employers* using unauthorised labour were introduced, provisions criminalising the facilitation of illegal immigration concluded with the so-called 'Texas Proviso': 'for the purpose of this section, employment (including the usual and normal practices incident to employment) shall not be deemed to constitute harboring'.[6] Having said that, unlike in Australia, entry without inspection in the USA is a criminal offence,[7] and some individual American states criminalise unauthorised work.[8]

Poignantly, there is no evidence of investigations or prosecutions of the s. 235 offence in Australia, presumably because of the overwhelming policy

2 Introduced by *Migration Amendment Act 1979* (Cth), s 19, the offence marked the reversal of the commitment to punish employers for unauthorised migrant labour in the early years after Federation: *Contract Immigrants Act 1905* (Cth), s 6.

3 In a cruel irony, the proscription on unauthorised work does not apply to work 'performed by an unlawful non-citizen who is detained in a detention centre' pursuant to s 235(6) and *Migration Regulations 1994* (Cth), reg 5.32A (*Migration Regulations*). See further *Hussein v. Secretary of the Department of Immigration and Multicultural Affairs (No 2)* [2006] FCA 1263 (*Hussein*).

4 *Migration Act* ss 235(4B) and 235(5); *Criminal Code 1995* (Cth), s 6.1.

5 *Immigration Act 1971* ss 24(1)(a), 24(1)(b)(i) and 24(1)(b)(ii).

6 *Immigration and Nationality Act*, Pub L 82-414, 66 Stat 163 (June 27, 1952, as amended) § 274(a).

7 Ibid. § 275(a).

8 E.g. *Alabama Code* § 31-13-11(a) (2011).

imperative to remove unauthorised migrants from Australia without delay. The Immigration Department has confirmed that, between 2007 and 2013, there were no successful prosecutions or evidence of any investigations in its system.[9] Instead, the punitive effects of the move to criminalisation play out more indirectly, such as in the realm of employment laws.

Workers compensation entitlements

These punitive effects across employment entitlements are uncertain, patchy and inconsistent. At least with respect to workers compensation legislation, the preeminent approach appears to be to deny coverage to unauthorised workers on the basis that their employment contract was void for illegality because it contravened the *Migration Act* offence. This is reflected in South Australian and Queensland superior courts judgments and tribunal decisions in New South Wales (NSW), which accord so much significance to the immigration law violation as to leave no room for the law to acknowledge any other legal implication of a non-citizen employee's presence in Australia. This renders legally irrelevant the value of the work, the power differentials in the employment relationship, the precariousness of the worker's employment, the consequences for the employee of this workplace injury and the employer's culpability for the injury itself. At the same time, there is another strand of reasoning in NSW courts and tribunal decisions that treats the employment contracts of unauthorised workers as valid, although they are reluctant to remedy the actual future losses to the worker resulting from the injury. When it comes to calculating remedies for loss of future earning capacity, these judgments betray a desire to 'offshore' the consequences of injuries sustained in the course of unauthorised work.

This section seeks to make sense of the courts' divergent approaches to the legality of the underlying contract by attending to their construction of the work relationship and the interpretive importance of the regulatory context within which this work is situated. It traces the origins of these principles in the English common law, which, however, has recently signalled moves towards a more inclusive posture toward unauthorised work.

Erasing employment relationships: the invalidity of employment contracts in Australia for the purposes of workers compensation

In Australia, each state and territory workers compensation scheme provides that where someone is injured in the course of their employment they may be entitled to lump sum and weekly workers compensation payments. While the legislative details vary, in general the injured person must show that they fall within the definition of 'worker' under a contract of service and are

9 Email to author from Jeanie Bruce, Director, National Employer Sanctions Support Team, Department of Immigration and Citizenship (DIAC), 19 July 2013; Explanatory Memorandum, Migration Amendment (Employer Sanctions) Bill 2006 (Cth), [7.4].

therefore covered by the statutory protection.[10] Industrial relations scholars have observed that, even in collectivised statutory labour law regimes such as Australia's, the common law contract provides the foundation for a range of statutory, common law and equitable entitlements.[11]

For those working in Australia without permission, this brings into play a common law doctrine inherited from the UK, which holds a contract void or unenforceable if contrary to a statutory prohibition, done for an illegal purpose or expressly vitiated by a statute.[12] Where legislation is silent as to the consequences of non-compliance, contemporary Australian courts consider whether the policy and scope of the vitiating rule suggest that it should produce contractual invalidity.[13] Very early statutory restrictions on migrant labour in Australia in the *Immigration Restriction Act 1901* (Cth) s. 11 explicitly provided that any employment agreement with an unauthorised worker was 'unenforceable and of no effect'. By contrast, neither the statutory prohibition in s. 235 nor the provision that preceded it (s. 83(2)) explicitly declare such employment contracts invalid. Therefore, judicial approaches to the validity of employment contracts of unauthorised migrant workers have been highly divergent. To be sure, difficulties related to this principle of illegality are certainly not limited to immigration regulation. The doctrine itself has been described as 'shadowy', plagued by 'many pitfalls', with case law marked by 'obscurities, supposed distinctions and questionable techniques of decision'.[14] But the controversial nature of immigration legislation compounds these ambiguities in case law on unauthorised work which commenced with a 1994 South Australian Supreme Court judgment.

In *WorkCover Corporation v. Da Ping*, the Supreme Court of South Australia denied a claim for workers compensation brought by a Chinese man, who had injured his right hand while working for San Remo Macaroni Company. The *Workers Rehabilitation and Compensation Act 1986* (SA) ss 30(1) and 3 provided that entitlement to compensation depends on the existence of a valid contract of service. However, Liang Da Ping was working in breach of s. 83(2) of the *Migration Act*, which was in effect from 1979 until the introduction of s. 235 in 1994 and provided that '[w]here a person who is an illegal entrant performs any work in Australia without permission, in writing,

10 E.g., in NSW a 'worker' for the purpose of the *Workplace Injury Management and Workers Compensation Act 1998* (NSW) is defined as a person who has entered into or works under a contract of service: sch 1.

11 Breen Creighton and Richard Mitchell, 'The Contract of Employment in Australian Labour Law' in L. Betten (ed.), *The Employment Contract in Transforming Labour Relations* (Kluwer Law International, 1995), 129, 136–7.

12 *Wilkinson v. Osborne* (1915) 21 CLR 89, 98 drawing upon *Holman v. Johnson* (1775) 98 ER 1120, 1121 (*Holman*).

13 *Fitzgerald v. JF Leonhardt Pty Ltd* (1997) 189 CLR 215 (*Fitzgerald*).

14 *Nelson v. Nelson* (1995) 184 CLR 538, 595 (*Nelson*); *Archbolds (Freightage) Ltd v. S Spanglett Ltd* [1967] 1 QB 374, 393; Walter Gelborn, 'Contracts and Public Policy' (1935) 35 *Columbia Law Review* 679, 679.

of the Secretary of the Department of Immigration, the person commits an offence'.[15] In relation to the common law principles governing the legality of contracts, the court noted Australian High Court authority that 'the cases are likely to be rare in which a statute prohibits a contract but nevertheless reveals an intention that it should be valid and enforceable'.[16] Applying this jurisprudence to the s. 83(2) offence, the South Australian Supreme Court found that the 'act to be performed under the contract [was] the very act forbidden by the statute', which strongly suggested an implication that the prohibition rendered the employment contract void.[17] Consequently, Da Ping was determined not to be a worker for the purposes of the legislation, and had no entitlement to workers compensation.

Four years later, the NSW Court of Appeal in *Nonferral (NSW) Pty Ltd v. Taufia* considered the implications of the s. 83(2) offence for workers compensation coverage, but arrived at the opposite result.[18] Silivenusi Taufia had entered Australia from Tonga in March 1992 on a tourist visa, subsequently overstayed, and began working at Nonferral aluminium foundry late that year. In May 1993, he injured his left lower leg when a block of aluminium fell onto him. While recovering from the injury, Taufia was arrested in August as an 'illegal entrant' (a term no longer in use) and deported within the week. After the NSW Compensation Court awarded him workers compensation benefits,[19] his employer appealed to the Court of Appeal. That court focused on two High Court judgments that had been delivered since *Da Ping*, in which the High Court had become somewhat more circumspect about rendering a contract illegal on the basis that its performance breached a statute. No longer presuming that a statutory prohibition would result in contractual invalidity, McHugh J observed in *Nelson v. Nelson* in 1995, that courts should only refuse to enforce rights associated with an unlawful purpose where:

> (a) the statute discloses an intention that those rights should be unenforceable in all circumstances; or (b) (i) the sanction of refusing to enforce those rights is not disproportionate to the seriousness of the unlawful conduct; (ii) the imposition of the function is necessary, having regard to the terms of the statute, to protect its objects or policies; and (iii) the statute does not disclose an intention that the sanctions and remedies contained in the statute are to be the only legal consequences of a breach of the statute or the frustration of its policies.[20]

15 *WorkCover Corporation v. Da Ping* (1994) 175 LSJS 469 (*Da Ping*).
16 *Yango Pastoral Co Pty Ltd v. First Chicago Australia Ltd* (1978) 139 CLR 410, 413 (*Yango Pastoral*).
17 *Da Ping* (1994) 175 LSJS 469, 473.
18 *Nonferral (NSW) Pty Ltd v. Taufia* (1998) 43 NSWLR 312 (*Taufia* appeal).
19 *Taufia v. Nonferral (NSW) Pty Ltd* [1995] NSWCC 30 (*Taufia* first instance).
20 *Nelson* (1995) 184 CLR 538, 613.

In 1997, in *Fitzgerald v. FJ Leonhardt Pty Ltd*, Dawson and Toohey JJ reiterated this narrower principle, noting that:

> [i]t has sometimes been said that a contract is illegal if its performance involves breach of a statute passed for the protection of the public but, stated in that way, the proposition is too broad. The purpose of the statute may be served by the imposition of a penalty, notwithstanding that it is for the protection of the public.[21]

Thus, the High Court now counselled that a statutory prohibition would render a contract void only where parliament intended this result. The contract would remain enforceable if the statutory penalty alone was sufficient to secure the object of the statute.[22]

In *Taufia*, the NSW Court of Appeal held, by majority, that neither the object nor intention of the *Migration Act* required the court to declare the contract invalid. Stein JA, with whom Cole JA agreed, examined the statutory prohibition more closely than had the South Australian Court in *Da Ping*. Noting that s. 83(2) prohibited the performance of work by an illegal entrant 'without the permission in writing of the Secretary of the Department of Immigration', he reasoned that this did not 'prohibit illegal entrants from working in Australia per se' but only from working without the Secretary's written permission.[23] Furthermore, the object of the *Migration Act* (which the court concluded was the protection of the public from unauthorised work) could be achieved without rendering void all contracts of service entered into without the Secretary's permission. The criminal penalty imposed under s. 83 (then, a fine of A$5,000) and the possibility of removal were sufficient to prevent unauthorised migrants from working. Stein JA then considered the 'drastic' consequences that could follow a finding of the contract of employment as wholly void and unenforceable. Denying the employee workers compensation would be disproportionate to the seriousness of his unlawful conduct. Furthermore, unscrupulous employers could deliberately recruit unauthorised migrants to avoid paying award wages since those workers could file no suit under a void employment contract. Indeed, an employer would be unable to enforce an unauthorised employee's obligations under a contract, for example, the duty of confidentiality. Hence, s. 83(2) did not implicitly render an unauthorised employment contract illegal, nor therefore prohibit the worker from receiving compensation for work-related injuries.

In a forceful dissent, Sheppard AJA would have held invalid Taufia's employment contract in order to give effect to the purpose of the *Migration Act*. His Honour noted that:

21 *Fitzgerald* (1997) 189 CLR 215, 220.
22 Ibid. 423.
23 *Taufia* appeal (1998) 43 NSWLR 312, 320.

> The *Migration Act 1958* (Cth), dealing as it does with the circumstances in which persons who are not Australian citizens may enter and remain in Australia and, if they remain, the conditions (if any) upon which they may do so is of substantial public importance. The operation of the Act is of national importance because it involves the protection and overall wellbeing of the Australian community.[24]

Sheppard AJA held that the *Migration Act* evinced a clear intention forbidding illegal entrants from working, under threat of monetary penalty and deportation. Taufia could not lawfully have performed the contract and his employer could not, therefore, have insisted on its performance.

The question came before the Queensland Court of Appeal in 2004 in *Australia Meat Holdings Pty Ltd v. Kazi*, this time in relation to the current provision prohibiting unauthorised work, s. 235, which had been introduced since *Taufia*.[25] A Bangladeshi man, Mainuddin Kazi, having overstayed his visitor visa valid to 1996, worked at a meatworks from February 1998. In the course of that employment, in August 2000, he injured his knee falling over the conveyor belt in the cold store and received medical treatment for the injury before ceasing employment in June 2002. The employer then sought a declaration that Kazi was not entitled to workers compensation. In the first instance at the Supreme Court of Queensland, Mullins J applied the reasoning in *Taufia* and held that, despite the stronger wording in the new s. 235(3), the sanction of declaring the contract of employment invalid was not necessary to protect the object of the *Migration Act*.[26]

However, the Queensland Court of Appeal, effectively reverting back to the position in *Da Ping*, reversed this judgment. It declared Kazi's employment contract invalid, finding him ineligible for redress under Queensland workers compensation legislation.[27] The majority emphasised that unlike the repealed s. 83, s. 235 absolutely proscribes work by a migrant contrary to visa conditions. It no longer envisages any circumstance in which an unlawful non-citizen may enter into an employment contract, for instance with the permission of the Departmental Secretary. Davies JA found the implications of this straightforward: '[i]f it is in the national interest to prohibit unauthorised migrants from performing work, it must also be in that interest ... to prohibit any such person obtaining rights under a contract to perform work'.[28] With Williams JA concurring, his Honour concluded that primacy should be accorded to border enforcement. Section 235 resulted in not just criminal penalty, detention and removal, but also, implicitly, the further punishment of withheld employment-related entitlements. McMurdo J

24 Ibid. 332.
25 *Australia Meat Holdings Pty Ltd v. Kazi* [2004] QCA 147 (*Kazi* appeal).
26 *Australia Meat Holdings Pty Ltd v. Kazi* [2003] QSC 225 (*Kazi* first instance).
27 *WorkCover Queensland Act 1996* (Qld), s 12(1).
28 *Kazi* appeal [2004] QCA 147, [23].

dissented, emphasising Stein JA's view in *Taufia* that a statutory prohibition should not be implied 'if it would lead to an unjust, unreasonable, inconvenient or absurd result'.[29] McMurdo J expressed concern that to invalidate an employment contract could have deleterious consequences on other people whose rights depended on the contract having legal effect: an employer might be prevented from enforcing common law duties of good faith and fidelity and third parties might have no claim in vicarious liability of the employer.

The question of the effect of s. 235 on workers compensation entitlements was next considered, but not resolved, by the Northern Territory Supreme Court in April 2013.[30] In 2007, Lior Navi was gored by a bull in cattle yards at Coniston Station in outback Northern Territory, injuring his leg. The employer's insurer rejected Navi's injury claim on the basis that any work contract was void for illegality because he was not entitled to work in Australia. Kelly J stayed proceedings concerning the workers compensation entitlements pending the determination of Navi's common law claim for damages, which at time of writing had not yet concluded.

Several scholars have submitted that the NSW Court of Appeal's reasoning in *Taufia* is preferable and that this precedent should be applied when the issue next arises.[31] Nevertheless, the Queensland Court of Appeal's approach to invalidity in *Kazi* has since been applied by tribunals in preference to *Taufia*, even in NSW, on the basis that *Kazi* dealt with the current statutory provision, s. 235. In *Yong Fu Zhang v. Mei Hu t/as Eden Furniture and the WorkCover Authority of NSW*, the NSW Workers Compensation Commission found the employment contract void pursuant to *Kazi*, although this did not negate an award of workers compensation because of a statutory discretion in NSW to treat an illegal contract as legal (discussed in more detail below).[32] In a second matter, the issue arose in relation to an unfair dismissal claim regarding a complex employment arrangement. Leanne Smallwood argued she was unfairly dismissed under s. 394 of the *Fair Work Act 2009* (Cth) (*FW Act*) by her employer Ergo Asia Pty Ltd.[33] She was on a 457 visa under a labour agreement sponsored by an on-hire company that provided workplace services to Ergo. The federal Fair Work Commission held that the on-hire arrangement, viewed as a whole, indicated that Smallwood did not have an employment contract with Ergo but rather the on-hire company. Although it was not strictly necessary to decide the point, the Commission also considered the legality of any employment contract between Smallwood and Ergo, if one existed, in light of the *Migration Act*. Because under the

29 Ibid. [69].
30 *MG Lines Pty Ltd t/as Coniston Station v Navi* [2013] NTSC 20 (*Navi*).
31 Robert Guthrie and Michael Quinlan, 'The Occupational Safety and Health Rights and Workers' Compensation Entitlements of Illegal Immigrants: An Emerging Challenge' (2005) 3(2) *Policy and Practice in Health and Safety* 69.
32 [2006] NSWWCCPD 15, [21] (*Zhang*).
33 *Smallwood v. Ergo Asia Pty Ltd* [2014] FWC 964.

Migration Regulations a 457 visa-holder must be directly employed by their sponsor, an employment contract between Smallwood and Ergo (who did not sponsor her) would be in breach of visa conditions and therefore s. 235. Applying *Kazi*, the Commission held that any such contract would be void for illegality on the basis that it is prohibited by s. 235.

Through these cases, the lens of the common law contractual doctrine of illegality illuminates the role of immigration regulation in giving meaning to employment arrangements and determining their enforceability. The criminalisation of unauthorised work tends to centre the courts' attention on the wrongs done by Da Ping, Kazi and Zhang within their relations with state authorities (in contravening immigration law), to the exclusion of wrongs committed within their employment relations. This results in a radical re-envisaging of the employment relationship in the majority judgments of *Kazi* and *Da Ping*, from that in *Taufia*.

One clue to the different approaches taken by the courts lies in the historical source of this area of contract law: the equitable doctrine that those who break the law cannot seek the law's redress.[34] Scholars have proposed that courts refuse to confer on those engaging in prohibited conduct any legal benefit flowing from the breach in order to protect 'the majesty of the law'.[35] The integrity and authority (and even the credibility[36]) of the law can only be restored if the law withholds its protective capacity. Formulating the rule in this way is highly evocative of Judith Butler's description of human responses to precariousness.[37] She notes that someone else's suffering often produces a heightened sense of our own fragility. Rather that responding with empathy and support, an individual, a community or even an institution may often instead move, defensively, to buttress itself by attempting to obliterate that individual's weakness, which becomes a threat. Faced with the unauthorised workers' law-breaking, the law moves to withdraw its protection entirely.

The need to protect the law's authority seems particularly acute when a contract violates immigration rules in particular. Even in *Taufia*, where the NSW Court of Appeal concludes that the employment contract is valid, the majority nevertheless cautions against trivialising the gravity of Taufia's immigration violation. In the first instance decision in Taufia's suit, Burke CJ had observed:

> I find it difficult to see anything particularly blameworthy in a citizen of a country less fortunate than ours doing the best he can to support

34 *Holman* (1775) 98 ER 1120, 1121.

35 Richard Austen-Baker, 'Comprehensive Contract Theory: A Four-Norm Model of Contract Relations' (2009) 25 *Journal of Contract Law* 216, 229.

36 In the context of immigration law violations, Peter Schuck describes 'the loss of credibility … that a legal apparatus suffers when it cannot effectively execute its own rules and intentions': 'The Transformation of Immigration Law' (1984) 84 *Columbia Law Review* 1, 77.

37 Judith Butler, *Precarious Life: The Powers of Mourning and Violence* (Verso, 2004), 131–40.

> himself, his wife and five children, even in the face of a statutory prohibition ... it is all a matter of perspective.[38]

All three appeal judges ruled that Burke CJ's discretion miscarried by understating the seriousness of the breach of the *Migration Act* in this passage.[39] The sanctity of the state's prerogative to control its territorial integrity looms even larger in *Da Ping* and *Kazi*. It is not simply that these plaintiffs approach the courts with unclean hands. Unlike anyone else in Australia whose labour produces a criminal offence, the wrong committed by Da Ping and Kazi relates not to what they have done, nor even the gravity of their criminal conduct, but who they are. In this respect they embody Arendt's archetypal stateless person whom, she said, is 'persecuted not because of what they had done or thought, but because of what they unchangeably were'.[40]

Unauthorised workers' very act of claiming employment-related rights reveals the vulnerability of governance structures seeking to police admissions to Australia and the terms of these admissions. Their presence in legal proceedings disrupts the illusion that the law depends for its existence, and for its legitimacy, on a fixed and delimited political community of nationals. A significant body of North American immigration law scholarship has exposed how immigration rules attempt to define the entire universe in which contests over employment (and all other) entitlements take place. In Linda Bosniak's words, immigration laws comprise 'constitutive boundary maintenance' of the national community.[41] This explains the unique position of unauthorised migrants, described by Mae Ngai as 'impossible subjects', a 'problem that cannot be solved'.[42] Unauthorised employment illuminates these contradictions as an ongoing state of affairs rather than a singular event. A declaration that the unauthorised worker infringed the *Migration Act* seems insufficient to shore up the efficacy of governance over national borders. Nothing short of a total rupture of the relationship between worker and employer, and a refusal to acknowledge the legal significance of the injuries sustained by these workers in Australian workplaces, seems to be required to restore the meaning of immigration laws.

Sadly, the return of the *Kazi* and *Da Ping* courts to border regulations as the final answer in the dispute between worker and employer actually works to diminish Australian governance of workplaces. The implications of these judgments is that unauthorised workers suffer no legal harms whatsoever when denied compensation. But in deregulating workers' conduct, the courts here deregulate employers' conduct as well. Refusing to entertain a

38 *Taufia* appeal (1998) 43 NSWLR 312, 334.

39 Ibid. 315 (Cole JA), 320 (Sheppard AJA), and 327 (Stein JA).

40 Hannah Arendt, *The Origins of Totalitarianism* (Harcourt Brace, 1951), 294.

41 Linda Bosniak, *The Citizen and the Alien* (Princeton University Press, 2006), 11.

42 Mae Ngai, *Impossible Subjects: Illegal Aliens and the Making of Modern America* (Princetown University Press, 2004), 5.

claim tainted with illegality denies any legal significance of the employers' responsibility for the workers' injuries.

To explain this, it might, at first, be supposed that a singular focus on the workers' wrongs must flow from the logic of the illegality of contracts doctrine itself. Since its historical purpose was for courts to avoid stepping in to aid a plaintiff with unclean hands, it might seem entirely appropriate that the loss 'lies where it falls'.[43] Even McMurdo J, ruling in favour of the unauthorised worker in *Kazi*, refers to the court's 'general power, based on public policy, to refuse its aid to a guilty party'.[44] However, in 1995, the High Court explicitly rejected this absolutist approach, counselling courts instead to consider unjust enrichment by either party alongside the plaintiff's statutory breach.[45] In balancing both parties' wrongs, the *Kazi* and *Da Ping* courts concede the employers' breaches of occupational health and safety obligations, but ultimately accord overwhelming precedence to the workers' breaches of immigration rules. In so doing, not a single judgment acknowledges in any way the employers' complicity in creating the unauthorised employment relationship in the first place.

By contrast, those judgments that uphold the validity of the employment contracts take a very different view of the purpose of those arrangements and what exactly is transacted in them. For instance, Burke CJ in Taufia's first instance decision finding for Taufia observes, '[t]he parties to this arrangement ... did not seek to further any illegal purpose or plan. One promised to work in a foundry and the other to pay for such work. One of the most ubiquitous contracts in our society'.[46] The mutual investment of, and interdependencies between, the employer and employee are vividly apparent in this passage. Situating the analysis squarely within the context of employment as much as that of border control illuminates more clearly what is at stake in these disputes.

The doctrine of illegality and unauthorised work in the UK

The doctrine of illegality as applied in *Kazi* hails from English common law. In Britain, the employment contracts of unauthorised workers are widely considered tainted by illegality and therefore void and unenforceable because the employer and (especially) worker are contravening criminal prohibitions.[47] As in Australia, the illegality of contract doctrine in the UK affects not only claims based on the employment contract itself, but also the assertion of statutory rights that depend on the existence of the contract.

43 *Muckleston v. Brown* (1801) 31 ER 934, 942.
44 *Kazi* appeal [2004] QCA 147, [70].
45 *Nelson* (1995) 184 CLR 538, 558–61 and 597.
46 *Taufia* first instance [1995] NSWCC 30.
47 It a criminal offence for an employer to hire an irregular immigrant (*Immigration, Asylum and Nationality Act 2006* s 15) and an offence to enter the UK without permission (*Immigration Act 1971* s 24).

Therefore, unfair dismissal protections have been denied by the Employment Appeals Tribunal on the basis that the contract of employment is illegal in its formation and, in any event, is tainted with illegality contrary to public policy, especially where the employee knowingly works in breach of their condition of entry.[48] In one matter, for instance, where an unauthorised worker subsequently regularised his immigration and employment status, the Tribunal held that, throughout the period where the employee was working illegally, the contract was unenforceable for reason of illegality. However, the contract was severable and was enforceable after his work became authorised.[49]

However, British jurisprudence has been far more complex in relation to tortious claims of discrimination by unauthorised workers. In 2004, in *Vakante v. Addey and Stanhope School*, the Court of Appeal denied such remedies to a Croatian asylum seeker who obtained work as a teacher he was not authorised to do by providing a fraudulent national insurance number.[50] In that matter, Mummery LJ held that, because the worker's illegal conduct arose at the formation of the employment relationship, his culpability barred him from any discrimination claim. However, ten years later, in 2014, the Supreme Court held that a different approach should be taken where the worker's loss was not inextricably linked to the illegal procurement of the employment contract and where the discrimination claim should be allowed as a matter of public policy.[51] In *Hounga v. Allen*, Ms Hounga arrived in the UK from Nigeria in 2007 to work in the Allens' home as a 'sort of *au pair*', having previously worked in Mrs Allen's brother's home in Lagos. She may have been as young as 14. Allen obtained a false passport and tourist visa for her and promised her £50 per month to look after the children. However, on arrival and for 18 months, Allen allegedly paid Hounga nothing and regularly physically abused her before eventually throwing her out of the house. Hounga brought a claim for wrongful dismissal, unfair dismissal, unpaid wages, discrimination and harassment. The employment tribunal dismissed all these claims on the basis of illegality of the underlying contract, except race discrimination; the Employment Appeal Tribunal agreed, awarding her £6,187. The Court of Appeal overturned this decision for

48 *Zarkasi v. Anindita and Tse Tan* [2012] UKEAT/0400/11/JOJ. See further Bernard Ryan, 'The Evolving Legal Regime on Unauthorized Work by Migrants in Britain' (2005) 27 *Comparative Labor Law and Policy Journal* 27, 45; Elaine Dewhurst, 'Models of Protection of the Right of Irregular Immigrants to Back Pay: The Impact of the Interconnection Between Immigration Law and Labor Law' (2014) 35 *Comparative Labor Law and Policy Journal* 217.

49 *Bamgbose v. Royal Star and Garter Home* [1996] EAT 841/95.

50 [2004] 4 All ER 1056, affirming *Vakante v. Governing Body of Addey and Stanhope School (No 2)* [2004] ICR 279.

51 *Hounga v. Allen* [2014] UKSC 47, overturning *Allen v. Hounga* [2012] EWCA Civ 609. See A. L. Bogg and T. Novitz, 'Race Discrimination and the Doctrine of Illegality' (2013) 129 *Law Quarterly Review* 12.

reasons similar to those in *Vakante*, holding the illegal contract fatal to the claim in tort.

On appeal, the Supreme Court upheld Hounga's race discrimination claim. In the majority, Lord Wilson (with whom Lady Hale and Lord Kerr agreed) held that illegal conduct was part of the context that constituted her vulnerability to racial abuse but was not 'inextricably bound up' with her tort claim of having been treated less favourably because of her race. Further, according to the majority judgment, the claim should be upheld as a matter of public policy, in particular the preservation of the 'integrity of the legal system'. Here, Lord Wilson noted that Hounga was not profiting from her own wrong or evading a penalty so upholding the racial discrimination claim did not encourage unauthorised work, while unscrupulous employers may well be attracted to unauthorised labour if they could breach their employment rights with impunity. Furthermore, Lord Wilson concluded that Hounga had been trafficked and, therefore, to deny her claim would be to undermine the public policy of English common law to protect victims of trafficking.

This recent turn in the British jurisprudence significantly reframes arguments about the effect of granting workplace entitlements to unauthorised workers on the integrity of the law. It is particularly striking that Lord Wilson's judgment acknowledges the regulatory failures (improperly rewarding employers) which can result from the doctrine of illegality in the context of unauthorised work, something barely considered in *Kazi*. To this extent, it is possible that *Hounga* may provide an alternative perspective on the doctrine for Australian courts. However, it is important not to overstate the force of *Hounga*, since the Court of Appeal's approach in *Hounga* is likely inapplicable beyond tort law: Lord Wilson explicitly distinguished the operation of the doctrine of illegality in contract from Hounga's tort claim noting that her claim for unfair dismissal must have failed. Lord Hughes in the minority upheld Hounga's discrimination claim, on narrower grounds, but also found that her breach of contract claims must fail because her contract was clearly illegal.

Moreover, in Australia, beyond judicial interpretations of the doctrine of illegality, further contradictions arise in the remedial effort. It is to this case law that the chapter now turns.

Australian workers compensation remedies and the borders of impairment

Under workers compensations schemes in two states, a finding that an employment contract is illegal is not conclusive of entitlements. Legislation in NSW and Western Australia bestow on decision makers a general discretion to deem such contracts valid, and permit the recovery of compensation.[52] This discretion is not available elsewhere in Australia, where the

52 *Workers' Compensation Act 1987* (NSW), s 24; *Workers Compensation and Injury Management Act 1981* (WA), s 192.

precedent in *Kazi* may therefore have greatest impact.[53] The ways that decision-makers in NSW award remedies to unauthorised workers illuminate complexities in responding to, or disavowing, the various vulnerabilities and harms at stake.

The discretion in s. 24 of the *Workers' Compensation Act 1987* (NSW) to treat the underlying employment contract as valid has overwhelmingly been exercised in favour of unauthorised workers.[54] Indeed, the NSW Court of Appeal in *Taufia*, which by majority found Taufia's employment contract valid, nevertheless considered the operation of this discretion. Sheppard AJA (the dissentient who found Taufia's contract invalid) would have exercised it to award him compensation, noting that the discretion requires the decision-maker to consider whether the legislators intended the illegality to be overlooked, whether the worker disadvantaged anyone in undertaking the employment, whether the work itself was illegal, and whether the employer was aware of the worker's statutory breach.[55]

Having found unauthorised workers entitled to workers compensation, these judgments grapple with the appropriate level of award. In addition to compensation for the injury itself, NSW legislation provides workers weekly payments for ongoing incapacity as a result of the injury.[56] Generally, these payments are determined by deducting the worker's current capacity to earn since the injury from what they would likely have earned without the injury and then allows for a further exercise of discretion. A great diversity of approaches has been taken to applying this formula to unauthorised work. In *Viliami v. National Springs*, in 1993, the NSW Compensation Court awarded nothing at all for ongoing incapacity due to the worker's unauthorised status.[57] The Tongan applicant, Penisimani Tuuhetau Tupa, came to Australia on a visitor visa, began working for National Springs in May 1989 and in June his right hand became tangled in a conveyor belt, seriously damaging his hand, wrist and the lower part of his arm. He received medical treatment and compensation and, indeed, later returned to work where he was provided with appropriately amended duties. Subsequently, immigration authorities appeared at the workplace and pointed out that Tupa was precluded from working in Australia, whereupon his employment was terminated. Burke J granted compensation for Tupa's permanent injuries, but not weekly payments for lost earnings. Since Tupa was not legally

53 See *Workers Rehabilitation and Compensation Act 1988* (Tas); *Workers Rehabilitation and Compensation Act 1986* (SA); *Accident Compensation Act 1985* (Vic); *Workers' Compensation and Rehabilitation Act 2003* (Qld).

54 *Zhang* [2006] NSWWCCPD 15; *Kaufusi v. Supre Pty Ltd* (1999) 18 NSWCCR 607 (*Kaufusi*); *Viliami v. National Springs* (1993) 9 NSWCCR 453 (*Viliami*); *Taufia* first instance [1995] NSWCC 30.

55 *Taufia* appeal (1998) 43 NSWLR 312, 336.

56 These cases all consider former s 40 of the *Workers Compensation Act*, which has since been replaced by ss 33 and 35.

57 *Viliami* (1993) 9 NSWCCR 453.

permitted to work in Australia, his Honour held that what he would have earned if he had not been injured was effectively nil. Noting that such payments must be calculated with reference to 'a reasonably accessible labour market', his Honour determined that Tupa had 'no labour market reasonably accessible to him by operation of law'.[58]

This conclusion illuminates a profound paradox in resolving the legal claims of unauthorised litigants. Political sociologist Christina Boswell notes the contradiction that arises where the law recognises that a plaintiff has rights by virtue of having been present in fact, but has 'no right to *be* present'.[59] Boswell observes that UK courts frequently confer retrospective remedies for past rights violations (contingent on previous actual – although unauthorised – presence) but not for ongoing rights violations that depend upon continued presence, to avoid any suggestion that the law tolerates the person's ongoing unauthorised residence. In *Viliami*, the court determined remedies by interpreting ongoing earning capacity as lawful earning capacity in Australia. While understandable as an effort to resolve the contradiction highlighted by Boswell, this approach effaces employment relationships that would have continued but for the injury for which the employer is responsible. It limits the appraisal of harm caused by the injury to the national borders: there is no attempt to measure Tupa's reduced future earning capacity for work legally undertaken after leaving Australia.

Two years later, in *Taufia*, at first instance, the NSW Compensation Court took a more sophisticated approach to remedies.[60] This time, Burke J awarded no payments for the period after the injury and before Taufia's return to Tonga (while he continued to work without authorisation in Australia) since he was precluded from working in Australia and unable, geographically, to work elsewhere. But, thereafter, his Honour calculated Taufia's probable earnings as an unauthorised (uninjured) construction worker in Australia, less the probable earnings in Australia of working without authorisation but with his injured ankle. Burke J then exercised discretion to reduce this amount to A$25 per week, to 'reflect the reality' of Taufia's lack of work permission in Australia, his current actual circumstance of working in the Tongan economy with considerably lower wages 'but recognising that he yet has a disability which would affect him in that environment'. In essence, Taufia obtained an award of weekly compensation because of an available labour market in Tonga. The NSW Court of Appeal affirmed these orders. Clearly this approach absorbs the complex reality of Taufia's precarious circumstances better than the outright rejection of ongoing relief in *Viliami*. Nevertheless, these decisions share an inconsistency. Compensation is awarded to Taufia and Tupa on the basis of

58 Ibid. 457.

59 Christina Boswell, 'The Elusive Rights of an Invisible Population' (2008) 22(2) *Ethics and International Affairs* 187, 189, 191 (emphasis in original).

60 *Taufia* first instance [1995] NSWCC 30.

employment contracts that are deemed legal yet recompense for ongoing loss of earnings is limited because the work was in fact illegal. Analysing these judgments, Robert Guthrie suggests that this result may be reconciled on the basis that the worker's inability to continue to work was a consequence of both the work injury and unauthorised status, so that the unauthorised status acquired an additional relevance to the calculation of future incapacity.[61]

By contrast, in 1999, the NSW Compensation Court assessed another unauthorised Tongan worker's loss of earnings as if he were legally working in Australia.[62] Two and a half years after arriving in Australia, Finau Kaufusi began working without authorisation as a storeman and cleaner at a factory run by Supre, handling large rolls of fabrics, some up to 2.5m long and weighing 100kg. In 1991, he injured his back and right leg while bending under a table to pick up rubbish. Kaufusi returned to work three months later doing somewhat lighter work but that ended in November 1992 when immigration compliance officers informed Supre that Kaufusi's employment breached s. 83(2) of the *Migration Act*. He was granted permanent residence in September 1995 but had not found employment since that date. Armitage J held that, having exercised discretion to overlook the illegality of the work under s. 24, he was required to calculate weekly compensation payments on that same basis, as though the worker could have continued working under a valid contract of service from the date of the injury.

In 2006, the NSW Court of Appeal considered a compensation claim for ongoing incapacity by a worker who was injured while working lawfully but subsequently lost his work rights.[63] Gurminder Singh was a truck driver working lawfully while holding a Bridging visa A, which temporarily regularised his status while his application was pending for a substantive visa. In 2000, while he was unloading groceries, a trolley fell on him, injuring his chest, neck, back and right arm. He received lump sum compensation and weekly payments for partial loss of earning capacity. When this visa was later cancelled and substituted with a Bridging visa E prohibiting work, the private insurer terminated his benefits. The Arbitrator focused on what Singh 'is able to earn in the labour market that's open to him'. Singh argued that a labour market existed for unauthorised workers in Australia, for instance in 'banana plantations in Queensland', testifying: 'If I was not injured … I would still be working despite my immigration status. I am aware of a lot of other people in my community that have had their visa status changed. These people in order to survive still find work for cash such as farming and restaurant work'. The Arbitrator rejected this claim concluding there was virtually no evidence that a 'person without a visa that entitled them to work,

61 Robert Guthrie, 'Illegal Contracts: Impropriety, Immigrants and Impairment in Employment Law' (2002) 27(3) *Alternative Law Journal* 116, 119.

62 *Kaufusi* (1999) 18 NSWCCR 607, [44] and [47].

63 *Singh v. TAJ (Sydney) Pty Ltd* [2006] NSWCA 330 (*Singh* appeal).

could obtain employment' in such a labour market.[64] The NSW Workers Compensation Commission ruled that, for the time that Singh was prohibited from working legally, the amount that he 'would have been earning but for injury' was zero (this marked a return to the approach in *Viliami*, which restricted loss of future earning capacity purely to the formal Australian labour market).[65]

On review, the NSW Court of Appeal held that the worker's immigration status was not a relevant consideration in determining what the worker would be able to earn in suitable employment, at least where the original employment in which the injury was suffered was legal.[66] The court rejected the contention of Singh's employer that this approach indicated approval of a commission of a crime, explicitly overturned *Viliami* and remitted the matter back to the Commission.[67] On re-hearing, the Commission deducted the amount Singh could hypothetically earn in Australia post-injury from the amount Singh hypothetically would have earned in Australia without the injury. Acting Deputy President Moore then exercised her discretion, considering Singh's lack of authorisation to work, lowering the weekly payments to A$70.[68]

Without question, this approach is more responsive to the ongoing impact of the injury on the worker than *Viliami*. Nevertheless, this remedial effort does continue to efface the actual consequences of the injury to the unauthorised worker. The reality of what an unauthorised worker might actually have continued to earn if not injured is simply not reflected in the award. Nor is there any appreciation of how the injury in fact influenced the worker's migration status. Indeed, it is probable (although none of these decisions address this) that the injury precipitated the worker's unauthorised status becoming known to authorities. One of the most likely consequences of the injury is the abrupt termination of the employee's ability, albeit without authorisation, to reside and work in Australia. The unique costs of unsafe work to unauthorised workers are not compensable.

Other employment entitlements: unfair dismissal and restitution

It is not yet clear what the implications are of this workers compensation case law for the eligibility of unauthorised workers for other employment protections. Unauthorised workers might be thought to be excluded from the *FW Act*, which governs the bulk of employment entitlements, because this applies to 'national system employees' and 'employee' is given 'its ordinary meaning', which typically requires a contract of employment.[69]

64 Discussed ibid. [16], [20] and [22].
65 *Singh v. Taj (Sydney) Pty Limited* [2006] NSWWCCPD 7, [46]–[49].
66 *Singh* appeal [2006] NSWCA 330, [52].
67 Ibid. [39].
68 *Singh v. Taj (Sydney) Pty Limited* [2007] NSWWCCPD 152.
69 *FW Act* ss 13 and 15; and see Andrew Stewart, *Stewart's Guide to Employment Law* (Federation Press, 4th edn, 2013), [5.11].

However, this question has not yet been subject to judicial consideration. Anecdotally, the Fair Work Ombudsman (FWO) pursues entitlements for unauthorised workers. However, its formal approach to the legal domain of unauthorised work is uncertain. In one court proceeding, for instance, where workers appeared to have worked without authorisation (reportedly some held tourist visas, which prohibit work), the FWO pursued contraventions in relation to maintenance of records but did not pursue known underpayments of wages.[70] The question of their immigration status was not expressly discussed. In an effort to track the legal regulation of unauthorised work, this section explores what scant case law there is in two further areas of employment protections: unfair dismissal and restitution for unjust enrichment that may be payable in the absence of an enforceable contract. The jurisprudence on the record offers little solace to unauthorised workers in Australia, in contrast to more inclusive approaches to labour protections taken in the USA and EU.

I turn first to unfair dismissal, termination at the initiative of the employer that is harsh, unjust or unreasonable (s. 385(b) of the *FW Act*). Relief is provided when a dismissal has a disproportionate effect on the employee, is not based on a 'valid reason' or does not show sufficient procedural fairness. The application of this remedy to authorised temporary workers was discussed in Chapter 3. However, when it comes to unauthorised workers, even if they are entitled to *FW Act* protections more broadly, two decisions indicate that unfair dismissal protections are not available to workers dismissed because of their unauthorised status. In 1997, the Industrial Relations Court of Australia refused unfair dismissal remedies to an unauthorised worker, Chen Wei Xin.[71] Chen commenced work as a guillotine operator for Allied Packaging in 1993. In June 1996, he injured his back when a wheel on a trolley he was pushing became stuck in a hole in the factory floor. He sought medical advice and forwarded a medical certificate to his employer confirming that he was unfit for work until July. Around two weeks later the managing director, Ray Doherty, phoned Chen asking him to come into work, and gave him a letter terminating his employment. On these facts the termination seems to have been harsh, unjust and unreasonable and in breach of unfair dismissal protections against termination due to temporary illness.[72]

However, Chen did not hold a valid visa at the time of the injury. After the injury, Doherty had asked immigration compliance officers about Chen's entitlement to work and was informed that Chen was a non-citizen not entitled to work in Australia. Doherty terminated Chen's employment the following day. Considering Chen's claim for unfair dismissal, Wilcox CJ

70 *FWO v. Honest and Frank Pty Ltd* [2010] SAIRC 23, [12].

71 *Wei Xin Chen v. Allied Packaging Co Pty Ltd* (1997) 73 IR 53 (*Chen*); further considered in *Cunningham v. Bensons Building Services Pty Ltd* [1998] SAIRComm 26.

72 *Workplace Relations Act 1996* (Cth), s 170CK(2), then in force.

acknowledged that 'it may be correct' that 'Mr Doherty used [Chen's] illegal status as an excuse to terminate his employment'. His Honour expressed 'considerable sympathy for Mr Chen's position' but nevertheless upheld the lawfulness of Chen's dismissal.[73] Citing s. 235 of the *Migration Act*, Wilcox CJ observed:

> It is also clear that, once Mr Doherty became aware of Mr Chen's status, any action by him that facilitated Mr Chen's illegal employment would itself be unlawful. Mr Doherty would become an accomplice and would himself be exposed to prosecution.

In other words, Wilcox CJ concluded that the employer would have been acting unlawfully if he had allowed Chen's criminal conduct to continue.[74] Chen's breach of s. 235 constituted a valid reason for termination.

After termination, Chen obtained a visa granting him work rights but Doherty refused to re-employ him. Wilcox J dismissed Chen's application for reinstatement to which he would otherwise have been entitled,[75] holding that Chen's subsequent permission to work in Australia was not relevant to the legality of the earlier termination. Interestingly, the court here does not appear to treat Chen's contract of employment as illegal, nor question the payment of workers compensation to Chen prior to his dismissal.[76]

A second reported case concerns Anthony Emurugat, recruited from Kenya in 2005 by an Australian company on a 457 visa to work on power lines in Australia. Once in Australia, it became clear that he lacked the necessary skills for the work; although the company attempted to train him he remained unable to perform work in his nominated position. Instead, the company continued to employ him in a lower position, in contravention of condition 8107 on his 457 visa. After monitoring this arrangement, immigration officials concluded Emurugat was working in breach of his visa conditions. His employer, Utilities Management Pty Ltd, dismissed him to avoid contravening immigration laws itself. Emurugat claimed before the Australian Industrial Relations Commission that the company should have trained him to the required standard, and failing to do so amounted to unfair dismissal. The Commission rejected this contention since 'there was a valid reason for the termination of Mr Emurugat's employment' as his continued employment was illegal under the provisions of the *Migration Act*.[77]

73 *Chen* (1997) 73 IR 53, 54.

74 His Honour is referring to the aiding and abetting offences attached to s 235 since this judgment was handed down one decade before employer sanctions were introduced in Australia, which are discussed in the following chapter.

75 *Workplace Relations Act 1996* (Cth), s 170DE.

76 See Robert Guthrie and Rebecca Taseff, 'Dismissal and Discrimination: Illegal Workers in England and Australia' (2008) 24 *International Journal of Comparative Labour Law and Industrial Relations* 31, 51.

77 *Antony Emurugat v. Utilities Management Pty Ltd* [2008] AIRC 1114, [33].

Plainly, an unfair dismissal could not occur where the cause for the termination is the worker's unauthorised status and unauthorised workers hold no right to reinstatement. However, these cases leave unanswered the consequences of an employer unfairly sacking a worker and only later uncovering the unauthorised status, or of an employer hiring an employee in full knowledge of their lack of work rights and later dismissing them unfairly or in retaliation for claiming entitlements (although the facts in Chen may come close to this). Of course, in Australia, another practical way to terminate an unauthorised worker's employment is to report them to immigration officials who generally will remove the worker as soon as practicable.[78] Generally, under s. 343 of the *FW Act*, employers are prohibited from taking 'adverse action' against an employee to coerce them not to exercise a 'workplace right', defined in s. 341 as an entitlement under a workplace instrument or law, or a complaint or inquiry to seek compliance. But it is unclear whether 'adverse action' includes terminating unauthorised employment. It almost certainly would not include reporting an employee's criminal conduct to immigration authorities. By contrast, US case law has declared unlawful an employer reporting an unauthorised worker to immigration officials in retaliation for claiming unpaid wages.[79] The uncertainty on this point in Australia is cause for great concern because, even if unauthorised workers are covered, in principle, by other employment protections, denying security of employment to unauthorised workers renders all other substantive protections meaningless since a threat to with dismiss a worker is easily used to secure their compliance with inferior working conditions.

Given the overall lack of clarity on unauthorised workers' access to all these employment protections, including especially those under basic contract law, the final area of law considered in this chapter concerns restitution or the equitable doctrine of unjust enrichment. This section reviews the small body of case law on the claims of unauthorised workers where an employer has benefited from work they have performed in the absence of a genuine agreement or where a contract is frustrated or has been determined to be void for illegality. Graeme Orr, who assisted legal counsel for Kazi, has suggested that an equitable action might be available even if a court has denied statutory workers compensation protections, for example. While workers compensation benefits are in fact commonly drawn from state-backed compensation funds, 'wages and conditions are questions of transactional justice between the worker and employer'.[80] Restitution claims might be treated differently because they focus squarely on the exchange between worker and employer, on the employer's culpability

78 *Migration Act* ss 198, 200–206.

79 *Singh v. Jutla*, 214 FSupp 2d 1056 (ND Cal 2002).

80 Graeme Orr, 'Unauthorised Workers: Labouring Beneath the Law?' in Christopher Arup *et al.* (eds), *Labour Law and Labour Market Regulation: Essays on the Construction, Constitution and Regulation of Labour Markets and Work Relationships* (Federation Press, 2006), 677, 692.

within that relationship, and on the relative bargaining power of each. Orr also recommends pursuing tortious claims for negligence because the legality of work contracts might be considered irrelevant to tort law, since working without a visa does not exacerbate the risk of injury (or therefore amount to contributory negligence). Indeed, Orr notes that the immigration department website has previously warned employers that even 'if an employee is not covered under workers' compensation, he or she is covered under common law and if injured, could pursue a civil claim'. This advice has since been removed.

However, the reported case law provides little to confirm that these avenues for relief are open to unauthorised workers. One unauthorised worker's common law claim for damages resulting from an injury on a cattle station in the Northern Territory has not yet progressed to judgment.[81] None of the judgments in the workers compensation cases discussed above conclusively determines the eligibility of unauthorised migrants for equitable remedies. Instead, at least three judgments in the superior court cases on workers compensation entitlements examined earlier in this chapter suggest in *obiter dicta* either that an illegal contract prevents the employee from recovering unpaid wages for work actually done or, at least, that any such entitlement is not necessarily available.[82] Indeed the possibility is raised that, in the event of an illegal contract, an *employer* could recover wages they actually paid even though they benefited from the work done. One Federal Court judgment (explored in more detail below) positively withholds equitable relief from an unauthorised worker. However, the unique characteristics of that case mean that this ruling may not be conclusive.

More helpfully, two reported matters in NSW appear to award equitable remedies to unauthorised domestic workers although their reasoning is undeveloped. The first, a brief 1999 judgment of the NSW Court of Appeal, leaves in place a lower court judgment granting an (apparently unauthorised) migrant, Satyendra Nath Midya, reasonable remuneration of A$21,840 for work performed, on the basis of *quantum meruit*.[83] Delivered one year after *Taufia*, the judgment does not expressly indicate Midya's immigration status or why the claim was assessed on the basis of *quantum meruit* rather than under contract or an industrial award.

The second was *Masri v. Santoso*, proceedings brought before the NSW Industrial Relations Commission flowing out of the circumstances recounted at the commencement of this chapter.[84] It will be recalled that Masri's employer had procured a fraudulent visitor's visa, on which Masri entered

81 See *Navi* [2013] NTSC 20.

82 See Stein JA in *Taufia* appeal (1998) 43 NSWLR 312, 319; Mullins J in *Kazi* first instance [2003] QSC 225, [26]; McMurdo J, in dissent in *Kazi* appeal [2004] QCA 147, [77].

83 *Midya v. Sagrani* [1999] NSWCA 187. The circumstances of this claim were discussed before parliament: Commonwealth, *Parliamentary Debates*, House of Representatives, 11 August 1999, 8506 (Tanya Plibersek, ALP).

84 *Masri v. Santoso* [2004] NSWIRComm 108, [3], [157]–[176] and [181].

Australia before unlawfully undertaking domestic work for the Santosos, 17 hours each day, seven days a week. Over four years Masri was paid a total of A$5,190. Turning first to the question of whether there was any legal relationship between the parties, Haylen J concluded that there was at least an 'arrangement', if not a contract, which was sufficient to ground the Commission's jurisdiction under s. 105 of the *Industrial Relations Act 1996* (Cth) and a mutual intention to employ Masri as 'a housemaid' with monthly wages. The Commission then declared this arrangement void under s. 106 of the Act because it was unfair:

> It was unfair to bring the applicant to Australia without discussing the terms of her employment; it was unfair that the applicant should perform this amount of work for the paltry sum she was paid; and it was unfair that she was not provided with the kind of working conditions enjoyed by employees, such as to permit breaks in the work and a life outside the house.[85]

Exercising its power to order payment in lieu of a voided unfair contract, and in the absence of an industrial award covering private domestic labour, the Commission awarded Masri A$95,000 in compensation. Although Haylen J made detailed findings on Masri's working conditions, his Honour did not squarely address the question of whether Masri's unauthorised status interfered with the Commission's jurisdiction.

A 2006 Federal Court judgment, on the other hand, expressly rejected an unauthorised worker's claim for *quantum meruit*. In *Hussein v. Secretary of the Department of Immigration*, Graham J dismissed claims for compensation brought by an unlawful non-citizen detainee against private immigration detention service providers. Motahar Hussein sought payment for work he did in detention at Villawood Immigration Detention Centre, under either a contract of employment or *quantum meruit*. The court found that, if Hussein was performing 'work', the criminal offence in s. 235 rendered any employment contract void for illegality, and precluded the recovery of payment on the basis of *quantum meruit* for work 'which retained its illegal character'.[86] Migration laws have since been amended clarifying that it is not unlawful for a person to perform 'work' in immigration detention.[87] Hussein also claimed in tort that the Immigration Department had breached its duty of care to him. Graham J dismissed these claims as 'manifestly groundless' but also observed that arguably the law would not condone the commission of a criminal offence against s. 235(3) by granting a civil remedy in tort.[88]

85 Ibid. [179A].
86 *Hussein* [2006] FCA 1263, [67]–[68].
87 *Migration Act* ss 235(6) and 235(7)(a); *Migration Regulations* reg 5.32A.
88 Citing *Gala v. Preston* (1991) 172 CLR 243, 277; *Yango Pastoral* (1978) 139 CLR 410, 433.

As Graeme Orr has noted, these cases all involve an element of fiction given the practical barriers to enforcement that most unauthorised workers face.[89] This chapter has sought to demonstrate that, even beyond practical difficulties, workers' in principle substantive industrial rights are undermined by layers of jurisprudential uncertainty. The following section, reflecting on this jurisprudence as a whole, considers some of the imagined policy objectives articulated by the courts to justify their approach, arguing that it strengthens neither the hand of resident workers nor the integrity of the legal system itself. As we will see, jurisprudence in the USA and EU has been more successful in absorbing these policy implications.

The imagined dangers of protecting unauthorised workers

Across this case law, judgments characterise the consequences flowing from the legal protection of unauthorised workers very differently, according to their outcome. Those judgments that uphold the validity of unauthorised workers' employment contracts are acutely focused on the broad social harms of invalidating employment contracts. Stein JA, in his leading judgment in *Taufia* in favour of upholding the workers compensation claim, concludes that a statutory prohibition should not invalidate a contract 'if it would lead to an unjust, unreasonable, inconvenient or absurd result'.[90] McMurdo J (dissenting in *Kazi* and also ruling for the worker) explicitly links this consideration to the judicial task of interpreting the implications of s. 235:

> The adverse consequences from such contracts being void could be so extensive that, compared with the extent which the implication would conduce to the object of the statute, it should not be inferred that Parliament intended to inflict them upon the public.[91]

Justice McMurdo's dissent goes furthest in attending to the precariousness of all affected parties. He notes that declaring the contract illegal might in fact prejudice the employer, who would not therefore be entitled to enforce common law duties such as good faith and fidelity. 'Innocent' third parties' interests in copyright or patents may be compromised or they may be precluded from relying on the employer's vicarious liability for the worker's tortious conduct. This judgment recognises the relationships of trust and law that arise within the workplace community regardless of migration authorisation and acknowledges reciprocal rights and obligations inhering within this relationship.

89 Orr, 'Unauthorised Workers', above n. 80, 693.
90 *Taufia* (1998) 43 NSWLR 312, 319.
91 *Kazi* appeal [2004] QCA 147, [69].

By contrast, the judgments that withhold legal protections from unauthorised workers rest strongly on the objective of deterrence. Punishing unauthorised work is thought to reinforce the position of resident and lawfully working temporary migrants who risk degraded working conditions when unauthorised workers undercut them.[92] Withholding entitlements is deemed necessary to avoid gifting unauthorised workers some 'un-bargained for reward'.[93] To justify the resulting precariousness, these judgments emphasise unauthorised workers' agency. Indeed, this characterisation of unauthorised workers' fault is redolent of broader policy debates. The premise that unauthorised workers choose their circumstances is vividly captured in the title of a 1999 Immigration Department discussion paper on unauthorised work: *The Hidden Workforce: Illegal Workers in Australia and Those that Would Join Them.* As Stephen Legomsky paraphrases: 'is it not *we* who are subjecting them to that risk. It is *they* who are creating that risk, by choosing to commit acts they know to be illegal'.[94] This view sees migrant workers as willing creators of their precarious circumstances, freely 'trading-off' employment protections in order to remain in the labour market in the country of employment.[95]

There are two difficulties with this perspective, however. The first is, as argued in Chapter 2, if ethical responsibilities flow from the *impact* of Australian employers on unauthorised workers, the fact that an unauthorised worker has been injured after having 'chosen' to stay in Australia becomes less relevant. Second, invoking notions of choice and consent obscures the role of the state in constructing the conditions of precariousness within which workers exercise agency. It is not just that laws actively shape migrants' life choices by assigning immigration status, thereby producing relations of domination and subordination, nor even that unauthorised migrants' fear of removal is a form of institutionalised uncertainty. Rather, jurisprudence, which invalidates the employment contracts of unauthorised migrants, itself structurally produces precarious work. This lays bare a contradiction within the regulatory framework. By declaring an employment contract void, the courts and the law are removing themselves from governance of this relationship, narrowing the reach of employment regulation. In the name of preserving the law as the sovereign expression of national community, this in fact brings about a diminution of sovereignty.

92 For an incisive account of broader social constructions of injuries caused by irregular migration see Bridget Anderson, 'Where's the Harm in That? Immigration Enforcement, Trafficking and the Protection of Migrants' Rights' (2012) 56 *American Behavioral Scientist* 1241, 1248.

93 Peter Marguiles, 'Stranger and Afraid: Undocumented Workers and Federal Employment Law' (1989) 38 *DePaul Law Review* 553, 554.

94 Stephen Legomsky, 'Portraits of the Undocumented Immigrant: Epiphany Through Dialectic' (2009) 44 *Georgia Law Review* 65, 79 (emphasis in original).

95 Martin Ruhs and Philip Martin, 'Numbers vs. Rights: Trade Offs and Guest Worker Programs' (2008) 42 *International Migration Review* 249, 254.

A further irony, of course, is that withholding work-related entitlements from unauthorised workers increases their appeal to unscrupulous employers. Employers gain a windfall from work the law denies ever occurred and profit even more when unauthorised workers are discouraged from reporting workplace violations. Even where substantive protections apply, employers can benefit from remedial rules that disadvantage unauthorised workers. The law's emphasis on the offence of illegal work in s. 235 works paradoxically to incentivise the employment of unauthorised migrants. Of course, employer culpability may be pursued separately to workers compensation liability. As recounted in the opening narrative of Chapter 2, Jin Woog Kim's employer was convicted of various health and safety offences without any formal liability for workers compensation.[96] Even so, re-establishing lawful regulation of all employment relationships in Australia with coverage across the full range of entitlements may decrease employers' incentives to hire unauthorised workers, better protecting residents from degraded employment standards and strengthening immigration compliance itself.

The broader frame in EU and US laws

It is these very policy objectives that drive the inclusion of worker entitlements in the EU Employer Sanctions Directive, adopted in 2009. This instrument obliges member states to ensure that employers are liable to acquit any unpaid wages in accordance with minimum wage rules, a collective agreement or common practice in a particular industry.[97] Indeed, this provision arguably builds on established regulatory practice since the majority of EU member states already honoured the employment contracts of unauthorised workers and any related statutory entitlements.[98] For example, Luxembourg requires employers to pay unauthorised workers their salaries and a social contribution, while Austria allows for a wage claim based on a collective bargaining agreement even if the employment contract is void for illegality.[99]

An approach linking deterrence of both immigration and labour law violations with protection rather than diminution of unauthorised workers' rights is also taken in the USA. The New York Court of Appeal has ruled that

96 *Inspector Lai v. Rexma Pty Ltd* [2008] NSWIRComm 78.

97 Directive 2009/52/EC of the European Parliament and of the Council of 18 June 2009 providing for minimum standards on sanctions and measures against employers of illegally staying third-country nationals, art 6.

98 Elaine Dewhurst, 'The Right of Irregular Immigrants to Outstanding Remuneration under the EU Sanctions Directive: Rethinking Domestic Labour Policy in a Globalised World' (2011) 13 *European Journal of Migration and Law* 389, 393–4; Michele LeVoy, Nele Verbruggen and Johan Wets, 'Protective and Repressive Measures in EU States' in Michele LeVoy, Nele Verbruggen and Johan Wets (eds), *Undocumented Migrant Workers in Europe* (Instituut voor de arbeid, Katholieke Universiteit Leuven, 2004), 31–7.

99 Luxembourg, 2008 Law on Freedom of Movement and Immigration art 146; Austria, Civil Code s 1152 and Aliens Employment Act s 25.

a worker's unauthorised status does not interfere with their right to benefits for loss of future wages in a personal injury law suit, explicitly because 'limiting a lost wages claim by an injured undocumented alien would lessen an employer's incentive to comply with the Labor Law and supply all of its workers the safe workplace that the Legislature demands'.[100]

At the same time, the US case law is unique in that there is no federal offence prohibiting unauthorised migrants working there. Instead, to the extent that courts have limited remedies for unauthorised workers, it is on the basis of offences criminalising employers' use of unauthorised labour.[101] In the preeminent case of *Hoffman Plastic Compounds, Inc v. National Labor Relations Board*, the US Supreme Court ruled that Jose Castro, an unauthorised worker, remained a statutory 'employee' protected by employment law.[102] However, when his employer was found to have illegally discharged him in retaliation for union activity, he was ruled ineligible for back pay, because this would run counter to the intention of statutory employer sanctions laws. An encyclopaedic body of scholarship in the USA has condemned the Supreme Court's attenuation of employment entitlements in this case, with most concluding that it may take decades to determine the impact of *Hoffman* on employment laws more generally.[103] Nevertheless, unauthorised migrants in the USA may still assert claims for unpaid wages for work already performed under the *Fair Labor Standards Act*, which guarantees minimum wage and overtime payments (as opposed to back pay for work foregone).[104] Discrimination cases are more mixed: remedies under Title VII and other anti-discrimination provisions have been granted to unauthorised plaintiffs in most circuits[105] although back pay for work foregone may not be available.[106] State courts are divided on whether *Hoffman* should be read to deny tort and workers compensation claims.[107] Reinstatement is generally not available under any head of claim since this would force employers to hire an unauthorised worker in violation of criminal prohibitions.

100 *Balbuena v. IDR Realty LLC*, 6 NY 3d 338 (NY, 2006).

101 *Immigration Reform and Control Act of 1986*, Pub L No 99-603, 100 Stat 3359.

102 *Hoffman Plastic Compounds Inc v. National Labor Relations Board*, 535 US 137 (2002).

103 Michael Wishnie, 'Emerging Issues for Undocumented Workers' (2004) 6 *University of Pennsylvania Journal of Labor and Employment Law* 497, 516; Jennifer Gordon, 'Tensions in Rhetoric and Reality at the Intersection of Work and Immigration' (2012) 2 *UC Irvine Law Review* 125, 132ff.

104 29 USC §§ 201-219 (2000). See e.g. *Chellen v. John Pickle Co*, 446 FSupp 2d 1247 (ND Okla 2006).

105 *Rivera v. NIBCO*, 364 F3d 1057 (9th Cir 2004); *Iweala v. Operational Techs Servs*, 634 FSupp 2d 73 (DDC 2009).

106 *Escobar v. Spartan Sec Serv*, 281 FSupp 2d 895, 896 (SD Tex 2003).

107 E.g. *Madeira v Affordable Housing Foundation, Inc.*, 315 FSupp 2d 504 (SDNY 2004) upholding the right to lost earnings in tort; *Asylum Co v. Dist of Columbia Dept. of Emp't Servs*, 10 A3d 619 (DC 2010) upholding workers compensation entitlements; *Rosa v. Partners in Progress, Inc*, 868 A2d 994 (NH 2005) refusing damages for lost wages; *Sanchez v. Eagle Alloy*, 658 NW2d 510 (Mich Ct App 2003) denying workers compensation wage loss benefits.

Although these protections are still patchy, the approaches taken in these jurisdictions attest to the fact that the sole source of legitimacy of the sovereign law is no longer (if it ever were) the national democratic community. These jurisdictions treat unauthorised migrants as members of the domestic workforce (even if they are not in other ways full members of the community) to a greater degree than do Australian courts. They recognise that robust labour standards for all workers (as well as territorial sovereignty) are best served by emphasising, rather than erasing, the temporary practical ties between unauthorised migrants and employers, without needing to disavow entirely the consequences of their unauthorised presence.

The case for repealing the criminal offence of unauthorised work

In Australia, various forms of legislative amendment of s. 235 could move closer to the ideals embodied in these models. Parliament might clarify in s. 235 that it intends that unauthorised workers' statutory and common law employment rights remain enforceable, despite a worker's breach.[108] Alternatively, coverage of unauthorised workers under numerous state and federal industrial statutes could be achieved by amending the scope of 'worker' to include workers who contravene a legislative provision. Otherwise, the discretion, in the NSW and WA workers compensation legislation, to deem an illegal contract valid could be inserted into other legislative schemes. These courses of action are made difficult by the sheer number of statutory instruments covering employment protections. The latter in particular is undesirable since a discretionary protection is far less secure than a legal entitlement.

Alternatively, s. 235 could be repealed. Given the significance of s. 235 in the jurisprudence explored in this chapter, it is poignant indeed that there are no recorded convictions of this offence. Apparently, the statutory duty to remove unauthorised migrants 'as soon as practicable' is accorded precedence over criminal prosecutions.[109] This raises the serious question of what purpose is served by maintaining this offence on the books. Certainly, this chapter has argued that no helpful regulatory role is played by s. 235. However, even if s. 235 were repealed, it is possible that criminal employer sanctions offences in Australia (introduced in 2007 and discussed in the following chapter) could still enable the contractual illegality arguments to be run. Further legislative clarification is required.

108 Alex Reilly has recommended this be done in favour of international students working in excess of their 40 hour fortnightly work limitation but this should be more broadly stated in favour of all unauthorised workers: Alexander Reilly, 'Protecting Vulnerable Migrant Workers: The Case of International Students' (2012) 25 *Australian Journal of Labour Law* 181, 206.

109 Explanatory Memorandum, Migration Amendment (Employer Sanctions) Bill 2006 (Cth), [7.4].

Some may object that maintaining a system of strictly policed visa-based work restrictions and a protective employment scheme for unauthorised workers seem to pull in different directions. However, this tension is not insurmountable. More nuanced laws can provide protections that acknowledge migrants' period of membership in the workplace, taking seriously the multiplicity of human interactions and the true exchange between worker and employer, without disavowing the fact of their unauthorised presence. The immigration violation may be acknowledged through removal powers without negating labour protections. Positioning migrant workers as subjects of employment law as much as objects of immigration law recasts unauthorised employment as labour exploitation of vulnerable workers. It also, crucially, foregrounds migrant workers' agency by acknowledging not only the adverse impact of employers' unscrupulous conduct on them but also their right to participate in the formation of a legal response.

Conclusion

This chapter confronted the criminalisation of unauthorised work in Australia under the *Migration Act* and its interference with the employment entitlements of unauthorised workers. At times, the jurisprudence has justified denying employment remedies to these workers as necessary to strengthen the labour market security of lawful workers or re-establish a comprehensive law and order response to violations of immigration law. This chapter argued that, in fact, withholding legal protections from unauthorised workers simply narrows the reach of employment regulation. Jurisprudence from the EU and USA demonstrates that by reducing the labour costs of unauthorised workers, this case law paradoxically incentivises employers' use of them. Chapter 7, which follows, argues that employer sanctions legislation (introduced in Australia in 2007 and amended in 2013) is also misguided in its approach.

7 Employer sanctions against unauthorised workers

Chee Mei Wong was a madam at an inner-Sydney brothel when she arranged for eleven women of Indian and Sri Lankan background to travel from Malaysia to Australia on student visas.[1] On arrival, she required them to undertake sex work in 17-hour shifts, from 11 am to 4 am, between August 2008 and July 2009. They were forced 'to perform unprotected and demeaning sex acts, put up with rough clients and work through illness and pain'. Reportedly, the women were threatened with physical harm or removal if they escaped. One woman had quit school at 12 to work when her parents died, and another was servicing her family's debts after her older brother's death. Wong was found guilty in April 2013 of conducting a business that involved sexual servitude. She was also convicted of the crime, introduced in the employer sanctions scheme under the *Migration Act* in 2007, of allowing a person to work in breach of visa conditions in circumstances of exploitation.[2] Sentencing Wong to a maximum of six years imprisonment, Judge Sweeney said she had treated the women 'not as human beings but as commodities – machines to make money'. Project Respect (a Melbourne-based trafficked persons' support agency) apparently assisted two of the women to find other work. Others reportedly continued to work in the sex industry.

The previous two chapters explored the ways in which unauthorised migrant labour, and the precariousness that so often attends it, are produced through intersections between immigration and labour laws. This chapter concludes Part II on unauthorised migrant labour by examining reforms introduced by the conservative Howard government in 2007 to punish those who employ non-citizens without authorisation to work. While punitive measures

1 This narrative is drawn from *R v. Chee Mei Wong* (unreported, DCNSW, Sweeney J, 5 July 2013); Andreas Schloenhardt and Jarrod Jolly, *Trafficking in Persons in Australia: Myths and Realities* (LexisNexis Butterworths, 2013), [2.20]; Stephanie Gardiner, 'Jail for Brothel Keeper Who Enslaved Women', *Sydney Morning Herald*, 6 July 2013, 5.

2 Under *Criminal Code Act 1995* (Cth), s 270.6(1) (*Criminal Code*) and *Migration Act 1958* (Cth), s 245C (since amended) (*Migration Act*).

targeting people-smuggling and arrivals of asylum seekers in Australia have been the subject of endless public deliberation and detailed academic scrutiny, virtually no scholarship has considered Australia's employer sanctions regime.[3]

A review of the criminal framework four years later found it to have been spectacularly ineffectual in deterring irregular migrant employment.[4] Since criminal offences were introduced, there have been only four convictions: the most recent was of Wong, in the narrative at the opening of this chapter. Two of the four involved sex trafficking. The number of visa-overstayers during this period (and, therefore, probably unauthorised workers) actually increased. One reason for this ineffectiveness lay in the prominence given to the criminalisation of unauthorised work itself. According to Howells, prosecutors experienced difficulty in meeting the criminal onus of proof partly because workers, who are best placed to provide evidence of employers' criminal conduct, are unable to testify because their credibility is impugned by their own criminal conduct (the offence of unauthorised work in s. 235 of the *Migration Act*) and, in any event, they almost certainly will have been removed from Australia already.

Striving to enhance enforcement outcomes, in 2013, the Labor government passed legislation creating a more graduated employer sanctions scheme, expanding the ambit of criminal offences and introducing strict liability offences with no-fault civil penalties for those who employ unauthorised workers.[5] Notably, the government made no amendments whatsoever to the regulation of unauthorised workers, whether by assisting them to remain in Australia to aid investigations of employer misconduct, or by ameliorating their precarious living and working conditions during their stay.

To explain the evolution of these offences, this chapter traces a history of strong ambivalence in Australia to holding employers accountable for breaches of immigration laws, with compliance resources reserved instead for unauthorised workers. It sets the recent introduction of employer sanctions in Australia against comparative perspectives from the USA, UK, the EU and Canada, where penalties for employers who use unauthorised labour have been on the books for far longer. While these governments have promoted employer sanctions as a means of preventing the exploitation of unauthorised workers, among other things, in almost every case such sanctions fail to address the existing needs of those currently experiencing exploitation or the precariousness of unauthorised migration status. Instead, they actually intensify the precarious position of unauthorised workers by

3 For the only extended analysis of this issue in Australia some years before the introduction of this legislation, see Matthew Osborne, 'An Arresting Subject: An Examination of Some Issues Raised by the Notion of Introducing Employer Sanctions in Australia' (1992) 51(1) *Australian Journal of Public Administration* 96.

4 Stephen Howells, *Report of the 2010 Review of the* Migration Amendment (Employer Sanctions) Act 2007 (Cth of Australia, 2011), 69ff.

5 *Migration Amendment (Reform of Employer Sanctions) Act 2013* (Cth).

driving unauthorised work further underground and prompting employers to devise ever greater subterfuge to circumvent migration law. In Australia, moreover, employer sanctions distract attention from a legal landscape (sketched in Chapters 5 and 6) that produces precarity by withholding basic labour protections from unauthorised workers, and by denying them pathways to regularisation.

This chapter begins by providing a brief survey of employer sanctions schemes in several English-speaking Western states. Arguably, the historical reluctance to target employers as violators of immigration rules has been even more evident in Australia, as can be appreciated from the evolution of early precursors of employer-focused offences, through to the explicit criminal offences introduced as recently as 2007 and the expanded civil penalty scheme that came into effect in 2013. I suggest that Australia has followed international counterparts in the primacy it accords to worker-focused immigration compliance activities, which entrenches precarious labour in a number of ways. The chapter concludes by considering how (or whether) these offences might influence the Australian jurisprudence concerning employment entitlements of unauthorised workers explored in Chapter 6. Overall, in Australia as elsewhere, employer sanctions are likely to do little to decrease the prevalence of unauthorised work but much to marginalise unauthorised workers further.

Comparative perspectives on employer sanctions laws

Australia is a definite latecomer to immigration regulation that is directed at the employer. The ILO Convention on Migration for Employment required the adoption of employer penalties as early as 1975.[6] Perhaps one reason for the prevalence of employer sanctions in Europe and North America is that, from a democratic perspective, employer sanctions focus regulation and punishment on residents rather than those with weaker membership status. Joseph Carens suggests that 'employers' moral duty to obey laws prohibiting them from hiring irregular migrants is arguably clearer and stronger than the duty of irregular migrants not to seek jobs without the state's authorisation'.[7] At the same time, this very dynamic has produced difficulties in enforcing these laws in virtually every country where they have been introduced, especially in the first decade(s) of each scheme.

Canada adopted employer sanctions legislation in 1976 that has subsequently been amended several times.[8] It is now an offence to employ a person who is not authorised to work, with a positive obligation on

6 Migrant Workers (Supplementary Provisions) Convention, 1975 (ILO No 143) opened for signature 24 June 1975, 1120 UNTS 323 (entered into force 9 December 1978) art 6.

7 Joseph H. Carens, 'The Rights of Irregular Migrants' (2008) 22(2) *Ethics and International Affairs* 163, 184.

8 *Immigration Act*, RSC, ch 52 (1976–1977).

employers to exercise due diligence to determine an employee's work authorisation.[9] If tried by indictment, the offence can attract a fine of C$50,000 and up to two years' imprisonment.[10] With 33 investigations leading to charges against employers between 2006 and 2012, enforcement has been described as functioning primarily on a symbolic level.[11]

The USA introduced penalties against employers who knowingly hire unauthorised workers a decade later, in 1986,[12] establishing two civil offences.[13] The first occurs where an employer knowingly hires, recruits or refers for a fee an unauthorised migrant or continues to employ a migrant knowing they have become unauthorised to work. Fines are currently US$375–3,200 per unauthorised worker for first time offenders. The second offence occurs where an employer fails to comply with requirements for verification of work authorisation and identity, with fines of US$110–1,100 per worker for first time offenders. To establish an affirmative defence against prosecution for either offence, employers must, in 'good faith', complete paperwork certifying they have reviewed newly hired employees' identity or work eligibility documents that reasonably appear genuine. Additional criminal penalties are reserved for those employers who establish a 'pattern or practice' of violations, punishable by additional fines and up to six months' imprisonment.[14] Later, in 1996, the USA introduced another criminal offence of knowingly hiring of at least ten unauthorised non-citizens during any twelve-month period, punishable by up to five years' imprisonment.[15]

Again, weak enforcement plagued the scheme from its beginning. In its first two decades, investigations and prosecutions were hampered by evidentiary burdens, judicial constraints on law enforcement practices, non-communication between government agencies and employer strategies to evade detection. This led Alexander Aleinikoff to bluntly observe in 2008 that '[i]f [the employer sanctions legislation] was intended to end undocumented migration in our time, it has obviously failed'.[16] Yet the Obama Administration moved to strongly implement the scheme, presiding over a 44-fold increase in criminal arrests for egregious breaches between 2002 and

9 *Immigration and Refugee Protection Act*, SC 2001, c 27, s 124(1)(c).

10 *Immigration and Refugee Protection Regulations*, SOR/2002-227, s 125.

11 Judy Fudge and Fiona MacPhail, 'The Temporary Foreign Workers Program in Canada: Low-Skilled Workers as an Extreme Form of Flexible Labour' (2009) 31 *Comparative Labour Law and Policy Journal* 5; Sarah Marsden, 'Law's Permissions, Law's Exclusions: Precarious Migration Status in Canada' (unpublished Ph.D., University of British Columbia, 2013), 208.

12 *Immigration Reform and Control Act of 1986*, Pub L 99-603, 100 Stat 3359.

13 8 USC § 1324a(a)-(h).

14 8 USC § 1324a(f)(1).

15 *Illegal Immigration Reform and Immigrant Responsibility Act of 1996*, Pub L No 104-208, § 203(b)(4), 110 Stat 3009.

16 T. Alexander Aleinikoff *et al.*, *Immigration and Citizenship: Process and Policy* (Thomson West, 6th edn, 2008), 1312.

2008 and tenfold increase in administrative arrests, although the bulk of criminal convictions in federal court continued to be against non-citizens for border-crossing related violations.[17] In 2012, Immigration and Customs Enforcement served more than 3,000 notices of inspections, resulting in US$12.5 million in fines, compared to only three notices of intent to fine in 2004.[18] Nevertheless, commentators point out that the main target of this action was not the punishment of employers but the mass dismissal of thousands of unauthorised workers (hoping they would leave the USA voluntarily).[19] In addition, in the context of historically low levels of federal immigration enforcement, a plethora of states and localities have introduced a range of legal mechanisms to punish employers who hire undocumented workers.

In 1997, the UK introduced, on its face, a far more stringent approach to employment of unauthorised labour. A summary criminal offence was introduced of hiring someone whose immigration status prohibited such employment, with fines initially set at up to £5,000 per employee.[20] The offence was later expanded to be triable on indictment, increasing the possible fine to an unlimited amount. Nevertheless, this scheme also faced grave enforcement shortcomings, with only 37 convictions in its first 10 years,[21] and was subsequently entirely overhauled. New civil penalties came into effect in 2008, making employers liable for a penalty for employing someone without permission to work.[22] There is no requirement for employers to check workers' work authorisation as such but a statutory defence is available for employers who demonstrate that they have taken all reasonable steps to check the validity of immigration documents according to the Home Office guidance (this defence is not available where the employer actually knows that the worker is unauthorised).[23] The maximum penalty for employers who fail to check prospective employees' work entitlements is £15,000 for a first offence per unauthorised worker, issuable as an 'on-the-spot' civil penalty fine.[24] The fine is reduced where the employer has made partial checks, or reported the unauthorised worker to, or otherwise cooperated with, the Border Agency.[25] This scheme seems to have been far more readily enforced,

17 US Immigration and Customs Enforcement, *Fiscal Year 2008 Annual Report: Protecting National Security and Upholding Public Safety* (2008), 17.
18 Stephen Lee, 'Screening for Solidarity' (2013) 80 *The University of Chicago Law Review* 225, 228.
19 David Bacon and Bill Ong Hing, 'The Rise and Fall of Employer Sanctions' (2010) 38 *Fordham Urban Law Journal* 77, 79.
20 *Asylum and Immigration Act 1996* s 8.
21 Home Office UK Border Agency, *Employers Against Whom Notices of Liability Have been Issued and Civil Penalties Imposed for the Use of Illegal Migrant Workers* (September 2008).
22 *Immigration, Asylum and Nationality Act 2006* ss 15-25; *Immigration (Restrictions on Employment) Order 2007*, SI 2007/3290.
23 *Immigration (Restrictions on Employment) Order 2004*, SI 2004/755.
24 *Immigration (Employment of Adults Subject to Immigration Control) (Maximum Penalty) Order 2008*, SI 2008/132.
25 UK Border Agency, *Code of Practice on Preventing Illegal Working* (May 2014), 9.

with 8,169 penalty notices issued to the end of 2012.[26] Also in 2008, a new indictable criminal offence was introduced of knowingly employing a person who lacks permission to work in the UK. This extended the original criminal scheme by introducing a knowledge element and the possibility of imprisonment (a maximum sentence of two years).

Lastly, in 2009, an EU Employer Sanctions Directive harmonised the EU framework of sanctions on employers who hire migrants with no right to remain in an EU state.[27] Under the Directive, before recruiting a third-country national, employers are required to check that they are authorised to stay, and to notify relevant authorities if they are not (the sanctions do not apply to lawful temporary residents who are working contrary to the terms of their stay). States must oblige employers to check and maintain copies of the immigration documents of third country nationals (art. 4) and introduce financial penalties for breach including covering the workers' repatriation costs (art. 5).

This scheme is unique among those considered here in two respects. First, it reaches into labour law. Employers are specifically made responsible for the repayment of worker's outstanding wages, taxes and social security contributions (art. 6) and states must provide effective procedures to ensure unauthorised workers can make claims against their employer or that such claims can be made on their behalf (art. 13). Contractors who knew that the subcontractor employed unauthorised migrants may have joint and severable liability for both subcontractors' financial sanctions and also any unpaid entitlements. Second, the scheme is linked to counter-trafficking measures through additional requirements on states to introduce criminal offences (art. 9). These relate to intentionally engaging in repeated infringements, employing a significant number of unauthorised workers or employing an unauthorised worker in exploitative working conditions, with knowledge that they are a minor or have been trafficked. The Directive applies to the 24 EU member states other than Denmark, Ireland and the UK. Overall, 27 EU states have introduced employer sanctions, although the severity of penalties varies widely.

Australian ambivalence and the evolution of employer sanctions

Given successive Australian governments' ongoing quest for effective regulatory control over illegal immigration, it may be somewhat surprising that employer sanctions were enacted as recently as 2007. Both this delay and their continuing failure to be comprehensively enforced may stem from

26 Bernard Ryan, 'Employer Checks of Immigration Status and Employment Law' in Cathryn Costello and Mark Freedland (eds), *Migrants at Work: Immigration and Vulnerability in Labour Law* (Oxford University Press, 2014), 239, 241.

27 Council Directive 2009/52/EC of the European Parliament and of the Council providing for minimum standards on sanctions and measures against employers of illegally staying third country nationals [2009] OJ L 168/24.

ambivalent attitudes around holding employers to account for unauthorised labour. Indeed, this is arguably reflected in the degree of confusion in the policy debates surrounding these offences when first introduced.

The supporters of sanctions explained that they were needed to address the apparent anomaly that migrants who engaged in unauthorised labour committed an explicit criminal offence while the other party engaged in unauthorised employment, their employers, did not.[28] However, in fact, employing unauthorised workers was already criminalised in ancillary offences, although this was barely acknowledged by policymakers at the time. As long as the criminal offence of unauthorised work has been on the books,[29] employers could be convicted of 'aiding and abetting' unauthorised workers, with a maximum penalty of A$10,000.[30] 'Harbouring' an unlawful non-citizen has also been an offence since 1973, punishable by up to 10 years' imprisonment and/or a A$170,000 fine.[31] Moreover, while there is no general obligation to inform the Department of Immigration and Border Protection (DIBP) if one is aware someone is living (or working) in Australia without authorisation, it is an offence to fail to comply with a notice served by government officers to obtain information from whomever the Minister believes may assist in identifying or locating an unlawful non-citizen.[32] (These provisions appear to be confined to hunting down a specific suspect and do not permit information to be obtained from employers who might be thought to be employing unlawful non-citizens. These provisions also do not extend to locating people working in breach of otherwise valid visas.)

Extremely low levels of enforcement may have caused policymakers to overlook these offences; two employers were prosecuted for accessorial liability in two decades. One pleaded guilty in 1999 to 15 counts of 'employing illegal foreign workers' and was fined A$15,000, after a joint Immigration Department/Australian Taxation Office operation in 1999.[33] Another was convicted in 2003 of unauthorised employment of people on visitor visas, and was placed on a A$1,000 good behaviour bond.[34] Only one recorded charge

28 Explanatory Memorandum, Migration Amendment (Employer Sanctions) Bill 2006 (Cth), [7.20] (Explanatory Memorandum, Employer Sanctions Bill 2006).

29 The first criminal offence of unauthorised work was introduced by *Migration Amendment Act 1979* (Cth), s 19.

30 *Criminal Code* s 11.2.

31 *Migration Act* ss 233E(2) and 233E(3) inserted by *Anti-People Smuggling and Other Measures Act 2010* (Cth). Previous harbouring offences were introduced by *Migration Legislation Amendment Act 1994* (Cth), *Migration Amendment Act 1989* (Cth) and *Statute Law Revision Act 1973* (Cth).

32 *Migration Act* ss 18 and 21.

33 Senate Legal and Constitutional Affairs Legislation Committee, Parliament of Australia, 'Question Taken On Notice 59/Output 1.3, Budget Estimates Hearing: 26 May 2004, Immigration and Citizenship Portfolio' (2004).

34 Commonwealth, *Parliamentary Debates*, House of Representatives, 6 February 2007, 89 (Sharon Grierson, ALP, Second Reading Speech for the Migration Amendment (Employer Sanctions) Bill 2006).

of harbouring could be identified related to employing unauthorised workers rather than people-smuggling: a 58-year-old Queensland man was charged in 2003 with harbouring unlawful non-citizens, allegedly to use them 'as cheap labour for seasonal work on fruit and vegetable crops'.[35] It has been somewhat more common for employers of unauthorised workers to face penalties related to their immigration status as sponsors or visa-holders themselves. For instance, one employer was barred from future sponsorship of 457 visa workers for three years because he allowed an employee on a tourist visa to work unlawfully before being granted the 457 visa.[36] Another Singaporean man was denied permanent residence on the basis that employing six unlawful non-citizens in the 12 months before his application constituted a 'history of involvement in business activities of a nature that is not generally acceptable in Australia', contrary to the criteria of the business skills permanent visa for which he had applied.[37]

To be sure, the reluctance attending the slow emergence of employer sanctions in Australia is reflected in the experience of other jurisdictions. Extreme ambivalence is generally acknowledged to exist in the USA where commentators have widely concluded that criminal employer sanctions have failed to deter or reduce unauthorised labour.[38] Kitty Calavita and Maria Isabel Medina have traced these attitudes throughout the inadequate enforcement, lenient penalties and lax attitudes on the part of enforcement agents in that country.[39] They also emphasise a pervasive cultural perception in the USA that employment of willing unauthorised workers is not seriously criminal behaviour: the disadvantage to resident workers (of increased labour market competition and lower wages) is highly disputed and attenuated and the harm caused by overburdening social services (by an increased market for public resources) is not sufficiently immediate or direct. Similarly permissive attitudes may also be evident in Australia, to a degree. One compelling study found that a large minority of employers in certain Australian industries (especially horticulture) believed that '[i]n some situations employers really have no choice but to employ people without a valid visa or the right to work'.[40] It is possible that, in these small

35 Australian Federal Police, 'Man Charged with Harbouring Illegal Immigrants' (media release, 25 July 2003).

36 *1101874* [2011] MRTA 2506.

37 *Aw v. MIAC* [2009] FMCA 566; *071555387* [2008] MRTA 1347.

38 Michael Wishnie, 'Prohibiting the Employment of Unauthorized Immigrants: The Experiment Fails' (2007) *University of Chicago Legal Forum* 193.

39 Maria Isabel Medina, 'The Criminalization of Immigration Law: Employer Sanctions and Marriage Fraud' (1997) 5 *George Mason Law Review* 669, 672; Kitty Calavita, 'Employer Sanctions Violations: Toward a Dialectical Model of White-Collar Crime' (1990) 24 *Law and Society Review* 1041, 1045.

40 Hall & Partners Open Mind, *Engagement Strategies Associated with Deterring Illegal Workers* (research report submitted to DIAC, 11 October 2012), 12; Peter Mares, *Labour Shortages in Murray Valley Horticulture: A Survey of Growers' Needs and Attitudes* (Swinburne Institute for Social Research, 2006), 14.

pockets, immigration compliance may correspondingly be slightly more circumspect. However, in general, it is not clear that social tolerance towards undocumented labour is as common in Australia, as I argued in Chapter 3.

Instead, in the Australian context, regulatory ambivalence stems less from the fact that unauthorised employment is not taken seriously, and more because the role of employers seems to be de-emphasised. Governments in Australia seem reluctant to introduce or enforce employer sanctions because the criminal law has historically been directed primarily at migrants rather than residents. This will be demonstrated in this chapter by tracing the heritage of employer sanctions in Australia, sketching early forerunners of these offences and the long history of recommendations made to government to introduce a multi-layered approach beginning in 1999 and only comprehensively implemented in 2013. It describes the limited criminal justice framework that was introduced in 2007 and how this was substantially expanded in 2013. I conclude that, after all this legislative activity, it is still unclear whether these reforms will generate significantly stronger enforcement outcomes.

Employer sanctions were first formally proposed relatively recently. After a parliamentary inquiry into unauthorised immigration in Australia in 1990,[41] employer sanctions were recommended by the Immigration Department in a 1999 report, *Review of Illegal Workers in Australia: Improving Immigration Compliance in the Workplace* (the 1999 Report), under the conservative Howard Coalition government.[42] Predictably, this report focused squarely on the adverse impact on 'the Australian taxpayer' of unauthorised work and other issues affecting residents, rather than the bleak living and working conditions of unauthorised workers themselves. The concluding statement of the introduction to the report (at 2.4) provides a salient example of its apprehension of the 'problem' of illegal workers:

> The Review found sufficient evidence to conclude that the extent of illegal workers in Australia is a significant problem that denies many Australians the opportunity to access a job. Illegal work also places an additional burden on the Australian taxpayer in terms of compliance costs, uncollected taxes and fraudulently claimed social security benefits.

The report recommended three tiers of employer sanctions: a fault-based criminal offence, a strict liability offence and a system of infringement notices. It also proposed that data-matching services be streamlined to enable employers and migrants to verify their work authorisation, along with

41 Joint Standing Committee on Migration Regulations, *Illegal Entrants in Australia: Balancing Control and Compassion* (Australian Government Publishing Service, 1990).

42 Department of Immigration and Multicultural Affairs (DIMA), *Review of Illegal Workers in Australia: Improving Immigration Compliance in the Workplace* (Australian Government Publishing Service, 1999), 15–16 (*Illegal Workers Report*).

a 'whole of government' approach involving stronger coordination between immigration and workplace compliance agencies.

The government responded slowly, adopting incremental measures only in the name of avoiding imposing additional regulatory burdens on business. In 2000, a 'Work Rights Information Line' was established (a fax-back system for employers and labour suppliers to check work permission of prospective employees), accompanied by an educational campaign for employers. In 2002, the Minister introduced a system of administrative warning notices to employers and labour suppliers found to have engaged or referred unauthorised workers (known as Illegal Worker Warning Notices (IWWNs)). In 2004, the department created the Visa Entitlement Verification Online (VEVO) service allowing registered employers to check online whether prospective employees have a current visa and permission to work. Immigration compliance activity followed, with around 2,280 IWWNs issued to employers and labour suppliers in 2004–5, including 90 employers who received multiple notices.[43] These numbers were small when compared with the 3,870 unauthorised workers who were reportedly detected that year, and the 18,341 people that year who were located having either overstayed their visa or breached visa conditions.[44]

In 2007, an election year, the Howard government introduced the *Migration Amendment (Employer Sanctions) Act 2007* (Cth), establishing four narrow fault-based criminal offences and a system of infringement notices. The first two offences occur where a person knowingly or recklessly 'allows an unlawful non-citizen to work' or knowingly or recklessly 'allows a non-citizen to work in breach of a visa condition relating to work'.[45] Two further offences occur if a labour supplier knowingly or recklessly refers such persons to work.[46] These offences are punishable by up to two years' imprisonment and/or fines of up to A$20,400 for an individual and A$102,000 for a body corporate, for each unauthorised worker.[47] Aggravated offences are committed if the worker is exploited and the employer or labour supplier knows or is reckless as to that fact.[48] 'Exploitation' is narrowly defined as 'slavery or a condition similar to slavery, servitude, forced labour, forced marriage or debt bondage', although this conduct need not necessarily be

43 Commonwealth, *Parliamentary Debates*, Senate, 4 September 2006, 126 (Joe Ludwig, ALP, Second Reading Speech for the Migration Amendment (Employer Sanctions) Bill 2006).

44 Commonwealth, *Parliamentary Debates*, House of Representatives, 6 February 2007, 66 (Stuart Henry, Liberal, Second Reading Speech for the Migration Amendment (Employer Sanctions) Bill 2006).

45 Respectively then *Migration Act* s 245AB(1), currently ss 245AB(3) and (4); and then s 245AC(1), currently ss 245AC(3) and (4).

46 Then ss 245AD(1) and 245AE(1), currently ss 245AE(3) and (4) and 245AEA(3) and (4).

47 Sections 245AB(3), 245AC(3), 245AE(3) and 245AEA(3) (former and current provisions are identical) and *Crimes Act* ss 4AA and 4B.

48 Then ss 245AB(2), 245AC(2), 245AD(2) and 245AE(2), currently ss 245AD and 245AEB.

committed by the person who allows the non-citizen to work.[49] Aggravated offences attract imprisonment for five years and/or fines of A$51,000 for an individual or A$255,000 for a body corporate.[50]

When first introduced, the scope of these offences was circumscribed in ways that raised doubts about the government's commitment to their full implementation. The Bill's Explanatory Memorandum promised that '[m]ost first-time offenders will be given a warning notice rather than being referred for prosecution'.[51] Furthermore, the offences applied only to those in a direct legal relationship with an unauthorised migrant worker. If a subcontractor engaged an unauthorised worker, the subcontractor alone (and not the head contractor) would be criminally responsible. At the same time, the offence of 'allowing' an unauthorised worker to work did encompass relationships beyond straightforward employment relationships, including the use of independent contractors, bailments, or lease agreements.[52] It therefore may be committed by taxi owners who lease their cab to an unauthorised worker or landlords who lease work premises, for example to an unauthorised sex worker.

Most significantly, the criminal knowledge requirement presented a high threshold for commission of the offence and the government declined to adopt the third tier that had been recommended in the 1999 Report, a civil offence subject to strict liability. To be 'reckless', an offender needed to be 'aware of a substantial risk that the circumstance exists or will exist and having regard to the circumstances known to him or her, it is unjustifiable to take the risk'.[53] Therefore, these offences stopped far short of requiring an employer or labour supplier universally (or even routinely) to check work rights. Instead, employers or labour suppliers were apparently required to check only where there was 'substantial risk' that a prospective employee is an unauthorised worker.[54] The Immigration Department underscored this interpretation in its information booklet, *Do Your Employees Have a Valid Visa to Work in Australia?*, which recommended to employers:

> If it is impractical for you to check every new worker, at a minimum you should check if:
>
> - Your business operates in an industry where the Department of Immigration and Citizenship (DIAC) locates a large number of illegal workers such as the hospitality, agriculture, manufacturing, construction, transport, retail or sex industries;

49 Sections 245AH and 245AI, and *Criminal Code* s 271.1A (former and current provisions are identical).

50 Then ss 245AB(2), 245AC(2), 245AD(2) and 245AE(2), currently ss 245AD(1), 245AD(2), 245AEB(1) and 245AEB(2) read with *Crimes Act* ss 4AA and 4B.

51 Explanatory Memorandum, Employer Sanctions Bill 2006 (Cth), [7.4.10].

52 Howells, *Report of the 2010 Review*, above n. 4, 69–70.

53 *Criminal Code* s 5.4(1).

54 Explanatory Memorandum, Employer Sanctions Bill 2006 (Cth), [7.4.23] and [7.4.27].

- You have already been given a warning notice for employing or referring an illegal worker; and
- You have information which suggests there is a possibility the person could be an illegal worker.[55]

This passage virtually *assumed* poor compliance with these laws.

It was therefore not unexpected that by mid 2010 the Labor government reported 'little progress ... in prosecuting employers and labour hire intermediaries',[56] and announced a review of the scheme by barrister Stephen Howells. Howells' report in 2011 was to the point, concluding that the criminal employer sanctions regime is 'wholly ineffective as a deterrent against the small number of employers and labour suppliers who engage or refer non-citizens to work who do not have lawful permission to work or who work in breach of their visa conditions'.[57] Howells' findings bore out the experience of inadequate enforcement in foreign jurisdictions.[58] He identified barriers to enforcement at all levels of implementation and found strong evidence that well-resourced and organised operations continued to employ non-citizens lacking permission to work. Ineffectiveness was apparent through an increase in the number of visa-overstayers over the life of the scheme, from 46,500 in 2007 to 58,400 in 2011 (although, of course the size of unauthorised worker population is far more difficult to estimate).[59]

It was also evident in poor criminal justice outcomes. Between 2007 and 2010, immigration officials had investigated only ten matters involving alleged deliberate and systematic use of unauthorised workers in significant numbers, revealing 'apparent abuse of the workers including sexual exploitation, unsafe work practices, underpayment, taxation and welfare fraud, and associated crime'.[60] Four of these were referred to the Commonwealth Director of Public Prosecutions who pursued only one prosecution. At the time of the report's release there had been only one uncontested conviction of an employer, in December 2010, who, upon entering a guilty plea acknowledging a prior criminal record, received a A$12,000 fine. Since then, three successful convictions have been reported for illegally using foreign workers. The first resulted in a fine of A$7,000 for migration fraud and recklessly supplying Filipino workers to Western Australian businesses without requisite work rights.[61] The second, *R v. Nantahkhum*, resulted in an employer's

55 DIAC, *Do Your Employees Have a Valid Visa to Work in Australia?* (2009), 9.
56 AAP, 'Australia Faces Surge in Illegal Workers', *Brisbane Times*, 21 May 2010.
57 Howells, *Report of the 2010 Review*, above n. 4, 14.
58 Huyen Pham, 'The Private Enforcement of Immigration Laws' (2007) 96 *Georgetown Law Journal* 777, 804–7.
59 DIAC, *Population Flows: Immigration Aspects 2006–07* (2008), 65; DIAC, *Population Flows: Immigration Aspects 2010–11* (2012), 71.
60 Howells, *Report of the 2010 Review*, above n. 4, 13.
61 Commonwealth, *Parliamentary Debates*, Senate Legal and Constitutional Affairs Legislation Committee, 17 October 2011, 130 (Robert Illingworth, DIAC).

convictions of allowing an unlawful non-citizen to work and allowing a non-citizen to work in breach of a visa condition that limits work, in aggravating circumstances of exploitation (related to sex slavery). On appeal, the sentence was adjusted to a total of two years and three months' imprisonment in relation to these charges.[62] The third, in *R v. Chee Mei Wong*, also involving a sexual servitude conviction, was described in the prelude to this chapter.[63] A number of further prosecutions are on foot. Among them, *R v. Song Chhoung Ea* involves a number of trafficking and sexual servitude charges as well as the charges of the offence of allowing a non-citizen to work in breach of visa conditions, after three Thai women were allegedly brought to Australia on student visas and taken to a brothel against their will. In another, *R v. Kartawidjaja*, a Nandos franchisee and her associates are being prosecuted for allegedly arranging for around 20 Indonesians to travel to Australia on student visas to engage in unauthorised work.

While enforcement has arguably been problematic in almost every jurisdiction in which employer sanctions have been introduced, in Australia Howells primarily blamed the complexity of the criminal offences and the heavy evidentiary burdens of making out the knowledge elements. He pointed to, in particular, the difficulties for a successful prosecution posed by the offence of unauthorised work in s. 235. He suggested that, because of this provision, obvious sources of evidence against the accused may often not be available, admissible or probative:

> The worker may well have been removed before the trial because their status does not allow them to remain and the DIAC has an obligation to remove them once they are located. The cost, inconvenience and risks of detaining them are considerable. Even if they remain they themselves will probably have committed an offence and would be entitled to claim privilege and would need to be accorded quarter. Their evidence will be tainted for that reason and the circumstances might give rise to telling cross-examination as to motivation.[64]

He also identified as pitfalls the narrow scope of the criminal offences (insufficient to cover non-standard relationships such as informal labour-hire and intermediaries) and the large gap in severity of sanctions between the provision of warnings and serious criminal penalties. He observed that '[o]ne brothel owner in NSW has posted dozens of IWWNs on the walls in his lobby apparently regarding them as trophies'.[65] Howells advocated a return to the three tiers of offences that had been recommended in 1999. To this end, he suggested introducing new strict liability offences,

62 Unreported, Supreme Court of the ACT, Refshauge J, 24 May 2012; *Nantahkum v. R* [2013] ACTCA 40.

63 Unreported, DCNSW, Sweeney J, 5 July 2013.

64 Howells, *Report of the 2010 Review*, above n. 4, 70.

65 Ibid. 69.

accompanied by broad statutory defences for employers who made reasonable efforts to check workers' immigration status, and infringement notices carrying a fine. His rationale (the same that drove reforms to employer penalties in Britain) was that the civil burden of proof is more easily discharged (on the balance of probabilities, rather than beyond reasonable doubt), while strict liability relieves the prosecution from needing to establish an employer's knowledge or recklessness.

In 2013, the Labor government broadly implemented Howells' recommendations, passing the *Migration Amendment (Reform of Employer Sanctions) Act 2013* (Cth) (the *Employer Sanctions Reform Act*). Twelve years after the recommendations first made in the 1999 Report,[66] and well after civil penalties had been introduced in the USA and UK, employer sanctions in Australia now range from warnings and infringement notices through to non-fault civil penalty offences and criminal prosecutions for serious breaches. The civil offences are made out where a person contravenes the physical elements of the employer sanctions offences (allowing or referring visa-overstayers to work or migrants to work in breach of their visa), without any fault element of knowledge or recklessness as to the worker's visa entitlements.[67] Maximum penalties are A$15,300 for an individual, and A$76,500 for a body corporate for each unauthorised worker.[68] The infringement notice scheme in place in relation to 457 visa sponsorship obligations, discussed in Chapter 4, was expanded to cover the employer sanctions offences as well, which attract fines of up to A$3,060 for an individual and A$15,300 for a body corporate for each unauthorised worker.

New comprehensive statutory defences are available for contraventions of both the civil penalty provisions and criminal offences (although not the aggravated offences).[69] Similar to those available in Britain, these defences place the burden on the employer to establish that they took 'reasonable steps at reasonable times to verify' that the worker was entitled to work in Australia including (but not limited to) using Visa Entitlement Verification Online (VEVO).[70] They do not create an obligation in employers to inquire as to employees' work rights, and their precise meaning will need to be explored by the courts.[71] However, regulations provide that steps which engage the defences include inspecting a 'document that appears to be the worker's Australian passport' or 'Australian birth certificate'.

The 2013 reforms also clarified the scope of the offences, whether civil or criminal. The offences are now confined to circumstances where the non-

66 *Illegal Workers Report*, above n. 42, 16.
67 *Migration Act* ss 245AB(5), 245AC(5), 245AE(5), 245AEA(5) and 486ZF.
68 Ibid. ss 245AB(5), 245AC(5), 245AE(5) and 245AEA(5), read along with ss 5(1) and 486R(5)(a) and *Crimes Act* s 4AA.
69 *Migration Act* ss 245AB(2), 245AC(2), 245AE(2) and 245AEA(2).
70 *Migration Regulations 1994* (Cth), reg 5.19G.
71 For an early consideration on anti-discrimination law implications see *Willmott v. Woolworths Ltd* [2014] QCAT 601.

citizen is working in breach of their immigration restrictions solely because of working for that employer.[72] In other words, the employer or referrer is not expected to know whether a migrant worker has breached work-related visa conditions because of the cumulative effect of their work for multiple employers. Thus, an employer will not be liable where their international student employee works fewer than 40 hours a fortnight for them but more than 40 hours per fortnight overall.

In addition, whereas the original offences occurred only within bilateral contractual relationships, the definition of 'allows to work' now encompasses any business participating in a non-standard 'arrangement' involving the performance of unauthorised work, including through sub-contractors, informal labour-hire or the use of unauthorised workers by various entities within a conglomerate (*Migration Act* s. 245AG(2)(ba)). Offences also extend to the conduct of executive officers of corporations, partners and members of an unincorporated association's committee of management. Such persons may now be criminally or civilly liable where they knew that the work-related contravention would occur (or were reckless or negligent as to this fact) and, being in a position to influence the conduct of the body corporate in relation to the convention, they failed to take reasonable steps to prevent the offence being committed (ss 245AJ and 245AK).

The Act also established new investigatory powers to overcome the situation where previously immigration officers had no powers related to search and seizure that were specific to these offences, instead needing to make use of police warrants. The Secretary of DIBP is now empowered to require a person to produce documents or provide information that the Secretary has reason to believe are relevant to a possible offence or contravention (s 487B). In addition, if they can demonstrate reasonable grounds for suspecting that there is, or may be, evidential material on the premises, immigration officers may obtain a search and entry warrant from a magistrate or judge, also permitting them to ask questions, require the production of documents and seize material relevant to a work-related contravention (ss 487D-487J).

Whether a new focus on civil sanctions will be more effective remains to be seen. The Bill's passage was accompanied by numerous conciliatory statements about encouraging employers' voluntary compliance. One parliamentarian, in support of the Bill, described it as 'moving from the heavy-handed civil or criminal action to facilitate voluntary compliance by issuing administrative warnings and avoid legal sanctions where possible'.[73] However, this seems to raise the prospect of lapses in effectiveness similar to those identified in US studies from the early days of employer sanctions

72 *Migration Act* ss 245AC(1)(d), 245AD(2)(d), 245AEA(1)(c)(iii) and 245AEB(2)(c)(iii).

73 Commonwealth, *Parliamentary Debates*, House of Representatives, 1 November 2012, 12981 (Stephen Jones, ALP, Second Reading Speech for the Migration Amendment (Reform of Employer Sanctions) Bill 2012).

there.[74] Socio-legal scholars in America have observed that significant criminal sanctions, which would deter unauthorised employment, were less likely to be applied by courts and law enforcement agencies, which are averse to treating unauthorised employment as serious criminal misconduct. However, civil sanctions, which are more readily applied, seemed not to create a strong enough disincentive for employers to refrain from hiring unauthorised workers.

In Australia, it is not yet clear whether even the civil employer sanctions will be more comprehensively enforced. As of June 2014, there was evidence only of a sharp increase in warnings, in the form of IWWNs and only one infringement notice had been issued to an employer under the scheme, with a fine of A$30,600.[75] This may be unsurprising since, unlike the bipartisan endorsement of the criminal offences in 2007, the civil scheme was not supported by the then conservative Coalition opposition, which assumed government in September 2013, on the basis that it goes 'beyond the notion of reasonableness and will impose excessive regulatory and compliance measures on employers'.[76] In submissions on the exposure draft of the amendments, numerous industry representatives (including the Australian Chamber of Commerce and Industry and the Australian Industry Group) also vigorously opposed the introduction of civil penalties (in contrast to criminal sanctions), generally arguing that the cost and inconvenience to business are disproportionate to the goals of immigration compliance. Clearly, the supervision of employers (who are almost invariably citizens, command considerable resources and demonstrate the ability and willingness to protest) is of an entirely different order to the surveillance of non-citizen workers. Heightened political pressure may lead the DIBP to deprioritise employers further as targets for immigration compliance.

Indeed, it seems significant that, of the four convictions of employers to date, two (including Wong) contained strong elements of trafficking-like circumstances. A further prosecution for employer sanctions offences was discontinued in a 2008 case against four defendants that also involved alleged trafficking, sexual servitude and debt bondage.[77] This raises questions about whether these migration offences were introduced as a reserve for prosecutions relating to servitude or human trafficking, especially since, until 2013, little middle ground existed between extremely serious offences of servitude, trafficking and slavery and the summary offence of debt

74 Linda Bosniak, 'Exclusion and Membership: The Dual Identity of the Undocumented Worker Under United States Law' (1988) *Wisconsin Law Review* 955, 1015; Calavita, 'Employer Sanctions Violations' above n. 39, 79–80.

75 609 IWWNs were issued in 2009–10, 515 in 2010–11, 397 in 2011–12, 302 in 2012–13 and 909 in 2013–14: Regulatory Impact Statement, Migration Amendment (Reform of Employer Sanctions) Bill 2012 (Cth), 6; DIBP, *Annual Report 2013–14* (2014), 164.

76 Commonwealth, *Parliamentary Debates*, House of Representatives, 1 November 2012, 12971 (Scott Morrison, Liberal, Second Reading Speech for the Migration Amendment (Reform of Employer Sanctions) Bill 2012).

77 A fifth pled guilty to unknown charges: DIAC, *2007–08 Annual Report* (2008), 112.

bondage (discussed in more detail in Chapter 8). It is also possible that these offences were applied only in aggravating circumstances of criminal exploitation because other employers' 'mere' contraventions of immigration law are seen to lack profile and priority. In either case, civil offences may be applied just as infrequently. Further diffidence is evident in the failure of these reforms to address the ways that attempts to hold employers accountable are compromised by the primacy accorded to worker-focused immigration compliance activities, as the next section explains.

Priority accorded to workers' violations over employer sanctions

The cautious approach to implementing employer sanctions has been especially striking when compared with the diligence of compliance activities pursuing non-citizens' immigration violations. This disparity seems likely to continue. Howells accepted the overriding priority of removing unauthorised migrants 'as soon as practicable', under s. 198, explaining that the cost and the administrative inconvenience of detaining them pending a trial would be prohibitive. He also noted that the deference accorded to the criminal offence of unauthorised work in s. 235 seriously impeded investigations and prosecutions, depriving employer prosecutions of unauthorised employees' probative evidence identifying the specific employer and proving their state of mind. The simplest evidence of an employer's 'knowing' violation of the law is an employee's admission to the employer that they do not have valid work authorisation. However, governments and Howells himself have assumed almost without demur that workers will never be available to testify as to the employers' conduct, because admissibility and weight of their evidence is impugned by their own culpability for breach of s. 235.[78]

Rather than reforming the s. 235 offence, amendments to employer sanctions offences in 2013 sought to circumvent these evidentiary problems in three ways. First, strict liability in the civil offences obviates the need to prove employers' state of mind. Second, the expanded definition of 'allows to work' includes a business simply participating in an 'arrangement' involving unauthorised work. This permits investigators and prosecutors to rely less on a paper trail and more on their eyesight during a raid (although one might imagine that this might increase the value of having unauthorised workers available as witnesses). Third, and most dramatically, the accused employer's privilege against self-incrimination has been removed in civil (although not criminal) proceedings, a stark departure from the Attorney-General's Department's standard practice.[79] The lengths to which this

78 Howells, *Report of the 2010 Review*, above n. 4, 14, 36; Regulatory Impact Statement, above n. 75, 7.

79 *Migration Act* s 487C(1); Explanatory Memorandum, Migration Amendment (Reform of Employer Sanctions) Bill 2012 (Cth), Attachment B – Statement of Compatibility with Human Rights, 4 (Explanatory Memorandum, Reform of Employer Sanctions Bill 2012).

legislation goes to alleviate the need for worker testimony underscores the absolute primacy accorded to workers' unauthorised status. If employer misconduct (and worker exploitation) were truly the chief evil at which employer sanctions were directed, s. 235 might be repealed to prevent workers' testimony against their employers being tainted by their own illegal conduct, a reform proposed in Chapter 6. Alternatively, Chapter 9 suggests measures that would postpone the removal of the primary source of evidence against employers – the worker themselves. Yet there is no suggestion in the Howells report, nor in any other commentary on the Australian scheme, that there may be a value in the workers themselves staying in Australia to see the prosecution of their employer, much less to seek legal redress for any labour law infringements they have suffered.

This also exposes a central contradiction in the aggravated offence of exploitation. As explored in more detail in the following chapter, the *Criminal Code* now recognises that an employer's threat to report a worker to immigration authorities may constitute one piece of evidence of coercion or exploitation (to make out one element of a human trafficking or forced labour offence, which is also an aggravating factor of the criminal employer sanctions offence).[80] It is, therefore, a sad irony that, in the absence of other blatant indicators of human trafficking or forced labour, a 'tip off' from an employer is just as likely to lead to detention and removal of the worker as it is to be treated as evidence of an aggravated offence by the employer.

Employer sanctions entrench the precariousness of unauthorised workers

Beyond the precariousness produced by s. 235 and its effect on employment protections discussed in the previous chapter, employer sanctions (while ostensibly directed at employers' misconduct) further intensify the precarious position of unauthorised workers. This can occur for at least three reasons.

First, employer sanctions (such as harbouring and other offences associated with unauthorised migrants) criminalise people who may only be peripherally involved with an unauthorised migrant or, indeed, assisting them. Beyond simply reinforcing the prohibition on unauthorised presence, these offences aim to deeply unsettle human relationships involving unauthorised migrants. They discourage unauthorised workers' efforts to establish ties in Australia and disrupt the attempts of advocates, community leaders and others to support them and inform them of their rights. Because work for the purpose of employer sanctions is defined to be 'for reward or otherwise', charities have expressed concern that they may even be liable for facilitating volunteer work in the community by asylum seekers on bridging visas without work entitlements. By casting uncertainty over the legality of so many social interactions of unauthorised migrants, these

80 *Criminal Code* s 270.1A.

offences serve symbolically to portray unauthorised migrants as devoid of social or employment interests in Australia, depicting them not as a workforce but as subterranean criminals, thereby avoiding complicated normative questions about their membership while in Australia.

Second, even with stronger penalties for employer misconduct, workers still have more to lose than their employers from the detection of unauthorised work. The criminal penalties for employers are serious but possibly less severe than the extreme personal upheaval for workers who are detected (possible visa cancellation, followed by almost certain detention and removal). In any event, we are unlikely to see application of the more serious sanctions. The introduction of infringement notices and civil penalties increases the repertoire of administrative penalties directed at employers at the lower end of severity and the government's 'illegal work targeting strategy 2013–16' explicitly promotes voluntary employer compliance through education and warnings. As mentioned above, no infringement notice had been issued to June 2014, with a sharp increase in warnings alone. By contrast, there are few second chances, or dispensations, for unauthorised workers. This asymmetry in consequences clearly reflects the precedence accorded to workers' immigration violations over employers', which also features prominently in foreign jurisdictions. In the USA, Obama's heightened commitment to employer sanctions may have seen, for the first time, many thousands of employers fined, but it has also resulted in hundreds of thousands of unauthorised workers fired and deported. Analysts suggest that, while this discrepancy may stem from the fact that employers' offences may be harder to prove than workers', it is also likely that compliance priorities have led employers to be immunised from prosecution for cooperating with US Immigration and Customs Enforcement officials.[81] The UK Border Agency is even more explicit about its commitment to rewarding employers for cooperating with authorities in identifying unauthorised workers. It is quite possible that Australian policy will follow this course, effectively treating employers as minor actors complicit in workers' criminal breaches of immigration laws, rather than serious criminals in their own right.

Furthermore, the new statutory defences for employers are not available for workers. Both UK and US studies document employers' efforts to evade liability by complying with the letter of the law without changing the substance of their business practices.[82] Such strategies are just as imaginable in Australia because of the ways that the employer sanctions scheme creates asymmetrical obligations between employer and employee. An employer who suspects that an international student is engaging in other work that cumulatively breaches their visa condition (and who takes advantage of that vulnerability) commits no offence unless the breach arises by work for that

81 Bacon and Hing, 'The Rise and Fall of Employer Sanctions', above n. 19, 91.

82 Yara Evans, *'Papers Please': The Impact of the Civil Penalty Regime on the Employment Rights of Migrants in the UK* (Migrants' Rights Network, 2008), 27; Pham, 'The Private Enforcement', above n. 58, 780.

employer alone. An employer who initially checks the work rights of a working holiday maker but allows them to continue working when their visa expires is also likely to make out a successful defence. Further, the Immigration Department has indicated that the statutory defence is intended to allow an employer to create a contractual obligation for another party to verify whether a worker has permission to work in Australia.[83] In other words, the employer can contract out of this scheme. The worker, by contrast, would have unequivocally breached s. 235 in each of these scenarios. These disparities entrench the differential power relations between unauthorised worker and employer.

An employer might also take advantage of the defence by examining documents that appear to be genuine but then collude with unauthorised workers to infringe immigration restrictions. To make out the defence introduced in 2013 of 'taking reasonable steps' to check work entitlements, DIBP recommends that employers use VEVO, its online information facility containing the immigration profile of most non-citizens in Australia. This database does not, however, contain details about Australian citizens. As a result, it is possible that to evade the constraints of VEVO while appearing to take 'reasonable steps', unauthorised workers may be encouraged (in some cases by employers) to produce fraudulent certificates of Australian citizenship. This is cause for concern given that employer sanctions in the USA are widely believed to have spawned a flourishing market in false documents.[84]

Having superficially satisfied the elements of the defence, the employer may hire unauthorised workers and then subsequently profess to have suddenly developed a belief that the worker is unauthorised and terminate them, anonymously alert the authorities or threaten the employee with either of these. This change in heart may coincide with a worker's attempts to assert their entitlements. This has led Linda Bosniak to suggest in the American context that 'employers and their undocumented employees usually share … an interest in avoiding enforcement of the immigration law. But some employers deploy … that same law against undocumented workers when their interests diverge'.[85] Indeed, in the UK, where employers are expressly promised more lenient treatment for assisting authorities, advocates have documented cases of employers using deception, such as inviting undocumented workers into a 'meeting' later revealed to be a Border Agency ambush.[86]

83 DIAC, *Policy Commentary: Migration Amendment (Reform of Employer Sanctions) Bill 2012* (2012) 4; Explanatory Memorandum, Reform of Employer Sanctions Bill 2012 (Cth), [88].

84 Jennifer Gordon, 'Transnational Labor Citizenship' (2007) 80 *Southern California Law Review* 503, 538.

85 Bosniak, 'Exclusion and Membership', above n. 74, 994.

86 Evans, *'Papers Please'*, above n. 82, 26–7.

Third, workers may also suffer from employer sanctions less directly. Evidence from the USA suggests that law-breaking employers tend to transfer the cost of penalties to the unauthorised worker, for instance, by lowering their salary to compensate for an anticipated fine.[87] Employer sanctions encourage employers of unauthorised workers to ensure they keep no records of employment. The 2013 reforms sought to circumvent such tactics by broadening offences to include a business that 'participates' in an 'arrangement', which is designed to permit prosecutions even in the absence of a documentary trail of evidence.[88] This goal might be even more effectively achieved, however, by introducing a presumption that a failure to keep wage records indicates unauthorised employment, in a similar way to courts inferring underpayment from an employer's failure to keep records.[89]

These harmful effects of employer sanctions on unauthorised workers expose as disingenuous the claims by supporters and parliamentarians that the scheme endeavoured, at least in part, to protect them against exploitation. The Australian Council of Trade Unions (ACTU) supported employer sanctions from as early as 1990, pointing to their capacity to prevent degraded working standards of both resident and unauthorised workers, and has reiterated its endorsement of the three tiered sanction regime now in place.[90] This contrasts with the position of organised labour in the USA: the American Federation of Labor and Congress of Industrial Organizations (AFL-CIO) Executive Council called for the abolition of employer sanctions in 2000 given their deleterious effects on migrant workers.[91] In fact, the Australian framework of employer sanctions deals directly with harm against only a very small subset of unauthorised workers. As in the UK, the concept of exploitation as an aggravating factor is narrowly defined to encompass only trafficking-like situations.[92] Most unauthorised workers, as willing co-conspirators in this breach of border and labour market security, fall outside those more extreme aggravating circumstances.

Indeed, most rancour in the parliamentary debate leading to the passage of the 2007 Act was directed at the need for protection from 'illegal workers'. Unauthorised migrants were presented as agentive criminals with obvious motive and opportunity: 'the lure of a nation as great as ours is simply too

87 Bosniak, 'Exclusion and Membership', above n. 74, 1013–15.

88 *Migration Act* s 245AG(2)(ba).

89 Eg *FWO v. Orwill Pty Ltd* [2011] FMCA 730.

90 'Unions Want New Clamp on Illegal Entrants' (1990) 250 *Australian Outlook* 3. ACTU, Submission to DIAC, *Exposure Draft Migration Amendment (Reform of Employer Sanctions) Bill 2012*, August 2012, 11.

91 AFL-CIO Executive Council, *Building a Strong Union Movement in Every State and Community* (2001).

92 *Migration Act* ss 245AH and 245AI, and *Criminal Code* s 271.1A (former and current provisions are identical).

much to resist for many of those who are not enjoying their lives in their own countries'.[93] The debate positioned resident workers and taxpayers as victimised by 'illegal workers who fly here to steal Australian jobs and undermine Australian working conditions each and every day'.[94] The conviction that unauthorised workers exploit public welfare protections for residents engulfed the possibility that the workers themselves are exploited, as in this statement in the Explanatory Memorandum (at [7.7]): '[t]here are indications that people in low-skilled positions are often paid below official rates; some may not pay tax, either at the correct rate or at all; and some are claiming social security benefits that they are not entitled to'. Naturally, territorial integrity was also constructed as vulnerable to violation by unauthorised migration. One senator from a progressive minor party actively distinguished the threat posed by unauthorised migrant workers from asylum seekers:

> People who do threaten our borders and aspects of the Australian economy and society are people who live here illegally for prolonged periods of time and work here illegally, under the radar. I am not saying that they are a threat in the way that the government likes to paint any of these people as threats, in the sense of being potential terrorists or anything like that, but they are people in the community, under the radar or in the black market, and we are not aware of where they are or who they are. That does not apply, I would have to say – and I have to emphasise this – to asylum seekers.[95]

Only one submission to the Senate inquiry into the 2007 Bill expressed concern for unauthorised workers who had endured exploitative work practices.[96]

93 Commonwealth, *Parliamentary Debates*, House of Representatives, 6 February 2007, 73 (Peter Slipper, Liberal, Second Reading Speech for the Migration Amendment (Employer Sanctions) Bill 2006).

94 Commonwealth, *Parliamentary Debates*, Senate, 6 September 2006, 2 (Glenn Sterle, ALP, Second Reading Speech for the Migration Amendment (Employer Sanctions) Bill 2006).

95 Commonwealth, *Parliamentary Debates*, Senate, 5 September 2006, 2 (Andrew Bartlett, Australian Democrat Party, Second Reading Speech for the Migration Amendment (Employer Sanctions) Bill 2006).

96 Melbourne Catholic Migrant and Refugee Office, Submission No 4 to the Senate Legal and Constitutional Affairs Committee, Parliament of Australia, 'Inquiry into the Migration Amendment (Employers Sanctions) Bill', 18 April 2006, 2. A rare example of compassion for unauthorised workers in the public debate is Suhad Kamand, 'Proposed Sanctions Against Employers who Employ Unlawful Workers' (2007) 78 *Immigration News* 10, 11.

The implications of employer sanctions for workers' precarious entitlements under labour law

Further questions arise as to the effect of the criminal employer offences introduced in 2007, or civil offences from 2013, on the jurisprudence explored in Chapter 6. That case law on the statutory and contractual implications of the criminal prohibition on unauthorised work mostly predates the criminal employer sanctions.[97] It treats the criminal conduct as the unauthorised worker's alone. This final section explores the potential for employer sanctions to further reshape unauthorised workers' substantive entitlements.

It is helpful first to recall Australian superior courts' basic approaches to the validity of employment contracts contravening the *Migration Act*. In the two leading cases, the Queensland Court of Appeal, in *Australia Meat Holdings Pty Ltd v. Kazi*, and the New South Wales Court of Appeal, in *Nonferral (NSW) Pty Ltd v. Taufia*, considered the criminal offence of illegal work in s. 235 (and its predecessor, s. 83).[98] The courts drew different conclusions about their effects but both relied on High Court authority that the validity of the contract depends upon statutory interpretation to determine whether parliament would have intended the legislative prohibition to invalidate the contract.[99]

The question arising since 2007, but yet to be judicially considered, is the validity of an employment contract which violates both s. 235 as well as the (criminal or, since 2013, civil) prohibitions on employing an unauthorised worker in ss 245AB–245AEA. It is uncertain whether the fact that unauthorised work may now trigger criminal penalties for *both* employee and employer should affect the legality of the underlying contract. As with s. 235, the employer sanctions provisions do not expressly articulate the intended impact of their breach on contractual validity. On the one hand, the employer sanctions offences arguably evidence parliament's intention to emphasise the seriousness of unauthorised employment, rendering void a contract facilitating such a criminal enterprise. Indeed, given that employers have in fact been criminally liable for aiding and abetting unauthorised work all along, this too might lead a court to conclude that nothing significant has changed since the most recent precedent in *Kazi*, which concluded that an employment relationship in violation of the *Migration Act* produced no valid contract.[100] In the USA, where there is no federal offence prohibiting

97 The 2007 Act is mentioned in *Antony Emurugat v. Utilities Management Pty Ltd* [2008] AIRC 1114 and *MG Lines Pty Ltd t/as Coniston Station v. Navi* [2013] NTSC 20, although these judgments do not squarely consider its impact on the validity of the employment contracts.

98 *Australia Meat Holdings Pty Ltd v. Kazi* [2004] QCA 147; *Nonferral (NSW) Pty Ltd v. Taufia* (1998) 43 NSWLR 312.

99 *Nelson v. Nelson* (1995) 184 CLR 538, 613.

100 The aiding and abetting offence was considered relevant to denying unfair dismissal protections for an unauthorised employee in *Wei Xin Chen v. Allied Packaging Co Pty Ltd* (1997) 73 IR 53, 54.

unauthorised migrants working, jurisprudence has considered the effect of criminal offences directed at employers who employ unauthorised workers on unauthorised workers' entitlements under labour law. The Supreme Court has ruled that an unauthorised worker remained a statutory 'employee' with employment protections but was ineligible for back pay (lost wages resulting from the unlawful termination), because this would run counter to the intention of statutory employer sanctions laws.[101]

On the other hand, a court might treat the new employer offences as emphasising parliament's disapprobation of employer misconduct, suggesting that the policy of the *Migration Act* offences is best served by leaving the validity of the employment contract intact and ensuring employers do not receive a windfall from their own criminal conduct. A precedent for this approach lies in the 2009 EU Directive on Employer Sanctions, which requires member states to penalise employers who hire unauthorised third-country nationals but also ensure that employers are liable for outstanding remuneration to the illegally employed worker.[102]

It is also conceivable that a court would find an employment contract valid in circumstances where the employer committed the criminal offence (knowing or being reckless to the fact that the worker was working without permission) but invalid where the employer's actions were merely a violation of the strict liability civil offence, not necessarily knowing of the worker's unauthorised status but simply failing to check. Indeed, the UK takes an approach that balances the relative culpability of employer and employee, in that contractual validity tends to depend on whether the employee commenced employment with knowledge of the illegality.[103] Alternatively (and perhaps confusingly), it is also possible that a court would construe the strict liability nature of the new civil offence as evidence of its seriousness. In *Hussein v. Secretary of the Department of Immigration* (discussed in Chapter 6), the Federal Court determined that any work contract was void for contravening s. 235 because, specifically, s. 235 was an offence of strict liability.[104] The precedential value of this case, however, might be limited by its unique factual background relating to a claim for employment entitlements in immigration detention, which was denied.

Until the judiciary considers this question afresh, employer sanctions will produce deeper precariousness for unauthorised workers, if nothing else by casting further uncertainty over workers' statutory and contractual entitlements. It is noteworthy that the amendments to the scheme in 2013 went to

101 *Hoffman Plastic Compounds Inc v. National Labor Relations Board*, 535 US 137, 147-51 (2002).

102 Council Directive 2009/52/EC of the European Parliament and of the Council providing for minimum standards on sanctions and measures against employers of illegally staying third-country nationals (2009) OJ L 168/24, art 6.

103 Bernard Ryan, 'The Evolving Legal Regime on Unauthorized Work by Migrants in Britain' (2005) 27(3) *Comparative Labor Law and Policy Journal* 27, 47.

104 *Hussein v. Secretary of the Department of Immigration and Multicultural Affairs (No 2)* [2006] FCA 1263, [67]–[68].

such lengths to prevent employers avoiding culpability by bypassing the niceties of contract law in their employment practices: to address highly informalised or non-contractual labour practices, the offences were expanded to ensure that anyone who participates in a chain of events resulting in unauthorised work may now be held liable.[105] It seems ironic then that these same offences may be used to invalidate the contractual entitlements of employees, nullifying employers' accountability for employment-related duties.

Indeed, more perniciously still, employer sanctions arguably serve as a distraction from the unauthorised employment jurisprudence discussed in Chapter 6. By foregrounding the criminally responsible employer, they portray irregular migration and abuse of unauthorised workers as problems caused by the misconduct of individuals. They obscure the way that irregular migration is an inevitable product of national immigration enforcement within a globalised economy.[106] By prescribing employer offences in the *Migration Act*, the exploitation of migrant workers is presented as an aggravated offence under immigration law rather than exploitation of labour.

Conclusion

This chapter has demonstrated that employer-focused immigration offences accentuate the underlying power differential in migrants' precarious employment. Here again, reforms introduced in the name of preventing unauthorised employment, and the exploitation that so frequently attends it, have been better adapted to punishing employers and workers than to providing redress. Indeed, these offences dangerously conflate employment of unauthorised workers (the basic offence) with exploitation of unauthorised workers (the aggravated offence). Such confusion arose during the parliamentary debates preceding the passage of the laws in 2007, as evidenced by one sitting member who observed that 'any person who is prepared to employ illegal non-citizens is exploiting those individuals'.[107] These offences may serve to obscure truly precarious employment by framing exploitation as an immigration violation rather than a labour abuse.

Employer sanctions intensify the precarious position of unauthorised workers, since workers continue to have more to lose from detection than employers, and significant primacy appears to be accorded to worker-focused immigration compliance activities. Consequently, these offences

105 See s 245AG(2)(ba). See also Explanatory Memorandum, Reform of Employer Sanctions Bill 2012 (Cth), 2.

106 For an argument about how this plays out in the trafficking context see Bridget Anderson and Rutvica Andrijasevic, 'Sex, Slaves and Citizens: The Politics of Anti-Trafficking' (2008) 40 *Soundings* 135, 142.

107 Commonwealth, *Parliamentary Debates*, Senate, 5 September 2006, 14 (Ruth Webber, ALP, Second Reading Speech for the Migration Amendment (Employer Sanctions) Bill 2006).

may actually increase incentives for employers to hire unauthorised workers, paradoxically expanding the prevalence of unauthorised labour. They also serve to distract from the background legal context, which generates substantial precariousness by withholding basic labour protections from unauthorised workers. In short, employer sanctions are likely to do little to decrease the prevalence of unauthorised work but much to marginalise such workers further.

Part III

Forced migrant labour

8 Working with coercion

Labour trafficking in Australia

In December 2000, Mr and Mrs Kovacs arranged to bring a young Filipina to Australia to work as a domestic servant in their remote Queensland home and takeaway shop.[1] Zoltan Kovacs and a friend travelled to the Philippines where they were introduced to a 25-year-old woman. She lived with seven family members and her son in a one-room galvanised iron shack in the slums of Manila without running water, electricity or phone. She agreed to a sham marriage with Kovacs' friend to secure her visa for Australia, her dying mother begging her to take this opportunity. Kovacs told her that she would 'have to work for five years before she could leave Australia', and she would receive A$800 for her work in Australia (which she assumed was a monthly wage) some of which would be withheld to cover her travel expenses.

When she arrived in Australia over a year later, Kovacs took the young woman to a motel in Cairns where he allegedly sexually assaulted her three times, before travelling to the remote town of Weipa in Far North Queensland.[2] The complainant was forced to work without rest in the Kovacs' shop and home, with very little pay. She was subjected to repeated sexual assaults, verbal threats and abuse, and control over her movement. Kovacs threatened that 'they would all go to gaol' if she spoke to police. The complainant also stated that 'shame and embarrassment in Filipino society, not just to her but also her ailing mother, had stopped her saying anything'. She tried to escape once but was found by the Kovacs who then confiscated her passport. She

1 Details of this narrative are drawn from *R v. Kovacs* [2009] 2 Qd R 51, [7]–[13] (*Kovacs*); Fiona David, *Labour Trafficking* (Research and Public Policy Series No 108, Australian Institute of Criminology, 2010), 19; Margo Zlotkowski, 'Marriage No Sham, Says Man', *Cairns Post*, 12 February 2010, 11; Andreas Schloenhardt and Jarrod Jolly, 'Honeymoon from Hell: Human Trafficking and Domestic Servitude in Australia' (2010) 32(4) *Sydney Law Review* 671.

2 The allegations of sexual assault form the basis of additional charges, which led to convictions in 2005, but a retrial was ordered in 2006 and again in 2007: *R v. KO* [2006] QCA 7; *R v. Kovacs* [2007] QCA 143.

successfully escaped on a second occasion with the assistance of Zoltan Kovacs' estranged daughter. After their first convictions were set aside by the Queensland Court of Appeal in 2008, Zoltan and Melita Kovacs were convicted of slavery and immigration fraud.[3]

Australian laws implementing the United Nations Protocol to Prevent, Suppress and Punish Trafficking in Persons, Especially Women and Children (Trafficking Protocol),[4] introduced in 2005, represented a revolutionary step towards greater inclusion of exploited non-citizens in this country. Criminal sanctions for trafficking strongly acknowledge Australia's responsibilities to prevent serious harms not only to nationals but all who have lived in this country only briefly and/or without authorisation, such as the woman terrorised, imprisoned and assaulted by the Kovacs. By granting trafficked people greater security of stay – including, in certain cases, residence as a gateway to citizenship – these policies extend the boundaries of the Australian political community to migrant workers who have lived or worked in situations of acute precariousness.

At the same time, the Australian government's counter-trafficking strategy has been criticised (like many others around the world and, indeed, the Protocol from which it flows) for being too limited in its response to labour trafficking and exploitation. Two key faults were its focus on sexual exploitation to the exclusion of other harms, and its criminalisation of conduct only at the extreme end of physical severity. Together this meant that Australian laws failed to grapple with labour exploitation as a continuum, with offenders frequently employing more subtle forms of psychological coercion.

The *Crimes Legislation Amendment (Slavery, Slavery-like Conditions and People Trafficking) Act 2013* (Cth) (*Slavery Act*), passed in February 2013, sought to address these concerns. All offences involving sexual exploitation now also encompass non-sexual exploitation, and the incremental range of trafficking is reflected by new stand-alone offences, such as forced labour, which target the end-point of serious exploitation without the element of transportation entailed in trafficking offences. The definitions of coercion and related concepts were enlarged to include the complainant's social context, their particular vulnerabilities and the variations in dependencies in their actual relationship with their employer.

This chapter celebrates this far more contextualised approach to labour exploitation. These reforms comprise a dramatic reversal of historical trends

3 They were convicted of intentionally possessing a slave (*Criminal Code 1995* (Cth), s 270.3(1)(a) (*Criminal Code*)), intentionally exercising power over/using a slave (s 270.3(1)(a)) and arranging a contrived marriage for immigration purposes (*Migration Act 1958* (Cth), s 240(1) (*Migration Act*)). Zoltan was sentenced to one year imprisonment for the marriage offence and eight years for the slavery offences, to be served concurrently. Melita was sentenced to four years for the slavery offences and one year imprisonment for the marriage, served concurrently: *Kovacs* [2009] 2 Qd R 51, [3]–[4].

4 Opened for signature 15 December 2000, 2237 UNTS 319 (entered into force 31 May 2004).

to target sex trafficking to the exclusion of other forms of forced labour. At the same time, they consolidate jurisprudential approaches, far more sophisticated than policing practice or media in this arena, which have long been cognisant of the fine degrees of coercion, freedom and psychological duress occurring in sexual and non-sexual exploitation alike. Nevertheless, the criminal justice framework is bound to target a tiny proportion of exploitative conduct because it proscribes only certain types of forced labour. These offences leave unchallenged the serious constraints on non-citizen workers' labour market options and larger social choices, which are legitimated by immigration controls and other structural social dynamics. Martha Fineman's analysis of choice in the context of structural disadvantage is helpful in illuminating how the counter-trafficking framework erases the subordinating effects of the globalised economy and national immigration laws.

This chapter commences with an outline of Australia's counter-trafficking framework, and the Protocol on which it is built. As we will see, early preoccupations with sexual exploitation, both internationally and in Australia, have given way to a wider view of trafficking that encompasses non-sexual forms of labour. At the same time, this chapter explores how, despite few prosecutions brought outside of the sex industry, superior courts for some time have been taking a highly sophisticated approach to coercion, applicable both to sexual and non-sexual exploitation. Consideration then turns to the key labour trafficking-related amendments in the *Slavery Act*, and the new forced labour offence in particular, unpacking their renewed emphasis on the nuances of complainants' particular vulnerabilities in their personal circumstances. The chapter concludes by considering the serious coercive effects of immigration controls that are left unexamined in this criminal justice approach. To set the scene, the next section presents a brief sketch of the evolution of counter-trafficking efforts in international law, before turning to Australia's criminal and immigration law initiatives.

Responses to trafficking in international and Australian laws

The first generation of anti-trafficking conventions, between 1901 and 1950, was conceived as a battle against the 'white slave trade': the sexual exploitation of women and girls across borders for the purpose of prostitution.[5] Feminist political consciousness in the 1970s re-awakened this concern. Some

5 International Agreement for the Suppression of the White Slave Traffic, opened for signature 18 May 1904, 1 LNTS 83 (entered into force 18 July 1905); International Convention for the Suppression of the White Slave Traffic, opened for signature 4 May 1910, 98 UNTS 101 (entered into force 14 August 1951); International Convention for the Suppression of the Traffic in Women and Children, opened for signature 30 September 1921, 53 UNTS 39 (entered into force 24 April 1950); International Convention for the Suppression of the Traffic in Women of Full Age, opened for signature 11 October 1933, 150 LNTS 431 (entered into force 24 August 1934); UN Convention for the Suppression of the Traffic in Persons and of the Exploitation of the Prostitution of Others, opened for signature 21 March 1950, 96 UNTS 271 (entered into force 25 July 1951).

contemporary feminists framed trafficking as a globalised manifestation of prostitution, which they saw as invariably connected to gender-based violence against women and children.[6] Other scholars and activists defended sex work, when properly regulated, as a legitimate expression of women's autonomy, and differentiated trafficking as involving exploitation or deception, rather than any migration for prostitution at all.[7] Thus conceived, trafficking could arise in low-status work in any industry, involving sexual, physical or psychological abuse.

International counter-trafficking initiatives of the 1990s took shape in the spaces of convergence between these two perspectives. The result was the Trafficking Protocol, which supplements the Convention against Transnational Organised Crime (UNTOC).[8] The Protocol adopted a comprehensive definition of trafficking, in article 3, comprising three elements: (a) *action* ('the recruitment, transportation, transfer, harbouring or receipt of persons'); (b) *means* ('threat or use of force or other forms of coercion, of abduction, of fraud, of deception, of the abuse of power or a position of vulnerability or of the giving or receiving of payments or benefits to achieve the consent of a person having control over another person'); and (c) the *purpose* of exploitation. Exploitation is defined to include 'exploitation of the prostitution of others or other forms of sexual exploitation, forced labour or servitude, slavery or practices similar to slavery, servitude or the removal of organs'. Consent to exploitation provides no defence. The elements of forced labour, slavery and 'practices similar to slavery' are not defined in the Protocol but in other international Conventions.[9] Servitude is not defined at all.[10]

6 See e.g. Dorchen Leidholdt, 'Prostitution and Trafficking: An Intimate Relationship' in Melissa Farley (ed.), *Prostitution, Trafficking and Traumatic Stress* (Haworth Press, 2003), 167.

7 See e.g. Jo Doezema, 'Who Gets to Choose? Coercion, Consent and the UN Trafficking Protocol' (2002) 10(1) *Gender and Development* 20.

8 Opened for signature 15 December 2000, 2225 UNTS 209 (entered into force 29 September 2003).

9 'Forced or compulsory labour' is defined as 'all work or service which is exacted from any person under the menace of any penalty, and for which the said person has not offered himself voluntarily': Convention Concerning Forced or Compulsory Labour (International Labour Organization (ILO) No 29) opened for signature 28 June 1930, 39 UNTS 55 (entered into force 1 May 1932) art 2(1) (Forced Labour Convention). Slavery is defined as 'the status or condition of a person over whom any or all of the powers attaching to the right of ownership are exercised': Convention to Suppress the Slave Trade and Slavery, opened for signature 25 September 1926, 212 UNTS 17 (entered into force 9 March 1927) art 1 (1926 Slavery Convention). The Supplementary Convention on the Abolition of Slavery, the Slave Trade, and Institutions and Practices Similar to Slavery, opened for signature 7 September 1956, 226 UNTS 3 (entered into force 30 April 1957) art 1 incorporates in 'practices similar to slavery' the practices of debt bondage, serfdom, servile forms of marriage and the sale of children for exploitation.

10 Servitude is proscribed in arts 8(1) and 8(2) of the International Covenant on Civil and Political Rights, opened for signature 16 December 1966, 999 UNTS 171 (entered into force 23 March 1976).

The fragile political consensus on which the Trafficking Protocol was based led to a compromise position on its scope. Trafficking was framed broadly, in gender neutral terms, extending to various forms of exploitation.[11] Yet, as the Protocol's name suggests, trafficking discourse maintained a gendered emphasis on the exploitation of women and children.[12] Within the context of the UNTOC, the Protocol was situated squarely within a law and order paradigm, concerned primarily to protect sovereign security interests and curb illegal migration, rather than promote human rights. Articles 5.1 and 5.2 contain strong mandatory obligations on states to criminalise trafficking and prosecute traffickers; victim support is more optional. Articles 6.5, 6.6 and 7 require states parties to provide victims the 'possibility' to obtain compensation, to 'endeavour' to provide for the physical safety of victims on their territory, and to 'consider' adopting measures that permit trafficking victims to avoid deportation to their state of origin with due regard to humanitarian factors. As Joanne Berman argues, this 'law and order' rhetoric collapses complex issues regarding transnational migration, exploitation and labour into a narrative that positions trafficking as much as a threat to the sovereign nation as potential victims.[13]

The ideological struggles over whether prostitution is like other work also neutralised efforts to conceptualise trafficking in terms of labour or precarious work. By hiving off criminal conduct, the Protocol implicitly distinguishes trafficking from both legally tolerated employment contracts and illegal but non-criminalised labour violations. Exploitation has become the 'key actionable element in the trafficking process',[14] but it remains undefined, along with the means-related elements of 'other forms of coercion', 'abuse of power' or 'of a position of vulnerability'.

With this definitional uncertainty, the Protocol allows conflicting interpretations of what degree of exploitative employment is sufficiently egregious, or how deceived a worker must be about their terms of employment to come within the criminal purview of trafficking. These questions are greatly disputed, and historically have galvanised organised labour's commitment to protect workers. In the absence of any global consensus on detailed minimum employment standards, it is extremely difficult to distinguish 'free and consensual' from 'unfree and coerced' employment relationships. These difficulties are even more acute for migrants, who may submit to exploitation because the exploitative conditions in the host country may be preferable to employment conditions at home.

11 Anne Gallagher, 'Human Rights and Human Trafficking: Quagmire or Firm Ground? A Response to James Hathaway' (2009) 49 *Virginia Journal of International Law* 789, 791.

12 Marie Segrave, 'Human Trafficking and Human Rights' (2009) 14(2) *Australian Journal of Human Rights* 71, 74.

13 Joanne Berman, '(Un)popular Strangers and Crises (Un)bounded: Discourses of Sex-Trafficking, the European Political Community and the Panicked States of the Modern State' (2003) 9(1) *European Journal of International Relations* 37.

14 Janice Raymond, 'The New UN Trafficking Protocol' (2002) 25(5) *Women's Studies International Forum* 491, 495.

Similar tensions accompanied Australian efforts to implement this international framework.[15] A comprehensive anti-trafficking strategy was announced in 2003, targeting detection and prosecution of traffickers, with support structures for victims who cooperated with the criminal investigations.[16] In 2005, a suite of trafficking offences was introduced in Division 271 of the *Criminal Code*.[17] Twelve separate offences pertained to organising or facilitating the transport of a victim into, out of, or within Australia, in a range of coercive, deceptive or exploitative circumstances. In their original form, these circumstances included: the use of force or threats to obtain the victim's compliance;[18] being reckless as to whether the trafficked person will be 'exploited';[19] and deception concerning the provision of sexual services, future exploitation, debt bondage or the confiscation of travel or identity documents.[20] Alternatively, trafficking could be made out where there was agreement as to the provision of sexual services, but deception as to the nature of those services, or the extent to which the person was free to leave their place of work or residence, the extent to which they are free to cease providing sexual services, or the existence or amount of any debt claimed to be owed.[21] Aggravated offences required an intention that the victim will be 'exploited', or subjected to cruel, inhuman or degrading treatment, or recklessness as to danger of death or serious harm to the victim.[22] Separate offences proscribe trafficking in children, which do not require the use of force or deception.[23]

Exploitation, for the purpose of these trafficking offences, was originally defined to occur where the exploiter caused the victim to enter into slavery, forced labour, sexual servitude, or forced organ removal.[24] Prior to the 2013 *Slavery Act*, the term 'forced labour', as an element of exploitation in trafficking, was defined as:

> the condition of a person who provides labour services (other than sexual services) and who because of force or threats:
> (a) Is not free to cease providing labour or services; or

15 Australia ratified the UNTOC on 27 May 2004, and the Trafficking Protocol on 14 September 2005.

16 Attorney-General's Department (AGD), *Australian Government's Action Plan to Eradicate Trafficking in Persons* (2004), iii.

17 Introduced by the *Criminal Code Amendment (Trafficking in Persons Offences) Act 2005* (Cth).

18 *Criminal Code* ss 271.2(1), 271.2(1A) and 271.5(1), as enacted in 2005. The maximum penalty for all trafficking offences is 12 years' imprisonment.

19 Sections 271.2(1B), 271.2(1C) and 271.5(2), as enacted in 2005.

20 Sections 271.2(2), 271.2(2A) and 271.5(2A), as enacted in 2005.

21 Sections 271.2(2B), 271.2(2C) and 271.5(2B), as enacted in 2005.

22 Sections 271.3(1)(a)-(c) and 271.6(1)(a)-(c), as enacted in 2005. Maximum penalty for these aggravated offences is 20 years imprisonment.

23 Sections 271.4 and 271.7, as enacted in 2005. The maximum penalty is 25 years' imprisonment.

24 The dictionary in the *Criminal Code*.

(b) Is not free to leave the place or area where the person provides labour or services.[25]

In turn, 'threat' was defined as: '(a) a threat of force; (b) a threat to cause a person's removal from Australia; or (c) a threat of any other detrimental action, unless there are reasonable grounds for the threat of that action'.[26]

The 2005 Act also created the summary offence of 'debt bondage'.[27] This offence occurred when a person pledged their services (or the services of another) as security for a debt, where the reasonable value of those services was not applied to repay the debt, where the debt was 'manifestly excessive' or where the length and nature of the services was not defined.

These trafficking offences were additional to pre-existing offences related to slavery, sexual servitude and deceptive recruiting for sexual services that are set out in Division 270 of the *Criminal Code*.[28] Section 270.1 defines slavery as 'the condition of a person over whom any or all of the powers attaching to the right of ownership are exercised, including where such a condition results from a debt or contract made by a person'. This definition is partly based on the 1926 Slavery Convention but expands the concept of slavery to cover more modern forms of slavery such as debt bondage or extremely exploitative contracts. Section 270.3(1) sets out the offences of reducing a person to slavery, intentionally possessing a slave, exercising powers of ownership over a slave and entering into a commercial transaction involving a slave.[29] Further offences occur where the offender is reckless as to whether an act involves a slave.[30] Additional offences proscribed sexual exploitation that was less severe than slavery but did not involve the transportation required for trafficking: sexual servitude and deceptive recruiting for sexual services.[31]

25 Forced labour was at that time defined in the dictionary of the *Criminal Code* by reference to s 73.2.

26 Section 271.1, as enacted in 2005.

27 Section 271.8, as enacted in 2005. When first introduced, the maximum penalty was 12 months' imprisonment.

28 The *Criminal Code Amendment (Slavery and Sexual Servitude) Act 1999* (Cth). Previously, slavery in Australia was criminalised by British Imperial anti-slavery laws: *Slave Trade Act 1824*.

29 These attract a maximum penalty of 25 years imprisonment.

30 *Criminal Code* s 270.3(2). The maximum penalty is 17 years' imprisonment.

31 Sexual servitude was defined identically to forced labour but only in relation to sexual services: former s 270.4(1). The maximum penalty was 15 years' imprisonment or 20 years for an aggravated offence (where the victim is under the age of 18). *Sieders v. R; Somsri v. R* (2008) 72 NSWLR 417 explains the meaning of sexual servitude. Deceptive recruiting for sexual services was set out in former s 270.7. The maximum penalty was 7 years' imprisonment, or 9 years for aggravated offence (where the victim is under the age of 18).

Between 2004 and 30 June 2014, the Australian Federal Police (AFP) undertook 469 investigations into human trafficking matters.[32] As at 30 June 2014, 17 people had been convicted of slavery and trafficking offences in the *Criminal Code*: ten of slavery, four of sexual servitude and three of human trafficking.[33] Noone has been convicted of the debt bondage offence.

According to official and academic sources, most cases identified in Australia are not reducible to stereotypical abductions of trafficked women: the deceptive and exploitative conduct mostly occurs in Australia rather than overseas.[34] Even once in Australia, physical restraint, overt control of victims and seizure of passports are rare.[35] Coercion and control have chiefly been achieved through 'threats of violence, obligations to repay debt, isolation, manipulation of tenuous or illegal migration situations and a general sense of obligation'.[36] In several cases trafficked people maintain a measure of freedom (access to public transport, internet and mobile phones, for example).[37] In the renowned slavery case *Wei Tang*, Justice McInerney found that while the victims were not locked inside the brothel in which they worked, they had been 'effectively restrained by the insidious nature of their contract'.[38] I return to these threshold standards of restraint in the final section of this chapter, which considers the level of coercion required to make out these criminal offences.

To accompany these criminal offences, in 2004, the government's Action Plan to Eradicate Trafficking in Persons introduced a range of visas to regularise the immigration status of potential victims who assist criminal investigations.[39] This framework was amended in 2009 following criticisms that the threshold requirements for these visas were too narrowly tied to a person's ability to contribute to criminal prosecutions.[40] Since 2009, the scheme includes three visas.[41]

32 Anti-Human Trafficking Interdepartmental Committee, *Trafficking in Persons: The Australian Government Response 1 July 2013–30 June 2014* (Cth of Australia, 2014), 1 (*IDC Report 2013–14*).

33 Ibid. 22.

34 Andreas Schloenhardt, Genevieve Beirne and Tony Corsbie, 'Human Trafficking and Sexual Servitude in Australia' (2009) 32(1) *University of New South Wales Law Journal* 27, 31.

35 Anti-Human Trafficking Interdepartmental Committee, *Trafficking in Persons: The Australian Government Response 1 May 2009–30 June 2010* (Cth of Australia, 2010), 23 (*IDC Report 2009–10*).

36 Jacqueline Joudo Larsen and Lauren Renshaw, 'People Trafficking in Australia' (2012) 441 *Trends and Issues in Crime and Criminal Law* 2.

37 Frances Simmons *et al.*, 'Human Trafficking and Slavery Offenders in Australia' (2013) 464 *Trends and Issues in Crime and Criminal Justice* 1, 10.

38 *R v. Wei Tang* [2006] VCC 637.

39 *Migration Amendment Regulations 2003 (No 11)* (Cth), sch 8.

40 Jennifer Burn and Frances Simmons, 'Rewarding Witnesses, Ignoring Victims: An Evaluation of the New Trafficking Visa Framework' (2005) 24 *Immigration Review* 6, 9.

41 *Migration Legislation Amendment Regulations 2009 (No 2)* (Cth), sch 8.

The Bridging F visa (BVF), valid for 45 days,[42] is available if an AFP or state or territory police officer communicates in writing to the Department of Immigration and Border Protection (DIBP) that the applicant has been 'identified as a suspected victim of human trafficking'.[43] The person need not assist any police investigation.[44] A second BVF is available if 'a person is willing but not able to assist police because of their current mental, physical or emotional state'.[45] After visiting Australia in November 2011, the UN Special Rapporteur on Trafficking in Persons, Especially Women and Children (Special Rapporteur) noted that in practice an additional BVF is rarely granted and only where the applicant evidences extreme trauma.[46]

Upon expiry of a BVF, a Criminal Justice Stay visa (CJSV) may be issued at the discretion of the Minister for Immigration.[47] CJSVs permit an otherwise unlawful non-citizen to remain in Australia where the Attorney-General has issued a Commonwealth Criminal Justice Stay Certificate stating that their presence is required for 'the administration of criminal justice'.[48]

Subsequently, a trafficked person may be offered a Witness Protection (Trafficking) (Permanent) visa (WPTV), but only if the Attorney-General certifies the person has 'made a contribution to, and cooperated with, the prosecution of a person who was alleged to have trafficked a person or who was alleged to have forced a person into exploitative conditions (whether or not the person was convicted)' or an investigation that the Commonwealth Director of Public Prosecutions (CDPP) has decided not to prosecute.[49] The minister must also be satisfied the person would be in danger if repatriated.[50] The WPTV grants the visa-holder and their immediate family permanent residence with access to Medicare and income support.

In addition, the government instigated the Support for Trafficked People Program (currently implemented by the Australian Red Cross), which offers government-funded emergency accommodation, financial support, medical services including counselling, a caseworker and legal assistance. This

42 *Migration Regulations 1994* (Cth), sch 2 cl 060.511(3)(b)(ii) (*Migration Regulations*).
43 Ibid. sch 1 cl 1306(3)(d)(i).
44 'There is no requirement that they be willing to assist with an investigation': DIBP, 'PAM3: Act – Compliance and Case resolution – Program Visa – Bridging F Visas', [2.2].
45 Ibid.
46 Joy Ngozi Ezeilo, *Report of the Special Rapporteur on Trafficking in Persons, Especially Women and Children*, UN Doc A/HRC/20/18 (18 May 2012), 54. A parliamentary inquiry recommended in 2013 that this extension be made more available to suspected victims: Joint Standing Committee on Foreign Affairs, Defence and Trade (Human Rights Sub-Committee), *Trading Lives: Modern Day Human Trafficking* (Parliament of Australia, 2013), viii (*Trading Lives Report*).
47 *Migration Act* ss 157 and 158.
48 Ibid. ss 141, 147.
49 *Migration Regulations* reg 2.07AK(3)(c)(i) and (ii).
50 Ibid. reg 2.07AK(3)(f).

support was originally available only to holders of a BVF or CJSV.[51] Since 2009, it has been extended to anyone identified by the AFP as a 'suspected victim of human trafficking', regardless of visa status.[52] To be eligible for further support beyond an initial period the person must be willing and able to contribute to criminal processes.[53]

Between 2004 and June 2014, 235 suspected victims of trafficking were assisted through the Support for Trafficked People Program.[54] In this period, DIBP granted 224 BVFs, 202 CJSVs and 110 WPTVs (figures include primary visa grants as well as to immediate family members).[55] Victims of trafficking in Australia historically are nationals of Thailand, Malaysia, the Philippines and South Korea,[56] and increasingly India, Indonesia and China.[57] The majority of people trafficked into Australia enter on visitor, student or working holiday visas.[58] Apparently, student visas are preferred by traffickers because they permit five years of residence, 40 hours of work per fortnight while course is in session, including sex work, and unauthorised work in excess of this and failure to meet course requirements are difficult to identify.[59]

Historical overshadowing of labour exploitation

For all their other strengths, Australian counter-trafficking efforts until recently have tended to neglect 'labour trafficking'. Before exploring these failings, a note on terminology. I distinguish trafficking for sex from labour trafficking outside of the sex industry not because I believe these are necessarily different categories of trafficking, but to highlight the historical preoccupation with trafficking for sexual exploitation, and because assistance needs may differ depending on type or degree of exploitation. I agree with Simmons and David that this distinction 'does not reflect the complex reality' of trafficking, which may involve sexual abuse in industries outside of the sex industry, or people's experiences of trafficking in the sex industry as labour exploitation.[60]

51 Australian National Audit Office (ANAO), *Management of the Australian Government's Action Plan to Eradicate Trafficking in Persons* (the Auditor-General Audit Report No 30, 2008-09 Performance Audit, 2009), 51.

52 Department of Families, Housing, Community Services and Indigenous Affairs, *Anti-Human Trafficking Strategy* (2012).

53 Ezeilo, *Report of the Special Rapporteur,* above n. 46, 14.

54 *IDC Report 2013–14,* above n. 32, 30.

55 Ibid. 34.

56 Anti-Human Trafficking Interdepartmental Committee, *Trafficking in Persons: The Australian Government Response 1 July 2011–30 June 2012* (Cth of Australia, 2012), 3 (*IDC Report 2011–12*).

57 Ezeilo, *Report of the Special Rapporteur,* above n. 46, 3.

58 Joudo Larsen and Renshaw, 'People Trafficking in Australia', above n. 36, 3.

59 *IDC Report 2009–10,* above n. 35, 30.

60 Frances Simmons and Fiona David, 'The Road to Effective Remedies: Pragmatic Reasons for Treating Cases of "Sex Trafficking" in the Australian Sex Industry as a Form of "Labour Trafficking"' (2012) 1 *Anti-Trafficking Review* 60, 63.

While criminal laws have clearly extended to exploitation outside of the sex industry, Australian criminal justice data (detected cases, identified victims and prosecutions) have been starkly concentrated in the sex industry. Only recently have enforcement efforts encompassed other sectors, after policy analysts and scholars advocated for an adjustment to priorities. Of the 469 AFP trafficking investigations between 2004 and July 2014, around 55 per cent related to trafficking for sexual exploitation and the remainder to other forms of labour exploitation or forced marriage,[61] although the proportion of labour trafficking has significantly increased over time (from 30 per cent in 2009–10).[62] An even larger proportion of identified suspected victims have been trafficked in the sex industry (as of May 2013, 164 of 209 victims, or 78 per cent) although here again the proportion of labour trafficking has increased significantly (43 per cent of newly identified people in 2013–14).[63] Only three out of at least 32 trafficking and slavery prosecutions to July 2013 related to labour (one of which ended in acquittal).[64] In one more recent matter, three employers were charged with forcing two Estonian welders on working holiday visas into debt bondage, but a Western Australian District Court judge ordered these charges be withdrawn in 2014.[65]

Naturally, these figures reflect the efforts and priorities of government authorities, their understanding of the issue and interpretation of the law, and priorities of investigative agencies, rather than the actual extent of labour (or sex) trafficking in Australia.[66] Australian Institute of Criminology (AIC) research suggests that labour trafficking may occur in the agricultural, cleaning, hospitality, construction and manufacturing industries, as well as in domestic work.[67] However, it is impossible to assess its true scope, not least because it has the 'potential to be conflated with breaches of migration and labour laws'.[68] The Special Rapporteur notes that a much larger and more diverse population of trafficking victims is discernible in the caseloads handled by civil society agencies than is reflected in official government statistics.[69]

61 *IDC Report 2013–14*, above n. 32, 18.

62 Anti-Human Trafficking Interdepartmental Committee, *Trafficking in Persons: The Australian Government Response January 2004–April 2009* (Cth of Australia, 2009), 19.

63 *Trading Lives Report*, above n. 46, 71; *IDC Report 2013–14*, above n. 32, 30.

64 *Kovacs* appeal [2009] 2 Qd R 51; *R v. Yogalingham Rasalingham* (Unreported, NSWDC, Puckeridge J, 2 November 2007); *R v. Trivedi* (Unreported, NSWDC, O'Connor J, 12 October 2011).

65 'WA Jury Discharged over Extortion Trial', *SBS*, 7 November 2014.

66 Marie Segrave, 'Trafficking in Persons as Labour Exploitation' in Chris Cunneen and Michael Salter (eds), *Proceedings of the Second Australian and New Zealand Critical Criminology Conference* (19–20 June 2008, Sydney, Australia), 322, 327–8.

67 David, *Labour Trafficking*, above n. 1, 6. See also Australian Crime Commission, Submission No 6 to the Joint Standing Commission on Foreign Affairs, Defence and Trade, Parliament of Australia, 'Inquiry into Slavery, Slavery-Like Conditions and People Trafficking', 24 September 2012, 4–5.

68 Joudo Larsen and Renshaw, 'People Trafficking in Australia', above n. 36, 4.

69 Ezeilo, *Report of the Special Rapporteur*, above n. 46, 12.

The next section reviews in more detail this early preoccupation with sexual exploitation in Australian counter-trafficking measures and more recent moves recognising the interconnections between labour trafficking, forced labour and trafficking policies. Mapping this trajectory against similar international trends, this section unpacks some of the historical, ideological and logistical reasons for the prominence of sex trafficking in literature and government policy.[70]

The sexual focus of early counter-trafficking interventions

Australia's response to trafficking grew out of community outrage following the death of Phuontong Simpalee, a girl or young woman from Thailand who was found working in a brothel during an immigration raid in 2001 and died of heroin withdrawal in an immigration detention centre three days later.[71] From those early days, many Australian policy analysts,[72] academics[73] and government policymakers[74] focused almost exclusively on female victims of sexual servitude. As recently as 2009, even prominent academic commentators have observed that '[h]uman trafficking in Australia is done almost exclusively for sexual purposes involving legal and illegal brothels'.[75] The early omission of labour trafficking from political consideration in Australia was illustrated by parliamentary debate preceding the introduction of trafficking offences in 2005, which centred almost entirely on sex trafficking

70 On this international preoccupation with sex trafficking, see Grace Chang and Kathleen Kim, 'Reconceptualizing Approaches to Human Trafficking: New Directions and Perspectives from the Field(s)' (2007) 3 *Stanford Journal of Civil Rights and Civil Liberties* 317, 319–21; Janie A. Chuang, 'Rescuing Trafficking from Ideological Capture: Prostitution Reform and Anti-Trafficking Law and Policy' (2010) 158 *University of Pennsylvania Law Review* 1655, 1657.

71 Pru Goward, Federal Sex Discrimination Commissioner, 'Trafficking in Women: Where Have We Come From and Where to From Here?' (Paper presented at Project Respect Forum, Melbourne, 12 August 2005).

72 Judy Putt, 'Human Trafficking to Australia: A Research Challenge' (2007) 338 *Trends and Issues in Crime and Criminal Justice* 2; Kerry Carrington and Jane Hearn, 'Trafficking and the Sex Industry: From Impunity to Protection' (Current Issues Brief No 28, Parliamentary Library, Parliament of Australia, 2002–03).

73 Erica Kotnik, Melina Czymoniewicz-Klippel and Elizabeth Hoban, 'Human Trafficking in Australia: The Challenge of Responding to Suspicious Activities' (2007) 42(3) *Australian Journal of Social Issues* 369, 370; Lisa Carson and Kathy Edwards, 'Prostitution and Sex Trafficking: What are the Problems Represented to Be? A Discursive Analysis of Law and Policy in Sweden and Victoria, Australia' (2011) 34 *Australian Feminist Law Journal* 63; Catherine Flynn, Margaret Alston and Robyn Mason, 'Trafficking in Women for Sexual Exploitation: Building Australian Knowledge' (2014) 57(1) *International Social Work* 27.

74 ANAO, *Management of the Australian Government's Action Plan,* above n. 51, 11; Parliamentary Joint Committee of the Australian Crime Commission, 'Inquiry into the Trafficking of Women for Sexual Servitude' (2004).

75 Andreas Schloenhardt, Genevieve Beirne and Tony Corsbie, 'Human Trafficking and Sexual Servitude in Australia' (2009) 32(1) *University of New South Wales Law Journal* 27, 31.

(although the offences in fact extended to labour trafficking).[76] Trade unions used other forums to highlight alleged instances of labour trafficking,[77] but did not make submissions to the parliamentary processes that preceded the 2005 or 2013 legislation.

Indeed, traces of the gendered presumptions that link women with trafficking and men with labour migration are evident in this book. It has not taken as its focus female migrant workers as such, in part because of the scarcity of gender disaggregated data on migrant labour in Australia. Further research remains to be done to grapple with the role that gender plays in the exploitative working conditions of women temporary migrant workers.[78]

The prominence given to sexual coercion clearly drew from the dominant understandings of trafficking that shaped the Trafficking Protocol.[79] The Protocol itself sets out a broad conception of trafficking, including forced labour outside of the sex industry, although its title betrays an historical bias.[80] The US government claimed for years that the majority of transnational victims are women and children 'trafficked into commercial sexual exploitation'.[81] The UN Office for Drugs and Crime (UNODC) points to a further 'visibility bias', arguing that trafficking for prostitution is more likely to be detected than trafficking for labour because prostitution is simply more visible than forced labour, since it involves attracting potential clients.[82]

Indeed, the International Labour Organization's (ILO) treatment of forced labour was initially very disconnected from UNODC work on trafficking for sexual or labour exploitation. In 1998, the ILO reaffirmed the elimination of forced labour as a universal and absolute principle binding all member states regardless of ratification of specific forced labour

76 Transcript of the Senate Legal and Constitutional Affairs Committee, 'Inquiry into the Criminal Code Amendment (Trafficking in Persons Offences) Bill 2004' (NSW State Library, Sydney, 23 February 2005). Only Senator Kerry Nettle (of the Australian Greens party) avoided this emphasis on sex trafficking, noting that '[p]eople are trafficked to provide labour and there is evidence that this extends to the construction industry, clothing and textiles, [and] domestic work': Commonwealth, *Parliamentary Debates*, Senate, 20 June 2005, 76.

77 For example, the Liquor, Hospitality and Miscellaneous Union, the Construction Forestry Mining and Energy Union (CFMEU), the Australian Council of Trade Unions (ACTU), the Australian Manufacturing Workers Union and the Australian Nurses Federation made submissions to the Australian parliament's Joint Standing Committee on Migration, 'Inquiry into Temporary Business Visas' (2007).

78 For an interesting scoping study of this area see Jennifer Burn *et al.*, *Hidden Exploitation: Women in Forced Labour, Marriage and Migration* (Anti-Slavery Australia and Jumbunna Indigenous House of Learning at UTS, 2012).

79 Jyoti Sanghera, 'Unpacking the Trafficking Discourse' in Kemala Kempadoo, Jyoti Sanghera and Bandana Pattanaik (eds), *Trafficking and Prostitution Reconsidered: New Perspectives on Migration, Sex Work and Human Rights* (Paradigm Publishers, 2005), 3.

80 Bernadette McSherry and Susan Kneebone, 'Trafficking in Women and Forced Migration: Moving Victims Across the Border of Crime into the Domain of Human Rights' (2008) 12(1) *International Journal of Human Rights* 67, 71.

81 United States Department of State, *Trafficking in Persons Report* (2008).

82 UNODC, *Global Report on Trafficking in Persons* (2007), 51.

conventions.[83] However, during negotiations of the Trafficking Protocol, the ILO was reluctant to propose labour protections for trafficked people because of internal debates over whether sex workers should be granted social and labour protections.[84]

The turn towards labour trafficking

Over time, the ILO, UNODC, civil society advocates and academics have come to incorporate forced labour and labour trafficking into their agendas.[85] It is now nearly universally accepted that labour trafficking is globally under-detected. This may stem from confusion about its threshold requirements, beliefs that labour exploitation is not worthy of redress as a serious act of violence, or difficulties in differentiating labour trafficking from employment law violations.

As a result, figures on the nature and extent of labour trafficking and forced labour worldwide are unreliable and seem to change dramatically over short periods of time.[86] In 2009 the UNODC estimated that 18 per cent of trafficking victims identified by state authorities globally have been victims of forced labour.[87] Conversely, the ILO's approach to this field appears to be evolving and the relationship between labour trafficking (under the Protocol) and forced labour (under the ILO Convention) remain unclear. In reports in 2005 and 2009, the ILO defined labour trafficking as a subset of forced labour involving movement or migration,[88] estimating that there were 12.4 million victims of forced labour, of which 2.4 million were trafficked.[89] Also in 2009, the ILO promulgated a list of operational indicators to enable states to detect

83 ILO, ILO Declaration on Fundamental Principles and Rights at Work (International Labour Conference, 86th sess, 18 June 1998) art 2. See also Susan Kneebone and Julie Debeljak, *Transnational Crime and Human Rights: Responses to Human Trafficking in the Greater Mekong Subregion* (Routledge, 2012), 34ff.

84 O'Connell Davidson argues that the ILO may have been reluctant to see sex workers as 'workers' for fear of losing US funding of its global alliance against forced labour: Julia O'Connell Davidson, 'Will the Real Sex Slave Please Stand Up?' (2006) 83 *Feminist Review* 4, 18.

85 E.g. Don Flynn, *Policy Brief – Human Trafficking and Forced Labour: What Perspectives to Challenge Exploitation?* (Platform for International Cooperation on Undocumented Migrants, 2007); Global Alliance Against Traffic in Women, *More 'Trafficking' Less 'Trafficked': Trafficking for Exploitation Outside the Sex Sector in Europe* (2011); Klara Skrivankova, *Between Decent Work and Forced Labour: Examining the Continuum of Exploitation* (Joseph Rowntree Foundation, 2010).

86 Sheldon X. Zhang, 'Measuring Labor Trafficking: A Research Note' (2012) 58 *Crime, Law and Social Change* 469, 480; Patrick Belser and Michaelle de Cock, 'Improving Forced Labor Statistics' in Beate Andrees and Patrick Belser (eds), *Forced Labor: Coercion and Exploitation in the Private Economy* (Lynne Rienner Publishers, 2009), 173.

87 UNODC, *Global Report on Trafficking in Persons* (2009), 50.

88 ILO, *A Global Alliance Against Forced Labour* (International Labour Conference, 93rd session, 2005), 10; ILO, *The Cost of Coercion: Global Report under the Follow-up to the ILO Declaration on Fundamental Principles and Rights at Work* (2009), 11.

89 ILO, *Global Alliance*, above n. 88, 6, 15–16.

victims of trafficking more effectively, including a subset that specifically targets labour trafficking.[90] The indicators are structured around six elements drawn from the trafficking definition: deceptive recruitment, coercive recruitment, recruitment by abuse of vulnerability, exploitative conditions of work, coercion at destination and abuse of vulnerability at destination. However, by 2012, the ILO estimated the number of people in forced labour globally at 20.9 million, and no longer distinguished between forced labour and trafficking.[91] In 2014, the ILO adopted a new protocol to the Forced Labour Convention that explicitly links forced labour to trafficking and fraudulent and abusive recruitment practices towards migrant workers.[92]

Unsurprisingly, Australian policies have mirrored this new growing global alertness to labour trafficking. Concern about trafficking for labour exploitation in Australia was first given voice by a former AFP agent as early as 2004, noting that 'we know that men are trafficked into circumstances of slave-like labour in kitchens and restaurants around Australia'.[93] A 2005 Immigration Department report followed, acknowledging that 'people trafficking can occur in any industry'.[94] In 2007, the US State Department, along with anti-trafficking campaigner Elaine Pearson, recommended that extreme exploitation of 457 visa workers should be investigated as potential trafficking, with media at the time describing the scheme as 'akin to slavery'.[95] By 2009, scholars recommended the application of trafficking, slavery and debt bondage laws to cases of serious migrant labour abuse.[96]

In 2010, ground-breaking research by the AIC into labour trafficking lifted the profile of this issue considerably.[97] This report concluded that labour trafficking had occurred in Australia, but was unreported or unrecognised, along with less serious unlawful treatment, including non-payment of wages, sexual harassment and deception or fraud about working conditions and sponsorship for permanent residency. Some of these forms

90 ILO, *Operational Indicators of Trafficking in Human Beings: Results from a Delphi Survey Implemented by the ILO and the European Commission* (2009), 3.

91 It observes, somewhat cryptically, that 'there is … a clear link between the Protocol and ILO Convention No 29': ILO, *Global Estimates of Forced Labour: Results and Methodology* (2012), 20.

92 ILO, Protocol of 2014 to the Forced Labour Convention, 1930, adopted Geneva, 103rd ILC session, 11 June 2014.

93 ABC Radio, 'Crime Experts Warn of Untold Story of Human Trafficking', *AM*, 30 April 2004.

94 Department of Immigration, Multicultural and Indigenous Affairs, *Managing the Border: Immigration Compliance 2004–05* (2005), 96.

95 United States Department of State, *Trafficking in Persons Report* (2007), 57; Elaine Pearson, 'Australia' in Global Alliance Against Trafficking in Women, *Collateral Damage: The Impact of Anti-Trafficking Measures on Human Rights around the World* (2007), 45.

96 Miriam Cullen and Bernadette McSherry, 'Without Sex: Slavery, Trafficking in Persons and the Exploitation of Labour in Australia' (2009) 34(1) *Alternative Law Journal* 4, 10; Stephanie Toh and Michael Quinlan, 'Safeguarding the Global Contingent Workforce? Guestworkers in Australia' (2009) 30(5) *International Journal of Manpower* 453, 454.

97 David, *Labour Trafficking*, above n. 1.

of mistreatment were presented as meeting one or two of the ILO indicators of labour trafficking. The report noted a general lack of understanding, except among experts in the sector, that trafficking offences are defined to include conduct outside the sex industry.[98] It identified risk factors that can worsen migrant workers' susceptibility to exploitation: immigration status and fear of deportation; physical or linguistic isolation from the broader community; family or community obligations; financial pressures (including debts in their home country) and longer-term goals of permanent residency.

The AIC proposed strategies to target a broader range of exploitative practices. It recommended new offences covering lesser forms of exploitative behaviour such as abuse of vulnerability for gain, forced labour and servitude for non-sexual services without the need to make out the element of movement. It suggested that intermediaries (agents and brokers) be more effectively regulated and monitored, and recommended stronger coalitions and better awareness-raising among criminal justice agencies, labour inspectors, unions and employers.[99]

Contemporaneously with this research, government agencies re-oriented their attention toward labour trafficking. In 2009, the Sex Discrimination Commissioner publicly noted that the Australian Human Rights Commission was 'beginning to see more cases of labour trafficking'.[100] The Commonwealth Attorney-General's Department noted in 2011 that:

> it is possible that women working in the sex industry are over-represented among statistics on identified victims of trafficking simply because other forms of exploitation are under-reported and under-researched.[101]

Further institutional changes followed. In 2009, the Fair Work Ombudsman (FWO) joined the federal Anti-Human Trafficking Inter-Departmental Committee, which implements national policy on trafficking. The Australian Building and Construction Commission (the government construction industry inspectorate) joined the Committee in 2010–11.[102] In 2011 the Australian government awarded unions (the ACTU and CFMEU), an employer association (the Australian Hotels Association) and non-governmental organisations (Australian Red Cross and Asian Women at Work)

98 Ibid. 48.

99 Ibid. 52–53.

100 Elizabeth Broderick, Sex Discrimination Commissioner, '(Non-Sex Industry) Labour Trafficking: A Forum to Discuss Trafficking in Persons in Contexts Other than the Commercial Sex Industry' (Speech delivered to the Australian Institute of Criminology, 18 June 2009), 2.

101 AGD, *The Criminal Justice Response to Slavery and People Trafficking, Reparation and Vulnerable Witness Protection* (Discussion Paper 2011), 6.

102 Anti-Human Trafficking Interdepartmental Committee, *Trafficking in Persons: The Australian Government Response 1 July 2010–30 June 2011* (2011) (*IDC Report 2010–11*). In 2014 it ceased its membership of the Committee because its regulatory oversight of wages and entitlements in the construction industry was transferred to the FWO.

almost A$500,000 to undertake projects to develop targeted awareness campaigns to combat labour exploitation in Australian industries. More cosmetically, in 2011, the 'National Policing Strategy to Combat Trafficking in Women for Sexual Servitude' was re-branded the 'Australian Policing Strategy to Combat Trafficking in Persons 2011–13' and the AFP specialist taskforce, the Transnational Sexual Exploitation Team, was renamed the Human Trafficking Team.

Selective bias towards sex trafficking persists

However, concerns about sexual exploitation and the victimisation of women still dominate Australian discussions about trafficking. Responsibility for trafficking within the Australian Human Rights Commission continues to fall to the federal Sex Discrimination Commissioner. The Trafficking Victims Support Program sits within a program related to violence against women in the Department of Social Services, although the programme is not restricted to female clients. In September 2011, the government appointed an Office of the Global Ambassador for Women and Girls, whose formal duties include efforts to end the trafficking of women and girls.

More troubling, some commentary continues to minimise the prevalence of labour exploitation. Several parliamentary inquiries, at the state level, have focused specifically on trafficking of women or men and women for sex work.[103] Prominent scholars of Australian counter-trafficking law recently observed that there 'is no significant evidence of persons being brought into Australia for forced labour in sweat shops or other forced employment'.[104] The US State Department's most recent *Trafficking in Persons Report* describes Australia as 'primarily a destination country for women subjected to forced prostitution'.[105]

Even measures explicitly designed to take an expansive, industry-neutral view of trafficking continue to be described or justified in gendered or sexualised terms. To take one astonishing example, even the Attorney-General, introducing into parliament the 2012 Bill that explicitly broadens slavery offences beyond the sex industry, explains the Bill's purpose as 'protecting vulnerable women and children, *and in some cases men*, from trafficking and slavery'.[106] Ironically, a press report discussing the UN Special

103 In 2012, the New South Wales Community Relations Commission launched its 'Inquiry into the Exploitation of Women through Trafficking'. In June 2010, the Victorian Parliament Drugs and Crime Prevention Committee tabled its report on the *Inquiry into People Trafficking for Sex Work*.

104 Andreas Schloenhardt and Mark Loong, 'Return and Reintegration of Human Trafficking Victims from Australia' (2011) 23(2) *International Journal of Refugee Law* 143, 147.

105 United States Department of State, *Trafficking in Persons Report* (2014), 81.

106 Commonwealth, *Parliamentary Debates*, House of Representatives, 30 May 2012, 6226 (Nicola Roxon, Attorney-General, Second Reading Speech on the Crimes Legislation Amendment (Slavery, Slavery-like Conditions and People Trafficking) Bill 2012) (emphasis added).

Rapporteur's view that the 'scale of the problem appears to be underestimated and under-reported, *with most victims outside the sex industry remaining unidentified*', bore the headline 'Sex Trafficking Bigger than Australia Thinks – UN'.[107]

Jurisprudence across the spectrum of coercion in slavery cases

In a 2011 discussion paper foreshadowing the legislative reforms of 2013, the Commonwealth Attorney-General's Department observed that the situations of many people trafficked for sex or labour in Australia do not reflect stereotyped victims involving abduction, violence and physical restraint. It described the Australian experience as involving 'more subtle forms of coercion and control'.[108] For these reasons, the AIC's *Labour Trafficking* report had proposed that migrant worker exploitation be treated as a 'spectrum' ranging from extreme forced labour at one end, to decent work and the full application of fair labour standards at the other.[109] This notion of exploitation as a 'continuum' drew from analysis undertaken by the ILO[110] and British scholars,[111] and was quickly adopted in Australian research.[112]

This section of the chapter draws on this more complex conceptualisation of exploitation to point out that government interventions, initially slow to tackle labour trafficking, actually lagged behind sophisticated judicial consideration of trafficking and slavery offences. While few prosecutions were brought outside of the sex industry, superior courts have nevertheless long been cognisant of the gradations in coercion, freedom and psychological duress, within both sexual and non-sexual exploitation.

The case against brothel owner Wei Tang involved the first jury conviction under Australia's slavery offences and the only High Court of Australia consideration of the slavery offences to date (the final court of appeal in Australia). Tang was accused of purchasing five Thai women who previously worked in the Thai sex industry and arrived in Australia in 2002–3 on fraudulent tourist visas. The women testified that they had voluntarily entered into agreements to work in Australian brothels with a broker in Thailand, and owed A$40,000– A$45,000 on these contracts. Tang required

107 Australian Associated Press, 'Sex Trafficking Bigger than Australia Thinks – UN', *Herald Sun*, 30 November 2011 (emphasis added).

108 AGD, *The Criminal Justice Response*, above n. 101, 96.

109 David, *Labour Trafficking*, above n. 1, 27.

110 ILO, *A Global Alliance Against Forced Labour* (International Labour Conference, 93rd session, 2005), 8; Patrick Belser and Beate Andrees (eds), *Forced Labor: Coercion and Exploitation in the Private Economy* (Lynne Rienner Publishers, 2009), 123.

111 Siobhán McGrath, 'Many Chains to Break: The Multi-Dimensional Concept of Slave Labour in Brazil' (2012) 45 *Antipode* 1005, 1010.

112 Bodean Hedwards, Hannah Andrevski and Sarah Gosper, *Trafficking in Persons in the Australian Construction Industry: Risks and Protections for Migrant Workers* (AIC, forthcoming).

the women to work in her Melbourne brothel six days a week over seven to eight months, with their debt reduced by A$50 (of the A$110 charged) per customer. They were permitted to work a seventh 'free' day, when they could retain A$50 per customer for themselves. The trial judge concluded the women were 'effectively restricted to the premises':[113] although they were not locked in, Tang withheld their passports and airline tickets. There was no other evidence of physical abuse by Tang. Two other women had repaid their debts and voluntarily continued to work as sex-workers. Tang was convicted of five counts of possessing and exercising a power of ownership over a slave and sentenced to ten years imprisonment.[114] Her appeal to the Victorian Court of Appeal was upheld in June 2007.[115] In August 2008, the High Court overturned that decision and restored the initial convictions.[116]

The key point of difference between the High Court and the Victorian Court of Appeal judgments was their interpretation of the elements of the offence. As explained earlier, slavery is defined in s. 270.1 as:

> the condition of a person over whom any or all of the powers attaching to the right of ownership are exercised, including where such a condition results from a debt or contract made by the person.

The Court of Appeal ruled that the prosecution had to prove Tang's subjective knowledge that she was exercising power related to ownership and intended to exercise those powers.[117] The High Court disagreed, holding that the prosecution need not prove what Tang believed specifically about her rights of ownership, or whether the women were slaves. In the majority, Chief Justice Gleeson conceived of slavery by reference to the degree of control exercised by the accused over the complainant.[118] But it is Justice Hayne's judgment that has been most influential in the literature.

To determine whether an offender has the 'requisite dominion over another person', Hayne J focused on the position of the complainant, specifically their lack of 'freedom of choice' (at [149]). While a person might voluntarily choose to enter into a relationship amounting to slavery, by definition they have no freedom once enslaved. His Honour acknowledged that the five women may willingly have travelled to Australia, intending to undertake sex work. But it was nonetheless open to the jury to conclude that

113 *R v. Tang* (2008) 237 CLR 1, [14], [16] (*Tang*).
114 Contrary to *Criminal Code* s 270.3(1)(a): *R v. Wei Tang* [2006] VCC 637.
115 *R v. Wei Tang* (2007) 16 VR 454, 457 (*Wei Tang*).
116 *Tang* (2008) 237 CLR 1.
117 *Wei Tang* (2007) 16 VR 454.
118 His Honour considered the following factors would indicate powers attaching to a right of ownership: commodification of an individual by treating him or her as an object of sale and purchase ([35]); control over a person's movement ([44]); using a person's services without commensurate compensation ([50]); and the power to use the complainants and their labour in a substantially unrestricted manner ([50]).

they were slaves if, after they arrived, they did not retain 'any freedom to choose what was done with them in Australia' (at [166]). Thus, Hayne J confirmed that slavery does not require detention or actual threats or force. Indeed, a crude focus on physical vulnerabilities was never envisaged in the slavery provisions, when first enacted. The means-related elements of these crimes were always intended to be satisfied by a broad range of abusive practices, such as withholding wages or identification papers, continually threatening to expose a worker's unauthorised status to authorities or using debt contracts.[119]

The High Court was cognisant of the need clearly to differentiate slavery (an offence with a maximum penalty of 25 years) from harsh employment conditions (which may not amount to criminal conduct at all). Gleeson CJ observed:

> It is important not to debase the currency of language, or to banalise crimes against humanity, by giving slavery a meaning that extends beyond the limits set by the text ... [H]arsh and exploitative conditions of labour do not of themselves amount to slavery.[120]

As Kirby J noted during the proceedings, 'there are an awful lot of people in this country working in back rooms of restaurants and in the rag trade [whose employers] would be susceptible to ... prosecutions for slavery and that cannot be what Parliament intended'.[121] Yet the question remained: how to discern an exercise of power attaching to ownership from powers attaching to a 'legitimate right' such as employment? As Rachel Harris and Katharine Gelber point out, typical signs of property ownership may also arise in legitimate relationships, such as control over movement or indebtedness.[122] Distinguishing legitimate from illegitimate constraints becomes even more challenging for the analysis of Hayne J, which focuses on the complainant's context. His Honour acknowledges:

> An absence of choice on the part of the complainant may be seen to result from the combined effect of multiple factors. Some of these, such as the complainant's immigration status or the conduct of third parties, may be present independently of the conduct of the accused.[123]

119 Revised Explanatory Memorandum, Criminal Code Amendment (Slavery and Sexual Servitude) Bill 1999 (Cth), [20].

120 *Tang* (2008) 237 CLR 1, [32].

121 *The Queen v. Tang* [2008] HCATrans 180.

122 Rachel Harris and Katharine Gelber, 'Defining "De Facto" Slavery in Australia: Ownership, Consent and the Defence of Freedom' (2011) 11(3) *International Criminal Law Review* 561.

123 *Tang* (2008) 237 CLR 1, [158].

In another slavery case involving extreme sexual degradation, this time in Sydney, *McIvor and Tanuchit v. The Queen*, the jury's attention was drawn to nine aspects of the victims' circumstances, which may be relevant to determining whether the defendant's course of conduct amounts to slavery. These included that the victims: (i) lived and worked in locked premises operated by the appellants after they arrived in Australia; (ii) did not have keys to the premises and were not permitted by the appellants to leave the premises unaccompanied; (iii) did not speak English; (iv) did not know anyone outside the brothel; (v) were housed, cooked for and fed by the appellants; (vi) were constantly put to work by the appellants; (vii) were controlled by the appellants in all aspects of their lives including where they went, what they ate, where they slept and with whom they associated; (viii) had a fear of immigration authorities fostered in their minds by the appellants; and (ix) were instructed by the appellants to hide in the event that authorities attended the brothel premises. The New South Wales Court of Appeal acknowledged that none of these, with the possible exception of (vii), could amount to slavery on its own,[124] and even though some of these circumstances may not have been produced by the defendants' conduct, the court confirmed the utility of focusing on evidence of the victims' circumstances, or inferences drawn from that evidence.

It is noteworthy that, despite the sensitivity of this jurisprudence to a range of conduct that can amount to slavery, very few prosecutions involving trafficking and slavery outside of the sex industry have been commenced, and fewer have resulted in conviction. The remainder of this section provides a brief account of this labour trafficking case law.

Prosecutions outside of the sex industry

The first labour trafficking prosecution in Australia, *R v. Rasalingam*, resulted in the defendant's acquittal of the trafficking charge.[125] Yogalingham Rasalingam, an Australian restaurant owner in the Blue Mountains west of Sydney, brought a 24-year-old Indian man (the son of Rasalingam's servant in India) to Australia on a 457 visa, fraudulently obtained for a more highly skilled position. The complainant testified that they had agreed, in India, that he would work all 365 days for the first year of his employment without payment. In return, Rasalingam would pay for his airfare and remit 10,000 rupees a month (A$283) to the worker's family. On arrival in Australia in June 2006, Rasalingam took the man's passport and plane ticket and forced him to sleep on the floor in an unheated lounge room in the middle of

124 *McIvor v. The Queen* (2009) 247 FLR 363. The Court of Appeal set aside the convictions and ordered a retrial on other grounds.

125 In *R v. Yogalingam Rasalingam* (Unreported, NSWDC, Puckeridge J, 2 November 2007). Details are drawn from transcript of proceedings, *R v. Yogalingam Rasalingam* (DCNSW, Puckeridge J, 9 October–2 November 2007) and James Madden, 'Chef was "Forced Labour"', *The Australian*, 10 October 2007, 5.

winter. He worked seven days a week, sometimes for more than 15 hours a day. In a related application for civil penalties, evidence was submitted that he came to Australia with no money, virtually no English language skills, and in a position of dependence on Rasalingam for food, money, accommodation and transportation.[126] No evidence was presented that the man ever received payment or that money was forwarded to his family. The young man was located after working for approximately one month. Rasalingam was charged with one trafficking offence of facilitating the entry of a person into Australia being reckless as to whether that person would be exploited (in a situation of forced labour).[127]

A key issue was whether the elements of forced labour were made out. The Crown case was that Rasalingam had implicitly threatened the complainant with deportation should he leave his employment. The complainant testified that Rasalingam had told him the story of another person who had left their employer and who had then been repatriated. The defence refuted that any threat was made, arguing that the complainant, holding a 457 visa, was simply concerned that he might have to return to India should he change employer sponsors, and this situation arises as a general aspect of immigration law.

A jury found Rasalingam not guilty of the trafficking offence, but guilty of one count of dishonestly influencing a commonwealth public official by photocopying the visa-holder's signature on the employment contract sent to the Immigration Department.[128] He was sentenced to four months' imprisonment, to be released forthwith upon entering a recognisance in the sum of A$5,000 to be of good behaviour for 12 months. The worker did, however, receive A$11,500 for underpayment of wages as a result of an action brought by the then Office of Workplace Services (the labour inspectorate that predated the FWO).[129] The Federal Magistrates Court found that Rasalingam failed to meet minimum standards of pay and entitlements – indeed, he admitted making no payment at all until the investigation commenced – and ordered a A$18,200 penalty given Rasalingam's lack of contrition and that, although not a slave, the complainant was at a considerable disadvantage in his dealings with Rasalingam.[130]

The second slavery prosecution outside of the sex industry, *R v. Kovacs*, took place after a Filipina was discovered in the horrific circumstances described at the opening of this chapter. For over five months, the 25-year-old woman was forced to work relentlessly in the Kovacs' takeaway shop and home in remote far north Queensland. During this time, she endured repeated sexual assaults, verbal abuse and constant surveillance. In 2007,

126 *Fryer v. Yoga Tandoori House Pty Limited* [2008] FMCA 288, [10] (*Yoga Tandoori*).
127 *Criminal Code* s 271.2(1B).
128 Ibid. s 135.1(7).
129 *Yoga Tandoori* [2008] FMCA 288.
130 Ibid. [10].

Zoltan and Melita Kovacs each were convicted of three counts of slavery and immigration fraud.[131] The sentencing judge noted that although not physically restrained, the complainant's ability to leave was constrained by family pressures, the removal of her passport, weak English language skills and her overall situation in Australia, finding that:

> She had no money. She had no-one in this country to turn to, who she knew, in any significant way. She had no vehicle, nor could she drive, if I understand the evidence correctly, and she was thus, in a very real sense, dependent upon the two of you.[132]

The Kovacs successfully appealed to the Queensland Court of Appeal, which set aside the slavery convictions in 2008.[133] That court ruled that a miscarriage of justice had occurred because inadmissible evidence had been erroneously admitted, and the judge had given inadequate directions when one witness gave evidence from behind a screen.[134]

Importantly, however, the Court of Appeal upheld the trial judge's direction to the jury that 'you do not have to be satisfied that 24 hours a day, seven days a week that [a] condition [of slavery] existed'.[135] The Court of Appeal also dismissed the appellants' argument that the complainant had 'a degree of personal freedom inconsistent with the existence of slavery' under the Code because she was not physically imprisoned, had access to a telephone, sent and received letters and understood funds were transmitted to her family.[136] These findings reflect the expansion of modern slavery espoused by the High Court, which also did not require the victims in *Tang* to be under utter 'lock and key' control. The Court of Appeal in *Kovacs* noted that a number of factors contributed to the complainant's lack of freedom:

> The complainant's family were in circumstances of dire poverty ... The complainant's mother was sick and the complainant did not want to let her down or trouble her. The complainant gave evidence to the effect that Mr Kovacs told her not to say anything to the police or they would all go to jail.
>
> ...

131 They were convicted of intentionally possessing a slave (s 270.3(1)(a)), intentionally exercising power over/using a slave (s 270.3(1)(a)) and arranging a contrived marriage for immigration purposes (*Migration Act* s 240(1)): *Kovacs* [2009] 2 Qd R 51, [3]–[4].

132 Transcript of proceedings *The Queen v. Zoltan John Kovacs and Melita Kovacs* (Supreme Court of Queensland, Criminal Jurisdiction, Justice Callinane, 6 December 2007), 3.

133 *Kovacs* [2009] 2 Qd R 51.

134 Ibid. [76]–[84].

135 Ibid. [33].

136 Ibid. [44] and [46].

> Other factors operating to the complainant's disadvantage were: her limited knowledge of the English language, at least in the first few months of her stay; her lack of Australian friends or associates; the unspecified amount of debt of which she had been informed and the remote location of the shop and house.[137]

This confirms that the indicia of slavery outlined in *Tang* can apply to enslavement in circumstances as diverse as retail or domestic servitude. Even where a victim has apparent physical ability to leave or report the situation, Australian courts have taken a holistic approach to the multitude of circumstances that work in combination to deprive the victim of choice. Upon retrial in 2010, Melita Kovacs was found guilty of using and possessing a slave and sentenced to four years' imprisonment with a non-parole period of 18 months; Zoltan pleaded guilty to the same charges and was sentenced to nine years' imprisonment with a non-parole period of three years and nine months.[138]

The third trafficking prosecution outside of the sex industry, and the last prior to the passage of the *Slavery Act*, was brought against restaurant owner Divye Trivedi.[139] This yielded the first conviction of labour trafficking (rather than slavery). Between August 2007 and December 2008, Trivedi forced an Indian 457 visa-holder to work in his Indian restaurant in Sydney. The worker laboured 12 hours a day, seven days a week with only one day off during this entire period, on Christmas Day, living and bathing in the restaurant storeroom. Since Trivedi held his passport, the worker believed he could not leave the restaurant until his travel costs to Australia had been paid. Although promised a remuneration package of A$45,616 in accordance with the requirements of the 457 visa, in fact less than A$7,000 was paid to the worker's wife in India over 16 months. Trivedi allegedly threatened that if the worker did not comply with his demands, Trivedi would confiscate his house and property in India and harm his family there. On 6 October 2011 Trivedi pleaded guilty to one count of human trafficking, having facilitated the victim's entry to Australia, being reckless as to whether the victim would be subject to labour exploitation.[140] On 8 May 2012 he received a minimal sentence of 250 hours of community service and a fine of A$1,000 by the New South Wales District Court. On 27 March 2015, the Federal Circuit Court awarded the worker A$186,000 in unpaid wages and entitlements.

These prosecutions provided the context for the introduction of the 2013 reforms that sought to significantly enlarge criminal law's capacity to

137 Ibid. [47]–[48].

138 Evan Schwarten, 'Qld: Couple Jailed for Slavery', *Australian Associated Press*, 18 February 2010; 'Kovacs Jailed for Slavery', *Cairns Post*, 19 February 2010.

139 Details are drawn from *Ram v. D&D Indian Fine Food Pty Ltd* [2015] FCCA 389; Jessica Minshall, 'Slavery in the Australian Suburbs', *SBS News*, 19 April 2015; *IDC Report 2011–12*, above n. 56, 22 and 91–2.

140 *Criminal Code* s 271.2(1B).

respond to labour exploitation. It is to these legislative amendments that the chapter now turns.

Forced labour, coercion and choice

The *Crimes Legislation Amendment (Slavery, Slavery-like Conditions and People Trafficking) Act 2013* (Cth) (*Slavery Act*), passed on 27 February 2013, was sweeping in scope, designed, in the government's words, to 'ensure the broadest range of exploitative behaviour is captured and criminalised'.[141]

Among many other innovations outside the scope of this study, these amendments expanded the offences of sexual servitude and deceptive recruitment for sexual services to encompass all forms of servitude and deceptive recruiting.[142] New offences of forced labour and harbouring a victim of trafficking criminalise the end-point of exploitation as itself a slavery-like or trafficking offence.[143] A substantially higher maximum penalty for debt bondage underscores the serious nature of that offence.[144] The definition of coercion in these offences focuses more squarely on the complainant's social context, their particular vulnerabilities and the fine variations in the dependencies between victim and offender.[145]

In these ways, these amendments criminalise an area of moderately severe labour exploitation that experts had complained was excluded from existing slavery and trafficking laws.[146] In *Tang*, Gleeson CJ cautioned that it was:

> unnecessary and unhelpful to seek to draw boundaries between slavery and cognate concepts such as servitude, peonage, forced labour or debt bondage [since those] who engage in the traffic of human beings are unlikely to be so obliging as to arrange their practices to conform to some convenient taxonomy.[147]

By articulating graduated offences across the spectrum of exploitation from slavery to debt bondage, the *Slavery Act* attempts to do just that. Under the

141 Brendan O'Connor, Minister for Home Affairs, Minister for Justice, Chris Bowen, Minister for Immigration and Citizenship and Kate Ellis, Minister for the Status of Women, 'Slavery-like Offences to Become Crimes' (media release, 23 November 2011).

142 *Criminal Code* ss 270.5 and 270.7.

143 Sections 270.6A and 271.7F. The Act also created offences in new areas such as forced marriage (s 270.7B) and organ trafficking (s 271.7B), clarified the slavery offence (s 270.3(1)), created new categories of aggravation for certain offences and marginally improved the availability of reparations to victims (*Crimes Act 1914* (Cth), s 21B(1)(d)).

144 Sections 271.8 and 271.9 increase the maximum penalty from 12 months imprisonment to four years, and from two to seven years imprisonment for aggravated offences.

145 Sections 270.1A, 271.1A, 271.2(1), 271.2(1A) and 271.5.(1).

146 See e.g. Jennifer Burn and Frances Simmons, 'Trafficking and Slavery in Australia: An Evaluation of Victim Support Strategies' (2006) 15 *Asian and Pacific Migration Journal* 553, 544.

147 *Tang* (2008) 237 CLR 1, [29].

original 2005 scheme, the offence of trafficking for forced labour only applied to an offender involved in a victim's *transportation*. This offence required the victim to be moved as well as exploited, and so excluded situations where a worker undertook a combination of independent and facilitated travel, or first encountered the person involved in their exploitation at their final destination. Furthermore, before 2013, outside of labour trafficking, offences criminalised extreme labour exploitation (slavery, involving the exercise of 'any or all of the powers attaching to the rights of ownership') or minor exploitation (debt bondage, a summary offence). Mid-range offences in between these polarities (the 'slavery-like' crimes of servitude and deceptive recruiting) were restricted to purely *sexual* services excluding non-sexual forms of labour. There were no stand-alone offences of forced labour or non-sexual servitude, and throughout the original scheme, elements emphasised the use or threats of physical force, excluding from coverage more subtle forms of coercion or deception.

The redrawn criminal offences go much further in conceiving a continuum of criminal exploitation, as the government has claimed. However, the remainder of this chapter contends that, for all their other strengths, this criminal framework leaves unchallenged the ways that immigration controls can seriously constrain migrant workers' labour market options. These structural forces can organise migrant workers into situations of forced labour without any specific effort by employers to exploit them. Naturally, criminal offences necessarily target only a tiny proportion of exploitative conduct. However, in its narrow scope, this legal intervention into trafficking has missed an opportunity to understand how intersections between employment and immigration regulations can magnify coercion for migrant workers. In making this argument this section focuses on the stand-alone forced labour offences introduced in 2013 and unpacks how they have reconceptualised the condition of coercion in ways that are both expansive and limiting in various respects.

There are two forced labour offences in s. 270.6A: engaging in conduct that causes a person to enter into or remain in forced labour; and conducting a business involving forced labour.[148] Forced labour is defined in s. 270.6 as:

> the condition of a person (the victim) who provides labour or services if, because of the use of coercion, threat or deception, a reasonable person in the position of the victim would not consider himself or herself to be free:
> (a) to cease providing the labour or services; or
> (b) to leave the place or area where the victim provides the labour or services.

148 These are subject to a maximum penalty of nine years imprisonment, or 12 years in circumstances of aggravation.

It is also plain that the coercion, threat or deception could occur against a third person (such as the victim's family). Section 270.6 continues:

> The victim may be in a condition of forced labour whether or not:
> (a) escape from the condition is practically possible for the victim; or
> (b) the victim has attempted to escape from the condition.[149]

This provision expresses a number of novel, and more expansive, understandings of the coercion or lack of freedom involved in the condition of forced labour.

First, the 'means' elements of achieving forced labour have been extended to cover 'coercion, threat or deception', which themselves are also broadly defined. Before 2013, the means of giving effect to forced labour (as part of a trafficking offence) was through the use of 'force or threats'.[150] The inclusion of 'coercion' is a significant expansion, especially since it is defined broadly to 'include coercion by force, duress, detention, psychological oppression, abuse of power or taking advantage of a person's vulnerability'.[151] This definition attends to power differentials, such that a broad range of relational dynamics might now be characterised as coercive. This new definition brings Australian law into greater conformity with the means-related elements of trafficking under the Trafficking Protocol, even though the concepts of 'psychological oppression' and 'taking advantage of a person's vulnerability' in the Protocol have been criticised as vague.[152]

The means elements of forced labour have likewise been extended through a broader definition of 'threat'. Before 2013, 'threat' was defined as 'a threat of force, or a threat to cause a person's removal from Australia, or a threat of any other detrimental action; unless there are reasonable grounds for that action'.[153] The amended definition is:

149 Section 270.6(3)

150 Former s 73.2 of the *Criminal Code* defined forced labour as 'the condition of a person who provides labour or services (other than sexual services) and who, because of the use of force or threats: (a) is not free to cease providing labour or services; or (b) is not free to leave the place or area where the person provides labour or services'.

151 Section 270.1A.

152 Recall that the Protocol defines trafficking in persons in art 3A as 'the recruitment, transportation, transfer, harbouring or receipt of persons, by means of the threat or use of force or other forms of *coercion*, of abduction, of fraud, of deception, of the *abuse of power* or of *a position of vulnerability* or of the giving or receiving of payments or benefits to achieve the consent of a person having control over another person, for the purposes of exploitation' (emphasis added). Some commentators have criticised this provision for stopping short of actually defining coercion: Commonwealth, *Parliamentary Debates*, Senate Legal and Constitutional Affairs Legislation Committee, 29 August 2012, 2 (John Dowd, President of the International Commission of Jurists Australia).

153 *Criminal Code* former s 271.1.

> a threat of coercion, a threat to cause a person's deportation or removal from Australia, or a threat of any other detrimental action, unless there are reasonable grounds for the threat of that action in connection with the provision of labour or services by a person.[154]

Thus, threats encompass indirect, non-physical means to obtain a victim's compliance. The definition of deception in s. 271.1 remains unchanged as 'mislead as to fact (including the intention of any person) or as to law, by words or other conduct'.

The second major innovation relates to the conception of deprivation of freedom in the forced labour offence. Previously, forced labour (as an element of trafficking rather than a stand-alone offence) was defined to occur where a person '*is not free to* [cease providing services or leave premises] because of the use of force or threats' (emphasis added). Now, the condition of forced labour is made out where, as a result of coercion, threats or deception, '*a reasonable person in the position of the victim would not consider himself or herself to be free*'.

This changes the calculus considerably. Where the original phrasing assumed that there was an objective reality to the person's freedom, which needed to be assessed, the question now raised is whether a reasonable person would consider themselves to be free to withdraw their labour or services, or to leave the workplace. The amendment retains an element of objectivity (that of a reasonable person – the victim's actual perception is not enough). However, crucially, the condition of forced labour now depends on the reasonable person's self-assessment of their freedom and the practical availability of escape does not preclude a finding of forced labour.[155] This re-framing acknowledges that deprivation of freedom does not exist as a prior category but is a state that can be embodied, and in determining that state, the reasonable person must be placed in the victim's actual position (although, as I suggest below, it remains to be clarified by courts precisely what circumstances their 'position' entails).

154 Ibid. s 270.1A. The Explanatory Memorandum expounds that a 'legitimate threat' is excluded, 'for example a threat of an employer to terminate employment due to sustained under-performance would not amount to a threat for the purposes of Division 270': Explanatory Memorandum, Crimes Legislation Amendment (Slavery, Slavery-Like Conditions and People Trafficking) Bill 2012 (Cth), 12.

155 Section 270.6(3). This new formulation is arguably in greater conformity with the ILO definition of forced labour as 'all work or service which is exacted from any person under the menace of any penalty and for which the said person has not offered himself voluntarily' (Forced Labour Convention art 2(1)). 'Menace of penalty' is understood to include psychological pressure and threats to denounce the victim to immigration authorities. However, the legislation's reasonable person approach may be narrower than the ILO's since 'lack of voluntariness' suggests a subjective approach to coercion. See further ILO, *Cost of Coercion*, above n. 88, 5–6; ILO, *Global Alliance*, above n. 88, 5–6.

This construction of freedom in the forced labour offence echoes the Queensland Court of Appeal's approach to the slavery offences in *Kovacs*. That court rejected the Kovacs' contention that their verdicts were unreasonable because the victim in this case had a 'degree of personal freedom inconsistent with the existence of slavery as defined in the Code'.[156] The defendants were pointing to the facts that the complainant was not physically restrained in the store or house where she worked, was not locked in her room, and could send and receive letters and use the telephone. The court concluded nonetheless that her physical freedom was ultimately 'illusory or non-existent' because of the atmosphere of psychological coercion and geographical isolation.

A third area of nuance in the understanding of coercion in these offences is a provision inserted by the 2013 amendments that clarifies that a victim's consent is not a defence to any slavery, slavery-like or trafficking offence, including forced labour.[157] This clarification sought to overrule some judges who have directed juries that consent may be relevant to an assessment of whether a person was in fact reduced to a state of slavery.[158] The significance of consent to the offence of forced labour is particularly fraught under international law. The Trafficking Protocol makes it clear that a victim's consent is irrelevant to the offence of labour trafficking.[159] The ILO Forced Labour Convention is more equivocal, since it defines forced labour as work 'for which the said person has not offered himself voluntarily'.[160] However, the UNODC has recommended that forced labour should be understood to occur, even when someone initially accepts an offer of work voluntarily, if that voluntariness is manipulated (for instance, by the retention of identity documents) or not based on informed consent, or where coercive mechanisms arise later to keep that worker in an exploitative situation or prevent them from leaving a job.[161] The *Slavery Act* puts these issues beyond doubt.

A fourth significant innovation of these provisions is explicitly to set out relevant matters a judge or jury may consider in determining whether a victim has been coerced, threatened or deceived into a trafficking or slavery-like situation, including of course forced labour, or has been caused to enter into debt bondage.[162] This non-exhaustive list includes: the economic

156 *Kovacs* [2009] 2 Qd R 51, [44]–[46].

157 *Criminal Code* ss 271.11B and 270.11.

158 Explanatory Memorandum, Crimes Legislation Amendment (Slavery, Slavery-Like Conditions and People Trafficking) Bill 2012 (Cth), 31. See e.g. *Ho v. The Queen*; *Leech v. The Queen* [2011] VSCA 344, [80], [83].

159 Trafficking Protocol art 3(b). Although many note that the compromise position on consent reached by the Protocol was ambiguous: Doezema, 'Who Gets to Choose?', above n. 7, 21.

160 Forced Labour Convention art 2(1).

161 UNODC, *Model Law Against Trafficking in Persons* (2009), 15.

162 *Criminal Code* ss 270.10 and 271.11A(2). Previously these were relevant only to the (now repealed) offence of deceptive recruiting for sexual services.

relationship between victim and offender, the terms of any written or oral agreement between them, the lawfulness of the victim's immigration status, their facility with English and their social and physical dependence on the offender. These elements constitute new and explicit recognition of myriad forms of constraint used by employers to compel migrant workers to submit to exploitation. For instance, accommodation arrangements made by an employer (perhaps as a 'package deal') can be used not just to deduct disproportionate sums from an employee's wages, but function also as a means of control, restricting a person's mobility, since to leave the job means losing their place to live. Confiscated identity documents can constrain an employee's physical mobility as well as act as a threat of disclosure of the unauthorised immigration profile. Perhaps most significantly, employers can use debt bondage not only to withhold payments but also as a highly personal and coercive means of confining a person in an employment relationship marked by pronounced dependency and asymmetry.[163]

In these four ways, at the very least, the offence of forced labour and the inclusion of a broadly defined element of coercion in the trafficking, servitude and deceptive recruiting offences go a long way to recognising the complex ways that employers can exert control over migrant workers. This is fitting since Gallagher has observed that 'coercion is central to the idea of trafficking'.[164] Indeed, Australia's trafficking framework, as amended in 2013, goes much further than earlier laws in recognising that precarious immigration status shapes workers' vulnerability to abuse. An employer's 'threat to cause a person's deportation or removal from Australia' may cause forced labour if it would lead 'a reasonable person in the position of the victim' to consider themselves not free to leave that employment.[165] This adopts the ILO's view that threats of deportation can constitute non-economic compulsion to exact forced labour from migrants, especially unauthorised workers.[166]

However, despite these advances, these offences continue to leave unaddressed the fact that the coercion inherent in unauthorised status can amplify the power differentials in employment relationships to such a degree that specific efforts by the employer to constrain liberty are unnecessary. An unauthorised worker does not need even an implied threat to understand that their employer can anonymously report their presence and bring about their removal. The complainant in *Kovacs*, for example, was simply warned by Kovacs not to 'say anything to the police or they would all go to jail'. The Queensland Court of Appeal observes that '[h]aving regard to the manner

163 Julia O'Connell Davidson, 'Troubling Freedom: Migration, Debt and Modern Slavery' (2013) 1(2) *Migration Studies* 176.

164 Anne Gallagher, *The International Law of Human Trafficking* (Cambridge University Press, 2010), 31.

165 *Criminal Code* s 270.1A.

166 ILO, *A Global Alliance*, above n. 88, 6.

in which she had gained entry to Australia, Mr Kovacs' warning would not have appeared exaggerated'.[167] The court here appreciates how compelling this indirect but highly effective threat would have seemed to the isolated victim, who had knowingly entered into a sham marriage to obtain a Partner visa. But it remains unclear whether Kovacs' statement itself would amount to a threat causing forced labour or instead whether there were 'reasonable grounds for the threat of that action in connection with the provision of labour or services by a person'. Similarly, in the context of the 457 visa scheme built upon employer sponsorship, it remains unclear whether a jury would construe as an implied threat of removal Rasalingam's alleged statement to his young employee that a former worker who had complained about working conditions had later been repatriated.[168]

Naturally, criminal laws target only a small proportion of exploitative conduct. Distinguishing trafficking from legitimate or lawful employment conditions holds considerable challenges, as evidenced by the absence of a definition of 'exploitation' in the Trafficking Protocol itself. Indeed, the question as to the point when tolerable working conditions become exploitative is almost universally contentious.

In drawing a necessary distinction between criminal and non-criminal exploitation, these trafficking offences settle upon the line between coercion and freedom. An unauthorised worker is only subject to coercion if her employer makes an explicit threat of constraint against her. She is not subject to coercion by virtue of her precarious immigration status alone. But, if trafficking offences are designed to protect the most abject workers, those who cannot extricate themselves from serious exploitation, it is a sad irony that labour trafficking laws are not extended to those unauthorised workers who, even in the absence of active physical or psychological coercion by an employer, are legally and literally unable to help themselves gain relief from exploitative working conditions, for fear of employer blackmail, detention or removal if they complain. This background context of coercive immigration regulation must be erased by counter-trafficking laws because the worker's 'deportability' goes directly to the validity of states' authority to control mobility. Therefore, while the trafficking, forced labour and slavery offences express liberal aspirations of freedom, they in fact allow for the imposition of myriad restrictions on people deemed otherwise supposedly to be free. Similar issues arise in relation to constraints on temporary workers' labour market mobility. Robert Miles and Bridget Anderson have argued that visa

167 *Kovacs* [2009] 2 Qd 51, 47–8.

168 Transcript of proceedings, *R v. Yogalingam Rasalingam*, above n. 125. Indeed, a 2013 study of nurses on 457 visas found that some migrants' perceptions about their lack of rights or the institutional dependency of their immigration status were based on mistaken beliefs that were not borne out by their objective legal position: Martina Boese *et al.*, 'Temporary Migrant Nurses in Australia: Sites and Sources of Precariousness' (2013) 24(3) *The Economic and Labour Relations Review* 316, 333.

conditions curbing migrants' entitlement to exercise their full labour power produce a form of unfree labour.[169] At the very least, such restrictions can make it profoundly difficult for workers to withdraw their labour. But these constraints do not appear in the legal calculus of coercion into forced labour.

Thus, the hard distinction between coercion and freedom in these criminal trafficking and slavery laws is at least partly fictional: the freedom of non-trafficked workers is oversold, and likewise the coercion of trafficked people may also be exaggerated. Indeed, although they connote force and captivity, trafficking, slavery and forced labour still can involve the enslaved or trafficked person being offered a choice between appalling alternatives.[170] Robert Steinfeld writes that, even in the context of historical slavery, slaves' labour was rarely elicited 'through overwhelming physical force' but instead 'by forcing slaves to choose between very unpleasant alternatives, such as death, torture and endless confinement on the one hand, or back-breaking work on the other'.[171] Unforced labour also involves a choice: starvation or difficult and dangerous work one would not otherwise agree to perform. Steinfeld continues, for 'both the slave and free wage worker, the parties may be said to have been coerced into performing the labour or to have freely chosen the lesser evil'.[172]

However, the crimes of trafficking and forced labour cannot withstand such a flattening of the distinctions between coercion and choice. To do so would involve seeing each of the workers depicted in this book – from the sex workers in *Tang*, to Guo Jiandong (whose death in a forest in remote southwest Queensland was described in Chapter 1), to the 18-year-old Masri (brought to Australia as a 'housemaid' as described in Chapter 6) – as suffering exploitation as a result of various constellations of constrained choices, emanating from limited options and financial obligations of various kinds. The difficulties are expressed in a comment from a law enforcement officer in Segrave, Milivojevic and Pickering's study of Australia's counter-trafficking strategies:

> There are a lot of women from South-East Asian countries here [in Australia] lawfully, I mean what they do, prostitution, is in a lot of states of Australia a lawful occupation and they're on a working holiday visa, [or a] student visa … so it's a lawful visa, lawful occupation and they're

169 Bridget Anderson, 'Where's the Harm in That? Immigration, Enforcement, Trafficking and the Protections of Migrants' Rights' (2012) 56(9) *American Behavioral Scientist* 1241, 1252; Robert Miles, *Capitalism and Unfree Labour: Anomaly or Necessity?* (Tavistock, 1987).

170 Julia O'Connell Davidson, 'New Slavery, Old Binaries: Human Trafficking and the Borders of "Freedom"' (2010) 10(2) *Global Networks* 244, 246.

171 Robert Steinfeld, *Coercion, Contract and Free Labour in the Nineteenth Century* (Cambridge University Press, 2001), 14.

172 Ibid. 15.

> happy to work in the industry ... Most of them only really become a victim when things go wrong for them ... there are very few people who ... go to Australia ... not knowing that they're going to be involved in the sex trade.[173]

However, unauthorised workers are routinely denied victim support and unscrupulous employers avoid criminal prosecution, because their dangerous work or deprivation of entitlements are characterised as flowing from voluntary decisions made by them within the structural constraints of the globalised economy and national immigration laws.[174] Indeed, the AIC has noted the 'difficulty of responding to situations in which both the employer and employees are essentially *complicit* in exploitative situations'.[175]

In her work on dependency, Fineman helpfully unpacks the assumptions that underpin the use of 'individual choice' as a justification for ignoring inequities and maintaining the status quo.[176] She writes that all choices are shaped by social conditions that 'funnel individual decision-making into prescribed channels, often operating along practical and symbolic lines to limit and close down options'.[177] However, by constructing behaviour as a 'choice' we assume consent to the underlying societal conditions that generated that choice.

The forced labour offences target the extreme commodification of migrant workers by offenders who exploit their structural advantage. Yet uncertainties as to their scope remain. The government unwisely rejected a Law Council of Australia recommendation that the test (a 'reasonable person in the position of the victim would not consider himself or herself to be free'[178]) be restated as 'a reasonable person of the same background and in the same circumstances'.[179] This leaves unresolved ambiguities about the characteristics of the reasonable worker. Does this assessment include the worker's personal background as well as their actual circumstances? What role must the perpetrator play in relation to these coercive circumstances? Does it include third party contractual pressures (via pre-existing debts to off-shore agents) or only the debts to the employer? Does it encompass

173 Marie Segrave, Sanja Milivojevic and Sharon Pickering, *Sex Trafficking: International Context and Response* (Willan Publishing, 2009), 51–2.

174 Jayashri Srikantiah, 'Perfect Victims and Real Survivors: The Iconic Victim in Domestic Human Trafficking Law' (2007) 87 *Boston University Law Review* 157, 188; Jennifer Chacón, 'Misery and Myopia: Understanding the Failures of US Efforts to Stop Human Trafficking' (2006) 74 *Fordham Law Review* 2977, 3021–4.

175 David, *Labour Trafficking*, above n. 1, xiii (emphasis added).

176 Martha A Fineman, 'Dependency and Social Debt' in David B. Grushky (ed.), *Poverty and Inequality* (Stanford University Press, 2005), 133, 141.

177 Ibid.

178 *Criminal Code* s 270.6(1).

179 Law Council of Australia, Submission No 21 to Senate Legal and Constitutional Affairs Committee, 'Inquiry into Crimes Legislation Amendment Slavery, Slavery-like Conditions and People Trafficking Bill 2012', 1 August 2012, 13.

broader social or structural constraints such as the lack of alternative income sources, welfare ineligibility or bleak labour conditions back home? It remains to be seen whether a criminal prosecution will be a productive forum for parsing the complex place of immigration law in exploitative labour.

This book has argued that responsibility for the legal and social forces determining the choices and outcomes for migrant workers cannot be located in the workers alone. Exploitative working conditions must be interrogated in a complex way that holds multiple perspectives around coercion and agency. It is salient to recognise, for example, that many workers may conceive of their migration as a period of suffering to be tolerated, because it offers a means of achieving particular goals. Scarce livelihood options mean that some workers engage in risky projects of labour migration with varying outcomes. This may involve approaching agents' fees in their home country as an 'investment' to facilitate access to a visa (legally or illegally) or a potential job and going into significant debt to pay them. Migrant workers, by running the risk of falling into a period of 'unfreedom', may be able to pay off their debt, send money home or save for themselves. Some people who are positively identified as trafficked do not perceive themselves as victims but as 'migrant workers who had some bad luck as a result of a bad decision'.[180]

Conclusion

This chapter considered Australia's moves to criminalise labour trafficking in a sophisticated way. Focusing on the forced labour offence in particular, it celebrates the ways this scheme builds on pre-existing jurisprudence to capture a range of criminal exploitation in various industrial settings. However, a criminal justice approach necessarily excludes certain forms of mistreatment, and leaves the highly coercive power of immigration status unexamined. The following chapter takes up in more detail this sharp disjuncture between criminal and non-criminal exploitation, arguing that, in addition to the nuanced spectrum of offences within the sphere of trafficking, more needs to be done to integrate counter-trafficking measures with broader labour protections.

180 Kemala Kempadoo, 'From Moral Panic to Global Justice: Changing Perspectives on Trafficking' in Kemala Kempadoo, Jyoti Sanghera and Bandana Pattanaik (eds), *Trafficking and Prostitution Reconsidered: New Perspectives on Migration, Sex Work and Human Rights* (Paradigm Publishers, 2005), vii, xxiv.

9 Getting our priorities straight

Connecting forced labour and labour

In early 2005, Kentwood Industries Pty Ltd, a building and construction business, employed a group of Chinese tradesmen on 457 visas.[1] They worked on the Chinese Garden of Remembrance in Kalgoorlie in regional Western Australia, a Chinese Temple at Springvale Cemetery in Melbourne and residential buildings in Perth. Recruited as tilers, carpenters and skilled builders, Kentwood's managing director and part-owner, Zhang Jian Yang, required the men to undertake a variety of skilled and unskilled work – as labourers, bricklayers, plasterers, renderers and welders. After 12 to 24 months of work, five of these men (Yuan Zhaolin, Zeng Zheng Shun, Hang Jian Qi, Shen Zongxin and Guo Jian Qi) sought back pay totalling A$242,000 plus A$65,000 in interest.

The men were recruited through Beijing Sunshine Aust-China Cultural Development Co Ltd, a recruitment agent in China, which Zhang also owned. Each worker agreed to pay Beijing Sunshine 15,000 RMB (more than A$2,300) for employment and visas, equivalent to four months' pay under their employment contract. Before leaving China, each worker signed an employment contract with Kentwood, with conditions below both applicable industrial standards and the minimum requirements of the 457 visa scheme. Whereas the legislative minimum salary payable to 457 visa workers at that time was A$39,100 per annum for a 38-hour week, the employment contracts promised annual salaries of 39,100 RMB for nine hours a day six days a week, roughly A$3 an hour. Although 457 visa workers are entitled to bring their dependents to Australia, one of the workers was promised that, only if he worked well, his wife and daughter might be brought to Australia for a visit as a bonus.

1 Details of this narrative taken from *Fair Work Ombudsman (FWO) v. Kentwood Industries Pty Ltd* [2010] FCA 98, [8] (*Kentwood*); *FWO v. Kentwood Industries Pty Ltd (No 2)* [2010] FCA 1156, [7], [79]–[95], [114], [118]–[119], [134]–[140], [165], [200]–[201] (*Kentwood No 2*); *FWO v. Kentwood Industries Pty Ltd (No 3)* [2011] FCA 579, [1], [25]–[27], [50]; Nicolas Perpitch, 'Builder Told to Pay "Exploited" Chinese Workers', *The Australian*, 1 June 2011; ABC Radio National, 'WA Company Accused of Exploiting Guest Worker', *ABC Transcripts*, 21 February 2007 (David Weber).

In Australia, one of these workers was not paid at all for ten months; three others worked three months until their first pay. The men lived in one house, up to three to each bedroom, at times sleeping on the floor. They worked up to eleven hours a day, six to seven days a week. They received A$600 monthly in their Chinese bank accounts. They were also paid A$20 cash for six hours of overtime work. Each worker was underpaid between A$28,000 and A$69,000, earning roughly one-fifth of their statutory minimum remuneration entitlements.

Zhang attempted to argue (unsuccessfully) that the real dispute was between the workers and the recruitment agent, Beijing Sunshine, rather than Kentwood. He told reporters that he had not underpaid the men but had deposited wages into an Australian bank account; Beijing Sunshine had then extracted A$14,000 in fees for the visa application, translation, airfares, food and living expenses in Australia. Zhang did indeed open Australian bank accounts for the workers, but had not given them key cards or the access code.

When one of the workers, Yuan, queried his entitlements, Zhang immediately terminated his employment. Soon after the Fair Work Ombudsman (FWO) first contacted Kentwood, Zhang asked three workers to sign statements that they had worked no more than 40 hours a week; they refused. The Department of Immigration and Citizenship (DIAC) found Kentwood to be in breach of its sponsorship undertakings, cancelled its existing sponsorships and barred it from using the 457 visa programme for five years. The workers found new sponsors and remained working in Australia until 2010. After protracted Federal Court proceedings, in 2011, four years after they left this work and five to six years after they began it, Kentwood was ordered to pay a fine of A$123,000; Zhang was fined a further A$24,600 and the workers were ordered to be paid a total of A$242,000 plus interest of A$65,000.[2]

While the previous chapter praised Australian trafficking offences for their sophisticated approach to criminalising a spectrum of labour exploitation in Australia, which may generate more successful prosecutions, this chapter fixes on what these criminal justice interventions have not yet accomplished. The support services and immigration concessions for suspected victims of trafficking are still primarily designed to achieve criminal justice outcomes; they do not systemically afford industrial justice through enforcement of employment entitlements. In any event, these social and immigration support structures are extended only to suspected victims of criminal offences, leaving an abrupt disjuncture between people subjected to

2 Kentwood was found to have failed to pay the guaranteed basic rate of pay, pay at the required frequency and pay leave entitlements, overtime, meal allowances and public holiday rates and to provide rostered days off (*Workplace Relations Act 1996* (Cth), ss 182, 189 and 235(2) and Notional Agreement Preserving the Western Australian Building Trades (Construction) Award 1987 cls 13, 15, 16, 17, 20, 22(7)(b)).

criminal exploitation and those working in abusive conditions below the criminal baselines.

In these ways, trafficking and slavery laws are premised on the disconnections between forced labour and labour, intimating that the trafficking framework is for migrants, while labour regulation is for locals. By detaching forced labour from labour, Australian trafficking interventions have missed an opportunity to understand how the employment–immigration nexus can magnify precariousness and exploitation. A 2011 government discussion paper on criminal justice responses to human trafficking has recommended 'a mixture of civil and criminal remedies' but this view has not been realised.[3] Thus, having refined a spectrum of criminal offences within the sphere of trafficking with the reforms introduced in 2013 and described in the previous chapter, further refinement is needed to integrate these measures with labour protections.

This chapter, therefore, calls for a reconsideration of the structural dimensions of policy responses to migrant labour exploitation in Australia. A truly emancipatory commitment to unforced labour would: (a) integrate trafficking and industrial or private remedies, and (b) cede immigration enforcement priorities to workplace justice. The excesses of migration law need to be moderated to afford migrants in precarious work access to a full range of legal remedies, regardless of immigration status or whether their circumstances make out a colourable criminal offence. The chapter reviews regulatory measures adopted in the European Union and USA in particular, which seek to 'quarantine' unauthorised workers' rights as workers from their status as potentially removable migrants. In Australia, it is proposed that a novel visa category should be adopted to regularise the status of migrant workers to facilitate pursuit of bona fide employment-related claims. In addition, institutional arrangements need to be developed to avoid immigration compliance operations undermining labour protections and serving the interests of nefarious employers.

How labour trafficking laws stop short of truly seeing exploitation as a spectrum

The forced labour and servitude offences, introduced in 2013, set out to better capture a 'continuum' of exploitation across slavery, trafficking and slavery-like conditions.[4] Early signs held promise of a new bridge between trafficking and labour policies. In parliamentary debate, the Attorney-General, Nicola Roxon, linked the new labour trafficking offences with industrial safeguards, stating '[i]t was Labor who repealed Tony Abbott's

3 Commonwealth Attorney-General's Department, *The Criminal Justice Response to Slavery and People Trafficking; Reparation; and Vulnerable Witness Protections* (Discussion Paper 2011), para 76.

4 Explanatory Memorandum, Crimes Legislation Amendment (Slavery, Slavery-Like Conditions and People Trafficking) Bill 2012 (Cth), 1.

unfair workplace laws. And it is Labor who is now introducing a new offence of forced labour'.[5] The Explanatory Memorandum describes the Bill's objective as safeguarding 'the right to work and rights in work: by criminalising forced labour and expanding deceptive recruiting to apply to all forms of work, therefore *promoting legal and safe working conditions*'.[6] Indeed, the opposition coalition criticised the 'ambiguously wide definition of "servitude"' in the *Crimes Legislation Amendment (Slavery, Slavery-Like Conditions and People Trafficking) Act 2013* (Cth) (*Slavery Act*) as not far enough away from labour policies, arguing that it 'could be misused in an industrial relations context'.[7]

In reality, however, these offences continue the bifurcation between serious criminal coercion or deception and lesser forms of exploitation, excluding from their scope employment relationships below the criminal baselines. The Attorney-General clarified that:

> [t]he forced labour offence does not apply in circumstances that arise from standard relationships between employees and employers, including industrial disputes [but instead] targets abhorrent and serious exploitative practices.[8]

The expanded offences were not designed primarily to achieve safe and just working conditions. Supporters of the Bill seemed motivated largely to eradicate trafficking rather than less serious forms of migrant labour exploitation. For instance, the Australian Institute of Criminology (AIC), a body chiefly focused on criminal conduct, has expressed the view that labour law violations against migrant workers should be attended to principally because these are 'potential breeding grounds for more serious forms of exploitation' rather than concerns in themselves.[9] Similarly, Frances Simmons, who has strongly advocated for industrial remedies for trafficked people, does so on the basis that, '[f]rom a [trafficking] prevention perspective, we need to understand where exploitation starts. It begins with bad working conditions

5 Commonwealth, *Parliamentary Debates*, House of Representatives, 30 May 2012, 6227 (Nicola Roxon, Attorney-General, Second Reading Speech on Crimes Legislation Amendment (Slavery, Slavery-like Conditions and People Trafficking) Bill 2012). Similarly, Senator Faulkner applauded the Bill, for reinforcing 'the key values of fairness, equity under the law and a fair day's pay for a fair day's work': Commonwealth, *Parliamentary Debates*, Senate, 27 February 2013, 1 (John Faulkner, ALP, Second Reading Speech on Crimes Legislation Amendment (Slavery, Slavery-like Conditions and People Trafficking) Bill 2012).

6 Explanatory Memorandum, above n. 4, 3 (emphasis added).

7 Commonwealth, *Parliamentary Debates*, Senate, 27 February 2013, 10 (Helen Kroger, Liberal, Second Reading Speech on Crimes Legislation Amendment (Slavery, Slavery-like Conditions and People Trafficking) Bill 2012).

8 Commonwealth, *Parliamentary Debates*, House of Representatives, 21 August 2012, 9491 (Nicola Roxon).

9 Fiona David, *Labour Trafficking* (Research and Public Policy Series No 108, Australian Institute of Criminology, 2010), xii and 45.

and discriminatory labour exploitation'.[10] These campaigns seek important gains for trafficked people. However, on a continuum, they separate and prioritise trafficking over generally degrading working conditions.

Disconnecting forced labour from labour occurs in international trafficking frameworks. It is discernible in the institutionalised separation between the UN Office for Drugs and Crime (UNODC) and the International Labour Organization (ILO). The criminal tests for trafficking and slavery at international law are set intentionally high: the prohibition on slavery is a peremptory norm of international law; trafficking is a crime against humanity.[11] 'Mere' labour exploitation, conversely, is considered a lesser harm – merely a failure to meet basic human rights standards for wages, working and living conditions.

The previous chapter suggested that one reason for distinguishing forced migrant labour from unforced (but precarious) migrant labour is that questions of freedom and coercion become acutely challenging when related to temporary and unauthorised migration. Lacking the right to enter or move freely in a foreign state, non-citizens' most fundamental right is to freely *leave* that state at any time.[12] This is what distinguishes temporary labour migration from indentured servitude. It is relatively uncontentious for Western states to protect foreign workers' fundamental right to not be enslaved, or be prevented from departing. Safeguarding migrant workers' ability to freely engage in labour in conditions comparable to nationals is, however, far more controversial and is perceived to come closer to compromising states' sovereignty.

But, in fact, the distinction between indentured and exploitative labour is tenuous, resting on narrow formulations of coercion that have been challenged in the preceding chapters. Theorists of forced labour such as Ben Rogaly and Siobhán McGrath, argue that within any labour relationship (even one of forced labour) there may be 'elements of freedom as well as unfreedom, degrees of manoeuvrability, negotiation and contestation', and that a range of constraints of varying intensity may operate on physical movement, freedom to change employers, or workers' ability to contest their working conditions.[13] This means that we cannot simply separate free labour

10 Frances Simmons, 'Pathways to Justice: Compensation for Trafficked People' (Paper presented at Anti-Slavery Project Seminar, The Criminal Justice Response to Trafficking and Reparations, UTS Law Faculty, 18 February 2011), 14.

11 Commission on Human Rights, Sub-Commission on the Promotion and Protection of Human Rights, *Contemporary Forms of Slavery, Working Paper* UN Doc E/CN.4/Sub.2/2000/3 (26 May 2000) prepared by David Weissbrodt and Anti-Slavery International.

12 Universal Declaration of Human Rights, GA Res 217A (III), UN GAOR, 3rd sess, 183rd plen mtg, UN Doc A/810 (10 December 1948) art 13(2) provides that '[e]veryone has the right to leave any country, including his own, and to return to his country'.

13 Ben Rogaly, 'Migrant Workers in the ILO's Global Alliance Against Forced Labour Report: A Critical Appraisal' (2008) 29(7) *Third World Quarterly* 1431, 1444; Siobhán McGrath, 'Many Chains to Break: The Multi-Dimensional Concept of Slave Labour in Brazil' (2012) 45 *Antipode* 1005, 1006.

from coercion as the legislation tries to do. To do so overlooks why trafficked and exploited workers are vulnerable in the first place. Instead, an approach connecting trafficking, forced labour and labour better recognises that migrant exploitation is generated from a constellation of transnational immigration, economic factors, globalisation and human intervention.

The need for greater participatory inclusion to address labour and forced labour abuses

The previous chapter hailed Australia's counter-trafficking laws for embracing suspected victims of trafficking into the broader community. Securing criminal justice, immigration relief and social support for non-residents has been hard fought and sustained the lives of many. Yet unfortunately, these steps still fall short of a stronger commitment to participatory inclusion in two ways. First, there is no systemic means for trafficked or non-trafficked migrant workers to achieve industrial justice through enforcement of employment entitlements. Second, support structures are available only to a narrowly circumscribed class of recipients. Both of these weaknesses stem from anchoring counter-trafficking efforts in a criminal justice rather than industrial framework.

It is trite to observe that the criminal justice system can divest victims of agency, both during the legal proceedings and subsequent outcomes.[14] While a victim may be involved in the way the trial unfolds,[15] and their circumstances taken into account for sentencing,[16] their role is nevertheless principally a passive one as a witness for the prosecution. Advances have been made to ameliorate the marginalisation of victims of trafficking crimes in Australia: a legislative amendment passed in 2013 provides for Victim Impact Statements to be introduced in sentencing for federal crimes.[17] This formalises the use of written or oral statements about the crime's impact on the victim, issued after conviction and before sentencing.

Still, an emphasis on the exploiters rather than the exploited is driven by the Trafficking Protocol itself, which, as James Hathaway observes, carries 'no obligation [on States parties] to do anything about the condition of being

14 Lynne N. Henderson, 'The Wrongs of Victim's Rights' (1985) 37(4) *Stanford Law Review* 937, 951.

15 Commonwealth Director of Public Prosecutions, *Victims of Crime Policy* (2009).

16 Commonwealth general sentencing principles provide that the court must take into account, where relevant and known to the court, the personal circumstances of any victim of the offence, as well as any injury, loss or damage resulting from the offence: *Crimes Act 1914* (Cth), s 16A(2) (*Crimes Act*).

17 *Crimes Legislation Amendment (Law Enforcement Integrity, Vulnerable Witness Protection and Other Measures) Act 2013* (Cth), sch 2 pt 2, inserting *Crimes Act* s 16AAA. Prior to this law, victim impact statements were nevertheless used in trafficking cases, such as *R v. McIvor & Tanuchit* [2010] NSWDC 310, [32]. In 2013, the Standing Council on Law and Justice (comprising representatives of commonwealth, state and territory governments) created a *National Framework for Rights and Services for Victims of Crime 2013–16*, committing to improve the welfare of victims of crime.

exploited, much less to provide a remedy to exploited persons'.[18] In Australia, the prosecution against Wei Tang (discussed in Chapter 8) illustrates how the welfare of trafficked people can be profoundly undermined in the name of criminal justice. The five women enslaved by Tang were initially granted Criminal Justice Stay visas (CJSVs) rather than permanent Witness Protection visas, leaving them susceptible to removal once proceedings had concluded in 2008. Their lawyer, David Manne, explained:

> [I]t left them in a twilight world, where they felt incredibly powerless, they felt on a limb and they felt in a sense as though this situation had left them in a sense of disempowerment and exploitation, and as if they were sort of in witness bondage, not debt bondage.[19]

The irony is striking. Hayne J in *R v. Tang* framed slavery in terms of degrees of deprivation of choice.[20] Yet counter-trafficking policies did not meaningfully enlarge the trafficked women's concrete capacity to seek justice or improve the material conditions of their lives short of leaving Australia.

The experience of these women pre-dated (and likely catalysed) the more generous changes to the trafficking visa scheme in 2009. They were granted permanent residence (although not until 2009),[21] and it is hoped that their experience no longer reflects the treatment of trafficked people under the scheme. Nevertheless, eligibility for any trafficking visa beyond an initial reflection period continues to depend on cooperation with police investigations. Parliamentary inquiries have urged the government to consider providing visas and support irrespective of victims' participation in the criminal justice system,[22] but the government has repeatedly rejected this proposal for fear of undermining prosecutorial success.[23] Yet, as Rachel Harris and Katharine Gelber conclude, it is 'unconscionable to exploit trafficked women's lack of freedom in the name of defending it'.[24]

18 James Hathaway, 'The Human Rights Quagmire of "Human Trafficking"' (2008) 49 *Virginia Journal of International Law* 1, 10.

19 Damien Carrick, interview with David Manne (ABC Radio National Law Report, 2 September 2008).

20 *R v. Tang* (2008) 235 CLR 1, [150].

21 Anti-Human Trafficking Inter-Departmental Committee, *Trafficking in Persons: The Australian Government Response 1 May 2009–30 June 2010* (2010), 9.

22 Senate Legal and Constitutional Affairs Committee, 'Inquiry into Crimes Legislation Amendment (Slavery, Slavery-like Conditions and People Trafficking) Bill 2012', September 2012, vii and 36; Joint Standing Committee on Foreign Affairs, Defence and Trade (Human Rights Sub-Committee), *Trading Lives: Modern Day Human Trafficking* (June 2013), rec 5 (*Trading Lives Report*).

23 Australian Government response to the Joint Standing Committee on Foreign Affairs, Defence and Trade Committee report: *Trading Lives: Modem Day Human Trafficking* (July 2014), 8 (Australian Government Response).

24 Rachel Harris and Katharine Gelber, 'Defining "De Facto" Slavery in Australia: Ownership, Consent and the Defence of Freedom' (2011) 11(3) *International Criminal Law Review* 561, 577.

Trafficking prosecutions also do not ensure meaningful access to economic entitlements for those exploited for others' profit. Financial redress could discharge migrant workers' debts or offer a degree of economic independence. Courts have only a highly circumscribed power to order financial reparation upon conviction of a federal offence, described by Frances Simmons as 'better suited to tax offences than trafficking' because it does not include compensation for non-economic losses such as pain and suffering.[25] It has not been exercised in relation to any trafficking or slavery offence. Advocates have strongly fought for payments for trafficked people through publicly-funded victims of crime compensation schemes. In the absence of a federal scheme, claims must be made pursuant to state or territory schemes.[26] The shortcomings of these have been trenchantly criticised: threshold requirements include sexual violence, permanent physical injury or severe psychological disorder, which exclude many trafficked people, especially those harmed non-physically through labour exploitation.[27]

The FWO has played a powerful role in securing industrial remedies for trafficked people, frequently after referrals by victims' lawyers.[28] Unfortunately, referrals do not yet seem to be made by various counter-trafficking agencies as a matter of course, apparently because of uncertainty as to the coverage of sex workers by the *Fair Work Act 2009* (Cth) (*FW Act*). The disconnect between trafficking and industrial interventions is illuminated by the fact that WorkCover NSW, a state workers compensation inspectorate, has to date conducted no investigations related to trafficked workers whatsoever, even though robust workplace health and safety regulation is powerfully linked to efforts to combat labour exploitation.[29]

This is important because promoting compliance with labour standards also vindicates important national interests. Holding employers accountable for profiting illegally from migrant labour, like resident labour, involves a structural challenge to markets prone to under-regulated labour practices.

25 Frances Simmons, 'Pathways to Justice', above n. 10, 6. *Crimes Act* s 21B empowers courts to make an order for reparation. This was slightly amended by the *Slavery Act*. Whereas previously, reparation could be awarded only to any person in respect of losses which were a 'direct result' of the offence, they may now compensate for losses suffered or expense incurred 'by reason of' the offence.

26 *Victims of Crime (Financial Assistance) Act 1983* (ACT); *Victims Rights and Support Act 2013* (NSW); *Victims of Crime Assistance Act 1996* (Vic); *Victims of Crime Act 2001* (SA); *Criminal Injuries Compensation Act 2003* (WA); *Victims of Crime Assistance Act 2009* (Qld); *Victims of Crime Assistance Regulations 2010* (Tas); *Victims of Crime Assistance Act 2006* (NT).

27 For example, Frances Simmons, 'Making Possibilities Realities: Compensation for Trafficked People' (2012) 34 *Sydney Law Review* 511, 528ff. A parliamentary inquiry recommended the establishment of a federal compensation scheme: *Trading Lives Report*, above n. 22, rec 6.

28 For example, *Fryer v. Yoga Tandoori House Pty Limited* [2008] FMCA 288.

29 NSW Community Relations Commission, *Inquiry into the Exploitation of People Through Trafficking, in All Its Forms in NSW* (2013), 30.

Access to communal employment protections, therefore, as much as criminal laws and rehabilitation, addresses the underlying causes of exploitation and trafficking.

As significant is the deeper political nature of migrants' full participation in the Australian legal and industrial systems, described in Chapter 2 as 'the right to claim rights'.[30] As Hannah Arendt understood, without membership in the political community, individuals stand exposed to violence, unmediated and unprotected by rights.[31] In a similar vein, Martha Minow frames a legal claim as a call to be heard that 'initiates a form of communal dialogue'.[32] I argued in Chapter 2 that, even if this does not yet generate fully equal membership for migrants in the national community, invoking rights at least constitutes the migrant worker as a 'self' in relationship with the Australian community. The use of law courts is an act of claiming political authority within sovereign institutional structures. Linda Bosniak describes a non-citizen's assertion of rights as 'a claim to be counted or recognized *as part of the context*'.[33] Seeking redress from an exploitative employer asserts a self-determining legal subject within the workplace relationship. Indeed, Stephen Lee goes so far as to argue that unauthorised workers advancing workplace claims should be granted membership rights on the grounds that such claims-making demonstrates workers' solidarity and strong social and economic bonds with citizen co-workers.[34]

Thus, civil claims are key exercises of participatory inclusion. Supporting migrants to enforce workplace rights situates them as participants in the Australian labour market rather than merely objects of immigration enforcement or victims of crime. Legal cognisance of such entitlements honours migrant workers' contributions within the national labour market. Since law can create a forum for negotiating power among individuals and between individuals and the state, assertion of rights provides an antidote to oppression and deprivation of choice, since unscrupulous employers are held liable directly to the victim and not just the state. This is one of the reasons why Frances Simmons and Fiona David have argued that trafficking responses should encompass industrial relations remedies.[35]

However, immigration concessions and social support, including legal advice, are only routinely extended to those identified as a 'suspected victim

30 The term is coined by Engin F. Isin, 'Citizenship in Flux: The Figure of the Activist Citizen' (2009) 29 *Subjectivity* 367, 371.

31 Hannah Arendt, *The Origins of Totalitarianism* (Harcourt Brace, 1951), 296–7.

32 Martha Minow, 'Interpreting Rights: An Essay for Robert Cover' (1986-7) 96 *Yale Law Journal* 1860, 1875.

33 Linda Bosniak, 'Persons and Citizens in Constitutional Thought' (2010) 8(1) *International Journal of Constitutional Law* 9, 27 (emphasis in original).

34 Stephen Lee, 'Screening for Solidarity' (2013) 80 *University of Chicago Law Review* 224.

35 Frances Simmons and Fiona David, 'The Road to Effective Remedies: Pragmatic Reasons for Treating Cases of "Sex Trafficking" in the Australian Sex Industry as a Form of "Labour Trafficking"' (2012) 1 *Anti-Trafficking Review* 60.

of human trafficking' by the Australian Federal Police (AFP).[36] This heightens the importance of policies guiding AFP officers' application of the threshold tests (such as through indicators of trafficking).[37] Victims come to the attention of the AFP primarily through external sources, in particular through referrals from the DIBP,[38] which therefore also holds significant power as a gatekeeper for counter-trafficking support. While the initial 45-day Bridging Visa F (BVF) does not require any criminal investigation to be on foot, further permission to stay in the form of a CJSV is available only for migrants certified by a state or commonwealth Attorney-General as required for 'law enforcement purposes'.[39] It is expected that the greater range of criminal activity introduced in 2013 (with new offences and more broadly defined elements of pre-existing crimes) will lead to more BVF grants. But even after these amendments, the overwhelming majority of migrants suffering severe deprivation at the hands of their exploiters, such as the employees of Kentwood, will be unable to convince the AFP and DIBP that their employers may have committed serious criminal offences. There needs to be a continuum between trafficking and labour exploitation.

However, some scholars object to trafficked people being treated as workers insisting that labour law mischaracterises the oppression they have suffered. Reducing a gross violation of human rights to an issue of financial compensation may constitute an affront or, at best, inappropriately trivialise the injury.[40] Some oppose civil remedies on the grounds that they are partial, and unlikely to ever completely recoup the victim's physical, emotional and financial losses and cannot replace the criminal justice framework as a suitable response to trafficking, forced labour or slavery.

My argument is that employment law, and other remedies, should complement the criminal process or provide an alternative to it, if prosecution is not an option or not an option the victim wishes to pursue. The nature of claims and redress must depend on the mistreatment. In all cases, choice should be restored to individual migrant workers and/or trafficked people who have been deprived of choice. Unfortunately, at present, the options for anyone who experiences exploitation and is not an Australian resident are ultimately determined by an assessment of them as a specific kind of victim, as this chapter has demonstrated, and by their migration status, as explored in the section that follows.

36 *Migration Regulations 1994* (Cth), sch 1 cl 1306(3)(d)(i) and reg 2.20(14)(a)(ii)(E) (*Migration Regulations*).

37 AFP Governance, *AFP Practice Guide on Human Trafficking Investigations* (2012), para 9.

38 Anti-Human Trafficking Interdepartmental Committee, *Trafficking in Persons: The Australian Government Response 1 July 2013–30 June 2014* (Cth of Australia, 2014), 20 (*IDC Report 2013–14*).

39 *Migration Act* ss 141, 147.

40 Beth Stephens, 'Translating *Filartiga*: A Comparative and International Law Analysis of Domestic Remedies for International Human Rights Violations' (2002) 27 *Yale Journal of International Law* 1, 12. See also Harris and Gelber, above n 24, 561.

Immigration enforcement imperatives undermine employment protections

A range of employment protections are available to temporary and unauthorised migrant workers in Australia. Chapters 3, 4 and 6 carefully charted protections including minimum pay rates and unfair dismissal under the *FW Act* and awards, workers compensation and restitution. The FWO National Overseas Workers initiative proactively monitors the working conditions of migrant workers. In 2012–13 the FWO conducted 2,018 investigations involving temporary visa holders recovering more than A$1,427,395 in unpaid entitlements. The same year, it finalised eleven legal proceedings concerning foreign workers, with A$613,048 awarded in penalties and A$362,596 in unpaid wages.[41] Actions for misleading and deceptive conduct are also available against employers who illegally charge potential job seekers for applying for work.[42] Pamela Stewart has proposed that civil actions are available for trafficked or exploited workers in Australia through the torts of deceit, conspiracy by unlawful means and 'intentional psychiatric injury'.[43]

However, the full benefits of these protections elude temporary and unauthorised workers. While this occurs for a number of reasons, discussed in more detail in Chapter 3, this section focuses on how these measures are undermined by DIBP's enforcement powers. DIBP's removal powers operate independently of employment regulators. The FWO acknowledges that it 'cannot control or influence when visa-holders are required to return to their country of origin'.[44] This contrasts with the AFP's power, through Attorney-General certification, to stay removal for suspected victims of trafficking. Alarmingly, in early 2013, in their expert study on unpaid work commissioned by the FWO, Andrew Stewart and Rosemary Owens:

> found it very difficult to gain a more complete understanding of how DIAC approaches the problem of dealing with migrants who are working unpaid and/or perhaps contrary to their visa conditions ... Often, it appears, it is only through individuals 'dobbing' in other workers that these matters are drawn to its attention.[45]

41 Anti-Human Trafficking Interdepartmental Committee, *Trafficking in Persons: The Australian Government Response 1 July 2012–30 June 2013* (Cth of Australia, 2014) 36 (*IDC Report 2012–13*).

42 *Competition and Consumer Act 2010* (Cth), s 18. It is unlikely that this statutory prohibition applies to recruiters or agents offshore.

43 Pamela Stewart, 'Tortious Remedies for Deliberate Wrongdoing to Victims of Human Trafficking and Slavery in Australia' (2011) 34(3) *UNSW Law Journal* 898.

44 Janine Dennis, 'The Fair Work Ombudsman' (Paper presented at Immigration Lawyers Association of Australasia Conference, Sydney, 10 March 2012).

45 Andrew Stewart and Rosemary Owens, *The Nature, Prevalence and Regulation of Unpaid Work Experience, Internships and Trial Periods in Australia: Experience or Exploitation?* (University of Adelaide, Report for the Fair Work Ombudsman, January 2013), 177.

For instance, there is no evidence that DIBP triages for labour abuses among unauthorised workers in immigration detention centres, who almost certainly would have outstanding claims for entitlements. In fact, only a handful of formal referrals from DIBP to FWO have been recorded across all visa classes.[46]

From 2013, the FWO's role in monitoring the compliance of 457 visa employer-sponsors, although applauded by unions, may actually further undermine visa workers' rights. As discussed in Chapter 4, if Fair Work Inspectors cease to be seen as a labour inspectorate and are instead viewed as an extended arm of border security, 457 visa workers and other migrant workers may be far less confident to lodge complaints with the FWO which risks severely threatening its monitoring function. Stewart and Owens have cautioned against such an arrangement:

> DIAC should not generally expect that FWO would in return focus on examining or establishing the elements of a case which concern compliance with visa conditions regarding work and then pass on any such information to DIAC. The integrity of the system of labour inspection means that all workers must be able to be confident that the primary focus of the agency is compliance with labour legislation.[47]

They point out that the 2006 ILO *General Survey on Labour Inspection* suggests that cooperation with migration authorities should be 'cautious ... keeping in mind that the main objective of the labour inspection system is to protect the rights and interests of all workers and to improve their working conditions'.[48] I would go so far as to suggest that monitoring immigration compliance may in fact be incompatible with the FWO's capacity to effectively enforce workplace rights. This is arguably the lesson learnt from a similar administrative experiment in the USA, explored during the Clinton presidency when, between 1992 and 1998, the Immigration and Naturalization Service and the Department of Labor (DOL) agreed that the latter

46 There were 12 in 2012–13: email from Michele Schiller, Monitoring and Free Trade Agreements Policy Section, DIAC to author, 9 August 2013.

47 Stewart and Owens, *The Nature, Prevalence and Regulation*, above n. 45, 182.

48 ILO, *General Survey of the Reports Concerning the Labour Inspection Convention, 1947 (No 81), and the Protocol of 1995 to the Labour Inspection Convention, 1947, and the Labour Inspection Recommendation, 1947 (No 81), the Labour Inspection (Mining and Transport) Recommendation, 1947 (No 82), the Labour Inspection (Agriculture) Convention, 1969 (No 129), and the Labour Inspection (Agriculture) Recommendations, 1969 (No 133)* (Report IIIB (Part IB), International Labour Conference, 95th session, 2006), 54. The Labour Inspection Convention, 1947 (ILO No 81), International Labour Conference, 30th sess, opened for signature 11 July 1947 (entered into force 7 April 1950), which Australia ratified on 24 June 1975, provides in article 3(2) that any further duties which may be entrusted to labour inspectors shall not be such as to interfere with the effective discharge of their primary duties or to prejudice in any way the authority and impartiality which are necessary to inspectors in their relations with employers and workers.

would investigate employers' immigration violations when investigating wage and hour violations.[49] Engaging in direct enforcement of immigration was ultimately found to undermine workers' confidence in DOL and therefore its ability to enforce labour laws more generally.[50]

In Australia, however, this is not simply a matter of bureaucratic priorities: the Australian legal framework governing immigration and labour compliance appears to demand that the former be preeminent. DIBP is given statutory power under s. 18 of the *Migration Act* to require the production of information or documents from anyone who they have reason to believe is relevant to ascertaining an unlawful non-citizen's identity or whereabouts, including information held by other commonwealth agencies. The FWO is also empowered to refer evidence of unlawful activity onto other government agencies, such as the DIBP.[51] Although it is unclear whether this occurs routinely, DIBP declares on its website that it works with the FWO 'to locate and identify illegal workers'.[52] The legislative requirement to detain anyone who an officer knows or reasonably suspects to be an unlawful non-citizen extends beyond DIBP personnel to federal and state police officers.[53] It is therefore unsurprising that one study of onshore policing networks revealed widespread fear among immigrant communities in Australia that seeking help from police could result in detention and removal.[54]

On detecting an unauthorised migrant, DIBP is legally incapable of deprioritising removal in order to achieve other objectives such as industrial justice. The primary avenues for regularising the status of unlawful non-citizens are the Bridging Visa E (BVE), which may be granted only if the minister is satisfied that the applicant is making acceptable arrangements to depart Australia (or has made a valid application for a substantive visa),[55] and the BVF, which may be granted if a police officer has identified the applicant as a 'suspected victim of trafficking'.[56] Indeed, one of the few causes for which immigration enforcement outcomes are sacrificed is in the service of the counter-human trafficking agenda.[57] A protocol between DIBP

49 *Memorandum of Understanding Between the Immigration and Naturalization Service, Department of Justice, and the Employment Standards Administration, Department of Labor*, 11 June 1992.

50 Stephen Lee, 'Monitoring Immigration Enforcement' (2011) 53 *Arizona Law Review* 1089, 1113.

51 *FW Act* s 682(e); FWO, *Operations Manual* (2010), [9.5.3] and [11.4.2.2].

52 DIBP, 'Fact Sheet 87 – Initiatives to Combat Illegal Work in Australia', 27 August 2014.

53 *Migration Act* ss 5 and 189.

54 Leanne Weber, 'Policing a World in Motion' in Jude McCulloch and Sharon Pickering (eds), *Borders and Crime: Pre-Crime, Mobility and Serious Harm in an Age of Globalisation* (Palgrave Macmillan, 2012), ch 2.

55 *Migration Regulations* sch 2 cl 050.212.

56 Ibid. sch 1 cl 1306(3)(d)(i).

57 Senator Boyce hailed the amendments to the trafficking regime as 'Labor has implemented a strong whole-of-government strategy to target human trafficking': Commonwealth, *Parliamentary Debates*, Senate, 27 February 2013, 8 (Sue Boyce, Liberal National Party, Second Reading Speech on Crimes Legislation Amendment (Slavery, Slavery Like Conditions and People Trafficking) Bill 2012).

and the AFP requires DIBP to refer all indicators of human trafficking to the AFP and to consult the AFP prior to undertaking any compliance operation involving a premises or person with suspected links to trafficking.[58] Equally, an empirical study of the policing of unauthorised migrants by Leanne Weber found that police may be particularly likely to check immigration status in cases of labour exploitation because they perceive victims' immigration as relevant to trafficking protections.[59] While understandable, this is concerning because, having notified DIBP of the presence of an unauthorised migrant, no bridging visa may be granted if they are ineligible for trafficking protections and 'merely' wish to pursue redress for employment or other abuses. In fact, Weber reported that police complain that witnesses of non-trafficking offences who lack immigration authorisation can be summarily removed by DIBP without notice.[60]

Consequently, DIBP priorities dictate the terms of labour enforcement, as part of a 'whole-of-government' approach to maximising compliance by unauthorised migrants.[61] DIBP coordinates with a range of agencies to facilitate data-matching, joint operations and the receipt of notifications to locate unlawful non-citizens, for instance with the Australian Taxation Office, state and territory police, road and transport authorities and the social security agency, Centrelink. Privacy protections that would normally prevent large-scale cross-agency exchange of personal information are not applicable because of DIBP's powers to obtain information about unauthorised migrants under s. 18.[62] There is considerable public support for such arrangements: the Construction Forestry Mining and Energy Union has recommended extending them to cover lawful non-citizens with a high propensity to work in breach of visa conditions, such as overseas students.[63] Indeed, DIAC had a Memorandum of Understanding (MOU) to access information from the Australian Building and Construction Commission to assist immigration officials, among other things, to consider whether to cancel 457 visas in the construction industry.[64]

In contrast, this whole-of-government approach is not routinely taken to labour rights enforcement among temporary or unauthorised migrants.

58 Indeed, it seems that if an alleged victim appeared to have been trafficked, DIBP would refer the person to the police even if this was against their wishes: Evidence to Senate Legal and Constitutional Affairs Legislation Committee, Parliament of Australia, Canberra, 29 August 2012, 36 (Ramzi Jabbour, AFP).

59 Leanne Weber, *Policing Non-Citizens* (Routledge, 2013), 71.

60 Ibid. 80.

61 Department of Immigration, Multicultural and Indigenous Affairs, *Review of Illegal Workers in Australia* (1999), 16.

62 Australian National Audit Office (ANAO), *Onshore Compliance: Visa Overstayers and Non-Citizens Working Illegally* (2004–05 Audit Report No 2, 2004), 88.

63 Construction Forestry Mining and Energy Union, 'Submission Re Implementation of Howells Review of Employer Sanctions Legislation 2011' (1 September 2011), 4.

64 *Memorandum of Understanding between DIAC and Australian Building and Construction Commission*, 6 April 2011, cl 6.3.

One rare instance where the costs of immigration compliance to labour priorities were acknowledged occurred during a multi-agency national project called 'Fruitlink' in 2001. Various state-based occupational health and safety agencies sought to develop safety training for transient, migrant and unauthorised horticultural workers. The federal government offered to fund the scheme but insisted that it be used to identify tourists, working holiday makers and visa-overstayers working illegally. The state agencies refused the funding, concerned that it would undermine industry and worker confidence in the scheme.[65] As we will see, in the section that follows, such efforts to prevent immigration compliance from providing unscrupulous employers with a disposable workforce, so exceptional in Australia, are more common in other jurisdictions.

An integrated approach to industrial citizenship beyond criminal justice

Clearer acknowledgement is needed in Australia of the labour consequences of immigration compliance operations. If migrant labour exploitation is genuinely conceived as a spectrum, it makes sense to extend (at least some of) the immigration concessions for trafficked people to other migrants who have endured seriously unlawful treatment at work. The rest of this chapter proposes a new concessionary visa framework to allow temporary or unlawful migrants who have experienced unlawful treatment at work to remain legally in Australia long enough to take action against their employers. I also suggest further measures to avoid DIBP's compliance operations serving the interests of nefarious employers. These proposals build in part upon Australia's trafficking immigration framework as an analogy. They also draw inspiration from regulatory models in the EU and USA, which promote industrial justice even for those with no right to be present to make the legal claim. I first explore efforts to 'quarantine' workers' immigration status from the enforcement of employment entitlements in these jurisdictions before outlining the reform proposals for the Australian context.

Compliance Priorities in the EU and USA

While the absolute primacy accorded to immigration compliance over industrial protections may seem pre-ordained in the Australian context, a comparative perspective indicates that it need not be so. The 2009 EU Employer Sanctions Directive (explored in Chapter 7) requires employers who are penalised under that scheme to pay any outstanding remuneration

65 Robert Guthrie and Michael Quinlan, 'The Occupational Safety and Health Rights and Workers' Compensation Entitlements of Illegal Immigrants: An Emerging Challenge' (2005) 3(2) *Policy and Practice in Health and Safety* 69, 75.

to non-EU unauthorised migrants.[66] This provision is not uncontroversial in Europe: Britain has not opted in to the Directive largely due to this requirement.[67] However, the Directive goes further, in art. 13 and paragraph 16 of the preamble, in ensuring that this right is practically enforceable by requiring EU countries to establish mechanisms that permit unauthorised workers or their representatives (and trade unions) to lodge complaints or a government authority to bring proceedings against the employer. EU states are required to inform all unauthorised migrants of the right to claim for unpaid entitlements before they are removed from their territory, and the Directive includes a presumption that employers have employed an unauthorised worker for a minimum of three months at minimum wages (art. 6(3)).

The EU Directive takes a more ambivalent approach to regularisation of unauthorised workers' stay in the member state in order to pursue such legal claims. On the one hand, in paragraph 15 of the preamble, the Directive recommends that an illegally employed non-EU national should not derive a right to stay and access to the labour market from the illegal employment relationship or back payment of remuneration. Yet the Directive also urges, in paragraph 27 of the preamble, that EU states 'should be free to grant residence permits of limited duration, linked to the length of the relevant national proceedings, to third-country nationals who have been subjected to particularly exploitative working conditions or who were illegally employed minors and who cooperate in criminal proceedings against the employer'. This provision extends protections for trafficked migrants to those who suffer other criminal exploitation. In this regard, the Directive arguably mirrors the approach taken to temporary immigration concessions in Australia that are available only for colourable claims of criminal victimisation.

By contrast, the USA has devised a much wider range of sophisticated institutional mechanisms to accommodate unauthorised workers' rights as workers before pursuing them as potentially removable migrants. Similar to the Australian CJSV, four-year temporary 'U visas' (and possible eventual permanent residence) are available to undocumented workers who are victims of serious criminal activity, if they are certified by the DOL as likely to be helpful in prosecuting an employer.[68] US policies also include an array of other immigration concessions that apply in the absence of criminal exploitation. For example, any removal that would cause irreparable injury or does not further the public interest may be stayed.[69] The Department of Justice

66 Council Directive 2009/52/EC of the European Parliament and of the Council providing for minimum standards on sanctions and measures against employers of illegally staying third-country nationals [2009] OJ L 168/24 (Directive), art 6(2).

67 Elaine Dewhurst, 'The Right of Irregular Immigrants to Outstanding Remuneration under the EU Sanctions Directive: Rethinking Domestic Labour Policy in a Globalised World' (2011) 13 *European Journal of Migration and Law* 389, 393–4.

68 8 USC § 1101(a)(15)(U)(i)(II). See further Leticia M Saucedo, 'Immigration Enforcement Versus Employment Law Enforcement: The Case for Integrated Protections in the Immigrant Workplace' (2010) 38 *Fordham Urban Law Journal* 303.

69 See e.g. 8 USC § 1231(c)(2)(A) (2006).

(DOJ) and Department of Homeland Security (DHS) (the agency responsible for immigration enforcement through Immigration and Customs Enforcement (ICE)) have prosecutorial discretion to terminate deportation proceedings or deprioritise the enforcement of immigration laws against individuals who are 'in the midst of a legitimate effort to protect their civil rights'.[70]

An MOU in effect since 1998 (now between DHS and DOL) commits ICE to suspend its enforcement activities when there is an ongoing DOL investigation at that worksite.[71] An ICE policy manual recommends that its officials avoid becoming involved in a labour dispute and be cautious of 'tips and leads' used by employers to manipulate employment disputes, to retaliate against employees for exercising labour rights or to frustrate the administration of labour laws.[72] ICE officers should proactively ask any informant whether a labour dispute is in progress, determine whether the employer has a history of labour violations and assist victims of labour law violations to remain in the country to pursue their claims. To be sure, this manual is advisory; it does not prohibit outright immigration enforcement that undermines employment protections. Nevertheless, at least one immigration judge has ruled to suppress evidence against immigrants in deportation proceedings because immigration authorities had relied on a tip from an employer during an ongoing labour dispute and had failed to follow these guidelines.[73]

Furthermore, labour enforcement is proactively encouraged by DHS beyond the activities of DOL or other labour inspectorates. Since 1998, immigration officials have been required to share with DOL any information suggesting that a particular employer may have violated any labour laws falling within the DOL's jurisdiction.[74] The current MOU also permits the DOL to interview undocumented workers detained after ICE's workplace raids.

Finally, US executive agencies have created what Joseph Carens calls 'firewalls' that 'quarantine' workers' precarious immigration status from their labour law entitlements.[75] These include barriers between the authorities

70 John Morton, Director, ICE, Memorandum for all Field Office Directors, Special Agents in Charge, Chief Counsel, *Prosecutorial Discretion: Certain Victims, Witnesses, and Plaintiffs* (17 June 2011). See also Shoba Sivaprasad Wadhia, *Beyond Deportation: The Role of Prosecutorial Discretion in Immigration Cases* (NYU Press, 2015).

71 Currently *Revised Memorandum of Understanding Between US Department of Homeland Security and US Department of Labor,* 31 March 2011.

72 On the books in various forms since 1996, this is now designated as *ICE Special Agents Field Manual,* 33.14(h).

73 *In re Herrera-Priego,* US DOJ, Decision and Order of the Immigration Judge (10 July 2003).

74 *Memorandum of Understanding between the Immigration and Naturalization Service, Department of Justice, and the Employment Standards Division, Department of Labor,* No 23, 23 November 1998 (*1998 MOU*). See Michael J. Wishnie, 'Emerging Issues for Undocumented Workers' (2004) 6 *University of Pennsylvania Journal of Labor and Employment Law* 497.

75 Joseph H. Carens, 'The Rights of Irregular Migrants' (2008) 22(2) *Ethics and International Affairs* 163, 167.

that act to guarantee labour standards and those enforcing immigration laws. For instance, since 1998, during any inspection triggered by a worker's complaint, DOL must not inquire into workers' immigration status, nor convey this information to ICE.[76] This was intended to avoid discouraging labour complaints from workers, and although officers are required to inform ICE if they discover suspected unauthorised workers in the course of DOL-initiated investigations, Shannon Gleeson has concluded from detailed empirical research that labour agency officials often go to great lengths not to elicit information about a worker's immigration status.[77] Interestingly, she attributes this not to an affinity toward undocumented workers but a commitment to achieving the agency's enforcement goals and avoid a perverse incentive for employers to hire unauthorised workers. At the state level, Californian legislation prohibits inquiries into a person's immigration status for the purposes of enforcing state employment laws.[78] In Texas, the form required for filing a wage claim clearly states that providing a social security number is optional, and the intake form used by the Texas Workplace Commission Civil Rights Division does not request it at all.[79] Indeed, similar strategies appear to have been adopted in Britain where the Health and Safety Executive (the work-related health, safety and illness watchdog in the UK) has trained its construction inspectors in Polish 'so that they can tell the workers they're not interested in migration status, only health and safety'.[80]

Another form of this firewall in the USA can occur through the courts, which have, on occasion, refused employers' efforts to inquire into (and publicise) immigration status in employment-related litigation.[81] This jurisprudence appears to be fractured and unclear since other courts have permitted such discovery,[82] while still others require immigrants to reveal their status to employers under a protective order that confines disclosure to the parties and the court.[83]

For all of its strengths, it is important to note that this regulatory landscape in the USA is riven with inconsistencies, exceptions and discretion. For instance, the MOU described above only prevents DHS activity from

76 *1998 MOU*, above n. 74.

77 Shannon Gleeson, 'Means to an End: An Assessment of the Status-Blind Approach to Protecting Undocumented Worker Rights' (2014) 57(3) *Sociological Perspectives* 301.

78 *California Labor Code* § 1171.5.

79 Texas Workforce Commission. 'Welcome, We're Here to Help. Resources, Tips and Tools to Build a Stronger Texas Workforce' (2012).

80 Bridget Anderson and Ben Rogaly, *Forced Labour in the UK* (COMPAS and TUC, 2005), 54.

81 See e.g. *Rivera v. NIBCO Inc*, 364 F3d 1057 (9th Cir 2004); *Avila-Blum v. Casa de Cambio Delgado Inc*, 236 FRD 190 (SDNY 2006).

82 See e.g. *Lopez v. Superflex Ltd*, No 01 Civ 10010, 2002 WL 1941484 (SDNY 21 August 2002).

83 *Catalan v. Vermillion Ranch Ltd P'ship*, No 06 Civ 01043, 2007 WL 951781 (D Colo 28 March 2007).

displacing the enforcement of labour goals when a DOL investigation is already on foot. It has far less application where the labour exploitation has not yet triggered an employee's complaint or come to the attention of DOL. In short, very little in any of these policies guarantees unauthorised workers access to industrial justice. Thus, courts in the USA have awarded damages against employers for threatening to report an unauthorised plaintiff to immigration officials in retaliation for workplace complaints.[84] However, where an employer does illegally report a worker to immigration authorities in such circumstances, this may still provide a lawful basis for removal.[85] Even so, these executive and judicial interventions are creative models of the possibilities for curbing the dominance of immigration enforcement.

A concessionary immigration framework for Australia

Australia has moved assertedly in the opposite direction. As described above, instead of quarantining immigration status, Australia has established policies of administrative linkage, encouraging public officials to report any contacts with unauthorised migrants to immigration authorities. The strategies for safeguarding the labour rights of unauthorised workers which have been devised in the USA may seem counter-intuitive in Australia where political debate is fixated on exclusionary policies and immigration compliance. Proactively protecting unauthorised workers from removal may seem more confronting still. Naturally, specific demographic realities, economic imperatives and complex enforcement structures shape each national jurisdiction in unique ways. I am not suggesting that measures which have been adopted overseas are necessarily politically viable in Australia. Nevertheless, comparative perspectives suggest alternatives to the legal and institutional status quo.

Instead, this chapter makes a number of proposals that are modest compared with the international models. First, building on the Australian trafficking visa framework, a new visa (perhaps named the Workplace Inclusion visa) should allow workers to remain in Australia long enough to seek legal advice and pursue bona fide claims against an employer (the duration might be determined in consultation with the FWO). Second, institutional arrangements need to be put in place to cede immigration enforcement imperatives to labour justice, creating forms of the firewall which has been adopted internationally.

The Workplace Inclusion visa should be made available to workers involved in an investigation of unlawful employment practices to promote the administration of industrial justice under commonwealth and state

84 E.g. at the federal level, *Fair Labor Standards Act*, 29 USC §§ 206-19 (2000); *Singh v. Jutla*, 214 FSupp 2d 1056 (ND Cal 2002). Many states, such as California, have comparable provisions. See also Annie Decker 'Suspending Employers' Immigration-Related Duties During Labor Disputes: A Statutory Proposal' (2006) 115 *Yale Law Journal* 2193.

85 8 USC § 1227(a)(1)(B) (Supp V 2006); *Montero v. INS*, 124 F3d 381, 384–85 (2d Cir 1997).

legislation. Ideally, the visa would be granted by way of application,[86] rather than relying upon the benevolence of DIBP. However, pragmatically, the integrity of the scheme might be better ensured by requiring the FWO or an industrial relations commission to certify that an investigation of unlawful employment practices is on foot. It is a concern, of course, that making the visa available on certification by these bodies and not by way of direct application by a worker would preclude administrative merits review of a rejection decision, which would risk legitimate claims not being properly detected. However, at the same time, a protracted administrative appeals process could leave workers with doubtful work authorisation for extended periods of time. Also, a certification-centred approach would relieve the worker of the need to adduce evidence for DIBP of their bona fide labour claim. It is crucial, however, that the Workplace Inclusion visa carries permission to work. This serves to acknowledge the migrant's employment contribution and is a necessary incentive for an unauthorised worker to identify themselves to the authorities.

While novel, this suggestion has precedents in Australia. The 2007 parliamentary inquiry into temporary work visas, for example, recommended that a comprehensive, confidential complaints mechanism be introduced allowing 457 visa workers to report abuses without provoking retaliatory action by employers.[87] The following year, Barbara Deegan recommended that even if 457 visa workers lose their employment, they be permitted to remain in Australia for the purpose of prosecuting health and safety complaints.[88] In a joint submission to the *FW Act* review in 2012, the Migration Alliance and the Transport Workers Union argued that visa cancellations under s. 116 of the *Migration Act* not take effect whilst any Fair Work investigations are pending.[89] These proposals differ from mine in that they assist only valid visa-holders rather than unauthorised workers and this book has urged against denying access to justice on the basis of immigration status alone.

There are, of course, a number of objections that might be made, particularly as this proposal empowers unauthorised workers. Some might baulk, perceiving it to 'reward' those who work without authorisation. Christina Boswell argues that upholding the employment rights of unauthorised migrants in Britain can lead to profound contradictions within that legal

86 In this respect, the process might more closely resemble the Australian family violence provisions than the trafficking visas. Family violence concessions permit applicants to apply for permanent residence on the basis of their close family relationship with an Australian sponsor who has engaged in violence in the family: *Migration Regulations* regs 1.21–1.27.

87 Joint Standing Committee on Migration, Parliament of Australia, *Temporary Visas … Permanent Benefits: Ensuring the Effectiveness, Fairness and Integrity of the Temporary Business Visa Program* (2007), rec 19.

88 Barbara Deegan, *Visa Subclass 457 Integrity Review: Final Report* (Cth of Australia, 2008), 57.

89 Migration Alliance and Transport Workers Union, 'Joint Submission to the *FW Act* Review', 17 February 2012.

system.[90] For rules to be consistently and fully instrumentalised, modern states strive to integrate different institutions and centralise data so that an individual's legal infringements are likely to become visible across systems. Once illegality has been observed by the state, it must (at least in principle) be resolved. Therefore, from the moment an unauthorised migrant is detected, any continued access even to remedies for past rights violations is possible, according to Boswell, only in the context of a pluralist or decentralised legal system. In short, '[t]he state cannot coherently embrace a commitment to carry on ensuring the welfare of someone whose presence it does not permit'.[91] However, by regularising a worker's unauthorised immigration status, the Workplace Inclusion visa arguably avoids this contradiction involving ongoing illegality. The visa would grant work rights for several months pending an FWO investigation. It permits unauthorised workers to recover retroactively for previous employment violations on the basis that entitlements accrue from unauthorised workers' de facto presence in the labour market.

To envisage the visa as an incentive to engage in unauthorised work misapprehends it entirely. A worker would have to alert government authorities of their unauthorised status (or feared future unauthorised status, for temporary visa-holders), thereby risking removal. Since the visa grant would depend on FWO discretion or DIBP approval, it is likely that gaining a Workplace Inclusion visa would be far from assured. This makes it unlikely that its availability will encourage unauthorised work. Rather, an unauthorised worker is likely to come forward only if their employment situation is desperate or perilous. In any event, the overwhelming majority of people who overstay their visas already present to compliance officers voluntarily, according to DIBP.[92] Proper incentive structures could encourage more unauthorised workers (as well as temporary migrants – such as 457 visa workers – who fear loss of status following an industrial dispute) to come forward to secure their rights, by offsetting the detriments of their precarious immigration status. If the ultimate goal is a reduction in unauthorised immigration, this proposal, while de-emphasising immigration status as a factor in considering whether to report workplace abuses, would have the effect of lessening unauthorised employment itself, as unauthorised workers become less appealing to employers. Arguably, such an arrangement would also enhance the effectiveness of the employer sanctions scheme (see

90 Christina Boswell, 'The Elusive Rights of an Invisible Population' (2008) 22(2) *Ethics and International Affairs* 187, 189.

91 Ibid.

92 In 2013–14, 13,875 of the 17,185 unlawful non-citizens located in the community were said to be detected voluntarily: DIBP, *Annual Report 2013–14* (2014), 169. The majority of students in breach of visa conditions apparently self-present to immigration authorities to clarify their immigration status: ANAO, *Management of Student Visas: Department of Immigration and Citizenship* (the Auditor-General Audit Report No 46, 2010–11 Performance Audit) (2011), 114.

Chapter 7), since it may help officials bring forward as witnesses unauthorised workers with intimate knowledge of their employer's unlawful practices.

Still, it is critical that the overriding goal here is industrial compliance rather than immigration compliance. The possibility of cooperation between employees and law enforcement provides a significant incentive for an employer to abide by immigration laws to avoid employer sanctions or treat employees well enough so that they do not become informants. This would afford unauthorised migrant workers a modicum of protection to improve their employment conditions.

Others may resist this visa proposal even if they accept the benefits of facilitating unauthorised workers' employment claims, namely that such a claim does not require a worker's presence in Australia: FWO inspectors pursue litigation for underpayment of entitlements under the *FW Act*;[93] legal proceedings may be initiated by a union,[94] or legal representatives;[95] and migrant workers may participate in hearings by video link,[96] or telephone.[97]

Yet, practically, employee plaintiffs who cannot remain in Australia face severe practical difficulties in obtaining legal advice, instructing lawyers, signing and serving documents and preparing oral and documentary evidence. Even the most determined plaintiff may find the dictates of long distance communication in a different language extremely difficult and expensive. In the absence of a Workplace Inclusion visa, and without automatic referrals of possible exploitation by DIBP to the FWO, most unauthorised workers will be unable to stay in Australia long enough even to register a grievance with the FWO, participate in FWO investigations or provide evidence. In several recorded matters, the FWO has struggled to identify or locate migrant workers in order to remit unpaid entitlements.[98] The national workplace relations tribunal, the Fair Work Commission, has dismissed workers' applications because of difficulties in contacting applicants who had returned overseas after being denied a visa extension.[99]

Indeed, this issue arose in the FWO's litigation against Kentwood, discussed at this chapter's opening. The availability of the workers to testify during

93 *FW Act* s 682.

94 In *Australian Licensed Aircraft Engineers Association v. International Aviations Services Assistance Pty Ltd* [2011] FCA 333, the ALAEA successfully represented a union member, pursuing a claim of unlawful dismissal in the Federal Court after he had returned overseas following termination of his employment and cancellation of his 457 visa.

95 Among the judgments in relation to unauthorised workers considered in Chapter 6, Silivenusi Taufia was in Tonga, Mainuddin Kazi, initially granted a Bridging visa, had been removed to Bangladesh and Gurminder Singh was in India.

96 See e.g. *Rajeev Prasad v. Alcatel-Lucent Australia Ltd* [2011] FWAFB 1515.

97 See e.g. *Applicant v. Respondent* [2010] FWA 4289.

98 Plaintiffs could not be identified or found in *FWO v. Glad Group Pty Ltd* [2012] FMCA 731. In *FWO v. Sanada Investments Pty Ltd* [2010] FMCA 401, a Sushi Train restaurant in Cairns owed total entitlements of A$90,021.78 to Japanese and South Korean working holiday maker employees who were unable to be located.

99 See, for example, *Edward Coupe v. International Motor Inn Pty Ltd* [2012] FWA 2117; *Ankitkumar Patel v. RPEP Holdings Pty Ltd* [2012] FWA 3915.

the Federal Court hearings rested entirely upon DIAC discretion. Yuan Zhaolin and the other workers were granted BVEs to remain in Australia but, amidst extensive delaying tactics by Kentwood, McKerracher J was concerned that 'extension of their visas was by no means certain'.[100] The court quoted at length from a letter addressed by DIAC to the FWO in relation to these workers' immigration status:

> BVEs are not granted for the purpose of attending court hearings that are unrelated to a migration or citizenship decision. However, a BVE holder may be engaged in matters unrelated to the purpose of the BVE while it is in effect. For example, a BVE granted on the basis that an applicant is making 'acceptable arrangements to depart Australia' may be granted for a period long enough to organise his or her travel during which time the client may also be attending court hearings, etc.
>
> ...
>
> DIAC cannot provide any assurances that Mr Yuan [a witness for the applicant] will be granted another BVE as this will depend on the BVE decision maker's assessment of the applicant's circumstances at the time of the application. However, if the decision maker is satisfied that Mr Yuan is making acceptable arrangements to depart Australia and that he will abide by any conditions that will be imposed on the visa, then it is likely that another BVE will be granted.[101]

Participatory inclusion requires far greater security of presence for migrant workers than the Kentwood workers were afforded.

A further practical objection concerns the challenges of ensuring the genuineness of visa applications. Offering protections from the full coercive force of immigration rules for those who have experienced exploitation at work may create incentives for non-citizens to exaggerate evidence or provide false information. Such concerns, along with related fears that immigration concessions open the floodgates, were also levelled at the trafficking visa scheme. A senior AFP officer with significant expertise in human trafficking has cited evidence of self-described victims of trafficking using 'false identities and [making] up stories in order to manipulate the system'.[102]

Indeed, a vital reason for the government's willingness to assist trafficked people is that trafficking is, rhetorically, set apart from unauthorised migration and people smuggling as uniquely deserving of dispensation or

100 *Kentwood No 2* [2010] FCA 1156, [17].
101 *Kentwood* [2010] FCA 98, [20].
102 Evidence to Senate Legal and Constitutional Affairs Legislation Committee, Parliament of Australia, Canberra, 29 August 2012, 33 (Chris McDevitt, AFP).

compassion.[103] Trafficking visas are premised on the exceptional entitlements of trafficked people under international law. The UN Trafficking Protocol encourages states to allow trafficking victims to remain in their territory temporarily or permanently, and to give them an opportunity to present their views.[104] States are also encouraged to withhold punishment from trafficked people for immigration status offences in connection with their situation as trafficked persons.[105] Relatedly, the UN Convention against Transnational Organised Crime affords victims a right to participate in legal action against their exploiters.[106] Part of the reason why such solid victim support outcomes have been achieved is because the anti-trafficking cause is so compelling. As Catherine Dauvergne observes, in relation to trafficking of children, '[i]s it even possible to be *too* concerned about selling children into sexual slavery?'[107] Slavery and trafficking generate an impression of political consensus, which in Australia, has manifested in extremely serious criminal offences, and possible residence and welfare services for vulnerable victims, with over A$150 million spent on counter-trafficking measures between 2003 and 2014.[108]

Since it leaves the precise scope of exploitation undefined, supporters of the Trafficking Protocol can promote it as intended to safeguard those victims trapped in situations of utterly overbearing coercion. Choosing to migrate for work purposes, on the other hand, taints the premise of innocence that is often presumed in trafficking narratives. A visa that regularises the immigration status of unauthorised workers who have suffered lesser forms of exploitation or coercion can be viewed as undermining this justification for extending rights to trafficking victims. Only the extreme vulnerabilities of trafficked people, it is thought, warrant the government overlooking serious breaches of immigration laws.

103 Julie Ham, Marie Segrave and Sharon Pickering, 'In the Eyes of the Beholder: Border Enforcement, Suspect Travellers and Trafficking Victims' (2013) 2 *Anti-Trafficking Review* 51.

104 United Nations, Protocol to Prevent, Suppress and Punish Trafficking in Persons, Especially Women and Children (Trafficking Protocol) opened for signature 15 December 2000, 2237 UNTS 219, Annex II (entered into force 31 May 2004) arts 6(2) and 7; Recommended Principles and Guidelines on Human Rights and Human Trafficking of the Office of the United Nations High Commissioner for Human Rights, UN Doc E/2002/68/Add.1 (Trafficking Principles and Guidelines) principle 8.

105 Conference of the Parties to the UNTOC, 'Report on the Meeting of the Working Group on Trafficking in Persons held in Vienna on 14 and 15 April 2009' UN Doc CTOC/COP/WG.4/2009/2, 21 April 2009, rec 1(H). See also Trafficking Principles and Guidelines principle 7.

106 Convention against Transnational Organised Crime, opened for signature 15 December 2000, 2225 UNTS 209 (entered into force 29 September 2003) art 25(3); Trafficking Protocol art 6(2)(b); Trafficking Principles and Guidelines principle 9, guideline 4.7.

107 Catherine Dauvergne, *Making People Illegal: What Globalization Means for Migration and Law* (Cambridge University Press, 2008), 69 (emphasis in original).

108 *Australian Government Response*, above n. 23, 2.

Trafficking is also extremely rare. Only 224 BVFs and 202 CJSVs have been granted in ten years,[109] which has assuaged fears about their floodgates dimensions. Conversely, roughly 100,000 people engage in unauthorised work in Australia at any one time.[110] It is unknown precisely how prevalent exploitation is among this workforce, nor among those working legally on valid temporary visas who may wish to avail themselves of the Workplace Inclusion visa upon expiry of their visa. The Workplace Inclusion visa would be accessible to remedy a broad range of illegal conduct, and might therefore trigger greater concerns about promoting the appearance of lax immigration enforcement. Nevertheless, an applicant for this visa will be required to make out a bona fide employment-related claim, possibly to the satisfaction of the FWO or another certifying body. Minimising exploitation of migrant workers is worth the possibility of a small proliferation of temporary visas that hold employers to account for labour law non-compliance.

This proposal would reduce migrant workers' precariousness but not eliminate it. Unauthorised workers may elect not to apply for this visa for calculated reasons. Shannon Gleeson argues that, '[b]y maintaining a low profile and "avoiding problems", many undocumented workers choose not to deploy their knowledge of workplace rights in order to maintain a modicum of certainty in their lives'.[111] Other workers will continue to be reluctant to come forward because of distrust of authorities, fear of not being able to regularise their status, and social stigma attached to their situation. The capacity of people to complain continues to be limited by the very factors that make them vulnerable to exploitation. While the process of seeking legal entitlements is empowering for many workers, participating in court proceedings may be too confronting for others. The challenges of bringing a civil action are illustrated in the 2004 case described at the opening of Chapter 6. A restitutionary claim for unpaid wages was brought by Masri, 'a young Indonesian girl of limited education and ... no bargaining power in her relationship' with a family for whom she worked as a 'housemaid' for four years. In fact, while she was eventually awarded A$95,000, she was forced to face cross-examination by her employer, who was representing himself.[112] Of course, this difficulty can also arise in trafficking prosecutions: one alleged victim was subjected to cross-examination that was so re-traumatising that she was later unwilling to act as witness in a retrial.[113]

109 *IDC Report 2013–14*, above n. 38, 34.

110 Stephen Howells, *Report of the 2010 Review of the* Migration Amendment (Employer Sanctions) Act 2007 (Cth of Australia, 2011), 12.

111 Shannon Gleeson, 'Labor Rights for All? The Role of Undocumented Immigrant Status for Worker Claims Making' (2010) 35(3) *Law and Social Inquiry* 561, 583.

112 *Masri v. Santoso* [2004] NSWIRComm 108, [58], [180].

113 Transcript of proceedings, *R v. Tran, Xu and Qi* (DCNSW, Blackmore J, 2005).

It is also important to acknowledge another limitation of the Workplace Inclusion visa, particularly as it compares with some much more thoroughgoing protections available in other jurisdictions. As merely a temporary 'reprieve' from the coercive power of immigration enforcement, my proposal comes, as Catherine Dauvergne notes with respect to other law reforms, 'from within the modern paradigm – established migration laws – rather than challenging it'.[114] As an exception to the general rule that those without a substantive visa are unlawful non-citizens and liable for removal, the visa proposal made here suspends the harshness of immigration laws while simultaneously reinforcing them.

The Workplace Inclusion visa would only partially disrupt the economic, social and legal conditions (including the conditions of national sovereignty itself) that make workers vulnerable to exploitation. The proposal is based more on what seems practically possible in the current Australian social and political context than on what is ethically required for the just treatment of authorised and unauthorised migrant workers. Yet, even this partial reform, curbing some excesses of migration law, would structurally reconfigure policy responses to migrant labour exploitation in Australia. Enhancing workers' abilities to advocate for their entitlements, even to this limited degree, would be a significant blow to power disparities in migrant workplaces. It should also be accompanied by a comprehensive audit of migrant workers' access to legal services, as one Australian trafficking agency has advocated.[115] An evaluation of the roles of the FWO and other labour inspectorates in enforcing the rights of migrant workers is also desirable. In addition, more is required by way of adjustment of immigration and employment enforcement priorities to support and supplement the Workplace Inclusion visa.

Workplace inclusion requires more than just a visa

The lack of mindful coordination between Australian immigration and employment geared towards promoting industrial justice stands in stark contrast to various measures that have been adopted in North America and parts of Europe. Far from a 'firewall', Australian law requires administrative linkages, which operate overwhelmingly in the service of immigration enforcement. While FWO officers report immigration violations to DIBP, DIBP does not apparently inquire into, or document, employers' breaches of labour laws.

DIBP should be pressed to adopt employment-conscious investigative procedures. These should include putting in place a protocol requiring

114 Dauvergne, *Making People Illegal*, above n. 107, 85.

115 Jennifer Burn *et al.*, *Hidden Exploitation: Women in Forced Labour, Marriage and Migration* (Anti-Slavery Australia and Jumbunna Indigenous House of Learning at UTS, 2012), rec 21.

DIBP to refer all apprehended unauthorised workers to the FWO for investigation (and certification for the purpose of the Workplace Inclusion visa) prior to removal. Sadly, some recent cooperative arrangements in favour of migrant workers' rights have been quickly wound back. In 2009, DIAC struck deals with workers compensation agencies in Victoria, New South Wales and Queensland to regularly exchange information on names of 457 visa-holders, their employers and details of workplace injuries and deaths,[116] but these agreements were all abandoned from 2012.

Alternatively, modelled on the EU Directive, Australia should explore the possibility of attaching a 'surcharge' to employer sanctions penalties (such as administrative warnings and infringement notices) which would be payable to unauthorised workers, with a presumption that three months' work has occurred, billed at minimum wage rates under an applicable award. A similar surcharge could be levied by DIBP together with penalties against employers for breaching sponsorship obligations under the 457 visa, which frequently relate to underpayments.

Conclusion

This chapter has argued that Australian trafficking interventions have missed an opportunity to understand how the employment – immigration nexus can magnify precariousness and exploitation. By contrast, establishing connections between criminal law, immigration law and employment laws opens up a plethora of ways of transforming precarious and exploitative labour and involving workers in gaining just treatment. To this end, the chapter called for reforms to integrate trafficking and industrial or private remedies (through a novel visa category to regularise the status of migrant workers pursuing bona fide employment-related claims) and develop institutional arrangements to cede immigration enforcement priorities to workplace justice.

116 Nick Toscano, 'Scheme to Help Protect 457 Visa Workers from Injuries Quietly Shelved', *Sydney Morning Herald*, 25 October 2014.

10 Conclusion

> Myung Yeol Hwang, 51, died in Sydney in August 2010.[1] He left South Korea after an economic downturn there and arrived in Australia on a tourist visa in 1998, easily finding work as a tiler in the years before the Sydney Olympics. He worked in Sydney for 12 years, moving from job to job, paid cash in hand on dozens of building sites. Unable to secure fixed accommodation, he stayed with friends in the Korean community. In 2009, he contracted a respiratory illness, likely from his construction work, but had no superannuation, no workers compensation and no medical insurance. He feared approaching a public hospital lest authorities discover his unauthorised status. Emaciated and having not washed for weeks, one of his friends called the Construction Forestry Mining and Energy Union for help. A Korean organiser brought him from a rundown house in Campsie to the union, which requested a meeting with the Department of Immigration and Citizenship to arrange a bridging visa and some medical attention. Tragically, Hwang died the next morning. The union, with public support, provided a cremation, burial and a candle memorial on a table in the union office.

This book ends, as it begins, with a death. The tragic and probably avoidable deaths of Guo Jiandong and Myung Yeol Hwang underscore the manifest vulnerability of many migrant workers, whether holders of temporary visas or visa-overstayers. In myriad ways, ineligibility for public welfare support, lack of political representation and disqualification for certain employment protections can leave workers susceptible to the raw impact of a weakly regulated labour market. This book has sought to reveal the ways in which not only their working conditions but also their employment relationships are re-constituted by immigration law, by immigration enforcement and by the interaction of immigration controls with other fields of government regulation.

1 Details are drawn from Erik Paul, *Neoliberal Australia and the US Imperialism in East Asia* (Palgrave Macmillan, 2012), 29; Deborah Snow, 'Silent Victims of Cut-Price Industry', *Sydney Morning Herald*, 20 September 2010, 2; Barbara Miller, 'Lonely Death Highlights Illegal Workers' Plight', *ABC News*, 20 September 2010.

Layers of law's precariousness

In a country that self-consciously pursued egalitarian labour conditions from its Federation, basic tenets of Australia's labour administration have sought to ensure that minimum terms and conditions of employment apply to temporary migrants. They enjoy, in principle, legal employment standards generally identical to residents. The Fair Work Ombudsman (FWO) actively pursues investigations and external audits on behalf of all workers, and in recent years has singled out for special attention those industries where migrant workers are known to be prevalent, such as fuel retailing for international students and horticulture for working holiday makers. Courts recognise some classes of temporary visa-holders and foreign-born resident workers as 'vulnerable' and the FWO regularly takes action to secure their entitlements.[2] In spite of these important efforts, migrants' experience of effective employment entitlements is frequently less robust than that of residents.

This book has suggested that this precariousness is produced by or perpetuated through law in at least four ways. Each of these four factors can intensify the superior bargaining strength of employers and enable them to exploit migrant workers' structural disadvantage, including circumstances that employers played no part in creating. First, precarious employment entitlements in countries of employment and of origin can result from broader social disadvantage, including inadequate welfare protections in their country of nationality, pre-existing debts, or poor labour market opportunity at home. A worker's position in a globalised economy can weaken their position in the local labour market.

Secondly, the coercive force of immigration law is channelled through conditions of entry and stay. Visa eligibility criteria mould the demographic profile of workers: their age, qualifications, language ability in the state of employment and the financial means (or debt) required of applicants. Visa conditions determine legally permissible behaviour once employed in the country of immigration. Aspirations for a future visa, too, can significantly shape the relationship between worker and employer. Those hopeful of attaining future residence may experience profound uncertainty as the requirements for permanent skilled visas perpetually change. For their part, application criteria valorising local work experience and employer sponsorship dramatically constrain temporary workers' labour market choices by increasing their incentives to stay in exploitative workplace relationships. These elements consign temporary migrants to a seriously differentiated labour market position from that of residents.

2 For example, *FWO v. Shafi Investments Pty Ltd (No 2)* [2013] FMCA 168, [56] (involving a worker on a secondary visa as a spouse of a student visa worker); *FWO v. Go Yo Trading Pty Ltd* [2012] FMCA 865, [15] (working holiday makers); *FWO v. Taj Palace Tandoori Indian Restaurant Pty Ltd* [2012] FMCA 258, [40] (a 457 visa worker); *Workplace Ombudsman v. Saya Cleaning Pty Ltd* [2009] FMCA 38 (a newly arrived resident worker from Iraq).

Further precariousness is engendered, thirdly, by the highly coercive, and sometimes uncertain, effects of immigration enforcement activities. Compliance operations, or fear thereof, gravely undermine enforcement of employment protections, as workers face great logistical barriers to pursuing claims from abroad after departing the country of employment. Even fear of instability (for instance concern that an employer may withdraw visa sponsorship in retaliation for a worker's complaint) may stifle lawful temporary workers' willingness to complain about inadequate conditions. Effective remedies are even more illusory for unauthorised workers (including temporary visa-holders who are working in excess of their visa privileges) because immigration compliance is almost inevitably prioritised over enforcement of labour laws.

Finally, workers' immigration status can reconfigure substantive and remedial employment entitlements in complex and unpredictable ways. In Australia, temporary migrant workers may be denied full remedies, especially in relation to unfair dismissal and workers compensation claims.[3] For unauthorised migrant workers, coverage of unfair dismissal, *quantum meruit* and workers compensation protections has regularly been withheld.[4] Complicating the picture, it is clear that some protections are offered in practice and the FWO has pursued redress for these workers.[5] Often without referencing the small body of case law withholding labour protections, courts have awarded employment-related remedies to apparently unauthorised workers.[6] Amidst such uncertain and inconsistent jurisprudence, recourse to legal protection for these workers is far from guaranteed.

Against the premise that regulatory intervention can either exacerbate precariousness or support resilience, this book has taken as a central case study specific immigration-based reforms introduced in Australia in the last decade in the name of addressing migrant labour exploitation in Australia. Given Australia's traditionally strong national consensus on taking a protectionist approach to migration and employment, mainstream policy debates on temporary migrant labour remain undeveloped. Pressure has intensified to follow other English-speaking developed countries in addressing the perceived harms of hosting a partly globalised workforce.

Aspects of these reforms have been highly effective at alleviating precariousness for migrant workers. Protective responses to human trafficking have extended the boundaries of the Australian political community to some migrant workers who have experienced acute exploitation, with greater security of stay including, in certain cases, residence as a gateway to citizenship. A raft of legislative amendments to this framework in 2013 dramatically

3 *Elgin Nogaliza v. Benale Pty Ltd ATF Fletcher Unit Trust t/as Fletcher International WA* [2010] FWA 2667, [29]; *Webster v. Mercury Colleges Pty Ltd* [2011] FWA 1807, [47].

4 *Australia Meat Holdings Pty Ltd v. Kazi* [2004] QCA 147; *Smallwood v. Ergo Asia Pty Ltd* [2014] FWC 964. Although cf. *Nonferral (NSW) Pty Ltd v. Taufia* (1998) 43 NSWLR 312.

5 See *FWO v. Shafi Investments Pty Ltd* [2012] FMCA 1150.

6 See *Masri v. Santoso* [2004] NSWIRComm 108; *Midya v. Sagrani* [1999] NSWCA 187.

reversed the historical tendency to prioritise sex trafficking over other forms of labour exploitation, and sharpened criminal laws' capacity to respond to the subtleties of coercion and psychological duress. Likewise, efforts to remodel the 457 visa in 2008 and 2013 did much to improve the bargaining capacity of sponsored workers, by reappraising salary requirements and lessening the worst excesses of workers' structural dependencies on employer sponsors.

However, other elements within these various legislative packages may have distracted attention from, or even accentuated, the legal constitution of precariousness in migrants' employment relationships. A common theme across these amendments is a concentration on punitive measures against employers: those who breach 457 visa sponsorship obligations, employ unauthorised workers, or engage in labour trafficking offences. Like the international models on which they have drawn, these policy responses have tended to locate the problem in unscrupulous employers and vulnerable migrant workers. This is problematic for two reasons. First, this approach tends to overlook the role of the regulatory environment of immigration controls itself in intensifying pre-existing power differentials in migrant workers' employment relationships. For example, employer sanctions distract attention from a legal landscape that produces precariety by withholding basic labour protections from unauthorised workers. Criminal justice responses to human trafficking obscure the larger background context of coercion, which characterises many migrants' working lives: those with precarious immigration status, denied pathways to regularisation, are afforded highly partial access to enforcement of employment entitlements. Second, law enforcement strategies that are directed at employers often leave migrant workers bearing the highest costs, unless they are accompanied by immigration-specific protections for workers. For instance, employer sanctions offences can have the effect of driving unauthorised work further underground and prompting employers to devise ever greater subterfuge to circumvent migration law.

The need for novel interventions in the Australian context

The narratives about migrant workers throughout this book evidence both the impermanence of national membership, and also just how greatly citizenship and political communities matter, in law and in fact. By including them at the beginning of each chapter I hoped to underline one of the book's key ethical frames, which calls for immigration laws to be assessed by their effect on all who are substantially impacted by them, and not just co-nationals in a democratic community. Since temporary and unauthorised workers remain an inevitable feature of the contemporary context, this perspective has intimated at possible legislative amendments that may reverse the subordination of temporary and unauthorised migrants in workplaces across Australia, many of which draw from creative policy interventions overseas, which have done much to promote industrial justice for, and social inclusion of, temporary migrant workers.

These proposals in this book are made at the intersection of two competing imperatives: that residents and migrants impact upon one another in significant ways that generate mutual responsibilities to lessen harm; but also that a fixed political community is necessary to achieve strong social welfare commitments. This involves accepting certain orthodoxies while rejecting others, acknowledging as significant national concerns both immigration controls, and also the precarious effects of these on migrant workers. Thus, this runs counter to contentions that the 'national interest' should always trump the interests of migrant workers, and that adequate labour security for resident workers demands – and justifies – higher levels of vulnerability in 'guest' workers. Such a position has been taken, for example, by a large federal union in Australia, which has argued that federal and state anti-discrimination laws should permit 'discrimination in employment on the basis of visa status or residency status'.[7] This raises difficult questions about to what degree temporary migrants should be accorded full labour market membership whilst in the country of employment. It also fails to absorb how more robust protections for temporary and unauthorised migrants can coincide with residents' interests.

The ethical approach taken in this book also challenges the notion that volition is the final arbiter of responsibilities, arguing instead that legal protections should flow not only to those who have consented to laws by virtue of naturalisation, but also to those who are affected by them. Within rhetoric describing immigration as a 'privilege', temporary entrants are taken to consent to whatever conditions attach to their stay, even if these are unilaterally changed over time. Consequently, so this rationale goes, if poor working conditions result from a marginal immigration status voluntarily acquired, this is seen as a necessary evil that migrants positively accept as the terms of their stay. Hence, unauthorised migrants, such as Myung Yeol Hwang (whose story opened this chapter), are frequently taken to have 'chosen' to stay and work in Australia without authorisation and therefore are deemed to be personally responsible for the fatal combination of dangerous work and lack of ready access to medical and legal support. When international students pay illegal and extortionate sums to someone holding themselves out as an employer's agent to transfer to a 457 visa, they are condemned as taking a 'backdoor' to residence or generating visa 'churn',[8] as though it is improper to apply for a visa for which one is eligible in the hopes of remaining in Australia with a view towards permanent residence.

7 Construction Forestry Mining and Energy Union, Submission No 382 to the Senate Standing Committee on Legal and Constitutional Affairs, Parliament of Australia, 'Inquiry into the Exposure Draft of Human Rights and Anti-Discrimination Bill 2012', 21 December 2012, 3.

8 Bob Birrell and Ernest Healy, *Immigration and Unemployment in 2014* (Centre for Population and Urban Research, Monash University, 2014), 4.

Workers and employers do, of course, exercise volition in ways that can intensify or ameliorate poor working and living conditions. The lens of precariousness, though, illuminates how the regulatory structures of immigration law (interacting with other Australian laws and the global economy) can constrain workers' agency, thus challenging the premise of voluntariness.

The frame of participatory inclusion, which was introduced in Chapter 2, captures an aspiration that migrant workers in Australia be invited and empowered to play an active part in shaping laws and policies that affect them. In order to be able to take account of the interests of actual and prospective non-citizens, policies need to be directed toward supporting migrant agency to ensure migrants' meaningful capacity to give voice to their perspectives to shape policy formation. This must involve supporting migrant workers' ability to participate in institutional structures that provide concrete redress. This leads to the recognition of all workers (whether resident, temporary or unauthorised) as active participants in the domestic labour market. It involves reducing dependencies on employers, enhancing labour market mobility and recasting migrant worker exploitation from an immigration law violation to a labour law abuse. Here follows some broad suggestions for a reorientation in approach to migrant labour.

De-crimininalising unauthorised work

The criminalisation of unauthorised work impedes the comprehensive enforcement of employment laws in Australian workplaces. *Migration Act 1958* (Cth) s. 235 not only renders partial and unpredictable the coverage of employment laws and remedies for unauthorised workers, it also seriously undermines the enforcement of criminal sanctions against employers using unauthorised workers. It is ironic indeed that there are no recorded convictions under s. 235 because the statutory duty to remove unauthorised migrants impedes such prosecutions. Taking seriously the inclusion of all whose interests are affected means highlighting migrants' roles as workers. As argued in Chapter 6, repealing or amending s. 235 to dull its effect on workers' entitlements as against their employers would go far in restoring unauthorised migrant workers as subjects of employment law rather than (only) as objects of immigration law.

Adjusting enforcement priorities

The immediate consequences of immigration compliance can operate to undermine labour enforcement. By law, immigration officials in Australia are afforded no avenue to regularise the status of unauthorised workers to pursue claims against employers: the mandatory requirement to remove an 'unlawful non-citizen' and to do so 'as soon as practicable' is absolute. Bridging visas are available only in highly confined circumstances: where an application for a substantive visa is being processed; while the visa-holder is awaiting the finalisation of an immigration matter or making arrangements to leave; or for suspected victims of trafficking. While labour entitlements may be held by migrant workers, their ability to be claimed rests, among other things, on their holding secure immigration status or having been identified by the Australian Federal Police as a certain sort of victim (of trafficking).

Therefore, Chapter 9 suggested introducing a 'Workplace Inclusion visa' to ensure a modicum of security of presence to promote the administration of industrial justice under commonwealth legislation. This is a case where justice for migrant workers may be better protected by providing them with particular rights to address the specific sources of their precariousness rather than simply affording non-citizens the formal rights available to citizens and residents in host states. Such temporary regularisation should be available to workers to seek legal advice and pursue bona fide claims against an employer. More robust integrity of the scheme might be achieved by requiring a labour compliance agency to certify that an investigation of unlawful employment practices is on foot. This should be accompanied by a comprehensive audit of access to legal services for vulnerable migrant workers in Australia and an evaluation of the roles of the FWO in enforcing the rights of migrant workers including those lacking permission to work.

Enforcement priorities must also be reordered. This may involve immigration compliance authorities adopting employment-conscious investigative procedures, such as referring all identified unauthorised workers to the FWO for investigation prior to their removal. Drawing inspiration from the 2009 European Union Employer Sanctions Directive,[9] a 'surcharge' might attach to administrative warnings under the employer sanctions scheme, payable to unauthorised workers to compensate for unpaid entitlements, with a presumption that three months' work has occurred, billed at minimum wage rates under an applicable award. A similar surcharge could be levied against employers who have breached sponsorship obligations under the 457 visa since these so frequently relate to underpayments.

Even more forceful would be the creation of a 'firewall' that quarantines workers' precarious immigration status from entitlements under other areas of the law. Barriers between the enforcement of immigration controls and labour standards arise in the USA through legal doctrines that extend most employment protections to unauthorised workers, in strong contrast to employment laws in Britain and Australia (as discussed in Chapter 6). In addition, in a number of ways, immigration enforcement priorities are mandatorily adjusted in the USA in favour of workplace entitlements (set out more fully in Chapter 9). Labour inspectors enjoy freedom from a requirement to convey workers' immigration status to immigration author-

9 Council Directive 2009/52/EC of the European Parliament and of the Council providing for minimum standards on sanctions and measures against employers of illegally staying third-country nationals [2009] OJ L 168/24, art 6(2).

ities. Courts have on occasion prevented employers from using discovery of immigration status as a means to curtail employment-related litigation. Immigration compliance officials have in some circumstances committed to suspend their activities in the course of employment disputes, and unauthorised workers have been awarded damages against employers threatening to report them to immigration officials in retaliation for them exercising workplace entitlements, including making a lawful complaint.

In Australia, a 'whole-of-government' approach has seen the enlistment of employment, tax and other social agencies in the pursuit of strong immigration compliance. Labour inspections are an important tool to detect and prevent employer violations. However, tight cooperation between labour inspection and immigration enforcement and exercise of immigration control duties by labour inspectors impedes coverage of migrant workers under employment protections. If the appointment since 2013 of federal Fair Work inspectors to police the sponsorship obligations of employers of 457 visa-holders results in bars on sponsorship, and loss of job and therefore of lawful immigration status for workers, migrant workers may become even more reluctant to denounce abusive working conditions or cooperate with labour authorities.

Softening the force of employer sponsorship

The sponsorship structure of the 457 visa and related pathways to skilled residence breeds migrant dependency on employers and narrows visa workers' labour mobility. These vulnerabilities risk degrading migrants' working conditions and thereby undercutting residents' entitlements. Of course, the linking of immigration status to employment in a specific position is prevalent in temporary labour programmes in the USA, Canada and the UK and expressly permitted by International Labour Organization Conventions for a period of time. It is doubtless motivated in part by a view that this affords temporary workers greater security of employment in a foreign labour market. However, this is true only on the assumption of a generally equal bargaining relationship between employee and employer.

The coercion that attends sponsorship may be alleviated by removing employer sponsorship altogether as the keystone of these schemes, as the United Nations Special Rapporteur on the Human Rights of Migrants recommended in 2014.[10] Other agencies, such as the Organisation for Security and Cooperation in Europe, the International Organisation for Migration and the International Labour Organization have recommended that employer-bonding be limited only to a short period, such as three months, after which migrant workers have unlimited rights to change employment.[11] Alternatively, the sponsorship restriction in condition 8107

10 François Crépeau, *Report of the Special Rapporteur on the Human Rights of Migrants*, Human Rights Council, 26th session, Agenda item 3, A/HRC/26/35, 3 April 2014, 19.

might be modified to lessen its coercive effects, for instance expanding the limitations on visa workers' employment to a particular occupation or industry sector rather than an employer. To avoid the correlative risk of unemployment of 457 visa-holders in the absence of the degree of certainty afforded by employer sponsorship, dedicated support for migrant workers will be required in sourcing alternative employment in their industry sector.

Recasting migrant workers as subjects not objects of public debate

Just as industrial citizenship cannot be the purview of only resident participants in a labour market, public debate cannot involve only citizens coming together to design laws merely to suit their needs. Temporary migrant workers contribute to the productivity, wealth and tax income in Australia and yet are not entitled to public healthcare or other welfare benefits. They achieve legal standing in the workplace for certain claims against their employers but immigration rules embed subservience into these employment relationships. They are governed by Australian laws and yet are not directly represented in the parliamentary deliberations that create those laws nor able to hold the executive to account through electoral processes. Chapter 2 examined in detail the perspective that governments need not be accountable to temporary migrants in exactly the same way they are to citizens (although some contend that no distinction should be drawn between citizens and permanent residents in relation to electoral rights). Yet, for all the reasons discussed there, the concerns and interests of temporary migrants cannot be discounted as irrelevant to policymaking. Indeed, non-citizen workers have a special right of consultation on immigration policies, both formal (via government or parliamentary processes) and informal (through public debate and membership in social structures that represent worker interests such as unions).

Unfortunately, in Australia, the interests of temporary migrants are frequently disregarded, as evidenced by the frank admission from former Labor Immigration Minister, Senator Chris Evans, that 'the desires of migrants – including overseas students who came in on temporary visas in order to gain permanent residence – should not be driving Australia's immigration policy'.[12] In documenting policy changes affecting international students, Peter Mares has quoted one student (as if in response to Minister Evans): '"I like Australia and I want to make a contribution here," he told me, "but it's hard if there is no reciprocity"'.[13] Joo-Cheong Tham has observed that temporary migrants' criticism of policy settings in general is often dismissed

11 Organisation for Security and Cooperation in Europe, International Organization for Migration and International Labour Organization, *Handbook on Establishing Effective Labour Migration Policies in Countries of Origin and Destination* (2006), 115.

12 Mary-Anne Toy, 'Migration Rules Set for Revamp', *The Age*, 31 August 2009.

13 Peter Mares, 'Lives on Hold', *Inside Story*, 2 May 2011.

'as illegitimate, or worse as shameful ingratitude'.[14] Indeed, he has traced this attitude through the executive law-making processes (through regulations and government gazetted skills lists) that effected the 2009 reforms to the 457 visa, in particular the absence of accountability mechanisms for the people arguably most impacted by these rules: the visa workers themselves.[15] The principal consultation in those legislative drafting processes occurred via the Skilled Migration Consultative Panel, which consisted of four state governments, the Australian Council of Trade Unions and four industry representatives. Tham points out that 457 visa workers received no adequate opportunity to comment on proposed changes, nor could it be assumed that 'trade unions were adequately representing such workers as distinct from the interest of Australian workers'.[16]

Lack of consultation coupled with unreasonably swift legal reforms continue to be the hallmark of this visa scheme. When major reforms were made to the 457 visa scheme in 2013, legislative amendments were rushed through parliament on the last sitting day before a federal election. The Law Council of Australia opposed these amendments because their hasty introduction and passage through parliament lacked adequate consultation.[17] The acute lack of parliamentary accountability might, for citizens, be marginally ameliorated by the opportunity to exact electoral accountability. Migrant workers, whose interests are among the most affected, are denied this opportunity to provide feedback. One of the many novel elements of the 2013 reform package was to enshrine in statute the role of the Ministerial Advisory Council on Skilled Migration, comprising unions, industry and government representatives to provide advice to the Minister.[18] The government-commissioned Azarias review reporting in 2014 strongly recommended the continuation of a tripartite ministerial advisory council,[19] but, throughout the life of the scheme, little meaningful endeavour has been made to consult with the hundreds of thousands of 457 visa workers in Australia over the years. It is, therefore, critical that an agency be established to organise migrant workers, consult with the migrant worker community and represent its interests and lobby government authorities on behalf of

14 Joo-Cheong Tham, 'Multiculturalism and Temporary Migration: Where Does Justice Fit?' (Paper presented to the Australian Multicultural Council, draft on file with author), 17.
15 Joo-Cheong Tham, 'Law-Making and Temporary Migrant Labour Schemes: Accountability and the 457 Visa Scheme' (2009) 17 *Australian Journal of Administrative Law* 18.
16 Ibid. 20.
17 Law Council of Australia, Submission No 24 to the Senate Standing Committee on Legal and Constitutional Affairs, Parliament of Australia, 'Inquiry into the Migration Amendment (Temporary Sponsored Visas) Bill 2013', 21 June 2013, 2. The Senate referred the Bill to the Senate Legal and Constitutional Affairs Legislation Committee on 18 June 2013; the opportunity for submissions to the Senate inquiry closed on 20 June 2013.
18 *Migration Act* s 140AB(2).
19 John Azarias *et al.*, *Robust New Foundations: A Streamlined, Transparent and Responsive System for the 457 Programme* (September 2014), 49.

workers' rights. It might also provide a portal for complaints, interpretation services and access to justice for non-citizen workers.

Temporary labour migration as revolution

Many have described the upswing in temporary labour migration as a revolution.[20] It comprehensively challenges the notion that industrial justice is achievable only if the labour market sits neatly within the community of residents. This (now antiquated) view was quintessentially embodied in the aspiration for the 'Australian standard' at Federation. In contemporary Australia, as in every nation in the world, temporary and unauthorised migrant workers live at once within multiple political communities of their home state, their destination state and of a globalised economy. Migrant workers contribute to the wider material well-being of each: home states benefit from remittances, migrants' skills acquired during migration and lesser pressure on domestic labour markets; states of employment benefit from workers' productivity, tax and increasing demand for goods and services. Workers have investments in each of these communities and leave an imprint on each.

Engagement between employees and employers, migrants and residents, inevitably creates mutual dependencies and obligations of care, out of which grows an ethic of reciprocity and obligation. Countries like Australia cannot 'will away' people like Hwang on whom it does not wish to have an impact. Under the influence of regulatory power in the country in which they work, temporary or unauthorised non-citizens like Hwang must be permitted a stronger voice in how it is exercised.

20 Mary Crock, *Immigration and Refugee Law in Australia* (Federation Press, 1998), 92; Andrew Markus, James Jupp and Peter McDonald, *Australia's Immigration Revolution* (Allen & Unwin, 2009).

Select bibliography

Secondary references

Agustin, Laura, *Sex at the Margins: Migration, Labour Markets and the Rescue Industry* (Zed Books, 2007).

Ahmad, Muneer, 'Developing Citizenship' (2011) 9(1) *Issues in Legal Scholarship* 8.

Alcorso, Caroline, 'Immigrant Employees in Hotels' (2003) 14(1) *Labour & Industry* 17.

Alcorso, Caroline, *Improving Occupational Health and Safety Information to Immigrant Workers in NSW* (report prepared for WorkCover NSW, 2002).

Aleinikoff, T. Alexander, *Semblances of Sovereignty: The Constitution, the State and American Citizenship* (Harvard University Press, 2002).

Anderson, Bridget, 'Migration, Immigration Controls and the Fashioning of Precarious Workers' (2010) 24 *Work, Employment and Society* 300.

Anderson, Bridget, 'What's in a Name? Immigration Controls and Subjectivities: The Case of Au Pairs and Domestic Worker Visa Holders in the UK' (2009) 29 *Subjectivity* 407.

Anderson, Bridget, 'Where's the Harm in That? Immigration Enforcement, Trafficking and the Protection of Migrants' Rights' (2012) 56 *American Behavioral Scientist* 1241.

Anderson, Bridget and Andrijasevic, Rutvica, 'Sex, Slaves and Citizens: The Politics of Anti-Trafficking' (2008) 40 *Soundings* 135.

Anderson, Bridget and Ruhs, Martin, 'Researching Illegality and Labour Migration' (2010) 16 *Population, Space and Place* 175.

Arendt, Hannah, *The Origins of Totalitarianism* (Harcourt Brace, 1951).

Australian Human Rights Commission, *Principles to Promote the Rights of International Students* (2012).

Azarias, John, Lambert, Jenny, McDonald, Peter and Malyon, Katie, *Robust New Foundations: A Streamlined, Transparent and Responsive System for the 457 Programme* (September 2014).

Baas, Michiel, 'Students of Migration: Indian Overseas Students and the Question of Permanent Residency' (2006) 14(1) *People and Place* 9.

Baird, Bruce, *Stronger, Simpler, Smarter ESOS: Supporting International Students. Final Report on the Review of the Education Services for Overseas Students Act 2000* (Department of Education and Workplace Relations, 2010).

Banivanua-Mar, Tracey, *Violence and Colonial Dialogue: The Australian Pacific Indentured Labor Trade* (University of Hawaii Press, 2007).

Bauböck, Rainer, 'Citizenship and Free Movement' in Rogers M. Smith (ed.), *Citizenship, Borders and Human Needs* (University of Pennsylvania Press, 2011) 343.

Bauböck, Rainer, *Transnational Citizenship: Membership Rights in International Migration* (Edward Elgar, 1994).
Bauder, Harald, *Labour Movement: How Migration Regulates Labour Markets* (Oxford University Press, 2006).
Benhabib, Seyla, *The Rights of Others: Aliens, Residents and Citizens* (Cambridge University Press, 2004).
Benhabib, Seyla, 'Twilight of Sovereignty or the Emergence of Cosmopolitan Norms? Rethinking Citizenship in Volatile Times' in Heather Gautney, Omar Dabour, Ashley Dawson and Neil Smith (eds), *Democracy, States and the Struggle for Global Justice* (Routledge, 2009) 79.
Berg, Laurie, 'At the Border and Between the Cracks: The Precarious Position of Irregular Migrant Workers under International Law' (2007) 8 *Melbourne Journal of International Law* 1.
Berg, Laurie, '"Mate, Speak English, You're in Australia Now": English Language Requirements in Skilled Migration' (2011) 36(20) *Alternative Law Journal* 110.
Berg, Laurie and Samson, Anna, 'Space for Economic Migrants? Poverty, Migrants and Australian Civil Society' in Helmut Anheier, Marlies Glasius and Mary Kaldor (eds), *Global Civil Society Yearbook 2009: Global Civil Society and Poverty Alleviation* (SAGE Publications Ltd, 2009).
Berman, Joanne, '(Un)popular Strangers and Crises (Un)bounded: Discourses of Sex-Trafficking, the European Political Community and the Panicked States of the Modern State' (2003) 9(1) *European Journal of International Relations* 37.
Bertone, Santina, *From Factory Fodder to Multicultural Mediators: A New Typology of Immigrant Work Experiences in Australia* (VDM Verlag, 2008).
Biao, Xiang, 'Structuration of Indian Information Technology Professionals' Migration to Australia: An Ethnographic Study' (2001) 39(5) *International Migration* 73.
Bibler Coutin, Susan, 'Prohibited Realities and Fractured Persons: Remaking Lives in Transnational Spaces' (2011) 9(1) *Issues in Legal Scholarship* Article 8.
Birrell, Bob and Healy, Ernest, *Immigration and Unemployment in 2014* (Centre for Population and Urban Research, Monash University, 2014).
Birrell, Bob and Healy, Ernest, *Immigration Overshoot* (Research Report, Centre for Population and Urban Research, Monash University, 2012).
Birrell, Bob, Hawthorne, Lesleyanne and Richardson, Sue, *Evaluation of the General Skilled Migration Categories* (Commonwealth of Australia, 2006).
Bissett, Michelle and Landau, Ingrid, 'Australia's 457 Visa Scheme and the Rights of Migrant Workers' (2008) 33 *Alternative Law Journal* 142.
Boese, Martina, Campbell, Iain, Roberts, Winsome and Tham, Joo-Cheong, 'Temporary Migrant Nurses in Australia: Sites and Sources of Precariousness' (2013) 24(3) *The Economic and Labour Relations Review* 316.
Bosniak, Linda, 'Being Here: Ethical Territoriality and the Rights of Immigrants' (2007) 8(2) *Theoretical Inquiries in Law* 389.
Bosniak, Linda, *The Citizen and the Alien* (Princeton University Press, 2006).
Bosniak, Linda, 'Membership, Equality, and the Difference that Alienage Makes' (1994) 69 *New York University Law Review* 1047.
Bosniak, Linda, 'Persons and Citizens in Constitutional Thought' (2010) 8(1) *International Journal of Constitutional Law* 9.
Boswell, Christina, 'The Elusive Rights of an Invisible Population' (2008) 22(2) *Ethics and International Affairs* 187.

Boucher, Anna and Carney, Terry, 'Social Security for Migrant Workers and Their Families in Australia: More Australian Exceptionalism?' in Pablo Arellano, Gisbert Vonk and Marius Olivier (eds), *Social Security and Migrant Workers* (Kluwer, 2013) 187.

Brubaker, Rogers, *Citizenship and Nationhood in France and Germany* (Harvard University Press, 1992).

Burn, Jennifer and Simmons, Frances, 'Rewarding Witnesses, Ignoring Victims: An Evaluation of the New Trafficking Visa Framework' (2005) 24 *Immigration Review* 6.

Burn, Jennifer and Simmons, Frances, 'Trafficking and Slavery in Australia: An Evaluation of Victim Support Strategies' (2006) 15 *Asian and Pacific Migration Journal* 553.

Burn, Jennifer, Hollonds, Jemma, Power, Kate, Simmons, Frances and Stewart, Pam, *Hidden Exploitation: Women in Forced Labour, Marriage and Migration* (Anti-Slavery Australia and Jumbunna Indigenous House of Learning at UTS, 2012).

Butler, Judith, *Frames of War: When is Life Grievable?* (Verso, 2009).

Butler, Judith, *Precarious Life: The Powers of Mourning and Violence* (Verso, 2004).

Calavita, Kitty, 'Employer Sanctions Violations: Toward a Dialectical Model of White-Collar Crime' (1990) 24 *Law and Society Review* 1041.

Campbell, Iain and Tham, Joo-Cheong, 'Labour Market Deregulation and Temporary Migrant Labour Schemes: An Analysis of the 457 Visa Program' (2013) 26 *Australian Journal of Labour Law* 239.

Campbell, Michael, 'Perspectives on Working Conditions of Temporary Migrant Workers in Australia' (2010) 18(2) *People and Place* 51.

Carens, Joseph, 'Aliens and Citizens: The Case for Open Borders' (1987) 49 *Review of Politics* 251.

Carens, Joseph, *The Ethics of Immigration* (Oxford University Press, 2013).

Carens, Joseph, *Immigrants and the Right to Stay* (MIT Press, 2010).

Carens, Joseph, 'The Rights of Irregular Migrants' (2008) 22(2) *Ethics and International Affairs* 163.

Carney, Terry, 'Securing Social Security for Migrant Workers: Orthodox Approaches or an Alternative (Regional/Political) Path for Southern Africa?' (2010) 18(1) *African Journal of International and Comparative Law* 24.

Castles, Stephen and Davidson, Alastair, *Citizenship and Migration: Globalization and the Politics of Belonging* (Macmillan, 2000).

Castles, Stephen and Miller, Mark, *The Age of Migration: International Population Movements in the Modern World* (Palgrave-Macmillan and Guilford Books, 2009).

Chacón, Jennifer, 'Misery and Myopia: Understanding the Failures of US Efforts to Stop Human Trafficking' (2006) 74 *Fordham Law Review* 2977.

Chang, Grace and Kim, Kathleen, 'Reconceptualizing Approaches to Human Trafficking: New Directions and Perspectives from the Field(s)' (2007) 3 *Stanford Journal of Civil Rights and Civil Liberties* 317.

Chuang, Janie A., 'Rescuing Trafficking from Ideological Capture: Prostitution Reform and Anti-Trafficking Law and Policy' (2010) 158 *University of Pennsylvania Law Review* 1655.

Colic-Peisker, Val, 'A New Era in Australian Multiculturalism? From Working-Class "Ethnics" to a "Multicultural Middle-Class"' (2011) 45(3) *International Migration Review* 562.

Collins, Jock, 'Globalisation, Immigration and the Second Long Post-War Boom in Australia' (2008) 61 *Journal of Australian Political Economy* 244.

Collins, Jock, *Migrant Hands in a Distant Land: Australia's Post-War Immigration* (Pluto Press, 2nd edn, 1991).

Costello, Cathryn, 'Accidents of Place and Parentage: Birthright Citizenship and Border Crossings' in O. Doyle (ed.), *The Citizenship Referendum: Implications for the Constitution and Human Rights* (Law School Trinity College Dublin, 2004) 5.

Crépeau, François and Samaddar, Ranabir, 'Recognizing the Dignity of Migrants' (2011) 37 *Refugee Watch – A South Asian Journal on Forced Migration* 55.

Crock, Mary, 'Contract or Compact' in Mary Crock (ed.), *Nation Skilling: Migration Labour and the Law* (Federation Press, 2002) 55.

Crock, Mary and Berg, Laurie, *Immigration, Refugees and Forced Migration: Law, Policy and Practice in Australia* (Federation Press, 2011).

Crock, Mary and Friedman, Leah, 'Immigration Control and the Shaping of Australia's Labour Market: Conflicting Ideologies or Historical Imperatives?' in Christopher Arup, Peter Gahan, John Howe, Richard Johnstone, Richard Mitchell and Anthony O'Donnell (eds), *Labour Law and Labour Market Regulation: Essays on the Construction, Constitution and Regulation of Labour Markets and Work Relationships* (Federation Press, 2006) 322.

Crock, Mary, Howe, Sean and McCallum, Ron, 'Conflicted Priorities? Enforcing Fairness for Temporary Migrant Workers in Australia' in Cathryn Costello and Mark Freedland (eds), *Migrants at Work: Immigration and Vulnerability in Labour Law* (Oxford University Press, 2014) 422.

Cronin, Kathryn, 'A Culture of Control: An Overview of Immigration Policy-Making' in James Jupp and Marie Kabala (eds), *The Politics of Australian Immigration* (Australian Government Publishing Service, 1993) 83.

Cullen, Miriam and McSherry, Bernadette, 'Without Sex: Slavery, Trafficking in Persons and the Exploitation of Labour in Australia' (2009) 34(1) *Alternative Law Journal* 4.

Dahl, Robert A., *After the Revolution? Authority in a Good Society* (Yale University Press, 1970).

Dauvergne, Catherine, *Making People Illegal: What Globalization Means for Migration and Law* (Cambridge University Press, 2008).

Dauvergne, Catherine and Marsden, Sarah, 'The Ideology of Temporary Labour Migration in the Post-Global Era' (2014) 18(2) *Citizenship Studies* 224.

David, Fiona, *Labour Trafficking* (Research and Public Policy Series No 108, Australian Institute of Criminology, 2010).

Deegan, Barbara, *Visa Subclass 457 Integrity Review: Final Report* (Commonwealth of Australia, 2008).

De Genova, Nicholas, 'Migrant "Illegality" and Deportability in Everyday Life' (2002) 31 *Annual Review of Anthropology* 419.

Department of Immigration and Multicultural Affairs, *The Hidden Workforce: Illegal Workers in Australia and Those that Would Join Them* (1999).

Department of Immigration and Multicultural Affairs, *Review of Illegal Workers in Australia: Improving Immigration Compliance in the Workplace* (1999).

Deumert, Ana, Marginson, Simon, Nyland, Chris, Ramia, Gaby and Sawir, Erlenawati, 'Global Migration and Social Protection Rights: The Social and Economic Security of Cross-Border Students in Australia' (2005) 5 *Global Social Policy* 329.

Deumert, Ana, Marginson, Simon, Nyland, Chris, Ramia, Gaby and Sawir, Erlenawati, *The Social and Economic Security of International Students in Australia: A Study of 200 Student Cases* (Monash Centre for Research in International Education, 2005).

Dewhurst, Elaine, 'Models of Protection of the Right of Irregular Immigrants to Back Pay: The Impact of the Interconnection Between Immigration Law and Labor Law' (2014) 35 *Comparative Labor Law and Policy Journal* 217.

Fineman, Martha A., *The Autonomy Myth: A Theory of Dependency* (The New Press, 2004).

Fineman, Martha A., 'The Vulnerable Subject: Anchoring Equality in the Human Condition' (2008) 20 *Yale Journal of Law and Feminism* 1.

Fineman, Martha A., 'The Vulnerable Subject and the Responsive State' (2010) 60 *Emory Law Journal* 251.

Fitzgerald, John, *Big White Lie: Chinese Australians in White Australia* (UNSW Press, 2007).

Fudge, Judy, 'Precarious Employment in Australia and Canada: The Road to Labour Law Reform' (2006) 19 *Australian Journal of Labour Law* 105.

Fudge, Judy, 'Precarious Migrant Status and Precarious Employment: The Paradox of International Rights for Migrant Workers' (2012) 34 *Comparative Labour Law and Policy Journal* 95.

Fudge, Judy and Owens, Rosemary (eds), *Precarious Work, Women, and the New Economy: The Challenge to Legal Norms* (Hart, 2006).

Gallagher, Anne, *The International Law of Human Trafficking* (Cambridge University Press, 2010).

Gibney, Matthew J., 'Is Deportation a Form of Forced Migration?' (2013) 32(2) *Refugee Survey Quarterly* 116.

Gibney, Matthew, *Precarious Residents: Migration Control, Membership and the Rights of Non-Citizens* (Human Development Reports Research Paper No 2009/10, United Nations Development Programme: 2009).

Glick Schiller, Nina, Basch, Linda and Blanc-Szanton, Cristina, *Towards a Transnational Perspective on Migration: Race, Class, Ethnicity and Nationalism Reconsidered* (New York Academy of Sciences, 1992).

Goldring, Luin, Berinstein, Carolina and Bernhard, Judith K., 'Institutionalizing Precarious Migratory Status in Canada' (2009) 13(3) *Citizenship Studies* 239.

Gordon, Jennifer, 'Tensions in Rhetoric and Reality at the Intersection of Work and Immigration' (2012) 2 *UC Irvine Law Review* 125.

Gould, Carol, 'Envisioning Transnational Democracy: Cross-Border Communities and Regional Human Rights Frameworks' in Heather Gautney, Omar Dabour, Ashley Dawson and Neil Smith (eds), *Democracy, States and the Struggle for Global Justice* (Routledge, 2009) 63.

Gould, Carol, *Globalizing Democracy and Human Rights* (Cambridge University Press, 2004).

Graycar, Adam, *Racism and the Tertiary Student Experience in Australia* (The Academy of Social Sciences in Australia, 2010).

Grewcock, Michael, 'Back to the Future: Australian Border Policing Under Labor, 2007–2013' (2014) 3(1) *State Crime* 102.

Griffith, Kati L., 'Discovering "Immployment" Law: The Constitutionality of Subfederal Immigration Regulation at Work' (2011) 29 *Yale Law and Policy Review* 389.

Guild, Elspeth, 'Who is an Irregular Migrant' in Barbara Bogusz (ed.), *Irregular Migration and Human Rights: Theoretical, European and International Perspectives* (Martinus Nijhoff Publishers, 2004) 3.

Guthrie, Robert and Quinlan, Michael, 'The Occupational Safety and Health Rights and Workers' Compensation Entitlements of Illegal Immigrants: An Emerging Challenge' (2005) 3(2) *Policy and Practice in Health and Safety* 69.

Guthrie, Robert and Taseff, Rebecca, 'Dismissal and Discrimination: Illegal Workers in England and Australia' (2008) 24 *International Journal of Comparative Labour Law and Industrial Relations* 31.

Habermas, Jürgen, 'Citizenship and National Identity' in Bart van Steenbergen (ed.), *The Condition of Citizenship* (Sage, 1994) 20.

Habermas, Jürgen, Cronin, Ciaran and De Greiff, Pablo (eds), *The Inclusion of the Other: Studies in Political Theory* (MIT Press, 1998).

Harding, Glenys and Webster, Elizabeth, *The Working Holiday Maker Scheme and the Australian Labour Market* (Melbourne Institute of Applied Economic and Social Research, University of Melbourne, 2002).

Harris, Rachel and Gelber, Katharine, 'Defining "De Facto" Slavery in Australia: Ownership, Consent and the Defence of Freedom' (2011) 11(3) *International Criminal Law Review* 561.

Hartley, Lisa and Fleay, Caroline, *Policy as Punishment: Asylum Seekers in the Community Without the Right to Work* (Curtin University Centre for Human Rights Education, 2014).

Hawthorne, Lesleyanne, 'How Valuable is "Two-Step Migration"? Labor Market Outcomes for International Student Migrants to Australia' (2010) 19 *Asian and Pacific Migration Journal* 5.

Hawthorne, Lesleyanne, '"Picking Winners": The Recent Transformation of Australia's Skilled Migration Policy' (2005) 39(3) *International Migration Review* 663.

Held, David, *Democracy and the Global Order: From the Modern State to Cosmopolitan Governance* (Polity Press, 1995).

Ho, Christina and Alcorso, Caroline, 'Migrants and Employment: Challenging the Success Story' (2004) 40(3) *Journal of Sociology* 237.

Honig, Bonnie, *Democracy and the Stranger* (Princeton University Press, 2001).

Howe, Joanna, 'The *Migration Legislation Amendment (Worker Protection) Act 2008*: Long Overdue Reform, But Have Migrant Workers Been Sold Short?' (2010) 24 *Australian Journal of Labour Law* 251.

Howe, Joanna, 'Is the Net Cast Too Wide? An Assessment of Whether the Regulatory Design of the 457 Visa Meets Australia's Skill Needs' (2013) 41 *Federal Law Review* 443.

Howells, Stephen, *Report of the 2010 Review of the* Migration Amendment (Employer Sanctions) Act 2007 (Commonwealth of Australia, 2011).

Hugo, Graeme, 'Temporary Migration and the Labour Market in Australia' (2006) 37(2) *Australian Geographer* 211.

International Labour Organization, *The Cost of Coercion: Global Report under the follow-up to the ILO Declaration on Fundamental Principles and Rights at Work* (International Labour Conference 98th Session: 2009).

International Labour Organization, *A Global Alliance Against Forced Labour* (International Labour Conference, 93rd session, 2005).

International Labour Organization, *Towards a Fair Deal for Migrant Workers in the Global Economy* (2004).

Isin, Engin F., 'Citizenship in Flux: The Figure of the Activist Citizen' (2009) 29 *Subjectivity* 367.

Jacobson, David, *Rights Across Borders: Immigration and the Decline of Citizenship* (Johns Hopkins University Press, 1996).

Jockel, Maria, *457 Visa Law: Addressing Australia's Skilled Labour Shortage* (Lawbook Co, 2008).

Johnstone, Richard, McCrystal, Shae, Nossar, Igor, Quinlan, Michael, Rawling, Michael, Riley, Joellen, *Beyond Employment: The Legal Regulation of Work Relationships* (Federation Press, 2012).
Jupp, James, *From White Australia to Woomera: The Story of Australian Immigration* (Cambridge University Press, 2002).
Kempadoo, Kemala, 'From Moral Panic to Global Justice: Changing Perspectives on Trafficking' in Kemala Kempadoo, Jyoti Sanghera and Bandana Pattanaik (eds), *Trafficking and Prostitution Reconsidered: New Perspectives on Migration, Sex Work and Human Rights* (Paradigm Publishers, 2005) vii.
Kinnaird, Bob, 'Current Issues in the Skilled Temporary Subclass 457 Visa' (2006) 14 *People and Place* 49.
Khoo, Siew-Ean, Hugo, Graeme and McDonald, Peter, 'Which Skilled Temporary Migrants Become Permanent Residents and Why' (2008) 42 *International Migration Review* 193.
Khoo, Siew-Ean, McDonald, Peter, Voigt-Graf, Carmen and Hugo, Graeme, 'A Global Labour Market: Factors Motivating the Sponsorship and Temporary Migration of Skilled Workers into Australia' (2007) 41(2) *International Migration Review* 480.
Kim, Kathleen, 'The Trafficked Worker as Private Attorney General: A Model for Enforcing the Civil Rights of Undocumented Workers' (2009) *University of Chicago Legal Forum* 247.
Kneebone, Susan and Debeljak, Julie, *Transnational Crime and Human Rights: Responses to Human Trafficking in the Greater Mekong Subregion* (Routledge, 2012).
Knight, Michael, *Strategic Review of the Student Visa Program 2011: Report* (Commonwealth of Australia, 2011).
Kymlicka, Wil, 'Citizenship in an Era of Globalization: Commentary on Held' in Ian Shapiro and Casiano Hacker-Cordón (eds), *Democracy's Edges* (Cambridge University Press, 1999) 112.
Layman, Lenore, 'To Keep Up the Australian Standard: Regulating Contract Migration 1901–1950' (1996) 70 *Labour History* 25.
Lee, Stephen, 'Monitoring Immigration Enforcement' (2011) 53 *Arizona Law Review* 1089.
Lee, Stephen, 'Screening for Solidarity' (2013) 80 *University of Chicago Law Review* 224.
Legomsky, Stephen, 'Portraits of the Undocumented Immigrant: Epiphany Through Dialectic' (2009) 44 *Georgia Law Review* 65.
MacDermott, Therese and Opeskin, Brian, 'Regulating Pacific Seasonal Labour in Australia' (2010) 83(2) *Pacific Affairs* 283.
Macklin, Audrey, 'Freeing Migration from the State: Michael Trebilcock on Migration Policy' (2010) 60 *University of Toronto Law Journal* 315.
Maclellan, Nic and Mares, Peter, 'Labour Mobility in the Pacific: Creating Seasonal Work Programs in Australia' in Stewart Firth (ed.), *Globalisation and Governance in the Pacific Islands* (ANU E Press, 2006) ch. 8.
Mares, Peter, 'Fear and Instrumentalism: Australian Policy Responses to Migration from the Global South' (2011) 100(415) *The Round Table: The Commonwealth Journal of International Affairs* 407.
Mares, Peter, 'The Permanent Shift to Temporary Migration' in Suvendrini Perera, Graeme Seal and Sue Summers (eds), *Enter At Own Risk? Australia's Population Questions for the 21st Century* (Black Swan Press, 2010) 65.
Marginson, Simon, 'Global Position and Position Taking: The Case of Australia' (2007) 11(1) *Journal of Studies in International Education* 5.

Marginson, Simon, Nyland, Christopher, Sawir, Erlenawati and Forbes-Mewett, Helen, *International Student Security* (Cambridge University Press, 2010).

Markus, Andrew, *Fear & Hatred: Purifying Australia & California 1850–1901* (Hale and Iremonger, 1979).

Markus, Andrew, Jupp, James and McDonald, Peter, *Australia's Immigration Revolution* (Allen & Unwin, 2009).

Martin, Philip, Abella, Manolo and Kuptsch, Christiane, *Managing Labor Migration in the Twenty-First Century* (Yale University Press, 2006).

Martin, Philip, and Ruhs, Martin, 'Independent Commissions and Labour Migration: The British MAC' (2014) 11(1) *Migration Letters* 23.

Mathew, Penelope, *Reworking the Relationship between Asylum and Employment* (Routledge, 2012).

McCallum, Ron, 'Australian Labor Law, Migration and the Performance of Work' (2002) 16 *Georgetown Immigration Law Journal* 637.

McDowell, Linda, Batnitzky, Adina and Dyer, Sarah, 'Global Flows and Local Labour Markets: Precarious Employment and Migrant Workers in the UK' in Jacqueline Scott, Shirley Dex and Anke C. Plagnol (eds), *Gendered Lives: Gender Inequalities in Production and Reproduction* (Edward Elgar, 2012) 123.

McGrath, Siobhán, 'Many Chains to Break: The Multi-Dimensional Concept of Slave Labour in Brazil' (2012) 45 *Antipode* 1005.

McGrath-Champ, Susan, Rosewarne, Stuart and Rittau, Yasmin, 'From One Skill Shortage to the Next: The Australian Construction Industry and Geographies of a Global Labour Market' (2011) 53 *Journal of Industrial Relations* 467.

McNevin, Anne, *Contesting Citizenship: Irregular Migrants and the New Frontiers of the Political* (Columbia University Press, 2011).

McSherry, Bernadette and Kneebone, Susan, 'Trafficking in Women and Forced Migration: Moving Victims Across the Border of Crime into the Domain of Human Rights' (2008) 12(1) *International Journal of Human Rights* 67.

Medina, Maria Isabel, 'Employer Sanctions in the United States, Canada and Mexico: Exploring the Criminalization of Immigration Law' (1996) 3 *Southwestern Journal of Law and Trade in the Americas* 333.

Medina, Maria Isabel, 'The Criminalization of Immigration Law: Employer Sanctions and Marriage Fraud' (1997) 5 *George Mason Law Review* 669.

Miles, Robert, *Capitalism and Unfree Labour: Anomaly or Necessity?* (Travistock Publications, 1987).

Minow, Martha, 'Lawyering for Human Dignity' (2002) 11 *American University Journal of Gender, Social Policy and Law* 143.

Motomura, Hiroshi, 'Designing Temporary Worker Programs' (2013) 80 *The University of Chicago Law Review* 263.

Motomura, Hiroshi, *Immigration Outside the Law* (Oxford University Press, 2014).

Motomura, Hiroshi, 'The Rights of Others: Legal Claims and Immigration Outside the Law' (2010) 59 *Duke Law Journal* 1723.

Nasu, Hitoshi, 'Reform of Subclass 457 Visa Scheme: Proposal of Three Models' (2008) 33(3) *Alternative Law Journal* 147.

Neilson, Brett and Rossiter, Ned, 'From Precarity to Precariousness and Back Again: Labour, Life and Unstable Networks' (2005) 5(22) *Fibreculture* 1.

Ngai, Mae M., *Impossible Subjects: Illegal Aliens and the Making of Modern America* (Princeton University Press, 2005).

Nicholls, Glenn, *Deported: A History of Forced Departures from Australia* (UNSW Press, 2007).

Nyland, Chris, Forbes-Mewett, Helen, Marginson, Simon, Ramia, Gaby, Sawir, Erlanawati, Smith, Sharon, 'International Student-Workers in Australia: A New Vulnerable Workforce' (2009) 22(1) *Journal of Education and Work* 1.

O'Donnell, Anthony and Mitchell, Richard, 'Immigrant Labour in Australia: The Regulatory Framework' (2001) 14 *Australian Journal of Labour Law* 269.

O'Connell Davidson, Julia, 'New Slavery, Old Binaries: Human Trafficking and the Borders of "Freedom"' (2010) 10(2) *Global Networks* 244.

Oke, Nicole, 'Temporary Migration, Transnational Politics? The Politics of Temporary Migration in Australia' (2012) 33(1) *Journal of Intercultural Studies* 85.

Ong, Danny and Ramia, Gaby, 'Study-Work-Life Balance and the Welfare of International Students' (2009) 20(2) *Labour and Industry* 181.

Orr, Graeme, 'Unauthorised Workers: Labouring Beneath the Law?' in Christopher Arup, Peter Gahan, John Howe, Richard Johnstone, Richard N. Mitchell and Anthony O'Donnell (eds), *Labour Law and Labour Market Regulation: Essays on the Construction, Constitution and Regulation of Labour Markets and Work Relationships* (Federation Press, 2006) 677.

Owens, Rosemary, Riley, Joellen and Murray, Jill, *The Law of Work* (Oxford University Press, 2nd edn, 2011).

Pickering, Sharon, Segrave, Marie, Tazreiter, Claudia and Weber, Leanne, 'Migration Control and Human Security' in Satvinder S. Juss (ed.), *The Ashgate Research Companion to Migration Law, Theory and Policy* (Ashgate, 2013) 535.

Piore, Michael J., *Birds of Passage: Migrant Labour and Industrial Societies* (Cambridge University Press, 1979).

Quinlan, Michael and Lever-Tracy, Constance, 'From Labour Market Exclusion to Industrial Solidarity: Australian Trade Union Responses to Asian Workers, 1830–1988' (1990) 14 *Cambridge Journal of Economics* 159.

Reilly, Alexander, 'The Ethics of Seasonal Labour Migration' (2011) 20(1) *Griffith Law Review* 127.

Reilly, Alexander, 'Protecting Vulnerable Migrant Workers: The Case of International Students' (2012) 25 *Australian Journal of Labour Law* 181.

Robertson, Shanthi, 'Time and Temporary Migration: The Case of Temporary Graduate Workers and Working Holiday Makers in Australia' (2014) 40(12) *Journal of Ethnic and Migration Studies* 1915.

Robertson, Shanthi, *Transnational Student-Migrants and the State: The Education-Migration Nexus* (Palgrave Macmillan 2013).

Robertson, Shanthi and Runganaikaloo, Anjena, 'Lives in Limbo: Migration Experiences in Australia's Education-Migration Nexus' (2014) 14(2) *Ethnicities* 208.

Rogaly, Ben, 'Migrant Workers in the ILO's Global Alliance Against Forced Labour Report: A Critical Appraisal' (2008) 29(7) *Third World Quarterly* 1431.

Rosewarne, Stuart, 'Globalisation and Commodification of Labour: Temporary Labour Migration' (2010) 20(2) *Economic and Labour Relations Review* 99.

Rubenstein, Kim, *Australian Citizenship Law in Context* (Lawbook Co., 2002).

Rubio-Marin, Ruth, *Immigration as Democratic Challenge: Citizenship and Inclusion in Germany and the United States* (Cambridge University Press, 2000).

Ruhs, Martin, *The Price of Rights: Regulating International Labor Migration* (Princeton University Press, 2013).

Ruhs, Martin and Anderson, Bridget, 'Semi-Compliance and Illegality in Migrant Labour Markets: An Analysis of Migrants, Employers and the State in the UK' (2010) 16 *Population, Space and Place* 195.

Ruhs, Martin and Martin, Philip, 'Numbers vs Rights: Trade-offs and Guestworker Programs' (2008) 42(1) *International Migration Review* 249.

Ryan, Bernard, 'Employer Checks of Immigration Status and Employment Law' in Cathryn Costello and Mark Freedland (eds), *Migrants at Work: Immigration and Vulnerability in Labour Law* (Oxford University Press, 2014) 239.

Ryan, Bernard, 'The Evolving Legal Regime on Unauthorized Work by Migrants in Britain' (2005) 27 *Comparative Labor Law and Policy Journal* 27.

Sassen, Saskia, *Losing Control? Sovereignty in an Age of Globalization* (Columbia University Press, 1996).

Schloenhardt, Andreas and Jolly, Jarrod, *Trafficking in Persons in Australia: Myths and Realities* (LexisNexis Butterworths, 2013).

Schloenhardt, Andreas and Loong, Mark, 'Return and Reintegration of Human Trafficking Victims from Australia' (2011) 23(2) *International Journal of Refugee Law* 143.

Segrave, Marie and Milivojevi , Sanja, 'Auditing the Australian Response to Trafficking' (2010) 22 *Current Issues in Criminal Justice* 63.

Segrave, Marie, Milivojevic, Sanja and Pickering, Sharon, *Sex Trafficking: International Context and Response* (Willan Publishing, 2009).

Shachar, Ayelet, *The Birthright Lottery: Citizenship and Global Inequality* (Harvard University Press, 2009).

Simmons, Frances, 'Making Possibilities Realities: Compensation for Trafficked People' (2012) 34 *Sydney Law Review* 511.

Simmons, Frances and David, Fiona, 'The Road to Effective Remedies: Pragmatic Reasons for Treating Cases of "Sex Trafficking" in the Australian Sex Industry as a Form of "Labour Trafficking"' (2012) 1 *Anti-Trafficking Review* 60.

Soysal, Yasemin, *Limits of Citizenship: Migrants and Postnational Membership in Europe* (University of Chicago Press, 1994).

Standing, Guy, *The Precariat: The New Dangerous Class* (Bloomsbury Academic, 2011).

Steinfeld, Robert J., *Coercion, Contract and Free Labor in the Nineteenth Century* (Cambridge University Press, 2001).

Steinfeld, Robert J., *The Invention of Free Labor: The Employment Relation in English and American Law and Culture, 1350–1870* (University of North Carolina Press, 1991).

Tan, Yan and Lester, Laurence, 'Labour Market and Economic Impacts of International Working Holiday Temporary Migrants to Australia' (2012) 18 *Population, Space and Place* 359.

Tham, Joo-Cheong, 'Law-Making and Temporary Migrant Labour Schemes: Accountability and the 457 Visa Scheme' (2009) 17 *Australian Journal of Administrative Law* 18.

Tham, Joo-Cheong and Campbell, Iain, 'Temporary Migrant Labour in Australia: The 457 Visa Scheme and Challenges for Labour Regulation' (Working Paper No 50, Centre for Employment and Labour Relations Law, University of Melbourne, 2011).

Toh, Stephanie and Quinlan, Michael, 'Safeguarding the Global Contingent Workforce? Guestworkers in Australia' (2009) 30(5) *International Journal of Manpower* 453.

Velayutham, Selvaraj, 'Precarious Experiences of Indians in Australia on 457 Temporary Work Visas' (2013) 24 *The Economic and Labour Relations Review* 340.

Vosko, Leah, *Managing the Margins: Gender, Citizenship and the International Regulation of Precarious Employment* (Oxford University Press, 2010).

Vosko, Leah, *Precarious Employment: Understanding Labour Market Insecurity in Canada* (McGill-Queen's University Press, 2006).
Walzer, Michael, *Spheres of Justice* (Basic Books, 1983).
Weber, Leanne, 'Policing a World in Motion' in Sharon Pickering and Jude McCulloch (eds), *Borders and Transnational Crime: Pre-Crime, Mobility and Serious Harm in an Age of Globalisation* (Palgrave Macmillan, 2012) 35.
Weber, Leanne, *Policing Non-Citizens* (Routledge, 2013).
Weissbrodt, David and Rumsey, Mary (eds), *Vulnerable and Marginalised Groups and Human Rights* (Edward Elgar Publishing, 2011).
Willard, Myra, *History of the White Australia Policy* (Melbourne University Press, 1923).
Wishnie, Michael, 'Emerging Issues for Undocumented Workers' (2004) 6 *University of Pennsylvania Journal of Labor and Employment Law* 497.
Wishnie, Michael, *'Labor Law After Legalization'* (2008) 92 *Minnesota Law Review* 1446.
Yarwood, Alexander Turnbull, *Asian Migration to Australia: The Background to Exclusion 1896–1923* (Melbourne University Press, 1964).
Young, Iris Marion, *Inclusion and Democracy* (Oxford University Press, 2002).
Young, Iris Marion, 'Responsibility and Global Justice: A Social Connection Model' (2006) 23 *Social Philosophy and Policy* 102.
Zhang, Angela, 'Will the Fair Work Act Bring Improvements for Migrant Women Workers?' (2010) 21 *Economic and Labour Relations Review* 69.

Legislation

Commonwealth legislation

Anti-People Smuggling and Other Measures Act 2010 (Cth).
Australian Citizenship Act 2007 (Cth).
Australian Citizenship Amendment Act 1986 (Cth).
Conciliation and Arbitration Act 1904 (Cth).
Constitution of the Commonwealth of Australia.
Contract Immigrants Act 1905 (Cth).
Crimes Act 1914 (Cth).
Crimes Legislation Amendment (Law Enforcement Integrity, Vulnerable Witness Protection and Other Measures) Act 2013 (Cth).
Crimes Legislation Amendment (Slavery, Slavery-like Conditions and People Trafficking) Act 2013 (Cth).
Criminal Code Act 1995 (Cth).
Criminal Code Amendment (Slavery and Sexual Servitude) Act 1999 (Cth).
Criminal Code Amendment (Trafficking in Persons Offences) Act 2005 (Cth).
Fair Entitlement Guarantee Act 2012 (Cth).
Fair Work Act 2009 (Cth).
Health Insurance Act 1973 (Cth).
Immigration Restriction Act 1901 (Cth).
Industrial Relations Act 1988 (Cth).
Industrial Relations Act 1996 (Cth).
Industrial Relations Legislation Amendment Act 1992 (Cth).
Migration Act 1958 (Cth).
Migration Amendment Act 1989 (Cth).
Migration Amendment (Employer Sanctions) Act 2007 (Cth).

Migration Amendment (Reform of Employer Sanctions) Act 2013 (Cth).
Migration Amendment (Temporary Sponsored Visas) Act 2013 (Cth).
Migration Legislation Amendment Act 1994 (Cth).
Migration Legislation Amendment (Sponsorship Measures) Act 2003 (Cth).
Migration Legislation Amendment (Student Visas) Act 2012 (Cth).
Migration Legislation Amendment (Worker Protection) Act 2008 (Cth).
Migration Reform Act 1992 (Cth).
Pacific Islander Labourers Act 1901 (Cth).
Social Security Act 1991 (Cth).
Statute Law Revision Act 1973 (Cth).
Workplace Relations Act 1996 (Cth).
Workplace Relations Amendment Act 2005 (Cth).
Workplace Relations Amendment (Work Choices) Act 2005 (Cth).

Commonwealth regulations

Fair Work Regulations 2009 (Cth).
Migration Regulations 1994 (Cth).

Australian Capital Territory

Victims of Crime (Financial Assistance) Act 1983 (ACT).

New South Wales

Act to Regulate and Restrict the Immigration of Chinese 1861 (NSW).
Annual Holidays Act 1944 (NSW).
Coloured Races Restriction and Regulation Act 1896 (NSW).
Industrial Relations (Commonwealth Powers) Act 2009 (NSW).
Occupational Health and Safety Act 2000 (NSW).
Victims Rights and Support Act 2013 (NSW).
Workers Compensation Act 1987 (NSW).
Workplace Injury Management and Workers Compensation Act 1998 (NSW).

Northern Territory

Victims of Crime Assistance Act 2006 (NT).

Queensland

Act to Regulate the Immigration of Chinese and to Make Provisions Against Their Becoming a Charge upon Colony 1877 (Qld).
Pacific Island Labourers Act 1880 (Qld).
Polynesian Labourers Act 1868 (Qld).
Queensland WorkCover Act 1996 (Qld).
Victims of Crime Assistance Act 2009 (Qld).
WorkCover Queensland Act 1996 (Qld).
Workers' Compensation and Rehabilitation Act 2003 (Qld).

Workplace Health & Safety Act 1995 (Qld).

South Australia

Act to Regulate and Restrict Chinese Immigration 1881 (SA).
Victims of Crime Act 2001 (SA).
Workers Rehabilitation and Compensation Act 1986 (SA).

Tasmania

Victims of Crime Assistance Regulations 2010 (Tas).
Workers Rehabilitation and Compensation Act 1988 (Tas).

Victoria

Accident Compensation Act 1985 (Vic).
Act to make Provisions for Certain Immigrants (Chinese) 1855 (Vic).
Act to Regulate the Residence of Chinese Population 1857 (Vic).
Sentencing Act 1991 (Vic).
Victims of Crime Assistance Act 1996 (Vic).

Western Australia

Criminal Injuries Compensation Act 2003 (WA).
Industrial Relations Act 1979 (WA).
Workers Compensation and Injury Management Act 1981 (WA).

Canada

Immigration Act, RSC, ch 52 (1976-1977).
Immigration and Refugee Protection Act, SC 2001, c 27.
Immigration and Refugee Protection Regulations, SOR/2002-227.

New Zealand

Immigration Act 2009 (NZ).

United Kingdom

Asylum and Immigration Act 1996.
Immigration Act 1971.
Immigration, Asylum and Nationality Act 2006.
Immigration (Employment of Adults Subject to Immigration Control) (Maximum Penalty) Order 2008, SI 2008/132.
Immigration (Restrictions on Employment) Order 2004, SI 2004/755.
Immigration (Restrictions on Employment) Order 2007, SI 2007/3290.
Slave Trade Act 1824.

Transportation Act 1717.
Transportation Act 1824.

United States of America

Constitution of the United States.
Illegal Immigration Reform and Immigrant Responsibility Act of 1996, Pub L 104–208, 110 Stat 3009.
Immigration and Nationality Act, Pub L 82–414, 66 Stat 163.
Immigration Reform and Control Act, Pub L 99–603, 100 Stat 3359.

Treaties

Australia Schedule of Specific Commitments: Supplement 1, GATS/SC/6/Suppl.1 (4 October 1995).
Convention against Transnational Organised Crime, opened for signature 15 December 2000, 2225 UNTS 209 (entered into force 29 September 2003).
Convention Concerning Forced or Compulsory Labour (ILO No 29), opened for signature 28 June 1930, 39 UNTS 55 (entered into force 1 May 1932).
Convention Concerning Labour Inspection in Industry and Commerce (ILO No 81), International Labour Conference, 30th sess, opened for signature 11 July 1947 (entered into force 7 April 1950).
Convention for the Suppression of the Traffic in Persons and of the Exploitation of the Prostitution of Others, opened for signature 21 March 1950, 96 UNTS 271 (entered into force 25 July 1951).
Convention to Suppress the Slave Trade and Slavery, opened for signature 25 September 1926, 212 UNTS 17 (entered into force 9 March 1927).
Directive 2009/52/EC of the European Parliament and of the Council of 18 June 2009 providing for minimum standards on sanctions and measures against employers of illegally staying third-country nationals [2009] OJ L 168/24.
International Agreement for the Suppression of the White Slave Traffic, opened for signature 18 May 1904, 1 LNTS 83 (entered into force 18 July 1905).
International Convention for the Suppression of the Traffic in Women and Children, opened for signature 30 September 1921, 53 UNTS 39 (entered into force 24 April 1950).
International Convention for the Suppression of the Traffic in Women of Full Age, opened for signature 11 October 1933, 150 LNTS 431 (entered into force 24 August 1934).
International Convention for the Suppression of the White Slave Traffic, opened for signature 4 May 1910, 98 UNTS 101 (entered into force 14 August 1951).
International Convention on Protection of the Rights of All Migrant Workers and Members of their Families, adopted by GA Res 45/158, UN GAOR, 45th sess, UN Doc A/RES/45/158, 18 December 1990 (entered into force 1 July 2003).
International Covenant on Civil and Political Rights, opened for signature 16 December 1966, 999 UNTS 171 (entered into force 23 March 1976).
International Covenant on Economic, Social and Cultural Rights, opened for signature 16 December 1966, 993 UNTS 3 (entered into force 3 January 1976).
International Labour Organization Declaration on Fundamental Principles and Rights at Work (International Labour Conference, 86th sess, 18 June 1998).

International Labour Organization, Multilateral Framework on Labour Migration: Non-Binding Principles and Guidelines for a Rights-Based Approach to Labour Migration (2006).
Labour Inspection Convention, 1947 (ILO No 81), International Labour Conference, 30th sess, opened for signature 11 July 1947 (entered into force 7 April 1950).
Marrakesh Agreement Establishing the World Trade Organisation, opened for signature 15 April 1994, 1867 UNTS 154 (entered into force 1 January 1995) annex 1B, GATS/SC/6/Suppl.1AUSTRALIA – Schedule of Specific Commitments.
Migrant Workers Recommendation, 1975 (ILO No 151), International Labor Conference, 60th sess (adopted 24 June 1975).
Migrant Workers (Supplementary Provisions) Convention, 1975 (ILO No 143), opened for signature 24 June 1975, 1120 UNTS 323 (entered into force 9 December 1978).
Migration for Employment Convention (Revised), 1949 (ILO No 97), adopted 1 July 1949, 20 UNTS 79 (entered into force 22 January 1952).
Migration for Employment Recommendation (Revised), 1949 (ILO No 86), International Labour Conference, 32nd sess (adopted 1 July 1949).
Protocol of 2014 to the Forced Labour Convention, 1930 (ILO No 29), International Labour Conference, 103rd sess (adopted 11 June 2014).
Protocol to Prevent, Suppress and Punish Trafficking in Persons, Especially Women and Children, opened for signature 15 December 2000, 2237 UNTS 219, Annex II (entered into force 31 May 2004).
Recommended Principles and Guidelines on Human Rights and Human Trafficking of the Office of the United Nations High Commissioner for Human Rights, UN Doc E/2002/68/Add.1.
Rome Statute of the International Criminal Court, opened for signature 17 July 1998, 2187 UNTS 90 (entered into force 1 July 2002).
Supplementary Convention on the Abolition of Slavery, the Slave Trade, and Institutions and Practices Similar to Slavery, opened for signature 7 September 1956, 226 UNTS 3 (entered into force 30 April 1957).
Universal Declaration of Human Rights, GA Res 217A (III), UN GAOR, 3rd sess, 183rd plen mtg, UN Doc A/810 (10 December 1948).

Cases

Ahmed and Kaka Enterprises Pty Ltd t/as Desi Hut [2012] NSWWCC 65.
Al Ferdous v. Minister for Immigration [2010] FMCA 824.
Al Ferdous v. Minister for Immigration and Citizenship [2011] FCA 1070.
Alam v. Minister for Immigration and Multicultural and Indigenous Affairs (2004) 187 FLR 120.
Alcantara v. Buildpower Pty Ltd (No 2) [2010] FMCA 763.
Angelika Erika Mertens and Mindpearl AG (Unreported, AIRC, 4 November 2002).
Ankitkumar Patel v. RPEP Holdings Pty Ltd [2012] FWA 3915.
Anthony Emurugat and Utilities Management Pty Ltd [2008] AIRC 247.
Antony Emurugat v. Utilities Management Pty Ltd [2008] AIRC 1114.
Applicant v. Respondent [2010] FWA 4289.
Armstrong v. Healthcare Recruiting Australia Pty Ltd [2008] FMCA 1050.
Australia Meat Holdings Pty Ltd v. Kazi [2003] QSC 225.

Australia Meat Holdings Pty Ltd v. Kazi [2004] QCA 147.
Australian Workers Union v. Machine Shearers' and Shed Employees Union [1902] AR 16.
Aw v. Minister for Immigration and Citizenship [2009] FMCA 566.
Awa v. Minister for Immigration and Multicultural and Indigenous Affairs [2002] FCA 291.
Awa v. Minister for Immigration and Multicultural and Indigenous Affairs [2002] FCAFC 63.
Braun v. Minister for Immigration and Local Government and Ethnic Affairs (1991) 33 FCR 152.
Chen v. Allied Packaging Co Pty Ltd (1997) 73 IR 53.
Chia Gee v. Martin (1905) 3 CLR 648.
Chu Kheng Lim v. Minister for Immigration (1992) 176 CLR 1.
Crowhurst v. North Sydney City Council (Unreported, No 35179 of 1998, 26 July 1999).
Cunningham v. Bensons Building Services Pty Ltd [1998] SAIRComm 26.
Daniel Coppard and Australian Cable & Telephony Pty Ltd (Unreported, AIRC, 14 January 2005).
De Silva v. Minister for Immigration and Multicultural Affairs [2001] FCA 962.
Dib v. Minister of Immigration and Multicultural Affairs [1998] FCA 415.
Director of the Fair Work Building Industry Inspectorate v. Tunc [2013] FCCA 438.
Edward Coupe v. International Motor Inn Pty Ltd [2012] FWA 2117.
Elgin Nogaliza v. Benale Pty Ltd ATF Fletcher Unit T/A Fletcher International WA [2010] FWA 2667.
Eugene Magoo v. Dwyer Engineering & Construction Pty Ltd [2006] WAIRComm 4244.
Fair Work Ombudsman v. ACN 146435118 Pty Ltd (No 2) [2013] FCCA 1270.
Fair Work Ombudsman v. Australian Sales and Promotions Pty Ltd [2013] FCCA 1502.
Fair Work Ombudsman v. Bedington [2012] FMCA 1133.
Fair Work Ombudsman v. Bosen Pty Ltd (Unreported, Magistrates Court of Victoria, Industrial Division, Magistrate Hawkins, 21 April 2011).
Fair Work Ombudsman v. Butler & Blackberry Melbourne Pty Ltd [2012] FMCA 846.
Fair Work Ombudsman v. DZ Import & Export Trading Co Pty Ltd (Unreported, Chief Industrial Magistrates Court NSW, Magistrate Bartley, 5 August 2010).
Fair Work Ombudsman v. Glad Group Pty Ltd [2012] FMCA 731.
Fair Work Ombudsman v. Go Yo Trading Pty Limited [2012] FMCA 865.
Fair Work Ombudsman v. Honest and Frank Pty Ltd [2010] SAIRC 23.
Fair Work Ombudsman v. Jooine (Investment) Pty Ltd [2013] FCCA 2144.
Fair Work Ombudsman v. Kentwood Industries Pty Ltd (No 2) [2010] FCA 1156.
Fair Work Ombudsman v. Kentwood Industries Pty Ltd (No 3) [2011] FCA 579.
Fair Work Ombudsman v. Kingsford Carwash Pty Ltd (No 2) [2012] FMCA 1210.
Fair Work Ombudsman v. Lightfield Investments Pty Ltd (Chief Industrial Magistrate's Court NSW, GJT Hart, 8 July 2010).
Fair Work Ombudsman v. Nu Life Organic Farms Pty Ltd [2010] FMCA 694.
Fair Work Ombudsman v. Orwill Pty Ltd [2011] FMCA 730.
Fair Work Ombudsman v. Sacborn Pty Ltd T/as Eagle Boys Cessnock [2012] FMCA 890.
Fair Work Ombudsman v. Sanada Investments Pty Ltd [2010] FMCA 401.
Fair Work Ombudsman v. Taj Palace Tandoori Indian Restaurant Pty Ltd [2012] FMCA 258.
Fair Work Ombudsman v. Ultra Tune Australia Pty Ltd [2012] FMCA 560.
Fitzgerald v. JF Leonhardt Pty Ltd (1997) 189 CLR 215.
Flattery v. Zeffirelli's Pizza Restaurant [2007] FMCA 9.
Fryer v. Yoga Tandoori House Pty Ltd [2008] FMCA 288.
Han and Minister of Immigration and Citizenship [2008] AATA 129.
Han v. Mt Gambier Chinese Medical Centre [2007] SAIRC 75.

Hannington and Minister of Immigration and Citizenship [2008] AATA 581.
Hanssen Pty Ltd v. Jones [2009] FCA 192.
Ho v. The Queen; Leech v. The Queen [2011] VSCA 344.
Hong Su [1998] IRTA 11373.
Hong v. Minister of Immigration and Multicultural Affairs [2004] FCA 1308.
Hortle v. Aprint (Aust) Pty Ltd [2007] FMCA 1547.
Hussein v. Secretary of the Department of Immigration and Multicultural Affairs (No 2) [2006] FCA 1263.
Inspector Cooper v. Chung [2012] NSWIRComm 79.
Inspector Lai v. Rexma Pty Ltd [2008] NSWIRComm 78.
Islam v. Minister of Immigration and Citizenship (2007) 158 FCR 579.
Johnson v. Minister for Immigration and Multicultural and Indigenous Affairs [2003] FCA 758.
Jones v. Hanssen Pty Ltd [2008] FMCA 291.
Joshua Iser v. Penang Kayu Nasi Kandar Pty Ltd (unreported, Magistrates Court of Victoria, Melbourne Industrial Division, Magistrate Kate Hawkins, 13 May 2009).
Kamely v. Minister of Immigration and Citizenship [2011] FCA 1071.
Kaufusi v. Supre Pty Ltd (1999) 18 NSWCCR 607.
Kelly v. Fitzpatrick [2007] FCA 1080.
Kim v. Minister for Immigration [2007] FMCA 1580.
Kim v. Witton (1995) 59 FCR 258.
Kirshnakanth v. Saai Bose Pty Limited [2010] FMA 4578.
Komiatis v. Education Training and Employment Australia Pty Ltd [2008] VMC 29.
Kumar v. Rahul Chauhan (t/as Swaad of India) [2008] SAIRC 46.
L and the Employer [2007] AIRC 457.
Lawlor v. Dartbridge Welding Pty Ltd [2007] FMCA 2119.
LL Baker and Flight Centre Limited [2007] AIRC 281.
Luke Webster v. Mercury Colleges Pty Limited [2011] FWA 1807.
M Izawa and Ocean Spirit Dive Pty Ltd (Unreported, AIRC, 4 May 2000).
Mason v. Harrington [2007] FMCA 7.
Masri v. Santoso [2004] NSWIRComm 108.
McIvor v. R, Tanuchit v. R [2009] NSWCCA 264.
MG Lines Pty Ltd t/as Coniston Station v. Navi [2013] NTSC 20.
Midya v. Sagrani [1999] NSWCA 187.
Minister v. Msilanga (1992) 105 ALR 301.
Minister for Immigration v. Roberts [2011] FMCA 77.
Minister for Immigration v. Sahan Enterprises Pty Ltd [2012] FMCA 619.
Minister for Immigration and Multicultural and Indigenous v. Alam (2005) 145 FCR 345.
Mitchell v. Central West Area Health Service (1997) 14 NSWCCR 526.
Motomu Izawa and Ocean Spirit Dive Pty Ltd (Unreported, AIRC, 2 February 2001).
Mrs Q, Mr J and Mr S and the Employer [2007] AIRC 695.
Nantahkum v. R [2013] ACTCA 40.
NK Collins Industries Pty Ltd and Peter Vincent Twigg (C/2009/56) Industrial Court of Queensland, 27 April 2010.
NK Collins Industries Pty Ltd and Peter Vincent Twigg (C/2009/56) (No 2) Industrial Court of Queensland, 22 March 2011.
NK Collins Industries Pty Ltd v. President of the Industrial Court of Queensland [2010] QSC 373.
NK Collins Industries Pty Ltd v. President of the Industrial Court of Queensland [2012] QSC 147.
NK Collins Industries Pty Ltd v. The President of the Industrial Court of Queensland [2013] QCA 179.

Nolan v. Minister for Immigration and Ethnic Affairs (1988) 165 CLR 178.
Pawel Kurgan and Stankap Pty Ltd t/as Excite Powder Coating Services [2008] AIRC 112.
Plaintiff M47-2012 v. Director General of Security [2012] HCA 46.
Poskus v. Minister for Immigration and Multicultural and Indigenous Affairs [2005] FCA 118.
Purvi Sudani v. HealthWise Management (Aust) Pty Ltd T/A HealthWise Pharmacies Group [2011] FWAFB 1022.
Qiu and Minister for Immigration and Multicultural and Indigenous Affairs [2004] AATA 1308.
R v. Chee Mei Wong (unreported, DCNSW, Sweeney J, 5 July 2013).
R v. DS (2005) 153 A Crim R 194.
R v. KO [2006] QCA 43.
R v. Kovacs [2007] QCA 143.
R v. Kovacs [2008] QCA 417.
R v. Kovacs [2009] 2 Qd R 51.
R v. McIvor & Tanuchit [2010] NSWDC 310.
R v. Nantahkhum (Unreported, Supreme Court of the ACT, Refshauge J, 24 May 2012).
R v. Netthip [2010] NSWDC 159.
R v. Sieders and Yotchomchin [2007] NSWDC 101.
R v. Tang (2008) 237 CLR 1.
R v. Trivedi (Unreported, NSWDC, O'Connor J, 12 October 2011).
R v. Wei Tang [2006] VCC 637.
R v. Wei Tang (2007) 16 VR 454.
R v. Yogalingam Rasalingam (Unreported, NSWDC, Puckeridge J, 2 November 2007).
Radeshar Pty Ltd v. Minister for Immigration [2011] FMCA 560.
Raghavadev v. Moonlight Mushrooms Pty Ltd [2010] NSWWCCPD 120.
Rahhal v. Minister for Immigration [2008] FMCA 933.
Rahhal v. Minister for Immigration (No 2) [2008] FMCA 935.
Rajeev Prasad v. Alcatel-Lucent Australia Ltd [2011] FWAFB 1515.
Raymond Cordero Pagkaliwangan v. Siganto & Stacey Pty Limited [2010] FWA 9104.
Re Lachmaiya and Minister for Immigration and Ethnic Affairs (1994) 19 AAR 148.
Re Tan and Minister for Immigration and Multicultural Affairs [2001] AATA 308.
Richard Paternella v. Electroboard Solutions Pty Ltd [2011] FWA 3323.
Robert Lim v. Downer EDI Mining [2009] FWA 457.
Robtelmes v. Brenan (1906) 4 CLR 395.
S Liu v. Sinotrans Group Australia Pty Ltd (Unreported, AIRC, 15 February 2000).
Salandra v. Risborg Services Pty Ltd [2008] FMCA 76.
Salemi v. MacKellar (No 2) (1977) 137 CLR 396.
Shaw v. Minister for Immigration and Indigenous and Multicultural Affairs (2003) 218 CLR 28.
Shim v. JMNE Pty Limited t/as Wooden Bowl Restaurant [2010] FWA 8230.
Sieders v. R; Somsri v. R (2008) 72 NSWLR 417.
Singh v. TAJ (Sydney) Pty Ltd [2006] NSWCA 330.
Singh v. TAJ (Sydney) Pty Ltd [2007] NSWWCCPD 7.
Smallwood v. Ergo Asia Pty Ltd [2014] FWC 964.
Su Hong and Rainbow (Australia) Pty Ltd (Unreported, AIRC, 10 November 1997).
Susilo and Minister for Immigration and Multicultural and Indigenous Affairs [2004] AATA 495.

Taufia v. Nonferral (NSW) Pty Ltd (1995) 12 NSWCCR 431.
The Queen v. Wei Tang [2006] VCC 637.
United Furniture Trade Society v. Hordern [1905] AR 125.
Usman Ali v. Industries Services Training Pty Ltd [2011] FWA 9177.
Viliami v. National Springs (1993) 9 NSWCCR 453.
Wan v. Minister for Immigration and Multicultural Affairs [2000] FCA 1822.
Wan and Minister for Immigration and Multicultural and Indigenous Affairs [2002] AATA 217.
Weerasinghe v. Prism Grafix Pty Ltd [2009] FMCA 728.
Weerasinghe v. Prism Grafix Pty Ltd (No 2) [2011] FMCA 675.
Wei Xin Chen v. Allied Packaging Co Pty Ltd (1997) 73 IR 53.
Willmott v. Woolworths Ltd [2014] QCAT 601.
Work Cover Corporation v. Da Ping (1994) 175 LSJS 469.
Workplace Ombudsman v. Golden Maple Pty Ltd [2009] FMCA 664.
Workplace Ombudsman v. Huang (Unreported, Chief Industrial Magistrate's Court NSW, GJT Hart, 21 October 2009).
Workplace Ombudsman v. KSN Engineering [2009] FMCA 538.
Xia and Minister for Immigration and Citizenship [2007] AATA 180.
Yabut v. Dartbridge Welding Pty Ltd [2007] QADT 29.
Yan v. Minister for Immigration and Multicultural and Indigenous Affairs [2002] FCA 140.
Yong Fu Zhang v. Mei Hu t/as Eden Furniture and the WorkCover Authority of NSW [2006] NSWWCCPD 15.
Young Sim Lee v. Jimmy's on the Mall Pty Ltd [2011] FWA 3386.

United Kingdom

Bamgbose v. Royal Star and Garter Home [1996] EAT 841/95.
Holman v. Johnson (1775) 1 Cowp 341.
Hounga v. Allen [2014] UKSC 47.
Mayor and Burgesses of the London Borough of Hounslow v. Klusova (Unreported, EAT, 5 October 2006).
Sharma v. Hindu Temple [1991] EAT 253/90.
Vakante v. Addey and Stanhope School [2004] 4 All ER 1056.
Zarkasi v. Anindita and Tse Tan [2012] UKEAT/0400/11/JOJ.

United States of America

Asylum Co. v. Dist. of Columbia Dept. of Emp't Servs., 10 A3d 619 (DC 2010).
Balbuena v. IDR Realty LLC, 6 NY 3d 338 (NY 2006).
Chellen v. John Pickle Co., 446 FSupp 2d 1247 (ND Okla 2006).
Escobar v. Spartan Sec Serv, 281 FSupp 2d 895 (SD Tex 2003).
Hoffman Plastic Compounds Inc. v. National Labor Relations Board, 535 US 137 (2002).
Iweala v. Operational Techs Servs, 634 FSupp 2d 73 (DDC 2009).
Madeira v. Affordable Hous. Found., Inc., 315 FSupp 2d 504 (SDNY 2004).
Plyler v. Doe, 457 US 202 (1982).
Rivera v. NIBCO, 364 F3d 1057 (9th Cir 2004).
Rosa v. Partners in Progress, Inc., 868 A2d 994 (NH 2005).
Sanchez v. Eagle Alloy, 658 NW2d 510 (Mich Ct App 2003).
Singh v. Jutla, 214 FSupp 2d 1056 (ND Cal 2002).

Index

Page numbers in **bold** denote tables.

For Product Safety Concerns and Information please contact our EU representative GPSR@taylorandfrancis.com
Taylor & Francis Verlag GmbH, Kaufingerstraße 24, 80331 München, Germany

www.ingramcontent.com/pod-product-compliance
Ingram Content Group UK Ltd.
Pitfield, Milton Keynes, MK11 3LW, UK
UKHW020020200926
475702UK00014B/1979
* 9 7 8 1 1 3 8 7 1 6 8 2 7 *